Palgrave Macmillan Memory Studies

Series Editors
Andrew Hoskins
University of Glasgow
Glasgow, UK

John Sutton
Department of Cognitive Science
Macquarie University
Macquarie, Australia

The nascent field of Memory Studies emerges from contemporary trends that include a shift from concern with historical knowledge of events to that of memory, from 'what we know' to 'how we remember it'; changes in generational memory; the rapid advance of technologies of memory; panics over declining powers of memory, which mirror our fascination with the possibilities of memory enhancement; and the development of trauma narratives in reshaping the past. These factors have contributed to an intensification of public discourses on our past over the last thirty years. Technological, political, interpersonal, social and cultural shifts affect what, how and why people and societies remember and forget. This groundbreaking new series tackles questions such as: What is 'memory' under these conditions? What are its prospects, and also the prospects for its interdisciplinary and systematic study? What are the conceptual, theoretical and methodological tools for its investigation and illumination?

More information about this series at
http://www.palgrave.com/gp/series/14682

Kate Darian-Smith • Paula Hamilton
Editors

Remembering Migration

Oral Histories and Heritage in Australia

Editors
Kate Darian-Smith
University of Tasmania
Hobart, TAS, Australia

Paula Hamilton
University of Technology Sydney
Sydney, NSW, Australia

Palgrave Macmillan Memory Studies
ISBN 978-3-030-17750-8   ISBN 978-3-030-17751-5   (eBook)
https://doi.org/10.1007/978-3-030-17751-5

© The Editor(s) (if applicable) and The Author(s) 2019
This work is subject to copyright. All rights are solely and exclusively licensed by the Publisher, whether the whole or part of the material is concerned, specifically the rights of translation, reprinting, reuse of illustrations, recitation, broadcasting, reproduction on microfilms or in any other physical way, and transmission or information storage and retrieval, electronic adaptation, computer software, or by similar or dissimilar methodology now known or hereafter developed.
The use of general descriptive names, registered names, trademarks, service marks, etc. in this publication does not imply, even in the absence of a specific statement, that such names are exempt from the relevant protective laws and regulations and therefore free for general use. The publisher, the authors and the editors are safe to assume that the advice and information in this book are believed to be true and accurate at the date of publication. Neither the publisher nor the authors or the editors give a warranty, express or implied, with respect to the material contained herein or for any errors or omissions that may have been made. The publisher remains neutral with regard to jurisdictional claims in published maps and institutional affiliations.

Cover illustration: Rick Piper Photography / Alamy Stock Photo. Reproduced with the permission of Smith Sculptors (Charles Smith & Joan Walsh-Smith)
Cover design: eStudioCalamar

This Palgrave Macmillan imprint is published by the registered company Springer Nature Switzerland AG
The registered company address is: Gewerbestrasse 11, 6330 Cham, Switzerland

ACKNOWLEDGEMENTS

In early 2017, we invited those researching in the area of migration and memory studies to a symposium at the University of Melbourne, and it was there that most of the chapters in this book were given their first airing. We are very grateful to all contributors to *Remembering Migration: Oral Histories and Heritage in Australia* for preparing their chapters for publication and for the expertise and insights they bring to our shared endeavour.

We express our thanks to those who assisted with the symposium and this collection: Hannah Loney and Kyle Harvey at the University of Melbourne, and Claire McCarthy at the University of Tasmania. The work of Bethany Phillips-Peddlesden, also at the University of Melbourne, on administrative and logistical matters, and contributing to manuscript preparation, is much appreciated. At Palgrave Macmillan, we acknowledge the interest of the general academic editors of the Memory Studies series, Andrew Hoskins and John Sutton. We have been guided and well-supported by editor Lucy Batrouney and by editorial assistant Mala Sanghera-Warren. Two anonymous peer reviewers provided excellent critical advice, and attention to these comments has resulted in a more coherent and improved volume.

Midway through this project Paula became ill and Kate took on the majority of the editing of the contributions, with the valuable assistance of Vesna Rapajic. The dedication and professionalism shown by Vesna in copy-editing and preparing the manuscript for submission has been exemplary, and we appreciate her hard work over the festive season. Jon Jermey also prepared a thorough index.

v

vi ACKNOWLEDGEMENTS

Research for some chapters in this volume has been supported by a grant from the Australian Research Council: LP150100202 "Migration, Cultural Diversity and Television: Reflecting Modern Australia," with investigators Kate Darian-Smith (Lead), Sukhmani Khorana, Sue Turnbull and research fellow, Kyle Harvey; and partner investigators, Moya McFadzean and Michael Reason from Museums Victoria, and Helen Simondson from the Australian Centre for the Moving Image. Additional assistance has been provided by the College of Arts, Law and Education at the University of Tasmania.

We are also grateful to all copyright holders who have granted permission for the reproduction of images in the volume.

Kate Darian-Smith and Paula Hamilton

CONTENTS

1   Remembering Migration   1
Kate Darian-Smith and Paula Hamilton

Part I   Oral Histories and Migration: Unsettling Memory
Narratives   15

2   "I Am No Longer the Same Person": Intimate History
and the Gendered Experience of Migration   17
Alistair Thomson

3   Oral Histories of Displaced Persons: "What for? The
Story Like Mine's Plenty Now"   29
Jayne Persian

4   Shifting Countries, Shifting Identities? Oral History and
Lesbian and Gay Migration to Australia   47
Shirleene Robinson

5   "To Be Who I Was, Really, Was To Be Different":
Memories of Youth Migration to Post-War Australia   59
Anisa Puri

viii CONTENTS

6 Memory, Migration and Television: National Stories of
the Small Screen 75
Kate Darian-Smith and Kyle Harvey

7 A Shared Social Identity: Oral Histories of an Urban
Community of Italian Market Gardeners in Adelaide
1920s–1970s 93
Madeleine Regan

8 Forgotten Women: Remembering "Unsupported"
Migrant Mothers in Post-World War II Australia 107
Karen Agutter and Catherine Kevin

9 Years of Separation: Vietnamese Refugees and the
Experience of Forced Migration After 1975 123
Nathalie Huynh Chau Nguyen

10 The Pear Tree: Family Narratives of Post-War Greek
Macedonian Migration 141
Andrea Cleland

11 Negotiating Trauma and Cultural Dislocation Through
Memory: South Sudanese in Western Sydney 155
Atem Atem

12 "I Leave *Everything*": Encountering Grief with an Hazara
Refugee 167
Denise Phillips

Part II   Migrant Heritage: Representation, Sources and
Genres of Memory 183

13 The Voices of Diversity in Multicultural Societies: Using
Multimedia to Communicate Authenticity and Insight 185
Andrew Jakubowicz

CONTENTS   ix

14 Oral History and First-Person Narratives in Migration
    Exhibitions: Tracking Relations Between "Us" and "Them"   203
    Andrea Witcomb

15 Personal, Public Pasts: Negotiating Migrant Heritage—
    Heritage Practice and Migration History in Australia   219
    Alexandra Dellios

16 Hard Landings: Memory, Place and Migration   237
    Susannah Radstone

17 Purposeful Memory-Making: Personal Narratives of
    Migration at Melbourne's Immigration Museum   255
    Moya McFadzean

18 Settled and Unsettled: The Spirit of Enterprise Project as
    (Post)Settler-Colonial Memory Activism   271
    Alison Atkinson-Phillips

19 In Search of "Australia and the Australian People": The
    National Library of Australia and the Representation of
    Cultural and Linguistic Diversity   285
    Klaus Neumann

20 Remembering the Child Migrant on Screen   301
    Felicity Collins

21 Politicizing the Past: Memory in Australian Refugee
    Documentaries   317
    Sukhmani Khorana

22 Memory and Meaning in the Search for Chinese
    Australian Families   331
    Sophie Couchman and Kate Bagnall

Index   347

Notes on Contributors

Karen Agutter is a migration historian with a particular interest in the receiving-society/migrant relationship. Karen is a Visiting Research Fellow at the University of Adelaide and her most recent publications include "Lost in Translation: Managing Medicalised Motherhood in post-World War Two Australian Migrant Accommodation Centres" (with Catherine Kevin), *Women's History Review*, 2018 and "Fated to be Orphans: The Consequences of Australia's Post-War Resettlement Policy on Refugee Children," *History Australia* 41, no. 3, 2016.

Atem Atem is a PhD candidate at the Australian National University, researching the settlement experiences of Sudanese families in Western Sydney. He holds a Master degree in public policy and a Bachelor degree in medical sciences. Atem has worked in various roles for non-government organizations and community organizations to support the settlement of newly arrived refugees and humanitarian entrants, including in consultancy services and advocacy to improve the participation of refugees in policy development. He is currently the Multicultural Community Project Officer at Fairfield City Council in South Western Sydney.

Alison Atkinson-Phillips is a research associate at the Oral History Unit and Collective, at Newcastle University, United Kingdom. She hold a PhD from the University of Technology Sydney, and is a social and cultural historian whose research explores how difficult pasts are dealt with in the present, public art and place-based memory work. She is the author of *Survivor Memorials: Remembering Trauma and Loss in Contemporary Australia* (2019).

xii NOTES ON CONTRIBUTORS

Kate Bagnall is an Australian Research Council Fellow in the School of Humanities and Social Inquiry at the University of Wollongong, where she is working on a comparative study of Chinese colonial citizenship in Australia, Canada and New Zealand. She has published on various aspects of Chinese Australian history and is editor of *Chinese Australians: Politics, Engagement and Resistance* (with Sophie Couchman, 2015). Her research has explored the women, children and families of Australia's early Chinese communities, and the transnational connections and *qiaoxiang* ties of Chinese Australians before 1940.

Andrea Cleland has completed a PhD at the University of Melbourne. Her thesis examines family narratives about post-war Greek Macedonian migration from Florina to Melbourne and Toronto, and the intergenerational narration and transmission of notions of family, home and identity. She has contributed chapters to the book collections *Greek Research in Australia* (2013) and *Discovering Diasporas: A Multidisciplinary Approach* (2015).

Felicity Collins is a Reader/Associate Professor in Screen Studies in the Department of Creative Arts and English at La Trobe University. She has written extensively on the mediation of cultural memory in Australian film and television, with recent publications on stranger relationality, radical hope and proxy performance in reconciliatory screen cultures. She is the author of *Australian Cinema After Mabo* (with Therese Davis) and editor (with Jane Landman and Susan Bye) of the *Wiley Companion to Australian Cinema* (2019). She is writing a monograph on the transformation of television genres by the Blak Wave.

Sophie Couchman is a freelance curator and public historian and is an Honorary Research Fellow at La Trobe University. She has researched and published in the field of Chinese Australian history and heritage, including as Curator at the Chinese Museum in Melbourne. Sophie has a particular interest in the creation and circulation of visual representations and how they shape our understandings of Chinese Australians. She has edited *Chinese Australians: Politics, Engagement and Resistance* (with Kate Bagnall, 2015).

Kate Darian-Smith has published widely on histories of war, childhood, media, migration, memory, place and heritage in Australia. She is Executive Dean and Pro-Vice Chancellor, College of Arts, Law and Education at the

University of Tasmania, and previously held senior positions at the University of Melbourne. Kate edited the path-breaking *Memory and History in Twentieth Century Australia* (with Paula Hamilton, 1994). Recent publications include the edited books *Designing Schools: Space, Place and Pedagogy* (with Julie Willis, 2017), *Conciliation on Colonial Frontiers: Conflict, Performance and Commemoration in Australia and the Pacific Rim* (with Penny Edmonds, 2015), *Children, Childhood and Cultural Heritage* (with Carla Pascoe, 2013). Kate led the research team on the Australian Research Council-funded project on "Migration, Cultural Diversity and Television: Reflecting Modern Australia."

Alexandra Dellios is a cultural historian and lecturer in the Centre for Heritage and Museum Studies at the Australian National University. She is the author of *Histories of Controversy: Bonegilla Migrant Centre* (2017), and has published on child migrants, commemoration and heritage, and post-war migration. She is currently researching heritage-making practices within migrant communities and the discursive interactions between grassroots groups and official heritage.

Paula Hamilton is an Adjunct Professor of History at the University of Technology Sydney and at Macquarie University. She is a cultural historian and memory scholar, who edited the path-breaking *Memory and History in Twentieth Century Australia* (with Kate Darian-Smith, 1994) and has since published widely in oral history and memory studies, exploring the intersection between personal and public memories. Paula has also collaborated in a range of historical projects with libraries, community groups, museums, heritage agencies and trade unions. Her most recent work is the edited *A Cultural History of Sound, Memory and the Senses* (with Joy Damousi, 2017).

Kyle Harvey is a Research Fellow at the University of Tasmania working on the Australian Research Council project "Migration, Cultural Diversity and Television: Reflecting Modern Australia." His research interests include migration and media history, oral history and the history of social movements and radical thought in Australia, the United States, and the Pacific. Kyle is the author of *American Anti-Nuclear Activism, 1975–1990: The Challenge of Peace* (2014), and he has also published articles in *History Australia*, *Labour History*, and the *Journal for the Study of Radicalism*.

xiv   NOTES ON CONTRIBUTORS

Andrew Jakubowicz is Emeritus Professor of Sociology at the University of Technology Sydney. He previously directed the Centre for Multicultural Studies at the University of Wollongong, and headed the research team that wrote *Racism, Ethnicity and the Media* (1994). He produces the web project *Making Multicultural Australia*, an analytical archive with over 300 interviews. Since 2010 he has worked with SBS TV on a series of documentaries, where he has helped shape their "multicultural narratives". He is the editor *For Those Who've Come Across the Seas: Australian Multicultural Theory Policy and Practice* (with Chris Ho, 2013), and joint author of *Cyber Racism and Community Resilience* (2018).

Catherine Kevin is a Senior Lecturer in History at Flinders University. Her research has focused on the history of reproduction, women and migration, and the making of *Jedda* (1955). Her most recent publications include "Maternal Responsibility and Traceable Loss: Medicine and Miscarriage in Twentieth-Century Australia," *Women's History Review* 26, no. 6, 2016 and "The 'Unwanteds' and 'Non-compliants': 'Unsupported Mothers' as 'Failures' and Agents in Australia's Migrant Holding Centres" (with Karen Agutter), *History of the Family* 22, no. 4, 2017.

Sukhmani Khorana is Senior Lecturer in Media and Cultural Studies, and Academic Program Leader (South West Sydney) at the University of Wollongong. She is the editor of an anthology titled *Crossover Cinema* (2013), and has published extensively on news television, diasporic film, and multi-platform refugee narratives. Sukhmani is the author of a research monograph titled *The Tastes and Politics of Inter-Cultural Food in Australia* (2018), and an investigator on the Australian Research Council project "Migration, Cultural Diversity and Television: Reflecting Modern Australia."

Moya McFadzean is the Senior Curator of Migration and Cultural Diversity at Museums Victoria, leading many exhibitions at the Immigration Museum and Melbourne Museum, including the award-winning *Identity: Yours Mine, Ours* (2011–) and *British Migrants: Instant Australians?* (2017–18). She has a PhD from the University of Melbourne, where she is an Honorary Fellow in the School of Historical and Philosophical Studies. Moya has published widely on museums as sites of migration histories and social activism, and is a partner investigator on the

Australian Research Council project "Migration, Cultural Diversity and Television: Reflecting Modern Australia."

Klaus Neumann works for the Hamburg Foundation for the Advancement of Research and Culture, and is an honorary professor at Deakin University and an adjunct research fellow at the Hannah Arendt Institute in Dresden. He has written widely on public memory, historical justice, refugee policy, postcolonial history and other topics; his most recent book is the award-winning *Across the Seas: Australia's Response to Refugees: A History* (2015).

Nathalie Huynh Chau Nguyen is an Associate Professor in the School of Philosophical, Historical and International Studies at Monash University. She has held two major Australian Research Council Fellowships, and visiting fellowships at the National Library of Australia and Oxford University. Nathalie is the author of several award-winning books, including *Voyage of Hope: Vietnamese Australian Women's Narratives* (2007), *Memory is Another Country: Women of the Vietnamese Diaspora* (2009) and *South Vietnamese Soldiers: Memories of the Vietnam War and After* (2016). She is currently working on an Australian Research Council-funded project on the refugee legacy for second generation Vietnamese in Australia.

Jayne Persian is a historian of twentieth century Australian and international history at the University of Southern Queensland. Jayne has published *Beautiful Balts: From Displaced Persons to New Australians* (2017), shortlisted for the Prime Minister's Literary Awards. She is investigator on an Australian Research Council-funded project on "Displacement and Resettlement: Russian and Russian-speaking Jewish Displaced Persons Arriving in Australia via the 'China' Route in the Wake of the Second World War."

Denise Phillips is completing a PhD at the University of New England. Using oral histories, her thesis explores experiences of loss and hope among Hazara refugees from Afghanistan. Her research has been published in *History Australia*, the *Oral History Association of Australia Journal* and in the collection *Listening on the Edge: Oral History in the Aftermath of Crisis* (2014).

Anisa Puri is a professional historian and a PhD candidate in the School of Philosophical, Historical and International Studies at Monash University.

She is the author (with Alistair Thomson) of *Australian Lives: An Intimate History* (2017). Anisa is also a past President of Oral History New South Wales.

Susannah Radstone is Professor of Cultural Theory at the University of South Australia and Adjunct Professor in the School of Historical, Philosophical and International Studies, Monash University. She has published extensively on psychoanalytic and feminist cultural theory, cinema studies and cultural memory studies. Her books include, as editor, *Memory: History, Theory, Debates* (with Bill Schwaz, 2010), *Memory, History, Nation: The Politics of Memory* (Katharine Hodgkin, 2005), *Memory Cultures: Subjectivity, Recognition and Memory* (Katharine Hodgkin, 2005). With Rosanne Kennedy, she co-edited a special issue of *Memory Studies* on memory research in Australia and she is also currently co-editing the *Palgrave Companion to Memory and Literature.*

Madeleine Regan is completing a PhD at Flinders University. She is Secretary of Oral History Australia branch in South Australia/Northern Territory, and has coordinated history projects with communities and local governments. Since 2008 she has collected interviews with descendants of Veneto market gardeners who settled in Adelaide's urban periphery in the 1920s, and in 2016 contributed to a Migration Museum exhibition on this project.

Shirleene Robinson is Senior Curator of Oral History and Indigenous Programs at the National Library of Australia. She is also an Honorary Associate Professor in the Department of Modern History at Macquarie University, where she previously held research fellowships and worked on Australian Research Council grants. Her recent books drawing on oral histories are *Serving in Silence? Australian LGBT Servicemen and Women* (with Noah Riseman and Graham Willett, 2018) and *Gay and Lesbian, Then and Now: Australian Stories from a Social Revolution* (with Robert Reynolds, 2016).

Alistair Thomson is Professor of History at Monash University. In 2018, he was President of Oral History Australia and was previously President of the International Oral History Association and an editor of the British journal *Oral History*. His oral history books include: *Anzac Memories* (1994, 2013), *The Oral History Reader* (1998, 2006, 2016 with Rob Perks), *Ten Pound Poms* (2005, with Jim Hammerton), *Moving Stories: An Intimate History of Four Women Across Two Countries*

(2011), *Oral History and Photography* (2011, with Alexander Freund), and *Australian Lives: An Intimate History* (2017, with Anisa Puri).

Andrea Witcomb is a Professor in Cultural Heritage and Museum Studies at Deakin University where she is the Deputy Director (Research) of the Alfred Deakin Institute for Citizenship and Globalisation. She is the author of *Reimagining the Museum: Beyond the Mausoleum* (2003), *From the Barracks to the Burrup: The National Trust in Western Australia* (with Kate Gregory, 2010), and editor of the volumes *South Pacific Museums: Experiments in Culture* (with Chris Healy, 2006, 2012) *Museum Theory* (with Kyle Message, 2015). The chapter in this collection is based on Australian Research Council-funded project on "Collecting Cultural Diversity in the Australian Collecting Sector."

LIST OF FIGURES

Fig. 2.1   Phyllis Cave and "The car we won," Dundas Migrant Hostel, Sydney, April 1970. Courtesy of Phyllis Cave   18

Fig. 2.2   "Phyl Sydney Wide," 1973. Courtesy of Phyllis Cave   26

Fig. 7.1   Johnny and Romano Marchioro, sons of pioneer Veneto market gardeners, Adelaide c. 1946. Courtesy of the Marchioro family   97

Fig. 13.1   Changing faces of White Australia: Miss Jessie Wong's third grade class, Sydney Grammar Edgecliff, 1957 (author rear row second from left). Courtesy of Andrew Jakubowicz   187

Fig. 16.1   Royal Terrace, Nicholson Street, Fitzroy. Photograph by Susannah Radstone   248

Fig. 17.1   Tea cup soundscape and story projection, *British Migrants: Instant Australians?* Exhibition, 2017–2018. Photograph by Jon Augier. Courtesy of Museums Victoria   263

Fig. 18.1   Enterprise Heritage Trail marker at Springvale Shopping Centre (design by Sinatra Murphy Pty Ltd). Photograph by Alison Atkinson-Phillips   278

Fig. 22.1   Richard Num paying his respects at a shrine in Qiaotou village, Kaiping, with Megan Neilson looking on. Photograph by Sophie Couchman   332

CHAPTER 1

Remembering Migration

Kate Darian-Smith and Paula Hamilton

As Andreas Huyssen noted about the "boom" in memory studies, diasporic memory has been "seriously understudied" in comparison with national memory.[1] This remains so, even in an overtly migrant nation such as Australia. In 2013, we identified the experiences of migration and settlement since World War II as a key area (alongside the Anzac tradition and the impact of European colonization on Indigenous peoples) of the oral history collecting undertaken by Australian cultural institutions, scholars and the community.[2] These oral histories have been utilized in a multitude of memory practices including research projects, books, radio and television documentaries, memoirs, films and websites, and are a central feature of specialist migration or community museum exhibitions and heritage sites. Digital technologies have also contributed to the increasing range of memory work and first-person testimony relating to migration heritage circulating in the public sphere.

K. Darian-Smith (✉)
University of Tasmania, Hobart, TAS, Australia
e-mail: kate.dariansmith@utas.edu.au

P. Hamilton
University of Technology Sydney, Sydney, NSW, Australia
e-mail: paula.hamilton@uts.edu.au

© The Author(s) 2019
K. Darian-Smith, P. Hamilton (eds.), *Remembering Migration*,
Palgrave Macmillan Memory Studies,
https://doi.org/10.1007/978-3-030-17751-5_1

Yet despite renewed interest from scholars in the historical dimensions of migration, there is a serious shortfall in the analysis of its remembrance.[3] In addition, many collections of migrant testimonies—as well as the built fabric and material culture associated with migration—lack adequate cohesion or interpretation and are not always meaningfully situated within mainstream histories of Australia. This is a notable absence given the changing demography of Australia's people from the mid-twentieth century. In the 2016 census, the Australian Bureau of Statistics found 33.3 per cent of the population was born overseas, an additional 34.4 per cent had both parents born overseas and a further 11.1 per cent had one parent born overseas.[4] The majority of Australians today have direct personal or parental knowledge of the experiences of migration from more than 100 different cultures and countries of origin. This is evident in a plethora of everyday ways, from the linguistic and belief systems practised in diasporic communities through to the emergences of cross-cultural forms, such as "fusion" cooking, that are often celebrated as successful and distinctive outcomes of a multicultural Australia.

It is now timely to examine the evolving and disparate ways that migration to Australia has been recorded and commemorated. The first waves of migrants who arrived after World War II from across Europe, as well as the large numbers who came from Britain, are now elderly. A suitcase is often used to symbolize their arrival in Australia with few goods. The dominant narrative trajectory of their experience is one of hard work followed by economic success and social mobility, despite the endemic prejudice against non-British migrants. For many, too, the freedom from oppression and the opportunities available have strengthened this pervasive and positivist interpretation of the migrant experience for those who settled in Australia in the late 1940s, 1950s and 1960s. The nuances and disappointments of individual experiences have often been left to this generation's children and grandchildren, who grew up in very different political and social contexts, to interpret publicly as well as within more closed family circles.

The 1970s brought about the end of the racially restrictive White Australia Policy and ushered in the official policy of multiculturalism. Some bold government provisions recognized the nation's cultural diversity, such as the establishment of the multilingual Special Broadcasting Service (SBS). However, the profile of migrants was changing and the arrival of humanitarian refugees from Vietnam, China and later the Middle East became more pronounced in public understandings of immigration policy and practice. By the 2000s, Australia was actively protecting its coastal borders from those arriving illegally and had introduced contentious policies of off-shore processing and mandatory detention centres for asylum seekers. The reputation of Australia as a welcoming haven for those fleeing famine, poverty and war has been replaced by that of a nation strictly guarding its migrant intake, with government policy focusing on attracting skilled migrants whilst maintaining a small humanitarian programme. These circumstances have influenced the memories of recent migrants and have been central to ongoing political debate and public perceptions of some cultural groups.

Key events in the history of post-World War II migration include, among many others, the arrival in 1947 of the first displaced persons from the Baltic states as well as Central and Eastern Europe, the "Beautiful Balts" from Lithuania, Estonia and Latvia; the celebration in 1955 of the millionth post-war migrant, British woman Barbara Porritt; the landing of the first boatload of Vietnamese refugees in Darwin Harbour in 1976; and the *Tampa* affair of 2001, which led to Australia's "border protection" policy. Such historical moments have been captured in press and official photographs; some are now iconic images. Indeed, the way that migration has been remembered *is* highly visual, with millions of family photographs and video footage recording personal stories of life in a new country, and keeping connections with the old one. The intertwining of oral history and photography is key to the methodologies, analysis and forms of commemorating migration in Australia.[5] So too is the collation and exhibition of objects and the material culture of migrant mobility, and, increasingly, efforts to memorialize sites of migration history, such as former government and community spaces associated with settlement.

Recognition of migrant heritage and experience has often been emotionally difficult and politically fraught. First-person testimonies have played a central role in inquiries that address past wrongs, as seen in relation to the 7000 child migrants who came to Australia, primarily from the United Kingdom, under a state-sanctioned scheme. Placed in government and religious institutions, many were neglected and abused. The testimonies of survivors underpinned an unqualified national apology in 2009, delivered by the Prime Minister, to the Forgotten Australians and Former Child Migrants. Some of the accounts of former child migrants also contributed to the evidence collected for a subsequent Royal Commission into Institutional Responses to Child Sexual Abuse, which led to a National Apology to Victims and Survivors of Institutional Child Sexual Abuse in

2018.[6] In a somewhat different way, the publication of several books of oral histories and memoirs collected from asylum seekers held in detention has alerted the Australian public to their plight. As scholars such as Kelly Jean Butler have argued, such witnessing—listening to the voices of asylum seekers and acting on their behalf—has been an influential tool of political advocacy within the public sphere over the past two decades.[7]

Drawing on rich case studies, detailed research and cross-disciplinary approaches, the chapters in *Remembering Migration: Oral Histories and Heritage in Australia* examine how individuals, communities and the nation have commemorated and recorded the experiences of migration to Australia over the past 70 years. These contributions are divided into two parts: the first exploring the role of oral histories, and the second examining the complexity of migrant heritage, and the sources and genres of memory writing. Each part is split between chapters that raise broader thematic issues and questions, and those that focus on detailed case studies of migrant remembrance and memory in contemporary Australia.

Oral Histories and Migration

The practice of oral history developed in Australia in parallel with post-war social and economic change, incorporating migration. From the early 1950s, for instance, sociologist Jean Martin compiled the life stories of displaced persons, tracking their integration into an Australian way of life.[8] In subsequent decades, the stories which migrants tell about the experiences have changed markedly, just as the public debates and the framework for questions pursued by oral historians have also shifted.

As the French philosopher Paul Ricoeur has argued, "personal testimony in the archive" is the "threshold document" between memory and the writing of history.[9] Today, there are many thousands of interviews with and by migrants held by collecting and cultural institutions, from major repositories such as the National Library of Australia and state libraries, archives and museums, through to municipal libraries and community organizations. These interviews have been commissioned or donated, usually as part of specific projects undertaken by migrant groups, or commissioned by government organizations. Another body of oral histories is held in university libraries, the result of student work on migrant-related topics, including for doctoral degrees. On occasion, collections have been driven by individuals, as in the case of Leonard Janiszewski and Effy Alexakis who have conducted oral histories in

English and Greek since 1982, and which now number over 2000, held at Macquarie University, Sydney.[10]

The diverse provenance of these collections indicates the valuable but somewhat haphazard and serendipitous nature of preserving the oral narratives of migration. Indeed, the issue of sources and collecting objectives for national institutions is a key one for migrant heritage and is examined by contributions to this collection. There have been attempts at a more coherent approach, such as support from the New South Wales government for a Migrant Heritage Centre with a central digital archive and major website presence, although this initiative has been discontinued. The diverse "migrant voices" that are celebrated as a record of experience across these varied collections are largely spoken memories elicited for a range of purposes, not simply disinterested documentary accounts. Many of these interviews are also difficult to access, although this issue has been party facilitated by digitization, especially at the larger institutions such as the National Library of Australia and the State Library of New South Wales.

However, further limitations beyond access characterize the thousands of oral histories which now reside in archives and libraries or online. Firstly, many of these projects are focused on a defined national or cultural ethnic group, such as "Italians" or "Greeks" or "Chinese". They foreground the status of the interviewees as "migrants", rather than exploring shifting identities and how factors such as gender, class, age or sexuality have shaped their life stories. This has led to an emphasis on the distinctiveness of each ethnic group's collective experience, rather than an exploration of what might unite migrants from different places and cultures. It has also reinforced a sense that the migrant experience is "outside" that of Australian society in general, and reified ethnicity as the main descriptive identifier of the "migrant"—even many decades after arrival. Secondly, the individualized or atomized nature of the interview has inhibited their integration into migration histories in general, except as small illustrations. There are few studies that use oral histories to compare the experiences of migrants from different countries or which examine the changing interactions between ethnic groups, including intercultural intimacy and marriage.[11]

Interviews with migrants reveal that identity is built from multiple sources, including media, and narratives may be laced with deep ambivalence about moving to Australia. While these oral histories can be disruptive of the standard historical accounts, the very process of remembering is historically contingent and memories are revised according to the context of their articulation. Recent migrants, as is evident from the chapters in this volume, are focused on overcoming everyday challenges, and the discontinuity and disorientation of unfamiliar cultural traditions. Many have faced the dissonance between a place imagined and a place experienced in Australia, continuing to compare the "new" country with the "old" place as the anchor of memory.

As well, Australian histories have considered migrants in a national context and from the moment of their arrival, with scant attention to personal agency and the complex decision underlying migration. This is despite oral history's predisposition to embrace narrators as principal actors in the shaping of their destinies.[12] Since the emergence of a more transnational orientation and transcultural theories of memory from the 1990s, it became apparent that migration was quintessentially a story that crossed national and local borders. Despite a continued focus by government policymakers on the national frame, economic migrants have increasingly imagined wider international possibilities for settlement that have been activated by the emergence of low cost mass travel and social media.

One key theme to emerge in oral histories of migration is the cross-generational possibilities for remembering and forgetting. Marianne Hirsch's concept of post-memory, or absent memory, for a second generation where parents refuse to tell their stories, has particular resonance for those who are children of Holocaust survivors or other migrants who have fled war and trauma. The traumatic silence whereby parents transmit the wounds of their past through affect and non-verbal communication has often led to family secrets or can disrupt the transmission of children's narrative inheritance.[13] Even more generally, many migrants from the immediate post-World War II period adhered to the modernist assumption that too many memories would hinder resettlement, and orientated their stories towards "adjustment" and a fresh start. The political emphasis on assimilation and "fitting in" with Australian culture has also made it difficult to publicly express memories which undermine or question this goal of integration.[14]

Indeed, the absence of a national metanarrative with which the vast array of migrant experiences could identify beyond that of "contribution" to nation-building has relegated these memories to the semi-privatized sphere of the family or close-knit communities. Sara Wills has argued that "the mnemonic role of histories *not* constructed around pride and nationhood were unavailable" for many migrants.[15] When migrant memories move from private to public arenas, they may both reinforce and challenge dominant narratives of experience.[16]

Experiences and emotions of individuals, families and communities of settling in Australia as narrated through oral histories are explored in the first part of this book. The life stories of individuals are, of course, shaped by many factors other than migration, and several chapters probe these broader influences. Alistair Thomson examines how oral history can illuminate the gendered history of post-World War II migration—and indeed the centrality of gender in shaping migrant experiences and forms of remembrance is a dominant thread that runs across the chapters in this collection. Jayne Persian analyses how oral histories can both reveal and heal the emotional pain felt by interviewees who were among the 170,000 displaced persons who arrived in Australia between 1947 and 1952, mostly from Central and Eastern Europe. Sexuality has been an unexplored dimension of migration, and as Shirleene Robinson points out, oral history provides a unique insight into the challenges and rewards encountered by lesbian and gay migrants to Australia. In a similar way, Anisa Puri chooses age as a category of analysis of how migration is experienced, and through this lens interprets the life story of the child of migrants from Poland. Mass migration coincided with the introduction of television to Australia in 1956. Kate Darian-Smith and Kyle Harvey examine how television, and its local and imported programming, is situated within migrant narratives of adjustment and belonging, and raise questions about the interconnections between migration, memory and the media.

The focused chapters that follow these thematic studies provide insights into many individuals and communities who have migrated to Australia across almost one century. Madeleine Regan looks at the shared identity of a market gardening community from the Veneto region of Italy who arrived in South Australia in the 1920s, drawing on multiple oral histories that are now available as a digital resource for subsequent generations. Karen Agutter and Catherine Kevin discuss those largely "forgotten" women who migrated as "unsupported" widowed or unmarried mothers, and argue that to understand their lives we need to examine multiple archival sources alongside the insights provided by oral histories. The first substantial population from Asia to settle in Australia were Vietnamese refugees, who were among the exodus of two million people who fled their homeland in the two decades following the end of the Vietnam War in 1975. Nathalie Huynh Chau Nguyen draws on oral histories to highlight the complexities and delays in the sponsored migration process, and the long-term consequences of separation for Vietnamese families. In a different context, cross-generational narratives are addressed by Andrea Cleland on migration from Florina, in the Macedonian region of Greece. Cleland considers how collective family memory can shape transnational notions of belonging, home and identity for second- and third-generation descendants. Atem Atem provides a rich discussion on his own community of South Sudanese living in western Sydney, to examine how the trauma of living through and fleeing civil war is the dominant theme of their complex and multidirectional collective memories and the shaping of new identities. Finally, Denise Phillips uses successive oral histories with a Hazara refugee from Afghanistan to focus on the difficulties and trauma of settlement, and to invite empathetic imaginings of the lived experiences of migration. She argues that the use of silence, metaphor and digressions within the interviews can be understood as part of the broader narrative of fleeing persecution and managing acute grief.

Migrant Heritage

Since 2000, the massive expansion in migration commemoration across a variety of cultural modes and platforms has transformed the public circulation and understandings of migrant heritage—or, perhaps more correctly, the heritage of particular ethnic and cultural groups. Much of this memory work was spurred by the determination of migrants and their communities to claim a place in the national story, visibly demonstrating and celebrating their contribution to nation-building. This heritage may be highly specific and localized, such as the Sikh Heritage Trail set up by the Australian Sikh Heritage Association in Adenia Park, Perth, at the exact site where in the 1930s Sikhs were cremated legally in Australia for the first time. It can also be broadly conceptualized and inclusive in its reach. For instance, the Welcome Wall, located at the Australian National Maritime Museum in Sydney, is inscribed with the names of migrants from around the world who came to Australia. In all cases, however, "remembering" through commemorative heritage is a public recognition of value.[17]

Museums have played a prominent role in this commemorative explosion, although it is notable that the history of migration to Australia is often conveyed through specialist museums rather than incorporated into those of mainstream social history: the National Museum of Australia is a prime exception. The nation's first dedicated Migration Museum was set up in Adelaide in 1986 in response to the 1970s government policies supporting multiculturalism and the preserving of migrant "heritage".[18] Since then the Immigration Museum, a campus of Museums Victoria, opened in 1998, and its innovative exhibition practices are discussed in more detail in this book. There are also numerous small community ethno-based museums and heritage centres now established in Australia's state capitals, with many others located in regional areas. In Melbourne, for instance, a group of five community organizations—the Chinese Museum, Co.As.It Italian Historical Society and Museo Italiano, the Hellenic Museum, the Islamic Museum of Australia and the Jewish Museum of Australia—have joined forces as Multicultural Museums Victoria, embarking on cross-institutional activities.

Inevitably, maritime museums focus on the moment of migrant arrival and frame the journey as a principal "site of memory". As Gillian Whitlock notes, "Ships carry the weight of maritime histories and migrations that percolate through living memory".[19] In fact, arrival is often a confusing and stressful time, so memories of the "new country" can be easily lost in the many years of settlement afterwards if they are not emphasized by those who help to shape the memories of migrants; and this begs the question, when do people stop being "migrants"?

The story of migrant "inclusion" into national and local histories can take many forms in the heritage context. The institutionalization of voluntary organizations or churches and political spokespeople for various ethnic groups, and interests, has also had an impact on the strength of a migrant voice within the public arena. More broadly, the closure or re-purposing of the many government hostels and reception centres that accommodated the waves of incoming migrants from the late 1940s to the early 2000s has created opportunities for migrant-initiated forms of remembrance. One key site is at the former Bonegilla Migrant Reception and Training Centre in northern Victoria, which ceased operations in 1971 after housing over 300,000 arrivals from mainly non-English-speaking backgrounds. This can now be experienced *in situ* with displays of photographs and objects in restored barracks, and has become a place of reunions and visits from the children and grandchildren of the original migrant inhabitants, many of whom share stories via social media and online platforms.[20] Second- and third-generation descendants of migrants are also increasingly "returning" to the places of family origin, whether in Europe, Asia or elsewhere, and in doing so consciously re-connecting with their cultural inheritance and forging or re-establishing family ties.

The second part of *Remembering Migration* brings together many perspectives on the multiple heritages of migration and the sources and genres of migrant memory writing. Its thematic chapters open with a study by

Andrew Jakubowicz that explores the place of oral sources in research into Australia's multicultural society, including his oversight of the web archive and documentary *Making Multicultural Australia*, and television documentaries about migrant communities living in Australian cities. Andrea Witcomb turns to museums, where she explores how the use of oral histories in exhibitions about migration can provide a personal layer of interpretation around objects, and can also drive the exhibition's narrative structure to create different kinds of relations for audiences between "us" and "them". From a broad survey of the sites of migrant heritage, including former reception centres and hostels, Alexandra Dellios then examines the negotiations between the private and community aspirations for heritage recognition of particular places, and the forms of the "public past" of migration as recognized by state-sanctioned heritage organizations. Drawing on her own experiences, Susannah Radstone meditates on the question of how migrants can make themselves at home in new worlds, and what sorts of memory work are involved in an evolving process of physical and psychical relocation.

Deeper analyses of the places, texts and images of migrant heritage and commemoration are examined in the subsequent focused chapters. Moya McFadzean looks at the idea of "purposeful memory-making" at the Immigration Museum in Melbourne from 1998 to the present, charting the changes to its collection development, approaches to the mounting of exhibitions and engagement with migrant communities. In her close study of a memory project around the Springvale Enterprise Hostel, which offered accommodation and settlement services for migrants from 1970 to 1990, Alison Atkinson-Phillips argues that the past has been mobilized to contrast a previous celebration of multiculturalism and welcome to new migrants with Australia's present policies of "turning back" many asylum seekers. Klaus Neumann investigates how the commitment of the National Library of Australia's collection policy to "build the nation's memory" has responded to the acquisition of sources about migration history and cultural and linguistic diversity. In her incisive discussion, Felicity Collins traces how the stories of British child migrants and inter-country adoptees have been told on screen, arguing that cinematic techniques of memoir and adventure quest—as seen in the mini-series *The Leaving of Liverpool* (1992) and feature film *Lion* (2016)—have been crucial to creating a distinctive public memory of child migrants to Australia. Sukhmani Khorana examines how migrant heritages are conveyed through recent Australian documentary films, exploring how refugees' narratives may be incorporated into the national collective memory where they can shape public discourse. In this volume's final contribution, Sophie Couchman and Kate Bagnall focus on the increasing interest in researching Chinese Australian family history from the nineteenth century onwards, and reflect on the emergence of "roots tourism" to China and the tensions between personal memory-making in the context of national and familial forgetting.

Migration Memories and the Future

As the topics and content of *Remembering Migration* have demonstrated, a new generation of scholars working in migration studies—many of whom have contributed to this volume—have continued to open up the traditional reified migrant memories in Australia. Some descendants of migrants, like George Kouvaros, have begun exploring the importance of technologies of memory, including photographs and film.[21] A recent online Australian Migration History Network has been established, and contains a mixture of historical material and individual or collective memories. One of the strengths of such a network apart from circulating information is the room for "small stories" or single accounts of migration that can paint a larger picture of process. Of course, the construction of memories is not one merely supported by historical scholarship or memoir—but is also an imaginative and creative exercise as seen by the increasing number of literary and artistic works that deal with the themes of migration and all that this means within contemporary Australia.

The memory of migration is currently being transformed through social media, such as Instagram, Facebook and blogs, particularly in relation to transnational memories where migrants retain links with their home country, but also create cyber "communities" across a global diaspora. These practices underline the shifting understandings of the nature of migration: it is no longer a journey that means a radical break with a past life or leaving a home that is seldom re-visited. In 2015 there were over 1.5 million "temporary" migrants in Australia mainly from India, China and the United Kingdom. Between 2003 and 2014 international student visas rose by 80 per cent, and international education is a major sector of the Australian economy. For those who may only be residing in Australia temporarily, a more complex and ambivalent relationship to the nation is emerging. Their narratives suggest that future understandings of "migration memories" will involve a broader imagining of identities and belonging, however much governments might want to control this ceaseless movement of peoples within nationally defined parameters.

NOTES

1. Andreas Huyssen, "Diaspora and Nation: Migration into Other Pasts," *New German Critique* 88 (Winter 2003): 147–64.
2. Kate Darian-Smith and Paula Hamilton, "Memory and History in Australia: The State of the Field," *Memory Studies* 6, no. 3 (2013): 372–85.
3. Ruth Balint and Zora Simic, "Histories of Migrants and Refugees in Australia," *Australian Historical Studies* 49, no. 3 (2018): 378–409.
4. Quickstats.censusdata.abs.gov.au/census_services/getproduct/census/2016/quickstat/036; Census 2016, Country of Birth of Person by Year of Arrival in Australia. http://stat.data.abs.gov.au/Index.aspx?DataSetCode=ABS_C16_T07_SA.
5. Alexander Freund and Alistair Thomson eds, *Oral History and Photography* (New York and Basingstoke: Palgrave Macmillan, 2011).
6. Prime Minister of Australia, "The Apology to Forgotten Australians and Former Child Migrants," 16 November 2009, http://pandora.nla.gov.au/pan/110625/20091116-1801/www.pm.gov.au/node/6321.html; "The Apology to Victims and Survivors of Institutional Child Sexual Abuse," 22 October 2018, https://www.pm.gov.au/media/national-apology-address.
7. Kelly Jean Butler, *Witnessing Australian Stories: History, Testimony and Memory in Contemporary Culture* (London and New York: Routledge, 2017 [2013]), 151–84.
8. Jean Martin, *Refugee Settlers: A Study of Displaced Persons in Australia* (Canberra: ANU Press, 1965).
9. Paul Ricoeur, *History, Memory, Forgetting* (Chicago: University of Chicago Press, 2004).
10. Carol McKirdy, *Practicing Oral History with Immigrant Narrators* (Walnut Creek, CA: Left Coast Press, 2015), 8–39. Email correspondence with Leonard Janiszewski and Paula Hamilton, 1 February 2018.
11. One exception is Rachel Stevens and Seamus O'Hanlon, "Intimate Oral Histories: Intercultural Romantic Relationships in Post-war Australia," *Australian Historical Studies* 49, no. 3 (2018): 359–77.
12. Paula Hamilton, "Speak Memory: Issues in Oral and Public History," in Paul Ashton and Alex Trapeznik eds, *What is Public History Globally?* (London and New York: Bloomsbury, 2019).
13. Marianne Hirsch, *The Generation of Postmemory: Writing and Visual Culture After the Holocaust* (New York: Columbia University Press, 2012).
14. Julia Creet, "Introduction," in Julia Creet and Andreas Kitzmann eds, *Memory and Migration: Multidisciplinary Approaches to Memory Studies* (Toronto, Buffalo and London: University of Toronto Press, 2011), 7.

15. Sara Wills, "Between the Hostel and the Detention Centre: Possible Trajectories of Migrant Pain and Shame in Australia," in William Logan and Kier Reeves eds, *Places of Pain and Shame: Dealing with "Difficult Heritage"* (London and New York: Routledge, 2009), 263–80.
16. Rosemary Baird, "Constructing Lives: A New Approach to Understanding Migrants' Oral History Narratives," *Oral History* (Britain) 40, no. 1 (Spring 2012): 57–66.
17. Paul Ashton, Paula Hamilton and Rose Searby, *Places of the Heart: Memorials in Australia* (Melbourne: Australian Scholarly Publishing, 2012), 13–30.
18. Eureka Henrich, "Mobility, Migration and Modern Memory," in Anna Maerker, Simon Sleight and Adam Sutcliffe eds, *History, Memory and Public Life: The Past in the Present* (London: Routledge, 2018), 101–25.
19. Gillian Whitlock, "Salvage: Locating Lives in the Migration Museum," *Life Writing* 14, no. 4 (2017): 427–40.
20. Alexandra Dellios, *Histories of Controversy: Bonegilla Migrant Centre* (Carlton, VIC: Melbourne University Publishing, 2017).
21. George Kouvaros, *The Old Greeks: Cinema, Photography, Migration* (Crawley, WA: UWA Publishing, 2018), 12.

Bibliography

Ashton, Paul, Paula Hamilton, and Rose Searby. *Places of the Heart: Memorials in Australia*. Melbourne: Australian Scholarly Publishing, 2012.

Baird, Rosemary. "Constructing Lives: A New Approach to Understanding Migrants' Oral History Narratives." *Oral History* (Britain) 40, no. 1 (Spring 2012): 57–66.

Balint, Ruth, and Zora Simic. "Histories of Migrants and Refugees in Australia." *Australian Historical Studies* 49, no. 3 (2018): 378–409.

Butler, Kelly Jean. *Witnessing Australian Stories: History, Testimony and Memory in Contemporary Culture*. London: Routledge, 2017 [2013].

Creet, Julia, and Andreas Kitzmann, eds. *Memory and Migration: Multidisciplinary Approaches to Memory Studies*. Toronto, Buffalo and London: University of Toronto Press, 2011.

Darian-Smith, Kate, and Paula Hamilton. "Memory and History in Australia: The State of the Field." *Memory Studies* 6, no. 3 (2013): 372–85.

Dellios, Alexandra. *Histories of Controversy: Bonegilla Migrant Centre*. Carlton, VIC: Melbourne University Publishing, 2017.

Freund, Alexander, and Alistair Thomson, eds. *Oral History and Photography*. New York and Basingstoke: Palgrave Macmillan, 2011.

Hamilton, Paula. "Speak Memory: Issues in Oral and Public History." In *What is Public History Globally?: Working with the Past in the Present*, edited by Paul Ashton and Alex Trapeznik. London and New York: Bloomsbury, 2019.

Henrich, Eureka. "Mobility, Migration and Modern Memory." In *History, Memory and Public Life: The Past in the Present*, edited by Anna Maerker, Simon Sleight, and Adam Sutcliffe, 101–25. London: Routledge, 2018.

Hirsch, Marianne. *The Generation of Postmemory: Writing and Visual Culture After the Holocaust*. New York: Columbia University Press, 2012.

Huyssen, Andreas. "Diaspora and Nation: Migration into Other Pasts." *New German Critique* 88 (Winter 2003): 147–64.

Kouvaros, George. *The Old Greeks. Photography, Cinema, Migration*. Crawley, WA: UWA Press, 2018.

Martin, Jean. *Refugee Settlers: A Study of Displaced Persons in Australia*. Canberra: ANU Press, 1965.

McKirdy, Carol. *Practicing Oral History with Immigrant Narrators*. Walnut Creek, CA: Left Coast Press, 2015.

Prime Minister of Australia. "The Apology to Forgotten Australians and Former Child Migrants," 16 November 2009. http://pandora.nla.gov.au/pan/110625/20091116-1801/www.pm.gov.au/node/6321.html.

Prime Minister of Australia. "The Apology to Victims and Survivors of Institutional Child Sexual Abuse," 22 October 2018. https://www.pm.gov.au/media/national-apology-address.

Ricoeur, Paul. *History, Memory, Forgetting*. Chicago: University of Chicago Press, 2004.

Stevens, Rachel, and Seamus O'Hanlon. "Intimate Oral Histories: Intercultural Romantic Relationships in Post-war Australia." *Australian Historical Studies* 49, no. 3 (2018): 359–77.

Whitlock, Gillian. "Salvage: Locating Lives in the Migration Museum." *Life Writing* 14, no. 4 (2017): 427–40.

Wills, Sara. "Between the Hostel and the Detention Centre: Possible Trajectories of Migrant Pain and Shame in Australia." In *Places of Pain and Shame: Dealing with 'Difficult Heritage'*, edited by William Logan and Kier Reeves, 263–80. London and New York: Routledge, 2009.

PART I

Oral Histories and Migration: Unsettling Memory Narratives

CHAPTER 2

"I Am No Longer the Same Person": Intimate History and the Gendered Experience of Migration

Alistair Thomson

Consider the 1970 photograph of British migrant Phyllis Cave standing beside her new family car at a migrant hostel in Sydney shortly after settling with her family in Australia. In the background we can see the hostel clothesline, and the corrugated steel "Nissen Hut" that was used as accommodation for new arrivals, and which migrants like Phyl recalled as baking hot in summer and freezing cold in winter (Fig. 2.1).

Phyl's evident pride in the new car signifies opportunities for economic success in the new country. Intriguingly, in her hand Phyl holds an envelope that hints at a coded message for her parents back in England. The contents of that envelope, and the fact that Phyl is holding it for the photograph, speak to the gendered nature and meanings of the migration experience, and to the ways in which those meanings, and Phyl's migrant identity, evolved between the photographic moment in 1970 and Phyl's memory of that moment four decades later. We'll return to this photograph and its evolving meanings.

A. Thomson (✉)
Monash University, Melbourne, VIC, Australia
e-mail: alistair.thomson@monash.edu

© The Author(s) 2019
K. Darian-Smith, P. Hamilton (eds.), *Remembering Migration*,
Palgrave Macmillan Memory Studies,
https://doi.org/10.1007/978-3-030-17751-5_2

Fig. 2.1 Phyllis Cave and "The car we won," Dundas Migrant Hostel, Sydney, April 1970. Courtesy of Phyllis Cave

This chapter draws upon migrant photographs, letters, oral histories and autobiographical writings that were collected in research by Jim Hammerton and myself about post-war British migration to Australia and the so-called Ten Pound Poms.[1] There are many sources that convey the public history of migration. Official statistics enumerate flows of people and patterns of mobility. Political speeches and government policies convey the intentions of receiving states and the nature of any support they provide for new arrivals, as well as political opposition to migrants and refugees. Media commentary and debate highlight perceptions of and attitudes about migrants and migration. Yet beneath the surface of these public sources is a more intimate layer of history, captured in different types of life stories, that conveys the personal experience and meanings of migration. Migrant life stories illuminate the lived experience of migration statistics, policy and commentary: why someone would uproot their family and move to the other side of the world; the bewilderment or excitement of arrival; the breach of family ties and the challenges of settlement; the pain of discrimination and the delight of acceptance; the never-ending sense of belonging to two places but not quite fitting in either. Migrant life stories show how migrants negotiate the material pressures and social expectations of migration, and they highlight how such negotiations take place within the intimate contexts of personal and family life. They highlight the thoughts and attitudes, feelings and impulses that animate migrant action and identities. They show how we make our lives in historical circumstances which are not always of our own choosing.[2]

Phyl Cave's migration story is one of four by post-World War II British migrant women which features in my book *Moving Stories: An Intimate History of Four Women Across Two Countries*.[3] In the book, the life stories of four women—Dorothy Wright, Gwen Good, Joan Pickett and Phyllis Cave—illuminate women's migration and the complex and sometimes contradictory experience of the domestic ideal for women that was at the heart of the post-war suburban dream.[4]

We know about these women's lives because they saved hundreds of letters and photographs they sent to family and friends back "home," and later recorded their migration experiences in writing and oral history interviews. Though migration is the connecting thread across these four lives, their collective story is not only about migration. Because these women were migrants, they recorded their lives in the letters and photographs they sent home. Wanting to describe, compare and explain their new life in Australia, they wrote in intimate detail and with acute sensitivity about aspects of Australian everyday life and women's experience that are often lost to history: about childcare and housework, depression and joy, friendship, family and married life. These women's life stories recall the recent but easily forgotten history of women's lives before the transformations led by feminists from the early 1970s.

My book *Moving Stories* was also a reflection on life stories, and about how historians can best use letters, photographs and memories to make sense of the past and of the potent resonance of the past in the present. Migrants narrate their experience throughout their everyday lives, as they explain their motivations to migration officials, share the trials and tribulations of departure and arrival with fellow migrants and recall their settlement experiences at family or community reunions. Only some of these migrant life stories are recorded, and even less survive for use by historians and curators. The most obvious records are the family photographs, often lovingly preserved in albums and faded through frequent use, that portray journeys to strange new worlds and the detail of migrant family life and achievement. Among British immigrants it was usually women who created family photo albums and sent photographs to relatives back home, and in so doing created visual representations of family life in Australia.[5] Women were also the primary correspondents in these migrant families, as they are in many families. Migrant women used letters to sustain transnational relations, to communicate and reassure and to make sense of migration and family life, and about themselves. Some migrants also kept journals (most commonly on a long sea voyage) that track day-to-day events, insights and surprises. Others wrote accounts long after arrival (or indeed after return), and these retrospective memoirs fuse the story about past events with reflections on the meanings of migration and the identity of the migrant in the present. Perhaps most important are oral history recordings that include stories that were neither photographed nor written down by people who did not have the time, resources or skills to create such records. Like memoir, recorded memories tell of both the past and its present meanings, yet they also capture the migrant's voice (in audio recording) and physical presence (in video recording) and offer multi-sensory audio-visual clues about the migrant experience, etched into the ways in which people perform significant stories from their lives.

Yet, migrant life stories are not straightforward mirrors of experience, and effective interpretation and curation requires acute awareness of the factors that shape each story.[6] Each life story mode comes with conventions that impact on their use—expectations about how to write a letter or frame a photograph, for example—and these conventions vary across time and culture. Communication and recording technologies also impact the account: the nineteenth-century hand-written letter that took months to reach its destination tells a rather different story compared with the instantaneous twenty-first century email or Facebook posting; the pocket cameras popularized by Kodak across the twentieth century—with perhaps 12, 24 or 36 negatives that were sent away for developing—were often used more carefully and selectively than cameras on today's smart phones that can take, edit and send innumerable images of just about anything (though both old and new photographic technologies have been used to capture and display personal achievement and success). The communicative relationships and motivations of the migrant narrator also influence the story that is shared. Letters may be intended to console or reassure, or perhaps to encourage others to leave home; migrant photographs that are preserved and displayed may highlight happy families and material achievements (the new house and car) so that failure or unhappiness is not apparent. Migrant accounts are also moulded by the cultural language and meanings that individual narrators adopt and adapt as they seek to find words and concepts to articulate their own experience; for example, in a migrant nation like Australia the popular narrative of forging a successful life against the odds in a new land is an attractive narrative genre. And as cultural meanings change—for example, from assimilation to multicultur-alism—individual narrators develop and negotiate new ways to tell their stories. That negotiation is, of course, individual as much as cultural, and changing personal feelings, understandings and identity—which historians often label "subjectivity"—also impact the story told, as narrators seek to create a past they can live with which makes sense and provides comfort in the present. The return migrant, for example, often negotiates both public sentiment and personal feelings about the perceived "failure" of their migration, and may well transform the migration story into a more affirm-ing account of self-discovery through travel and adventure.[7]

Migrant life stories are thus not simply a source to illustrate the events of departure, arrival and settlement. Personal narratives, in whatever form, also articulate the meanings of such events, at the time and as those mean-ings change over the course of the migrant's life. And the ways in which the story is told—the framing of the photograph, the self-censorship of the letter or the composure of a comforting memoir—can suggest as much about the migration experience as the contents of the account. The medium is part of the message.

Let me now return to the photo of Phyllis Cave to show how migrant life stories can illuminate the ways in which gender constraints and expecta-tions shape the experience of migration, just as migration may in turn trans-form women's roles and opportunities. This case study draws upon a range of life story sources that Phyl has shared with me over the years. These include a written account of her family's migration that she sent to my British-based research project in 2000, letters that Phyl sent to her parents and other relatives between 1969 and 1974, a set of family photographs and an oral history interview we conducted on the Isle of Wight in 2006.[8]

Phyl, her husband Colin and their three primary-school-age children arrived in Sydney in 1969. Colin had been a farm worker in southern England where the family lived in a series of rented farm cottages that were "tied" to the job. Farm work was seasonal and Colin struggled to hold down a job, and every time he lost his job the family had to move home. Phyl was the driving force behind the decision to take up the assisted passage to Australia, which she hoped would offer a new start for Colin and a more settled future for the family.

22   A. THOMSON

Like many other British migrants, Phyl sent home letters and photographs that portrayed a beautiful country and wonderful lifestyle, and which asserted the success of their migration. In her letters Phyl described the novelties of Australian life and landscape and reassured her anxious family that their migration was a good decision. The photos could, quite literally, show off this success, and they offered a potent sense of visual authenticity. Four months after arriving in Australia, Phyl's letter to her parents included a set of photographs depicting their day trips out of Sydney. Phyl's letter explained that:

> Some of these are Palm Beach & some are Jenolan Caves & some Katoomba & Fitzroy Falls [...] I certainly think we've made the right decision coming here—don't you? I think you'll have to join us later too when we get our own house. I'd love you to see the country. As you can see from the photos it really is very beautiful.[9]

Buying their own home in Australia was central to the Cave family's migration aspirations, as it was for so many post-war migrants from Europe. For the Cave family, whose English life had been blighted by constant changes in rental accommodation, Australia offered the promise of more secure employment and a home of their own. In their first Australian year the Caves lived in a Sydney migrant hostel as they saved for a house on the cheapest fringes of outer western Sydney. Colin found steady work building cool-rooms for farmers. Phyl, who had taken in piecemeal machine-knitting work in England while she raised three small children, found her skills in great demand in Australia and took a full-time job promoting knitting machines and patterns in department stores. Given Colin's work history, Phyl had strong personal reasons for getting a job, but she was not unusual among married migrant women in post-war Australia who took up paid work at a higher rate than native-born mothers.[10]

Hostel life made it easier for both parents to work. The hostel restaurant reduced family domestic labour and a small Nissen Hut (sometimes divided and shared with another family) was comparatively quick to clean. Eleven-year-old Heather Cave was now old enough to walk with her two younger siblings to school, and at the hostel the children were relatively safe among hordes of hostel playmates as they waited for working parents to come home.

Even so, raising the funds for the home deposit was a real struggle, especially when the children got sick in the unhealthy hostel and Phyl had to stop work. Their home dream looked to be dashed when the man who drove Colin to work each day left the hostel, and it seemed that Colin, who could not afford a car, would have to give up his job on the other side of town. Out of the blue, the family had a memorable lucky break, and the new home was secured, when Colin won a new Ford Cortina in a lottery. Phyl sent home the photo of herself standing beside the new car, in an ecstatic letter that reported that the car was worth $2180 ("a bl-dy fortune") and Colin was "like a cat with two tails." She concluded that "our luck has certainly changed."[11]

In 1970, this photo represented the family's changing fortunes in Australia and their optimism for the future. In 2000, when Phyl included this image with the set of her "best" migration photos that she sent to our research project, she added a new caption explaining that this was "The car we won and our hut [at the migrant hostel] was the first one at the back by the fence." Phyl's written migration story which accompanied the photos emphasized the importance of the lottery win at a time of financial difficulties while they were living in the hostel and saving for a house, and in our interview six years later at her home on the Isle of Wight she told the same story with great enthusiasm.

The day after I interviewed Phyl, I returned with my laptop and we browsed through photographs from her collection that I had scanned onto the computer. Tiny Kodak Instamatic images from the 1970s now filled the computer screen in dramatic detail. As Phyl looked at each image, they triggered stories that often spiralled off in unexpected directions and enriched my understanding of the photos and the moments they pictured. The photo of the lottery car now sparked a very different memory, as Phyl pointed to the envelope in her hand and explained that it contained her first Australian pay check.

In 1970, when Phyl sent this photo to be circulated among relatives in England, including both Phyl and Colin's parents, her letter celebrated the lottery win and the car, but for Phyl the image had another, more intimate meaning that became increasingly significant over time. The more we talked, the more Phyl opened up about her migration experience. She now explained that Colin had not just been unlucky at work in England, he had lost jobs because he was an unreliable worker who sometimes mixed in the wrong circles. Phyl had been the driving force for the family's emigration because she wanted to take Colin away from bad influences in England so the family could begin a better life on the other side of the world. She had been determined to get a job in Australia so she could guarantee a secure home of their own that was not dependent on

Colin's work. As Phyl recalled in our interview, "If I could work, it didn't matter what he did, I was secure, and I could keep the home. That was what was behind that. First, last, and in the middle."[12]

This first pay check was thus especially significant, and when Phyl sent the lottery car photo to her own parents—who knew about Colin's troubled work history—they understood the hidden significance of the envelope in Phyl's hand. It signified that Phyl was working and the family's future was thus secured, regardless of Colin.

In fact, Phyl's Australian job blossomed into a successful professional career. Over the next few years Phyl's letters were effusive about her burgeoning machine-knitting career, and they highlight the ways in which Phyl's life and identity were transformed through migration. In 1973 she wrote home that she was "in charge of 36 [machine knitting] demonstrators in the metropolitan area."

> I travel from store to store and have driven 7,000 miles since May! [...] I work at home sometimes as I also supervise the writing of the knitting patterns and it's my job to check them and type them up for the printers & to organize the photography etc. Quite an interesting job and an experience I wouldn't have missed. Next year I have to train girls from all over N.S.W. It wouldn't matter where I went now I would know someone! I must admit that I am no longer the same person who was tied to the kitchen sink at home and I certainly would find it very difficult to go back to that again! Australia is a beautiful country.[13]

For Phyl, "beautiful country" was both a literal and a metaphorical expression, capturing both the wonder of the Australian landscape and the opportunities she was enjoying in the new country. Though Phyl did not describe herself as a feminist, she was clearly influenced by feminist criticisms of the constraints of women's domestic role that had "tied" her to "the kitchen sink" in England, and she was relishing the self-confidence and financial independence she was gaining through her Australian career.

That career was cut short in 1976, when Phyl had an unplanned fourth child. More importantly, Colin had lost his job, resented Phyl's success and wanted to reassert his preeminent role in the family. He began to complain of homesickness and insisted that Phyl and the children return with him to England. Phyl had been planning childcare so she would restart at work, but now struggled to imagine life as a single mother in Australia. Though she considered the option of remaining in Australia with the children, Phyl had no relatives in Sydney for emotional support or to help with childcare, she doubted that any government support for a single parent would be sufficient, and she did not want to break up the family.

Reluctantly, she agreed to return to England. Seventeen-year-old Heather, the eldest child, refused to leave Australia and the family went back to England without her. Phyl was heartbroken about the disintegration of the family and the loss of her daughter, and bitterly disappointed about the end of her career. Life back in England was difficult. Colin contracted rheumatoid arthritis and never worked again. Phyl's initial success with a wool shop ended with bankruptcy in the recession of the early 1990s and the loss of their home. In 1995 she and Colin separated and he died a few years later.

When Phyl now looks back on her life, the years in Australia, and especially her tremendously successful though short-lived career, are a highlight. In our interview, and when we looked over her old photos, Phyl emphasized the skill and success of her Australian working life. A picture of Heather in their Sydney backyard triggered a story about the dress she is wearing, which Phyl had made and which she used at work to demonstrate the clothes you could create on a knitting machine. In another photo, the front corner lights of Phyl's company car peaked out from the edge of a sunlit and smiling photo of Phyl and Colin watering the new rose bushes in their Sydney garden, and prompted a story about learning to drive (despite Colin's scepticism) so that she could supervise her team of knitting-machine demonstrators. The 1973 publicity shot of Phyl working as a knitting-machine demonstrator for Lemair Helvetia reminded Phyl that she had knitted the jumper and skirt she was wearing and that her smile displayed a new set of dentures because "I'd had all my top teeth out the day before." The photo then sparked a detailed account of the skills of pattern-making and sales demonstration (Fig. 2.2).

In 2000 Phyl had sent me the photo clipped to the 1973 letter that exclaimed that she was "no longer the same person who was tied to the kitchen sink at home." She captioned the image, "Phyl Sydney Wide." *Sydney Wide* was the name of the discount shop where she was demonstrating the machine, but the caption also evokes the many miles across metropolitan Sydney that Phyl travelled for work and a potent memory of expansive opportunities in her Australian years. In 2000, and even more emphatically during our interview in 2006, Phyl was quite clear that this photo of her at work best matched the sentiments of the 1973 letter, and that her Australian career was the time of her life.

Fig. 2.2 "Phyl Sydney Wide," 1973. Courtesy of Phyllis Cave

Taken together, Phyl Cave's photos, letters and memories illuminate both the gendered nature of the migration experience *and* the changing meanings of migration. They show how family circumstances and gender relations shaped the migration experience, and that migration might in turn transform family roles and gender identities. They show how migration might open up new opportunities for women, but how gender expectations and material circumstances might then limit those opportunities. Yet, they also show that once change was experienced it was never forgotten and that those memories would shadow and shape Phyl's life thereafter. They highlight a sense of the challenges faced and the opportunities gained and lost by a woman migrant of Phyl Cave's generation and circumstances.

NOTES

1. See A. James Hammerton and Alistair Thomson, *Ten Pound Poms: Australia's Invisible Migrants* (Manchester: Manchester University Press, 2005); A. James Hammerton, *Migrants of the British Diaspora Since the 1960s: Stories from Modern Nomads* (Manchester: Manchester University Press, 2017).
2. On oral history and migration see Rena Benmayor and Andor Skotnes eds, *International Yearbook of Oral History and Life Stories, Vol. III, Migration and Identity* (Oxford: Oxford University Press, 1994); Alistair Thomson, "Oral History and Migration Studies," *Oral History* 27, no. 1 (1999): 24–37; A. James Hammerton and Eric Richards, *Speaking to Immigrants: Oral Testimony and the History of Australian Migration* (Canberra: Research School of Social Sciences, Australian National University, 2002); Nathalie Huynh Chau Nguyen, *Memory is Another Country: Women of the Vietnamese Diaspora* (Santa Barbara, CA: Praeger, 2009).
3. Alistair Thomson, *Moving Stories: An Intimate History of Four Women Across Two Countries* (Manchester and Sydney: Manchester University Press and UNSW Press, 2011).
4. Thomson, "'Tied to the Kitchen Sink?' Women's Lives and Women's History in Mid-twentieth Century Britain and Australia," *Women's History Review* 22, no. 1 (2013): 126–47.
5. On migrant oral history and photography see Lynda Mannik, "Remembering, Forgetting, and Feeling with Photographs," in Alexander Freund and Alistair Thomson eds, *Oral History and Photography* (New York: Palgrave Macmillan, 2011), 77–96.
6. Alistair Thomson, "Life Stories and Historical Analysis," in Simon Gunn and Lucy Faire eds, *Research Methods for History* (Edinburgh: Edinburgh University Press, 2011), 104–21.
7. Thomson, "I Live On My Memories: British Return Migrants and the Possession of the Past," *Oral History* 31, no. 2 (2013): 55–65.
8. Copies of Phyllis Cave's letters, photographs and unpublished manuscripts are held in the British Australian Migration Collection, Mass Observation Archive, University of Sussex Special Collections, Brighton, England; Phyllis Cave, interviewed by Alistair Thomson, 5 June 2006, Isle of Wight, British Australian Migration Collection, Mass Observation Archive, University of Sussex Special Collections, Brighton, England, cassette recording with transcript. Phyllis Cave has granted permission for use of her words and photographs in my writings.
9. Phyllis Cave, Letter to Mum and Dad, 10 April 1970. I have written about my research relationship with Phyl Cave, and the challenges of "sharing authority" in interviewing and interpretation in Alistair Thomson, "Moving Stories, Women's Lives: Sharing Authority in Oral History," *Oral History* 39, no. 2 (2011): 73–82.

10. Hammerton and Thomson, *Ten Pound Poms*, 230–37.
11. Phyllis Cave, Letter to Mum and Dad, 10 April 1970.
12. Phyllis Cave, interview, 2006.
13. Phyllis Cave, Letter to Peter and Patricia Cave, 16 December 1973.

BIBLIOGRAPHY

Benmayor, Rena, and Andor Skotnes, eds. *International Yearbook of Oral History and Life Stories, Volume III, Migration and Identity*. Oxford: Oxford University Press, 1994.

Cave, Phyllis. Interviewed by Alistair Thomson, 5 June 2006, Isle of Wight. British Australian Migration Collection, Mass Observation Archive, University of Sussex Special Collections, Brighton, England. Cassette recording with transcript.

Hammerton, A. James. *Migrants of the British Diaspora Since the 1960s: Stories from Modern Nomads*. Manchester: Manchester University Press, 2017.

Hammerton, A. James, and Eric Richards. *Speaking to Immigrants: Oral Testimony and the History of Australian Migration*. Canberra: Research School of Social Sciences, Australian National University, 2002.

Hammerton, A. James, and Alistair Thomson. *Ten Pound Poms: Australia's Invisible Migrants*. Manchester: Manchester University Press, 2005.

Mannik, Lynda. "Remembering, Forgetting, and Feeling with Photographs." In *Oral History and Photography*, edited by Alexander Freund and Alistair Thomson, 77–96. New York: Palgrave Macmillan, 2011.

Nguyen, Nathalie Huynh Chau. *Memory is Another Country: Women of the Vietnamese Diaspora*. Santa Barbara, CA: Praeger, 2009.

Thomson, Alistair. "I Live On My Memories: British Return Migrants and the Possession of the Past." *Oral History* 31, no. 2 (2003): 55–65.

Thomson, Alistair. "Life Stories and Historical Analysis." In *Research Methods for History*, edited by Simon Gunn and Lucy Faire, 104–21. Edinburgh: Edinburgh University Press, 2016.

Thomson, Alistair. *Moving Stories: An Intimate History of Four Women Across Two Countries*. Manchester and Sydney: Manchester University Press and UNSW Press, 2011a.

Thomson, Alistair. "Moving Stories, Women's Lives: Sharing Authority in Oral History." *Oral History* 39, no. 2 (2011b): 73–82.

Thomson, Alistair. "Oral History and Migration Studies." *Oral History* 27, no. 1 (1999): 24–37.

Thomson, Alistair. "'Tied to the Kitchen Sink?' Women's Lives and Women's History in Mid-twentieth Century Britain and Australia." *Women's History Review* 22, no. 1 (2013): 126–47.

CHAPTER 3

Oral Histories of Displaced Persons: "What for? The Story Like Mine's Plenty Now"

Jayne Persian

As a girl in inter-war Poland, Helena Turkiewicz was orphaned, made homeless by the age of 9 and raped by her employer when she was 12. During World War II she was jailed by the Russians and sent to Siberia, then made her way with Polish compatriots through Uzbekistan and Africa, bearing a daughter to an Italian prisoner of war in Tangiers, before arriving in Australia. She has been the subject of her filmmaker daughter's autobiographical documentary, as well as the inspiration for her daughter's 1984 movie *Silver City*, a romance played out in Australia's post-war immigration camps.[1] However, she was not keen to be interviewed as part of the National Library of Australia's "Polish Australians Oral History Project." Helena argued against being an interesting subject: "What for? The story like mine's plenty now."[2]

This chapter aims to answer that question, using qualitative data from oral history interviews I carried out with post-war displaced persons (DPs) and their offspring from Europe and China.[3] It focuses on the utility of oral histories to the displaced persons themselves, and explores how oral histories add to historical understandings of migration, and reflects on emotion in oral history, particularly in the transmission of family memories.

J. Persian (✉)
University of Southern Queensland, Toowoomba, QLD, Australia
e-mail: Jayne.Persian@usq.edu.au

© The Author(s) 2019   29
K. Darian-Smith, P. Hamilton (eds.), *Remembering Migration*,
Palgrave Macmillan Memory Studies,
https://doi.org/10.1007/978-3-030-17751-5_3

Approximately 170,000 predominantly Central and Eastern Europeans arrived in Australia as International Refugee Organization (IRO)-sponsored refugees between 1947 and 1953. These displaced persons (DPs) were part of a million-strong group made up of people who found themselves in Germany at the end of the war: Jewish concentration camp survivors, voluntary and forced labourers of the Reich, non-German soldiers in military units withdrawing westwards and civilian evacuees fleeing west from the oncoming Russian Army.[4] They refused repatriation to Soviet bloc countries and were joined by others attempting to outrun the encroaching Iron Curtain in the post-war period. The DPs were settled in Australia under a two-year indentured labour scheme; accommodation was organized in migrant camps and families were often separated. European DPs were joined by approximately 7000 anti-Soviet Russians and Russian-speaking Jews resident in China who were resettled after the Chinese Communist Revolution in 1949, both by the International Refugee Organization and privately. For both groups, Australia was interested not in their stories, but in their capacity to work, and to assimilate.[5]

Stories of displaced persons have historically been silenced as politically inexpedient or relegated to ethnic, community or family history. Daniel G. Cohen argues that issues for historians attempting to "resurrect" DP memory include the cohort's lack of collective identity and sense of historical agency.[6] Glenda Sluga has noted the "isolation" of post-war migrants in Australia from "any shared community input of historical awareness" until they were "approached by an eager oral historian."[7] In recent decades, however, increased interest in oral and social history has brought these stories into the public domain, with historians arguing that "the common folk and the dispossessed have a history and that history must be written."[8] Oral testimonies also "personalise" history, telling us, as Alessandro Portelli argues: "not just what people did, but what they wanted to do, what they believed they were doing and what they now think they did."[9]

Oral histories, collected in libraries, museums and by ethnic communities, have thus sought to address the lack of information regarding post-war migrants to Australia, while also giving voice to the migrants themselves. So influential has this methodology become that it is now rare to come across any writing on migration that does *not* incorporate some form of oral history.

Former Ukrainian displaced person Kateryna Olijnyk Longley has emphasized the importance of oral history and memory in relation to her own family history. Although stories told by the DPs were initially "simply not welcome in Australia," Longley believes that for some migrants the telling of these stories is psychologically important. They are "drawn by the past, however appalling its memories might be, because there at least some semblance of stability can be achieved by packaging the past as a set of rehearsed stories." This storytelling is a "way of forcing attention on the bodily experience of suffering, which is obscured by historical narrative's smooth stylizing gestures." A "re-narration of the past" assists in rendering it "bearable, speakable and containable as a basis for building the future."[10]

Some displaced persons have participated in oral history projects partly for the sake of their children. For families, oral testimony can work to fix identity or to contextualize in narrative form a story of how a DP ended up in Australia. Longley has argued that telling stories, particularly among family members, can become a "ritualised process" of performance art. Such tales are an "intensely personal act of self-invocation, a conjuring of the old lost self, a frozen self, into the new living reality, across an impossible chasm."[11] Writer John Hughes concurs, commenting about his Ukrainian grandfather:

> what interested me most about my grandfather was his memories. ... As with most migrants, his memories were what interested him most about himself. Memories were his currency—it was how he defined himself—and he dealt in them as a means of filling in the temporal emptiness of his new place.[12]

While perhaps psychologically beneficial, this sort of "re-narration of the past" can be problematic for the historian. Once taken out of the familial sphere, migrant memories are subject to a new re-narration, to fit into "canons of appropriateness and rhetorical stereotypes."[13] British historian Kathy Burrell found in interviews with former Polish DPs that they emphasized turning points, survival and autonomy in an attempt to reduce the "distance between the story, the narrator and the listener," so as to make a dramatic account more accessible in modern-day Britain.[14] Soviet historian Gelinada Grinchenko has warned against those she terms "professional witnesses," noting their narratives are "chronologically and topically logical, well structured, and are stable, multiple-approved constructs."[15] Linda McDowell, interviewing Latvian DPs in Britain, has further noted that "Many of these people were able to take advantage of the post-war confusion, to rewrite their identities, affiliation and previous histories, raising complex questions for an oral historian about contested histories and memories that have been expunged."[16]

In Australia, these "approved constructs" in oral interviews are usually framed in national rather than transnational terms. They can be one-dimensional, celebrating assimilation through stories of "exemplary citizens with successful careers," who overcame personal difficulties to positively contribute to Australian society.[17] Other narratives offer simplistic and somewhat anachronistic accounts of ethnic community culture and/or multiculturalism. Often, the point of arrival to Australia is seen by migrants, and oral historians, as the endpoint of their stories. A transnational experience is thus locked into a well-known genre of laudatory national remembering.

Migrant stories are no longer ignored by the wider community, but they are more commonly collated than analysed. As ethnicity is deemed central to multicultural histories, the political affiliations, class, family, gender and sexuality of individuals can be sidelined or ignored.[18] The contexts of war, trauma and displacement are also hard for many who are born in Australia to empathize with. One pioneering migrant oral history interviewer exclaimed while interviewing a Hungarian DP: "It is so hard to imagine. ... I could really make a film from all this."[19] Burrell has identified a "disjuncture between ordinary people relating such extraordinary experiences, and the strange sensation of wartime traumas being revisited in people's living rooms."[20] Sometimes emotional trauma is ignored "partly because writers have not always understood the novelty and difficulty of what they are trying to do."[21] But not all those DPs interviewed have traumatic stories. Some interviewees, including former forced labourers under the Nazis, refuse to see anything unique in their life experiences, and may confound narrative expectations by putting a positive spin on their wartime lives.[22]

ANECDOTE

One of the primary utilities of oral history for migration historians is the anecdote or "narrative snapshot," which can add colourful detail to a previously outlined chronology.[23] Czech DP and historian Michael Cigler noted that "the essential humanity of the migrant experience, in all its diversity, complexity and contradictiveness, is readily expressed through the spoken word and often summed up in anecdote."[24] These recollections, referenced here from other collections as well as my own study, can be

3 ORAL HISTORIES OF DISPLACED PERSONS: "WHAT FOR? THE STORY... 33

ambivalent and can work against a celebratory national narrative, perhaps "combining gratitude at rescue from Europe with resentment at exploitation by the Australian authorities," and/or the prejudiced attitudes of locals.[25]

One Latvian identified the DPs in Australia as the "White Slaves of the twentieth century."[26] Olga Iszczyszyn, a Ukrainian DP, bleakly noted: "[we] were indentured to work to pay off our grim passage to freedom."[27] Many women DPs accommodated as "dependents" at migrant holding centres felt they were "held as hostages" for the breadwinner's "parole": "The difficulty was that we were not together with a family—with husbands. For us, it was: as long as we are together, and we are not."[28] Eugenia Bakaitis, a Lithuanian DP, described how she felt after travelling to the largest migrant camp at Bonegilla in north-east Victoria:

> Bonegilla was in the middle of nowhere. There was not a tree, not a flower, just an empty army barracks in an empty, hot, dusty place. There was barbed wire all around it like a German concentration camp. And the heat. The supervisor used to tell us to bring bucket after bucket of cold water and pour it on the floor and then we would all sit in it. We felt this enormous sense of deepening isolation. We didn't know where we were, we just knew that there was no way back.[29]

Anecdotes can also highlight the historical agency of the displaced persons, even under trying conditions. Kati Toth, a Hungarian DP, later admitted how her husband had evaded the work contract:

> Julius was not used to hard physical work. He had to do the jobs allocated to him under the DP work contract. ... He could not cope with such a strenuous job and needed to take on other work. He swallowed some chocolate wrapping which showed up on the x-ray as an ulcer. He was advised to take it easy for a while. This is how he got out of the contract.[30]

Oral histories also show that some migrants were not focused on assimilation into a new host community, but upon their place within their own émigré communities. "Snowy" explained the origins and benefits of his small Ukrainian community in Melbourne:

> We'd been set up in Europe to look after our people who might arrive, it was our future job. ... Nobody knew where he was going but wherever we went we would make sure that we stuck together, remember who we are, keep

our traditions. Life in the camps strengthened us. In camp we met people from many hundred kilometers from our villages and developed a liking, respect and trust.[31]

Relations within DP communities could, however, be complex. There were existing class issues, between the "intelligentsia" and the "peasants" in Europe, and between "city" and "country" Russians in China. There were also divisions between pre-war and post-war migrant communities: Croatian DP "Joe" described the reaction of "Yugoslav[s] already resident in Australia to his DP cohort":

We were quite isolated and unpopular; they avoided us. ... They called us Ustashis, fascists, Nazis, throatcutters, butchers, gangsters, all sorts of things because we wanted to call ourselves Croatian.[32]

For the Polish community, Soviet spies were a concern. George Klim, prominent in the Polish community in Newcastle, explained:

there were certainly a few people [who] ... did what the Communist regime instructed them to do, or suggested to them to do. There was a very small group which was financed by the Communist Consul-General here until 1990. They usually formed either sport associations, or Polish-Australian cultural groups, they called themselves.[33]

Soviet spies were also an issue within the Russian community from China, and spying in general is a theme that comes up surprisingly often in interviews. In my interview with "Evdokia," whose family arrived in Australia via China and Hong Kong, she noted in an aside that her policeman uncle engaged in espionage during World War II for the British and Americans, and that upon arrival in Australia he worked for the Commonwealth Special Intelligence Bureau.[34]

For many, a sense of transnational diaspora was paramount. Bohdan Mykytiuk, a child of DPs, admitted to a mythologized nostalgia, referring to his vision of Ukraine as a "garden of Eden."[35] Suzanna Prushynsky recalled that her family was so involved in the Ukrainian community that the children "were not allowed to speak English at home."[36] Highlighting a lack of understanding between the émigré and the host culture, Latvian displaced person "Irma" recalled attempting to raise money for a Lutheran children's home at the Ladies' Guild and the Young Women's Christian Association (YWCA):

3 ORAL HISTORIES OF DISPLACED PERSONS: "WHAT FOR? THE STORY... 35

I [wore] my national costume with all the jewelry. Then they asked about the times back in Germany and I know that there were a lot of people—old people—who needed help back there, and I hoped that they would open their hearts and their purses and help us a bit. And after I told the sad story they gathered round me and admired my jewelry and my national costume and said, 'Oh, how nice' [laughs].[37]

Conversely, Gunna Kinne, a Latvian nationalist, described attending a rally after Australia accorded *de jure* recognition to the Soviet occupation of the Baltic States in 1974 (this decision was reversed by the subsequent government): "Usually we felt as second-grade citizens in Australia, we all stood out only in a bad way. This was sort of standing out in a good way, even if only externally."[38]

Some of the casually recalled anecdotes in my oral history interviews have contained unique research leads. Ukrainian migrant "Nastasia"[39] told me a shocking story: at an Austrian DP camp, women drowned themselves and their babies in the river, and "six families were shot by their fathers," who then shot themselves, to avoid forced repatriation to the Soviet Union. Nastasia and her husband hid in the mountains for three months. This story has since led to further work on the so-called Lienz Cossacks, who were forcibly repatriated to the Soviet Union by the British in mid-1945.[40]

In another case, "Leo," a Polish Jew, described his meeting with Australian selection officers ("consuls"):

There were two consuls, there was a young one and an old one. ... The old one wouldn't let any Jew through. The secretary was a refugee, so you would go in with a carton of cigarettes, American cigarettes, you would give it to the secretary ... she knew it ... that carton of cigarettes came from the International Refugee Organization.[41]

This anecdote fills in the detail of the vagaries of the anti-Semitism involved in Australian migration selection practices.[42] Being white and non-Jewish was more important to some Australian officials, cancelling out a history of Nazi collaboration. "Jakub," a Czech, confided that former Nazis were let into Australia as DPs: "There were some guys ... on the job they had to keep their sleeves down [due to their SS blood group tattoo]. You know the reason [but] we don't talk about that."[43] These anecdotes confirm some of the scholarship around Nazi infiltration of the DP migration scheme.

Emotion and Family Transmission

Oral testimonies can open up the intimate spaces of private emotion. Mark Cave notes such emotional access is the "key to understanding the actions and attitudes of interviewees."[44] Analysing what these emotions *mean* are as important for the oral historian as noting their existence: why were *these particular* memories remembered?[45] This is particularly relevant when interviewing second- and third-generation descendants of migrants, who are not perhaps as well-rehearsed in "public stories," and sometimes share private stories, described by Longley as:

> Stories of intense suffering, humiliation, exclusion from all possible worlds, stories so painful that they may be untellable even now except within the security of the immediate family or deeply trusted friends. ... They have not yet been transformed into acceptable stories. To tell them is almost to relive them.[46]

Some DPs did not cope well with their migration to Australia. Upon arrival, "the migrants did the dirty jobs the Australians were not interested in."[47] "Robert," whose Polish Ukrainian father-in-law was sent to work for BHP at Port Kembla in New South Wales, remembered:

> Our people were basically off the land, so working in heavy industry was a bit of a culture shock. A lot of our blokes are heavy drinkers and I know with my father-in-law the things that he went through and he used to drink and a lot of it was to blot out the things, you know.[48]

Krystyna, a daughter of Polish DPs, participated in a university assignment requiring her to question her parents regarding their migration experiences. One of the questions was whether her parents regretted coming to Australia. She says: "I always remember what my father said, which was that he was very unhappy, he didn't care for Australia and he seemed very bitter. ... He basically said: 'What's there to be happy about? Sure I earn a salary but that's it.'" Krystyna lamented: "The unspoken pain behind that statement!"[49]

Oral histories are thus a valuable way in which to tease out themes of intergenerational and intercultural transmission, with a focus on "individual and family lives."[50] As noted by Maurice Halbwachs, family memory is a "living link between generations" which contributes to identity formation. However, it is very hard to isolate family oral history from community oral history or, indeed, any other dominant memory discourse.[51] Writer Tom Shapcott has argued that children of migrants tend to reject, or minimize, their language and cultural and family memory in order to fit in. In contrast, by the third generation "there is often a profound wish by that stage to rediscover the past and the abandoned culture."[52]

In my own oral history interviews I was interested in the traces of memory in individual testimony, and how this was evident in the importance of family and a definite ethnic culture. Some have already grappled with these questions. Hughes writes:

> We're taught it's essential that we remember. 'Lest we forget', we are told. But how can you forget what you never had a chance to remember? Memories you never had? How can you forget experiences that are not your own? Because this is what the injunction boils down to in the end: 'Remember the memories of somebody else'.[53]

This aspect of family transmission was usually raised by interviewees. Most DPs felt that they wanted to educate their children about their family history. Many expressed a desire to write their own autobiography for family members or a wider audience.

For second- and third-generation interviewees, a lack of access to their family's past was a common complaint. "Michael" learnt most about his father's past from his Australian mother. The arrest of his brother by Communist officials in Czechoslovakia prompted his father to "flee the Soviet system."[54] A teacher in Czechoslovakia, he worked as a labourer in Australia, drinking heavily. "Michael" explained: "He wouldn't talk, he would talk shit, he would talk a lot of drivel and a lot of stuff he's heard at the club ... it's not my place to pry. ... But it's interesting and it's always fascinated me."[55]

Second-generation Polish Ukrainian Peter Skrzynecki admitted, "My mother would tell me very little, my father told me nothing." However, this disinclination to dwell on the past worked to encourage rather than suppress Skrzynecki's innate curiosity. When he visited the National Archives to find out more about his family's history: "I sat there like a baby crying. ... It was like I had discovered a secret about myself. That piece of the puzzle that fitted together, occupations, date of births, religion, their places of birth." Skrzynecki, a poet who has written on issues of family memory, particularly in two autobiographical works, has also become an advocate of the national commemoration of post-war migrants.[56]

"Andrew," another second-generation Polish Ukrainian, was not told much about his family background. His mother even refused to apply for forced-labour compensation from the German government because that process involved dredging up the past: "Just forget about it."[57] When "Andrew's" children visited the National Archives to access family migration documents, it was an emotional experience: "This is my story and I didn't know anything about it." According to "Andrew," a "can of worms opened up—I've now got relatives everywhere!"[58]

For the most part, the DPs I talked to were interested in handing down family memory to their children and grandchildren. Their focus was on the individual and familial rather than the national or diasporic. The second and third generations also seem to be interested in family memory for reasons unrelated to ethnicity or nationality, but these individual and family memories are not always so easy to access.

While the "the vast structure of recollection"[59] can now feel intimidating or confusing, the work of a historian focusing on migration to Australia is, as Sara Wills has noted, "to produce histories based as much on the fact of migrancy as the myth of nation." In doing so, using an oral history methodology provides "scope for the remembrance of loss, disinheritance and the lack of a sense of belonging."[60] Individual memories provide illuminating anecdotes, traces of emotion and are also important ways in which to interrogate the transmission of memory in "individual and family lives."[61] This follows Longley's emphasis on recovering "life stories from lost worlds," as well as integrating Janis Wilton and Richard Bosworth's concern with "the small and beautiful"[62]—themes such as personal trauma and relationships with(in) family, culture and community—with the wider themes of national narrative, memory and commemoration.

Notes

1. Sophia Turkiewciz (Director), *Once My Mother* (Change Focus Media in association with Kalejdoskop Film, 2013); Sophia Turkiewicz (Director), *Silver City* (Limelight Productions, 1984).
2. Helena Turkiewicz, interviewed by Barry York, 9–10 April 2001, Adelaide, "Polish Australians Oral History Project," National Library of Australia, Oral TRC 4714.
3. All oral history interviewees mentioned here participated in oral history interviews with the author in either 2007, 2008 or 2018. The 2007/8 interviews were part of the author's PhD research at the University of

Sydney and interviewees were either directly requested, or they responded to a newspaper advertisement. The 2018 interview was carried out under Australian Research Council DP160101528, with ethics approval from the University of Southern Queensland. Names of all interviewees, who are displaced persons or their descendants, are anonymized for their privacy. Recordings and transcripts remain with the author.

4. It is estimated that only around 500 Jewish displaced persons arrived in Australia as part of the International Refugee Organization cohort. Suzanne Rutland, "Subtle Exclusions: Postwar Jewish Emigration to Australia and the Impact of the IRO Scheme," *The Journal of Holocaust Education* 10, no. 1 (Summer 2001): 56–57.

5. Jayne Persian, *Beautiful Balts: From Displaced Persons to New Australians* (Sydney: NewSouth Books, 2017).

6. Daniel G. Cohen, "Remembering Post-War Displaced Persons: From Omission to Resurrection," in Mareike Konig and Rainer Ohliger eds, *Enlarging European Memory: Migration Movements in Historical Perspective* (Ostfildern, Germany: Jan Thorbecke Verlag, 2006).

7. Glenda Sluga, "The Migrant Dreaming," *Journal of Intercultural Studies* 8, no. 2 (1987): 42.

8. Gary Y. Okihiro, cited in Kathleen M. Ryan, "'I Didn't Do Anything Important': A Pragmatic Analysis of the Oral History Interview," *The Oral History Review* 36, no. 1 (2009): 25, 35.

9. Alessandro Portelli, cited in Alan Young, "Oral History as Emergent Paradigm," *Special Issue: Oral History and Its Challenge(r)s, Oral History Association of Australia Journal*, no. 28 (2006): 5.

10. Kateryna Olijnyk Longley, "Remembering Rublivka: Life Stories from Lost Worlds," *Life Writing* 1, no. 1 (2004): 112–16.

11. Longley, "Remembering Rublivka," 112; see also Alexander Freund, "A Canadian Family Talks About Oma's Life in Nazi Germany: Three-Generational Interviews and Communicative Memory," *Oral History Forum D'histoire Orale, Special Issue: Remembering Family, Analysing Home: Oral History and the Family* 29 (2009): 25.

12. John Hughes, *The Idea of Home: Autobiographical Essay* (Artarmon, NSW: Giramondo Publishing, 2004), 21–22.

13. Elizabeth Tonkin, cited in Kate Darian-Smith, "Remembrance, Romance, and Nation: Memories of Wartime Australia," Selma Leydesdorff, Luisa Passerini and Paul Thompson eds, *International Yearbook of Oral History and Life Stories, Volume IV, Gender and Memory* (Oxford: Oxford University Press, 1996), 158.

14. Kathy Burrell, "Personal, Inherited, Collective: Communicating and Layering the Memory of Forced Polish Migration," *Immigrants and Minorities* 24, no. 2 (2006): 145, 149.

40   J. PERSIAN

15. Gelinada Grinchenko, "Ukrainian Ostarbeiters of the Third Reich: Remembering Patterns on Forced Labour in Nazi Germany," *Oral History Association of Australia Conference*, 2007: 13.
16. Linda McDowell, "Workers, Migrants, Aliens or Citizens? State Constructions and Discourses of Identity among Post-War European Labour Migrants in Britain," *Political Geography* 22 (2003): 870.
17. Maximilian Brändle, *Refugee Destination Queensland* (Kangaroo Point, QLD: Multicultural Writers & Arts Friendship Society, 1999), 4.
18. Donna R. Gabaccia, "The Multicultural History of Nations," in Lloyd Kramer and Sarah Maza eds, *A Companion to Western Historical Thought* (Malden, MA: Blackwell Publishing, 2007), 443.
19. Edith Noetel, interviewed by Janis Wilton, 9 June 1982, "The Oral Histories Project of the Ethnic Affairs Commission of NSW," State Library of New South Wales, CY MLOH 18/25.
20. Burrell, "Personal, Inherited, Collective," 148.
21. Alan Atkinson, "Do Good Historians Have Feelings?," in Stuart Macintyre ed., *The Historian's Conscience: Australian Historians on the Ethics of History* (Carlton, VIC: Melbourne University Press, 2004), 25.
22. Christoph Thonfeld, "The Shaping of Memory: Individual, Group and Collective Patterns of Recollection of Slave and Forced Labour for National Socialist Germany," *Proceedings of the 14th International Oral History Conference*, Sydney, Australia (12–16 July 2006).
23. Penny Summerfield, "Culture and Composure: Creating Narratives of the Gendered Self in Oral History Interviews," *Cultural and Social History* 1, no. 1 (2004): 89.
24. Barry York, *Michael Cigler: A Czech-Australian Story, From Displacement to Diversity, Studies in Australian Ethnic History Series, No 11* (Canberra: Centre for Immigration and Multicultural Studies, Research School of Social Sciences, Australian National University, 1996), 8.
25. James Jupp, *Immigration* (Melbourne: Oxford University Press, 1998), 105.
26. Ramunas Tarvydas, *From Amber Coast to Apple Isle: Fifty Years of Baltic Immigrants in Tasmania, 1948–1998* (Hobart, TAS: Baltic Semicentennial Commemoration Activities Organising Committee, 1997), 90.
27. Olga Iszczyszyn (Alexandra), "Immigration Bridge Australia," http://www.immigrationbridge.com.au/www/248/1001127/displayarticle/1011104.html?pub=1&pagemode=2&objectid=1037201; see also "Thousand Migrants Have Broken Work Contracts," *Sydney Morning Herald*, 7 March 1951.
28. Inese Petersons (1947–), interviewed by Allison Murchie, 2002, "South Australians Acting for Change: Welcoming Refugees Oral History Project," J. D. Somerville Oral History Collection, State Library of South Australia,

OH 636/2; "Irma" (1919–), interviewed by Karobi Mukherjee, 1989, "Lives of Older Women of Non-English Speaking Background and their Adaption to and Contribution to Life in South Australia," J. D. Somerville Oral History Collection, State Library of South Australia, OH 18/15.

29. Phillip Knightley, *Australia: A Biography of a Nation* (London: Vintage, 2001), 219.

30. Kati Toth, cited in Brändle, *Refugee Destination Queensland*, 121.

31. Andrew Markus and Eileen Sims, *Fourteen Lives—Paths to a Multicultural Community* (Clayton, VIC: Monash Publications in History: 16, Department of History, Monash University, 1993), 112.

32. "Joe," cited in Val Colic-Peisker, *Split Lives: Croatian Australian Stories* (Fremantle: Fremantle Arts Centre Press, 2004), 62.

33. Dr George Klim, interviewed by Barry York, 16–17 September and 1 October 1996, Canberra, "Polish Australians Oral History Project," National Library of Australia, Oral TRC 3498.

34. "Evdokia," interviewed by Jayne Persian, 2018, Brisbane, digital recording in author's possession.

35. Bohdan Mykytiuk, interviewed by Rob Willis, 21 October 2004, Bassendean, Western Australia, Rob and Olya Willis Folklore Collection, National Library of Australia, Oral TRC 5373/21–23.

36. Suzanna Prushynsky, interviewed by Rob Willis and Graham Seal, 26 October 2004, Rob and Olya Willis Folklore Collection, National Library of Australia, Oral TRC 5373/21–22.

37. "Irma" (1919–), interview, 1989.

38. Guna Kinne, cited in Karen Schamberger, Martha Sear, Kirsten Wehner, Jennifer Wilson and the *Australian Journeys* Gallery Development Team, National Museum of Australia, "Living in a Material World: Object Biography and Transnational Lives," *Transnational Ties: Australian Lives in the World*, Desley Deacon, Penny Russell and Angela Woollacott eds (Canberra: Australian National University EPress, 2008), 287.

39. "Nastasia", interviewed by Jayne Persian, 2007 and 2015, Sydney, cassette recording and handwritten notes in author's possession.

40. See Jayne Persian, "Cossack Identities: From Russian Emigres and Anti-Soviet Collaborators to Displaced Persons," *Special Issue: Refugee Family & Memory, Immigrants & Minorities* 36, no. 2 (2018): 125–42.

41. "Leo", interviewed by Jayne Persian, 2007, Sydney, cassette recording in author's possession.

42. Persian, *Beautiful Balts*, 61–66.

43. "Jakub", interviewed by Jayne Persian, 2007, Sydney, cassette recording in author's possession.

44. Mark Cave, "Reflections on Crisis Oral History," in Mark Cave and Stephen M. Sloan eds, *Listening on the Edge: Oral History in the Aftermath of Crisis* (Oxford: Oxford University Press, 2014), 96.

45. Paula Hamilton and Linda Shopes, "Introduction: Building Partnerships Between Oral History and Memory Studies," in Paula Hamilton and Linda Shopes eds, *Oral History and Public Memories* (Philadelphia: Temple University Press, 2008), viii–ix.
46. Kateryna Longley, "The Fifth World," *Ukrainian Settlement in Australia: Fifth Conference, Melbourne, 16–18 February 1990* (Melbourne: Slavic Section, Monash University, 1993), 129–30.
47. "Robert", interviewed by Jayne Persian, 2008, Wollongong, cassette recording in author's possession.
48. "Robert", interview, 2008.
49. Catherine Murphy, and United Trades and Labor Council (SA), *Boatload of Dreams: Journeys by European Immigrant Workers 1947–1994* (Adelaide, SA: United Trades and Labor Council (SA), 1994), 62.
50. Eric Richards, "Hearing Voices: An Introduction," in A. James Hammerton and Eric Richards eds, *Speaking to Immigrants: Oral Testimony and the History of Australian Migration*, Visible Immigrants (6). History Program and Centre for Immigration and Multicultural Studies, Research School of Social Sciences, Australian National University (Adelaide: Flinders University Press, 2002), 2.
51. Maurice Halbwachs cited in Anne Muxel, "Family Memory," in Daniel Bertaux and Paul Thompson eds, *Between Generations: Family Models, Myths, and Memories*, International Yearbook of Oral History and Life Stories, Volume II (Oxford University Press, 1993), 192, 193.
52. Tom Shapcott, "Multicultural Literature and Writing in Australia," in Jacques Delaruelle, Alexandra Karakostas-Sêdá and Anna Ward eds, *Writing in Multicultural Australia 1984: An Overview*, papers presented at the Multicultural Writers' Weekends in Sydney, 13 and 14 October 1984, and in Melbourne, 27 and 28 October 1984. (North Sydney: Australia Council for the Literature Board, 1985), 5–6.
53. Hughes, *The Idea of Home*, 16.
54. "Michael", interviewed by Jayne Persian, 2007, Sydney, cassette recording in author's possession.
55. "Michael", interview, 2007.
56. Peter Skrzynecki, *Old/New World* (St Lucia: University of Queensland Press, 2007); Peter Skrzynecki, *The Sparrow Garden* (St Lucia: University of Queensland Press, 2004); Peter Skrzynecki's Web Site, http://www.peterskrzynecki.com.
57. "Andrew", interviewed by Jayne Persian, 2008, Newcastle, handwritten notes in author's possession.
58. "Andrew", interview, 2008.
59. Proust, cited in Peter Read, *Returning to Nothing: The Meaning of Lost Places* (Cambridge: Cambridge University Press, 1996), 201.

60. Sara Wills, "Unstitching the Lips of a Migrant Nation," *Australian Historical Studies* 118 (2002): 71.
61. Richards, "Hearing Voices: An Introduction," 2.
62. Janis Wilton and Richard Bosworth, *Old Worlds and New Australia: The Post-War Migrant Experience* (Ringwood: Penguin Books Australia, 1984), 37.

Bibliography

"Andrew". Interviewed by Jayne Persian, 2008, Newcastle. Handwritten notes in author's possession.

Atkinson, Alan. "Do Good Historians Have Feelings?" In *The Historian's Conscience: Australian Historians on the Ethics of History*, edited by Stuart Macintyre. Carlton, VIC: Melbourne University Press, 2004.

Brändle, Maximilian. *Refugee Destination Queensland*. Kangaroo Point: Multicultural Writers & Arts Friendship Society (Queensland), 1999.

Burrell, Kathy. "Personal, Inherited, Collective: Communicating and Layering the Memory of Forced Polish Migration." *Immigrants and Minorities* 24, no. 2 (2006): 144–63.

Cave, Mark. "Reflections on Crisis Oral History." In *Listening on the Edge: Oral History in the Aftermath of Crisis*, edited by Mark Cave and Stephen M. Sloan, 1–16. Oxford: Oxford University Press, 2014.

Cohen, Daniel G. "Remembering Post-War Displaced Persons: From Omission to Resurrection." In *Enlarging European Memory: Migration Movements in Historical Perspective*, edited by Mareike Konig and Rainer Ohliger, 87–98. Ostfildern, Germany: Jan Thorbecke Verlag, 2006.

Colic-Peisker, Val. *Split Lives: Croatian Australian Stories*. Fremantle: Fremantle Arts Centre Press, 2004.

Darian-Smith, Kate. "Remembrance, Romance, and Nation: Memories of Wartime Australia." In *International Yearbook of Oral History and Life Stories, Volume IV, Gender and Memory*, edited by Selma Leydesdorff, Luisa Passerini and Paul Thompson, 151–64. Oxford: Oxford University Press, 1996.

"Evdokia". Interviewed by Jayne Persian, 2018, Brisbane. Digital recording in author's possession.

Freund, Alexander. "A Canadian Family Talks About Oma's Life in Nazi Germany: Three-Generational Interviews and Communicative Memory." *Oral History Forum D'histoire Orale, Special Issue: Remembering Family, Analysing Home: Oral History and the Family* 29 (2009): 1–26.

Gabaccia, Donna R. "The Multicultural History of Nations." In *A Companion to Western Historical Thought*, edited by Lloyd Kramer and Sarah Maza, 432–46. Malden, MA: Blackwell Publishing, 2007.

Grinchenko, Gelinada. "Ukrainian Ostarbeiters of the Third Reich: Remembering Patterns on Forced Labour in Nazi Germany." *Oral History Association of Australia Conference*, 2007, 1–14.

Hamilton, Paula, and Linda Shopes. "Introduction: Building Partnerships between Oral History and Memory Studies." In *Oral History and Public Memories*, edited by Paula Hamilton and Linda Shopes, vii–xvii. Philadelphia: Temple University Press, 2008.

Hughes, John. *The Idea of Home: Autobiographical Essay*. Artarmon, NSW: Giramondo Publishing, 2004.

"Irma" (1919–). Interviewed by Karobi Mukherjee, 1989. "Lives of Older Women of Non-English Speaking Background and their Adaption to and Contribution to Life in South Australia," J. D. Somerville Oral History Collection, State Library of South Australia, OH 18/15.

Iszczyszyn (Alexandra), Olga. "Immigration Bridge Australia". http://www.immigrationbridge.com.au/www/248/1001127/displayarticle/1011104.html?pub=1&pagemode=2&objectid=1037201.

"Jakub". Interviewed by Jayne Persian, 2007, Sydney. Cassette recording in author's possession.

Jupp, James. *Immigration*. Melbourne: Oxford University Press, 1998.

Klim, George. Interviewed by Barry York, 16–17 September and 1 October 1996, Canberra. "Polish Australians Oral History Project," National Library of Australia, Oral TRC 3498.

Knightley, Phillip. *Australia: A Biography of a Nation*. London: Vintage, 2001.

"Leo". Interviewed by Jayne Persian, 2007, Sydney. Cassette recording in author's possession.

Longley, Kateryna Olijnyk. "Remembering Rublivka: Life Stories from Lost Worlds." *Life Writing* 1, no. 1 (2004): 109–20.

Longley, Kateryna. "The Fifth World." *Ukrainian Settlement in Australia: Fifth Conference, Melbourne, 16–18 February 1990*. Melbourne: Slavic Section, Monash University, 1993.

Markus, Andrew, and Eileen Sims. *Fourteen Lives—Paths to a Multicultural Community*. Clayton, VIC: Monash Publications in History: 16, Department of History, Monash University, 1993.

McDowell, Linda. "Workers, Migrants, Aliens or Citizens? State Constructions and Discourses of Identity Among Post-War European Labour Migrants in Britain." *Political Geography* 22 (2003): 863–86.

"Michael". Interviewed by Jayne Persian, 2007, Sydney. Cassette recording in author's possession.

Murphy, Catherine, and United Trades and Labor Council (South Australia). *Boatload of Dreams: Journeys by European Immigrant Workers 1947–1994*. Adelaide, SA: United Trades and Labor Council (SA), 1994.

Muxel, Anne. "Family Memory." In *Between Generations: Family Models, Myths, and Memories*, International Yearbook of Oral History and Life Stories, Volume II, edited by Daniel Bertaux and Paul Thompson. Oxford: Oxford University Press, 1993.

Mykytiuk, Bohdan. Interviewed by Rob Willis, 21 October 2004, Bassendean, Western Australia. Rob and Olya Willis Folklore Collection, National Library of Australia, Oral TRC 5373/21–23.

"Nastasia". Interviewed by Jayne Persian, 2007 and 2015, Sydney. Cassette recording and handwritten notes in author's possession.

Noetel, Edith. Interviewed by Janis Wilton, 9 June 1982. "The Oral Histories Project of the Ethnic Affairs Commission of NSW," State Library of New South Wales, CY MLOH 18/25.

Persian, Jayne. *Beautiful Balts: From Displaced Persons to New Australians.* Sydney: NewSouth Books, 2017.

Persian, Jayne. "Cossack Identities: From Russian Emigres and Anti-Soviet Collaborators to Displaced Persons." *Special Issue: Refugee Family & Memory, Immigrants & Minorities* 36, no. 2 (2018): 125–42.

Petersons, Inese (1947–). Interviewed by Allison Murchie, 2002. "South Australians Acting for Change: Welcoming Refugees Oral History Project," J. D. Somerville Oral History Collection, State Library of South Australia, OH 636/2.

Prushynsky, Suzanna. Interviewed by Rob Willis and Graham Seal, 26 October 2004, Kiara, Western Australia. Rob and Olya Willis Folklore Collection, National Library of Australia, Oral TRC 5373/21–22.

Read, Peter. *Returning to Nothing: The Meaning of Lost Places.* Cambridge: Cambridge University Press, 1996.

Richards, Eric. "Hearing Voices: An Introduction." In *Speaking to Immigrants: Oral Testimony and the History of Australian Migration*, Visible Immigrants (6), edited by A. James Hammerton and Eric Richards, 1–20. History Program and Centre for Immigration and Multicultural Studies, Research School of Social Sciences, Australian National University. Adelaide: Flinders University Press, 2002.

"Robert". Interviewed by Jayne Persian, 2008, Wollongong. Cassette recording in author's possession.

Rutland, Suzanne. "Subtle Exclusions: Postwar Jewish Emigration to Australia and the impact of the IRO Scheme." *The Journal of Holocaust Education* 10, no. 1 (Summer 2001): 50–66.

Ryan, Kathleen M. "'I Didn't Do Anything Important': A Pragmatic Analysis of the Oral History Interview." *The Oral History Review* 36, no. 1 (2009): 25–44.

Schamberger, Karen, Martha Sear, Kirsten Wehner, Jennifer Wilson and the *Australian Journeys* Gallery Development Team, National Museum of Australia. "Living in a Material World: Object Biography and Transnational Lives." In

Transnational Ties: Australian Lives in the World, edited by Desley Deacon, Penny Russell and Angela Woollacott, 275–97. Canberra: Australian National University E Press, 2008.

Shapcott, Tom. "Multicultural Literature and Writing in Australia." In *Writing in Multicultural Australia 1984: An Overview,* Papers presented at the Multicultural Writers' Weekends in Sydney, 13 and 14 October 1984, and in Melbourne 27 and 28 October 1984, edited by Jacques Delaruelle, Alexandra Karakostas-Sêdá and Anna Ward. North Sydney: Australia Council for the Literature Board, 1985.

Skrzynecki, Peter. *Old/New World.* St Lucia: University of Queensland Press, 2007.

Skrzynecki, Peter. *The Sparrow Garden.* St Lucia: University of Queensland Press, 2004.

Sluga, Glenda. "The Migrant Dreaming." *Journal of Intercultural Studies* 8, no. 2 (1987): 40–49.

Summerfield, Penny. "Culture and Composure: Creating Narratives of the Gendered Self in Oral History Interviews." *Cultural and Social History* 1, no. 1 (2004): 65–93.

Tarvydas, Ramunas. *From Amber Coast to Apple Isle: Fifty Years of Baltic Immigrants in Tasmania, 1948–1998.* Hobart, TAS: Baltic Semicentennial Commemoration Activities Organising Committee, 1997.

Thonfeld, Christoph. "The Shaping of Memory: Individual, Group and Collective Patterns of Recollection of Slave and Forced Labour for National Socialist Germany." *Proceedings of the 14th International Oral History Conference,* Sydney, Australia, 12–16 July, 2006.

Turkiewicz, Helena. Interviewed by Barry York, 9–10 April 2001, Adelaide. "Polish Australians Oral History Project," National Library of Australia, Oral TRC 4714.

Wills, Sara. "Unstitching the Lips of a Migrant Nation." *Australian Historical Studies* 118 (2002): 71–89.

Wilton, Janis, and Richard Bosworth. *Old Worlds and New Australia: The Post-War Migrant Experience.* Ringwood: Penguin Books Australia, 1984.

York, Barry. *Michael Cigler: A Czech-Australian Story, from Displacement to Diversity, Studies in Australian Ethnic History Series, No 11.* Canberra: Centre for Immigration and Multicultural Studies, Research School of Social Sciences, Australian National University, 1996.

Young, Alan. "Oral History as Emergent Paradigm." *Special Issue: Oral History and Its Challenge(r)s, Oral History Association of Australia Journal,* no. 28 (2006).

CHAPTER 4

Shifting Countries, Shifting Identities? Oral History and Lesbian and Gay Migration to Australia

Shirleene Robinson

Histories of both migration and the lesbian and gay community in Australia have been considerably enhanced by oral history, which provides a unique method of recovering and incorporating the perspectives of individuals and groups often left out of broader narratives. In 2008, Eithne Luibheid noted that the majority of global migration discourse assumes the implicit heterosexuality of subjects.[1] It is important to challenge the positioning of migrants as innately heterosexual, as sexuality that falls outside of this categorization has been a powerful driving force behind migration and has also impacted and shaped the subsequent experiences of migrants. This chapter investigates the intersections between sexuality and migration further by deploying four in-depth oral histories conducted as part of the "Australian Lesbian and Gay Life Stories" oral history project in collaboration with the National Library of Australia. It argues that, although the decision to migrate is a complex one that can be prompted by a range of factors, shifting countries has both helped and hindered individuals in reconciling their sexuality.

S. Robinson (✉)
Macquarie University, Sydney, NSW, Australia
e-mail: shirleene.robinson@mq.edu.au

© The Author(s) 2019
K. Darian-Smith, P. Hamilton (eds.), *Remembering Migration*,
Palgrave Macmillan Memory Studies,
https://doi.org/10.1007/978-3-030-17751-5_4

Gender and race have been critical factors, and this chapter utilizes interviews that allow for greater consideration of these intersections. Women have emphasized the new possibilities offered as part of the decision to migrate, indicating that gendered expectations impact significantly on lesbian migrants. Furthermore, accounts from lesbian and gay narrators show that just as heterosexual migration has been shaped by race, class and support networks, so too has the experience of lesbian and gay migrants.

Between 2012 and 2015, a team of researchers from three universities worked with the National Library of Australia on an oral history project, exploring the way that social change had played out in the lives of gay men and lesbian women over the past sixty years.[2] At the time of its initiation, the project was internationally unique. While a growing body of oral history—within Australia and held in international repositories such as the British Library—had been deployed very effectively to capture the voices of lesbian and gay activists, there had been much less focus from archival repositories on the lives of "ordinary" gay men and lesbian women. Researchers on the "Australian Lesbian and Gay Life Stories" project were guided by feminist and queer historical practice. As Nan Alamilla Boyd asserts, these have both aimed for empowerment and have trusted the voices of interviewees "positioning narrators as historical experts, and interpreting narrators' voices alongside the narrators' interpretations of their own memories."[3]

Researchers were keen to ensure that the project captured the diversity of contemporary Australia, including a significant migrant population. From the outset, interview targets were set to ensure that interviewees born overseas were represented in the collection. This target was based on the 2006 Australian Census, which indicated that 22 per cent of Australians were born overseas. The most common countries of birth for migrants in the 2006 Census were England, New Zealand, China and Italy.[4] We began the project with the assumption that it might not be possible for our collection to replicate the Census in terms of including individuals who were either lesbian or gay and migrants and were also from the top countries of origin. At the project's conclusion, though, we found that applicants had largely reflected the broader pattern of Australian migration. Most applicants who had migrated to Australia were originally from England or New Zealand, although we had applicants who together spanned all continents, barring Antarctica.

The "Australian Lesbian and Gay Life Stories" team was inspired by the groundbreaking "Australian Generations" project, led by Alistair Thomson. In this project, generational change was used as the key analytical tool in analysing oral histories from 300 different Australians.[5] The "Australian Lesbian and Gay Life Stories" project explored the changing nature of lesbian and gay life and lesbian and gay cultural narratives. The focus was deliberately directed towards the lives of non-activist gay men and lesbian women as this project wanted to consider what it might be like to live a more "ordinary" gay or lesbian life at a time when broader social attitudes were undergoing a significant shift. Interviews were conducted with participants born between 1921 and 1992 who self-identified as same-sex attracted. Interviews ranged between two and six hours and were conducted as life history oral histories.[6] Bertram J. Cohler and Andrew Hostetler have argued that the life story model is particularly useful for investigating lesbian and gay lives as, for these individuals, unique historical events and social change have "defined the meaning of identity and desire."[7]

While there has been an impressive body of scholarship that has explored the experiences of non-heterosexual migrants, the majority of this research has emerged from the field of cultural geography or does not focus on Australia.[8] There is still a dearth of research that deploys oral history to place migration to Australia by non-heterosexual individuals into historical context. It is important to fill this lacuna. As Vera Mirhady has argued, "there is a lack of research and policy focus on the specific challenges that queer migrants face."[9] Furthermore, oral histories indicate that for many individuals, sexuality has been a key impetus driving the decision to migrate. Cultural geographer Andrew Gorman-Murray asserts "prior research and anecdotal evidence suggests that sexuality—as a key element of their subjectivities—more often than not" has played a major role in the migratory decisions of non-heterosexuals.[10]

Participants in the "Australian Lesbian and Gay Life Stories" project who migrated to Australia did so as a result of numerous factors. Those who migrated as children or adolescents with their families did not make the decision themselves. Most commonly, their families opted to migrate to Australia for improved work and educational opportunities. For participants who migrated to Australia at an older age and made this decision themselves, a range of factors could be at play and sometimes these overlapped. This was consistent with Gorman-Murray's study, which used data from 2004 to 2005 to investigate lesbian and gay migrations patterns within Australia, considering "migration decisions, motivations, paths and experiences over the life course."[11] He primarily focused on the domestic migration of Australian-born subjects but did include some overseas-born men and women.

Migration and Identity

The interviews conducted with migrants as part of the "Australian Lesbian and Gay Life Stories" project align with broader research that indicates that shifting countries provides opportunities to reconfigure or re-evaluate sexual identities. As Gorman-Murray points out, feminist work on migration has explored the role of subject and identity formation through the process of migration. He argues, "identity is correlated to movement through agentic needs and desires as well as the affects of structural forces."[12] This emerged as a particularly strong theme in interviews conducted with female participants across generations. Historian Rebecca Jennings has also found that travel—and migration—across the British world played a notable role in lesbian identity formation in the mid-twentieth century.[13]

The importance of migration and mobility in constituting a sexual identity came through strongly in an interview conducted with one of the project's older female participants. Catherine (Cate) Turner, who was born in 1928 in New Zealand, made the decision to first travel to Australia in 1954 when her brother announced that he was planning on spending some time travelling around the country. A brilliant student, she had attended teaching college and gained work as a teacher, before the growing realization that she was attracted to women made her feel that she was unfit to teach. She then worked for an airline, where she had her first relationship with another woman. Still struggling with sexuality, she also saw a psychiatrist at this time to try and "cure" her homosexuality.[14]

Her brother's decision to travel around Australia at this time was certainly an important part of her motivation guiding her first trip. But given the context of her sexuality and unhappiness, the option of spending time away from New Zealand must have also seemed particularly appealing. After a year spent exploring Australia, Cate returned to work in the airline industry in New Zealand, also attempting an unsuccessful heterosexual relationship. Four years later in 1958, at the age of thirty, she returned to Australia, spending a number of years in Melbourne and Maitland. The move seemed to represent both a physical and psychological break with her past. There were no further heterosexual encounters afterwards.

In Maitland, Cate formed a relationship with a woman, a librarian. She then moved to Sydney to live in a relationship with another woman, a relationship that lasted twenty-one years. When her interviewer asked if she had told her parents about her sexuality, she stated:

I didn't. I couldn't just, I somehow just couldn't tell them because I didn't think that they would understand. Not that they would have been cruel or anything, but I just didn't want to disappoint them I suppose.[15]

Later during the course of her interview, Cate also noted that as a young woman in New Zealand, there had been some degree of pressure placed on her to marry and have children. This was not something that happened for Cate "and of course it disappointed my family, my parents would have loved me to have married. My father wanted it."[16]

A geographical shift was also important for another female participant to fully live and express her sexuality. Jennie Partington, who was born in England in 1949, had realized she felt an attraction to other girls as a teenager, but struggled with this as "you want to be accepted as so-called 'normal,' and you want to be normal, but you feel as though you're not quite normal."[17] It was not until she came to Australia on a working holiday in her twenties that she fully accepted her sexuality. In 1975, aged twenty-six and in a small town in Western Australia, she embarked on a relationship with another woman, who was a fellow nurse. The search for mobility and independence are recurring motifs throughout her interview. She notes directly at one point in her interview that "I certainly wouldn't have travelled independently and I probably wouldn't have ended up in Australia, least of all Western Australia" if she hadn't been a lesbian.[18] Similarly to Cate, she emphasizes the enormous pressure placed on women of her generation to marry and have children. This social expectation would have been further reinforced had she remained in England. Although she did return to England for a time in the 1980s when she was comfortable with her sexuality and had a partner, she eventually decided to permanently migrate to Australia in 1987.

A participant from the project's younger cohort, Sophie Partridge, who was born in England in 1984, also emphasized that migration to Australia from England presented different possibilities and freedoms. Growing up in Derby with an identical twin, along with other siblings, she had felt that:

People's perceptions of lesbians are 'they can't get men,' or it was still very much defined against a heterosexual perception if that makes sense. So it was like 'oh, they can't get men,' or 'they're unattractive' or 'they're this.' Or there's some element to which being a lesbian is inferior to being heterosexual. I think that's probably what was the hardest thing for me.[19]

Given this atmosphere, it is perhaps not surprising that Sophie did not fully explore her sexuality until she moved away to university. Subsequent weekends in London introduced her to a vibrant lesbian culture. In London, she met an Australian woman. In her interview, she noted that she migrated for her partner and that she found the process of leaving her family to be difficult. However, the relationship had introduced her to a world that felt more "Technicolor." Sophie noted that her partner of that time had travelled extensively and had experienced "such a full and rich life" and had a "you can do anything" approach to life.[20] Sophie notes:

> I hadn't really felt like that. I think probably partly because of where I'd grown up and our economic situation. Everything always felt quite difficult and the move to Australia just felt enormous.[21]

After making an initial visit to Australia in 2009, Sophie was convinced to make the move to Australia the following year. She adds that, by then, she "already had this impression Sydney was a very open place for gay and lesbian people." When asked to expand on this, she continues:

> I don't know where that must have come from. I watched a TV show once and Sydney got described as gay and lesbian Mecca and there was a big feature on the Mardi Gras parade and things like that. So there'd always been a big perception for me that that Sydney was a really great place if you were gay. So I think that was a big factor as well and I think partly as well, I always felt like I didn't really belong in Derby and I knew I wanted to do more things in my life. So it wasn't as big a stretch moving to Australia as it might have been. But it was still a pretty big thing to do, yeah.[22]

Initially coming over on a working visa, Sophie later had to prove the validity of her relationship to Australian authorities in order to be able to remain in the country. Audrey Yue has noted that, in 1985, Australia became one of the first countries in the world to accept same-sex relationships as the basis of migration.[23] Sophie emphasizes that she was aware that being able to migrate to Australia on the basis of a same-sex relationship was quite progressive.

> I remember at the time feeling quite lucky that in Australia you can be same-sex partners and the de facto visa is for everybody. I remember because I had some friends who tried to move to other countries and it wasn't as easy as that. So yeah, I thought that was pretty cool. This is a pretty cool place.[24]

While that relationship ultimately did not last, Sophie did not regret her decision to move to Sydney, describing it as "amazing" and also noting that she feels "I do feel it's so much easier to be gay and lesbian in Sydney." At the time her interview was conducted, she was enjoying developing a relationship with someone she had very strong feelings for. Elaborating on the impact of migration for her personally, she observed that the process of migrating may have afforded her an opportunity to reshape or more fully live out her identity.

> I do think I feel like I'm a really different person here from what I was when I lived in the UK, so maybe it's just part of that moving out of your regular space, that you feel you can carve a new self or something like that.[25]

At the time of the interview, Sophie was the President of a soccer club in Sydney, described as the largest lesbian soccer club in the world with 120 players.

Intersecting Identities

Interviewees who migrated to Australia from non-English speaking parts of the world sometimes found the experience more hostile, with racism and extra cultural pressures to contend with. Migrants who came to Australia as children or adolescents felt these pressures more keenly. Joey Yung, who was born in Hong Kong to Chinese parents in 1987 and was twenty-six at the time of his interview, moved to an outer Sydney suburb in Australia with his mother and sister in 1997, when he was aged ten. His father, a businessman, was predominantly based in China but travelled to Australia when he was able. Joey remembers his arrival in Australia as a "culture shock" after experiencing a more disciplined upbringing with an emphasis on academic achievement in Hong Kong.[26] After Joey and his family were able to secure Australian permanent residency, they returned to Hong Kong where Joey joined an international school. When Joey reached the final two years of his high school education, he was sent back to Australia, where his aunt and uncle were still living, to board at an Anglican school.

While he came to realize his sexuality during high school, the pressure to achieve academically, coupled with the negative messages he received in school about homosexuality, saw him avoid focusing on this. It was not till he began university in 2006 that he first started to explore gay sites on the internet, including dating sites. As his financial resources were very connected to his family, he felt a considerable degree of pressure to conceal his sexuality. Eventually, though, this became increasingly hard for him and he raised the issue of homosexuality with his uncle. After this, he also had a discussion with his mother, which he remembers as being very hard and he was subsequently also berated by his father, who it turned out had cancer. His mother told him that he was to return to Hong Kong as soon as his university semester was over.

While in Hong Kong, his Christian aunt arranged for Joey to attend a Pentecostal Church, which he found helped him deal with an extremely emotionally turbulent time. He was not able to reconcile his sexuality with his faith at this time. Due to his mother's association of Australia with homosexuality, he was then sent to university in China, where he was based in an international student area and formed a friendship with an accepting straight man from San Francisco. After six months, with his father being hospitalized, he returned to Hong Kong. His father died, and in the aftermath he was sent to Australia again.

The process of reconciling his sexuality with his faith took some time. He found the gay world in Sydney intimidating and judgmental, and also experienced racism. Other interview subjects from non-English speaking backgrounds who participated in the project have also emphasized this point.[27] When Joey attempted to go out to the Sydney gay scene and nightclubs based around Oxford Street, he remembers "I was just feeling judged because I think because I'm—well, firstly because I'm Asian, and secondly because I'm new and I don't know much about the gay clubbing scene."[28]

Ironically, Joey felt the church community, in particular "gay church groups," provided a much greater degree of acceptance and less racism. He described this contrast in his interview. On the gay dating platform Grindr "there's a lot of, 'yeah, no Asians, no rice, no …'—all those kind of racist remarks."[29] When his interviewer asked what it had felt like to read comments such as this, Joey responded by saying, "I felt really more excluded. I felt more convinced of the fact that, wow, it's very exclusive the gay community."[30] The LGBTIQ-inclusive Metropolitan Community Church provided Joey with a way of feeling he could be true to both his faith and his sexuality. Joey's mother was living in Hong Kong at the time his interview was conducted, and he mentioned the fact that he hoped his mother would eventually come to accept his sexuality. When his interviewer asked whether it was "easier for you to be gay in Sydney than it would be in the bosom of the family kind of stuff?," Joey replied, "absolutely" before expanding to add, "absolutely, that makes it a little easier, but at the same time it will—the problem will not—the issue will not be resolved unless my parents accept it."[31]

CONCLUSION

It is evident from interviews undertaken for the "Australian Lesbian and Gay Life Stories" project that migration was a significant marker of experience for those participants who came to Australia from other countries. As Alessandro Portelli has asserted, "what is really important is that memory is not a passive depository of facts, but an active creation of meanings."[32] In the narratives developed, this creation of meaning through memory was evident. The process of shifting countries was remembered and articulated as a significant symbol of change in the life course. While the experience of migration varied and was remembered differently by narrators depending on their own subjectivities, it served as a way of ordering and composing life stories.

Oral history accounts provided by lesbian and gay narrators show that leaving one country for another is a process bringing both challenges and opportunities. It is also clear that gender, race, class and a range of other factors impact on the experiences of lesbian and gay migrants. Furthermore, the significance of migration—and the way the narrative of migration is composed and remembered by individuals—shifts and develops over time.

For lesbian women of earlier generations, leaving the place of birth offered opportunities to avoid pressures and societal expectations regarding marriage and children. Today, migration can still offer an opportunity to reshape and live out newly forged identities. Many participants—from both younger and older generations—referred to immigration as a way of developing and expressing a more open sexual identity. The project also revealed that migrants who came from non-English speaking backgrounds experienced subsequent challenges that could involve contending with racism and reconciling sexuality alongside cultural expectations that might sit apart from the gay and lesbian scene available in Australia. While a number of themes were evident in the narratives, the strongest was the process interviewees described of linking migration to a more explicit consideration and realization of their sexuality.

Notes

1. Eithne Luibheid, "Queer/Migration: An Unruly Body of Scholarship," *GLQ: A Journal of Lesbian and Gay Studies* 14, no. 2/3 (2008): 169.
2. Robert Reynolds and Shirleene Robinson, *Gay and Lesbian, Then and Now: Australian Stories from a Social Revolution* (Melbourne: Black Inc., 2016).
3. Nan Alamilla Boyd, "Who is the Subject?: Queer Theory Meets Oral History," *Journal of the History of Sexuality* 17, no. 2 (May 2008): 177–78.
4. Australian Bureau of Statistics, "2006 Census QuickStats," http://www.censusdata.abs.gov.au/census_services/getproduct/census/2006/quickstat/0?opendocument&navpos=220.
5. Alistair Thomson, "Australian Generations? Memory, Oral History and Generational Identity in Postwar Australia," *Australian Historical Studies* 47, no. 1 (2016): 41–57 and Anisa Puri and Alistair Thomson, *Australian Lives: An Intimate History* (Melbourne: Monash University Publishing, 2017).
6. Robert Reynolds and Shirleene Robinson, "Australian Lesbian and Gay Life Stories: A National Oral History Project," *Australian Feminist Studies* 31, no. 9 (December 2016): 363–76.
7. Phillip M. Hammack and Bertram J. Cohler, "Narrative, Identity and the Politics of Exclusion: Social Change and the Gay and Lesbian Life Course," *Sexuality Research and Social Policy* 8, no. 3 (September 2011): 164.
8. For international work, see Jasbir K. Puar, "Circuits of Queer Mobility: Tourism, Travel and Globalization," *GLQ: A Journal of Lesbian and Gay Studies* 8, no. 1–2 (2002): 101–37 and Nathaniel M. Lewis, "Moving 'Out', Moving On: Gay Men's Migration through the Life Course," *Annals of the Association of American Geographer* 104, no. 2 (2014): 225–33. For Australian scholarship, see Andrew Gorman-Murray, "Rethinking Queer Migration through the Body," *Social and Cultural Geography* 8, no. 1 (2007): 105–21 and Andrew Gorman-Murray, "Intimate Mobilities: Emotional Embodiment and Queer Migration," *Social and Cultural Geography* 10, no. 4 (June 2009): 441–60.
9. Vera Mirhady, "Canadian Perspectives on Queer Migration," *Undercurrent Journal* 8, no. 2 (Fall/Winter 2011): 56.
10. Gorman-Murray, "Intimate Mobilities," 441–60.
11. "Intimate Mobilities," 441–60.
12. "Intimate Mobilities," 442.
13. Rebecca Jennings, "'It was a Hot Climate and a Hot Time': Lesbian Migration and Transnational Networks in the Mid-Twentieth Century," *Australian Feminist Studies* 25, no. 63 (March 2010): 31–45.

14. Catherine Turner, interviewed by Julia Miller, 19 February 2015, Sydney, Australia, National Library of Australia, ORAL TRC 6510/51.
15. Catherine Turner, interview, 19 February 2015.
16. Catherine Turner, interview, 19 February 2015.
17. Jennie Partington, interviewed by Shirleene Robinson, 9 December 2014, Denmark, Western Australia, National Library of Australia, ORAL TRC 6510/49.
18. Jennie Partington, interview, 9 December 2014.
19. Sophie Partridge interviewed by Robert Reynolds, 13 December 2014, Newtown, New South Wales, Australia, National Library of Australia, ORAL TRC 6510/50.
20. Sophie Partridge, interview, 13 December 2014.
21. Sophie Partridge, interview, 13 December 2014.
22. Sophie Partridge, interview, 13 December 2014.
23. Audrey Yue, "Same-Sex Migration in Australia: From Interdependency to Intimacy," *GLQ: A Journal of Lesbian and Gay Studies* 14, no. 2–3 (2008): 239.
24. Audrey Yue, "Same-Sex Migration in Australia."
25. Audrey Yue, "Same-Sex Migration in Australia."
26. Joey Yung, interviewed by Robert Reynolds, 26 April 2014, Chatswood, New South Wales, Australia, National Library of Australia, ORAL TRC 6510/22.
27. Reynolds and Robinson, *Gay and Lesbian, Then and Now*, 105–24.
28. Joey Yung, interview, 26 April 2014.
29. Joey Yung, interview, 26 April 2014.
30. Joey Yung, interview, 26 April 2014.
31. Joey Yung, interview, 26 April 2014.
32. Alessandro Portelli, "What Makes Oral History Different?," in Alessandro Portelli ed., *The Death of Luigi Trastulli and Other Stories: Form and Meaning in Oral History* (New York: SUNY Press, 1991), 52.

Bibliography

Australian Bureau of Statistics. "2006 Census QuickStats." http://www.census-data.abs.gov.au/census_services/getproduct/census/2006/quickstat/0?opendocument&navpos=220.

Boyd, Nan Alamilla. "Who is the Subject?: Queer Theory Meets Oral History." *Journal of the History of Sexuality* 17, no. 2 (May 2008): 177–78.

Gorman-Murray, Andrew. "Intimate Mobilities: Emotional Embodiment and Queer Migration." *Social and Cultural Geography* 10, no. 4 (June 2009): 441–60.

Gorman-Murray, Andrew. "Rethinking Queer Migration through the Body." *Social and Cultural Geography* 8, no. 1 (2007): 105–21.

Hammack, Phillip M., and Bertram J. Cohler. "Narrative, Identity and the Politics of Exclusion: Social Change and the Gay and Lesbian Life Course." *Sexuality Research and Social Policy* 8, no. 3 (September 2011): 164.

Jennings, Rebecca. "'It was a Hot Climate and a Hot Time': Lesbian Migration and Transnational Networks in the Mid-Twentieth Century." *Australian Feminist Studies* 25, no. 63 (March 2010): 31–45.

Lewis, Nathaniel M. "Moving 'Out', Moving On: Gay Men's Migration through the Life Course." *Annals of the Association of American Geographers* 104, no. 2 (2014): 225–33.

Luibheid, Eithne. "Queer/Migration: An Unruly Body of Scholarship." *GLQ: A Journal of Lesbian and Gay Studies* 14, no. 2/3 (2008): 69.

Mirhady, Vera. "Canadian Perspectives on Queer Migration." *Undercurrent Journal* 8, no. 2 (Fall/Winter 2011): 56.

Partington, Jenny. Interviewed by Shirleene Robinson, 9 December 2014, Denmark, Western Australia. National Library of Australia, ORAL TRC 6510/49.

Partridge, Sophie. Interviewed by Robert Reynolds, 13 December 2014, Newtown, New South Wales. National Library of Australia, ORAL TRC 6510/50.

Portelli, Alessandro. "What Makes Oral History Different?" In *The Death of Luigi Trastulli and Other Stories: Form and Meaning in Oral History*, edited by Alessandro Portelli, 52. New York: SUNY Press, 1991.

Puar, Jasbir K. "Circuits of Queer Mobility: Tourism, Travel and Globalization." *GLQ: A Journal of Lesbian and Gay Studies* 8, no. 1–2 (2002): 101–37.

Puri, Anisa and Alistair Thomson. *Australian Lives: An Intimate History*. Melbourne: Monash University Publishing, 2017.

Reynolds, Robert, and Shirleene Robinson. "Australian Lesbian and Gay Life Stories: A National Oral History Project." *Australian Feminist Studies* 31, no. 9 (December 2016): 363–76.

Reynolds, Robert, and Shirleene Robinson. *Gay and Lesbian, Then and Now: Australian Stories from a Social Revolution*. Melbourne: Black Inc., 2016.

Thomson, Alistair. "Australian Generations? Memory, Oral History and Generational Identity in Postwar Australia." *Australian Historical Studies* 47, no. 1 (2016): 41–57.

Turner, Catherine. Interviewed by Julia Miller, 19 February 2015, Sydney, Australia. National Library of Australia, ORAL TRC 6510/51.

Yue, Audrey. "Same-Sex Migration in Australia: From Interdependency to Intimacy." *GLQ: A Journal of Lesbian and Gay Studies* 14, no. 2–3 (2008): 239.

Yung, Joey. Interviewed by Robert Reynolds, 26 April 2014, Chatswood, New South Wales, Australia. National Library of Australia, ORAL TRC 6510/22.

CHAPTER 5

"To Be Who I Was, Really, Was To Be Different": Memories of Youth Migration to Post-War Australia

Anisa Puri

Researchers from many disciplinary perspectives in the social sciences and humanities have examined the role of age in life story interviews. Their approaches range from sociologists' and psychoanalysts' studies of life course theory and life stages, to memory theorists' research on the relationships between age, life stages, identity, and autobiographical memory.[1] This chapter first considers how oral historians and migration scholars have used age as a category of analysis,[2] and then turns to a close reading of one life story interview to illustrate how age, intersecting with ethnicity and gender, is a useful frame through which to interpret memories of migration.

AGE AS A CATEGORY OF ANALYSIS

While Valerie Yow argues that practitioners can benefit from learning about human developmental stages in order to understand interviewees' experiences within "the context of emotional needs of others in the same

---

A. Puri (✉)
Monash University, Melbourne, VIC, Australia
e-mail: anisa.puri@monash.edu.au

© The Author(s) 2019   59
K. Darian-Smith, P. Hamilton (eds.), *Remembering Migration*,
Palgrave Macmillan Memory Studies,
https://doi.org/10.1007/978-3-030-17751-5_5

age group,"[3] oral historians rarely employ the category of age to interpret historical *experience*. Rather, their focus has been on intergenerational interviewing dynamics, how the age of elderly interviewees shapes the form and content of narrated memories, and the connections between the fields of gerontology and oral history.

Migration-focused oral history literature has often overlooked the influence of age. British oral historians Paul Thompson and Joanna Bornat explain that "[a]lthough age is as important an element in the migration experience as gender, there is little oral history on this issue."[4] Age is also underexplored in Australian post-war migration histories. Young migrants dominated Australia's post-war migrant population, as national immigration policies privileged the young. However, although migration history often details the experiences of young migrants, it rarely *explicitly* considers age as a lens for analysis. There are a few notable exceptions. A. James Hammerton and Alistair Thomson consider youthful "sojourners" in the 1950s and 1960s as historical antecedents of today's backpacking generation, and examine how emigration could constitute a "rite of passage, and in many cases, a dramatic coming-of-age" for young and independent British migrants.[5] In her study of the memories of Greek children who were removed from Greece during the Civil War in the late 1940s and eventually migrated to Australia, Joy Damousi argues that "the notion of 'national identity' became deeply problematic for many of these children in adulthood, after their experience of crossing several borders and nation-states during their formative years."[6] Recent historical work on how child refugees experienced arrival and resettlement in Australia explores memories of family separation and reunification, and young peoples' changing relationships to friends and family in their country of origin and with ethno-specific community groups in Australia.[7]

Age is not the sole determining factor of migration experience, but it can be just as instructive as other categories of analysis, such as gender or ethnicity. Experiences of age and life stage are gendered, culturally determined, and influenced by social class, so employing age as an analytical frame requires consideration of these intersecting factors. Age and life stage can influence how, and with whom, an individual migrates—whether as an accompanied or unaccompanied child migrant or refugee, as a young and single person, as a couple, as a parent with one's own child or family, or as an elderly parent or grandparent migrating with family, or perhaps joining family who have already emigrated. Age, life stage, and gender also influence the extent to which a person has *agency* in their decision to migrate including when, and where, to go.

Donat Santowiak: A Case Study

I use a life story interview with Donat Santowiak, recorded by the Australian Generations Oral History Project in 2014, to demonstrate the value of using age as a category of historical analysis when interpreting migration experiences and memories.[8] I use his interview not as a representative study of youth migration to post-war Australia, but rather, as an illuminating case study. In 1964, Donat migrated from Poland as a 13-year-old, with his parents and younger sister. Donat's interview highlights how inextricably linked experiences and memories of youth and migration can be for young migrants: his youth shaped his migration, and his migration shaped his youth. Youth is commonly recognized as the "most important period of identity-construction,"[9] and migration can often be a formative experience.

Before turning to the interview, it is worth briefly considering a definition of youth.[10] Youth is historically, culturally, and socially contingent. It is best understood as a relational category, bridging childhood and adulthood, though understandings of when childhood ends and adulthood begins change over time and across culture. Youth is regularly characterized in Western countries as a period in which individuals become independent, or transition from school to employment or further education. The rise of the "teenager" in the 1950s and the emergence of new youth subcultures in post-war Australia[11]—particularly in the 1960s and 1970s— shape understandings of experiences, and personal and popular memories, of youth in Australia. Today, the ages 18 and 21 hold social significance in many Western nations, where they serve as markers of the transition to adulthood. Official definitions of youth are usually age-specific—15–24 is a common definition—yet experiences of transitioning out of youth are not necessarily determined by age. I employ a flexible interpretation of youth to explore how Donat experienced this life stage and conceptualized his own youth.

Donat was interviewed in his home by Alistair Thomson, in the town of Moe in the Latrobe Valley, about 130 kilometres east of Melbourne. This interview was one of 300 life stories recorded by the Australian Generations project with "ordinary" people across Australia, who were born between 1920 and 1989. Donat was aged 64 when the interview was recorded over two consecutive days in 2014, totaling just under five hours of recorded material. Donat's interview takes a predominately chronological approach, though his narrative also moves fluidly between various periods of his past, and between the past and the present.

Over half of Donat's interview focuses on his childhood, youth, and migration to Australia at the age of 13. This is perhaps unsurprising given the formative influence of both youth and migration. Memory theorists and psychologists have examined the prominent place of youth in autobiographical memories, and refer to the increased remembering of youth in later life as the "reminiscence bump."[12] Yet the emphasis Donat places on his adolescent life and migration experience—50 years after he migrated—reveals this as a watershed in his life. About three minutes into the interview, and in response to a question about his family background in Poland, Donat launches into a narrative about his family's arrival to Australia. Although the focus of the interview was not on migration, Donat places his migration as a pivotal experience with severe and wide-ranging effects on his youth and later life.

Donat was born in Katowice in Upper Silesia in Southern Poland in April 1950 to a communist Catholic Polish father and a Lutheran mother who had converted to Catholicism. Some of his mother's family migrated to Australia as Displaced Persons in 1950. The Polish population in Australia was small before the late 1940s—the 1933 census showed that there were 3241 Polish-born individuals in Australia.[13] Donat and his immediate family left Poland for Australia in 1964, and were part of a new group of Polish immigrants who migrated directly to Australia under the family reunion scheme from the late 1950s.[14] They headed to the Latrobe Valley, where post-war migrants from countries including the Netherlands, Italy, Germany, Malta, and Poland[15] were drawn to the industrial region's employment opportunities in coal and electricity.

Donat, at age 13, did not have any role in the family's decision to migrate, but his interview demonstrates how he asserted his agency in other aspects of his migrant experience. As Mary Jo Maynes argues, a broader interpretation of what constitutes historical agency—beyond the typical positioning of a historical actor as "autonomous, driven by the imperatives of rational choice, aware of how the world works"—is necessary when examining young peoples' power and agency.[16] After starting school in Morwell, Donat decided to "assimilate" to reduce the verbal and physical bullying he endured at school and in the town. Donat found a job at a local milk bar, owned by a Polish couple, so he no longer had to rely on his parents for pocket money. (His father's qualifications were not recognized in Australia, so Mr Santowiak started work as a "pick-and-shovel type labourer" for the State Electricity Commission, and the family's financial circumstances took a "nosedive," after being "quite well-off" in Poland.)

Donat spent his first pay on a reel-to-reel tape recorder, which he used each evening, along with his Polish-to-English dictionary, to record his voice, practice English, and eradicate his Polish accent. Donat's decisions to secure employment, to select how to spend his disposable income, to change his accent, and to determinedly study the English language demonstrate how he actively shaped his early experience as a migrant in Australia.

Social isolation and loneliness often characterize teenagers' memory, and this particularly defined Donat's teenage life. Social exclusion was painful and was exacerbated by Donat's migrant status, so that he felt significant discomfort about his migrant identity for many decades. His secondary school was ill-equipped to deal with students with a limited grasp of English; Donat had to rely on assistance provided by fellow students who responded to the school's announcement for Polish or German speakers to act as "interpreters." Donat made a German Polish friend early on, but it wasn't until a year or two after arriving in Australia that he started playing soccer and found his "only real social connection with a group of people." When asked if there were other Polish kids for him to bond with at school, he responds, "probably, you know, there were but I didn't connect." He fondly remembers time spent with "the Koori [Aboriginal] kids," another group of "outsiders," with whom he felt "safe" and like he "belonged," although "there was no conversation because I could hardly speak English." He had no Anglo-Australian friends.

A lack of family support, and dysfunctional family relations, intensified the difficulties Donat experienced upon arrival. He was told that the reason for his immediate family's migration was to join his mother's relatives in Australia. His family stayed with these relatives in Maffra during their first few months in Australia, but after they moved to Morwell "certain issues came up" and there was little contact with their extended family. Donat's parents argued, as tensions in their marriage were exacerbated by financial difficulties and their struggle to adapt to Australia. The pushbike Donat's parents bought him became a "lifesaver" when the family home was "a bugger of a place to be." His father had a "nervous breakdown," which Donat partly attributes to the stress of migration and his father's difficulties finding suitable employment. Donat also considers whether genetic predisposition or war experience played a role in his father's paranoia. His father "set up listening devices in the house," and once "chased us with a knife"—"he was gonna kill us." Neighbours called the police, and Mr Santowiak spent a few weeks at Larundel Mental Asylum. Donat wonders: "How do you readjust to some kind of sense of *normality* in terms of living together after you've been threatened with your *life*, you know?" He explains that his pet dog Bobby was "probably responsible for keeping my wellbeing" during his lonely teen years. But one night, his parents had an argument, the police were called, and Bobby bit the policeman. They were ordered to put the dog down. Donat's voice quivers with emotion as he describes the distress he felt walking to the pound to have his "mate" Bobby "gassed." Donat's experience reveals the extent to which dysfunctional family relations can influence migration experiences, particularly for dependent minors.

Donat relays his early life in Australia through a solitary lens. Although Donat migrated with his family, he did not rely on them for emotional support during this transition. Donat's parents regretted their decision to migrate and argued about it, but he did not discuss this with them. Donat and his much younger sister had separate experiences of settling—"in that time ... we just didn't know one another which is really odd." He focused on himself "like having blinkers [blinders] and not seeing those other things that people are experiencing." Gender may have influenced Donat's account, as studies of migration memories have shown that men tend to place themselves as central and autonomous within their narratives, while women more often draw on relationships with others in their accounts.[17]

Donat's childhood experiences in Poland provide further insight into why he may have felt detached from his family. Donat spent his early years living with two "German-German" "elderly spinsters"—Hadla and Truda—in a flat across the hallway from his parents' flat. He describes his time with these women as "the only time in my life ... I felt like I really bonded" and speaks nostalgically of their "wonderful" capacity to embrace him. The reasons for his separation from his parents are unclear, but "the way I understand it, a lot of it was partly because of lack of accommodation." After Donat's sister was born, when he was eight, the two women and his parents swapped apartments, and he then lived in the larger apartment with his immediate family. Donat was separated from his family again when his father was drafted into the national service: he went to stay "with these [unidentified] people" in the country town where the army base was located, while his father was in the army reserve "over the fence," and his mother was "back at home." "I still don't know the full story" he explains. Donat also went on to stay with his father's relative shortly before the family's emigration, but again, is not sure why. Finally, upon arrival in Maffra, Donat was placed in his aunt's home, while his parents and sister lived with his grandmother. Donat's childhood separation from his parents, later separation from the two loving "spinsters", and further unexplained temporary separations from his parents, perhaps contributed to his subsequent sense of being abandoned and unloved.

Donat's struggle to adjust to life in Australia is clearly evident when he describes his engagement with 1960s youth cultures and the fashions that identified different groups. The mods in Morwell were "kind of aspiring hippies" with long hair and flared pants, while the sharpies donned "very baggy grey pants—pinstriped," had shorter hair, and preferred the colour maroon. Donat was "struggling for an identity," and "ended up growing my hair long and then getting it cut off" in "desperation (laughs) to, to *fit in somewhere.*" While Donat wanted to be "undetectable," he also "wanted to be notable" and used clothing to assert his individuality. "The fashion sense in Australia when we came was like in the Dark Ages," dominated by "beige and grey"—a sharp contrast to the flared pants and Carnaby Street shirts that he and his friends wore in Poland. In Australia, Donat's uncle, a tailor, made his clothing for him, and he was teased at school for his outfits. "It wouldn't have mattered whether I was a so-called wog in those days—just because I dressed like that I would have been a *target.* But, I, I did it regardless." His desire to dress distinctively contributed to the attention and rejection he endured at school, as a migrant but also as a newcomer who was different.

Donat's involvement in Polish folk dancing was another arena in which his ambivalence about his emerging migrant identity, Polish background, and choice of dress played out. Performing for a migrant audience "wasn't an issue," but dancing at "an Aussie cabaret" was "very awkward." He feared he would be "exposed" wearing his national costume—especially to fellow school students—as this clothing branded him as "a different entity" and displayed the Polish ethnicity he sought to reject. Donat "didn't *really* deep down want to" participate in Polish Australian culture. He can't recall whether he chose to participate in folk dancing or his parents made that decision: "but if I had to—although I had to, I say you '*had to*', I didn't, I—I suppose I had to." Youth is often a period during which young people's identities develop and stabilize, and for Donat this meant his experiences of youth and migration coalesced. His engagement with youth culture in Australia portrays the conflicting desires he was negotiating as a teenager: to fit in, to become invisible, to assert his individuality, to shed his accent and other markers of ethnicity, and to perform his migrant heritage.

For Donat at 17 a motor car was a key to masculine independence. By now, in 1968, he had finished grade 11 at Morwell Technical School (although he had to repeat English at night school) and had begun a five-year apprenticeship in design drafting at the State Electricity Commission (a major employer of local migrant men). He purchased a Holden Torana but it was a "false freedom": because it was the family's first car, his mother helped select the vehicle, and Donat served as a "family taxi" until his father bought a Holden FJ a couple of years later.

Yet, the car expanded Donat's social life. He connects the purchase of his first car with the beginning of his romantic life, which he had so longed for—two markers of emerging manhood. He and his Polish girlfriend would "go parking": they parked in the street, bought food, listened to the radio, and talked. The car held particular significance for Australian youth—along with independence, the car provided young people with access to private space.[18] Buying a car was especially important for Donat, given the threat of abuse in public space—he was thrown out of shops, and beaten by teens on the street. A car afforded Donat greater mobility, the ability to travel safely in public, and it legitimized his masculinity.

Donat also found refuge in alcohol. Drinking released the "tenseness" and anxiety he felt, and from the age of 18, he drank "more seriously," and grew dependent on alcohol. Donat had dangerous experiences driving while intoxicated, and at 20, he considered suicide. He is acutely aware of how lucky he was to survive, though "in a strange way I think that [alcohol] sort of saved my life."

In 1972, aged 22, Donat experienced a more clear-cut transition into adulthood. He married his first wife, a recently arrived English migrant. His social life expanded as he became acquainted with her English friends and family. The couple moved into a Ministry of Housing flat in Traralgon, in the Latrobe Valley. His marriage was his "exit point out of the family home," and he reflects that this may have played some role in the decision to marry. They had a daughter and bought a new house and block of land in the new town of Churchill. This period was "all about having a wife, having a child, *providing*," which is suggestive of the increasingly significant role that work played in his adult male identity. The marriage failed in the late 1970s, and Donat descended further into alcoholism, along with prescription drug use. Despite this, he managed at work, which was "the centrepiece of my life, in terms of a constant." For Donat, the beginning of his relationship with a woman who he later married marked the end of this challenging period, although his alcohol addiction continued and that marriage later ended.

In later life Donat experienced three particularly defining transitions. First, when he committed to sobriety on 23 December 1987; second, when he left secure employment after 27 years at the State Electricity Commission in the mid-1990s for a new career in human resources, adult education, and community development; and third, when he experienced a reconfiguration of his migrant identity in the 2000s. From 1998 to 2000, Donat worked at the Gippsland Migrant Resource Centre. He wondered if he was immigrant enough when he applied for the role: "I had changed so much and become so much of a—(sighs) I don't know … *an Aussie* I guess." Perhaps his application suggests a desire to question and reframe his identity. He began working on the West Sale Migrant Memorial Project, which commemorated the West Sale Migrant Camp. This project was a catalyst for Donat. After the project's physical memorial was unveiled in 2005, he became severely unwell. Although he lost about "19 kilos in seven weeks and became very debilitated," doctors struggled to produce a medical diagnosis. Donat felt that this process was a physical manifestation of emotionally releasing his "discomfort about not being okay with who I was" as a migrant. "It was like a kind of a coming out." In "coming out" Donat reconnected to the Polish language and reverted from the name "Don" to "Donat." This reconnection to his migrant identity continued when he returned to Poland for the first time in 2008 and traced his emigration journey: he "cried a lot" and it was "a strong component of growth."

Donat's adult experiences influence how he remembers and narrates his youth and migration. At 37, he turned to Alcoholics Anonymous (AA) for help fighting his alcohol addiction and experienced a transformative "*total rebirth.*" He draws on concepts he learnt through AA to explain his life story. By the time of his interview, Donat had "spent endless hours with counsellors and psychologists," which contributed to his ability to recount his life in depth and detail, identify experiences that most influenced his life, and examine how they shaped his identity.

While Donat did not fully understand the causes and effects of his discontentment as a teenager, he is now able to interpret those emotions. Polish folk dancing had "just felt awkward," but Donat can now explain that his participation "was negating my wanting to assimilate to the nth degree … placing me back to be someone that doesn't belong again—as I know today." As Kate Douglas writes: "Childhood memories are evoked by contemporary knowledge."[19] By his interview, Donat is familiar with prevalent social and cultural narratives about how post-war migrants experienced Australia's assimilation policy in the 1960s. Donat can now historicize his experience and draw on ideas and language—such as "wanting to assimilate"—that he has acquired as an adult. His use of the phrase "as I know today" emphasizes how he is aware that this interpretation occurred after the event, and after his youth. Donat's memories of childhood and youth have been reshaped by public narratives about European history, too—about a year before the interview, he read a book about the Iron Curtain, and explains, "I can now read myself into that."

Migration is the central experience through which Donat remembers his childhood and youth. His memories of his life in Poland are often vague compared to his detailed memories of his teen years as a migrant in Australia. He does not "have vivid memories" of the major transitions he experienced in Poland, such as moving in with his parents at age eight. "The bits that I can *vividly* remember from my childhood are probably [from] about the time when we came here." He has "little slides in my head of that time [in Poland], but nothing hugely vivid." His description of pre-migration life contains clichés and nostalgia: it was an "idyllic" childhood, "a wonderful childhood—almost fairy-tale occurrence." The fondness with which he recalls Poland may be influenced by his lonely teenage experience in Australia.

Donat's life story illuminates how *he* saw his migration as a defining experience that shaped his youth and adult life. He remembers the conse-quences of migration as the primary cause of his father's "breakdown," increased tensions in his parents' marriage, and his teenage unhappiness. Some of these difficulties likely stemmed from Donat's earlier life in Poland. In fact, Donat knows that he probably has "some heavy-duty stuff" around "abandonment" as a result of his childhood separation from his parents, and as we have seen, he contemplates how his father's army experience may have influenced Mr Santowiak's subsequent mental health in Australia, and he describes alcohol as relaxing a "tenseness" that he felt "24/7 for all those years" in Poland as well as Australia. Yet, he points to migration as predominately responsible for many of the troubles in his youth and early adult life, or at the very least as a tipping point. He remem-bers his "horrendous" first few years in Australia as "the worst time." Perhaps one way in which Donat found composure in his life story account was by explaining migration as primarily responsible for the hardships in his life. Perhaps this was an easier and more comfortable interpretation of his past to live with in the present[20] than one that attributed the difficulties in his young life in Australia to a range of complicated feelings about his Polish childhood, including his formal and distant relationship with his father, and his childhood separations from his parents and from the two German women. His lack of knowledge about certain aspects of his Polish childhood may have contributed to the importance he assigns to his migration in his life story. Donat's later employment at a migrant resource centre, his embracing of his migrant roots in 2005, and his 2008 retracing of his emigration journey demonstrate that he now wants to revisit his migration and create a more positive migrant identity.

CONCLUSION

My close reading of this interview shows how, for Donat, simultaneously experiencing youth and migration was a potent and challenging mix. Social exclusion, verbal and physical bullying and abuse, the lack of English language support, dysfunctional family dynamics, the lack of contact with his extended family, and the absence of tangible assistance from his school, all affected Donat's experiences of both migration and youth. Donat's experience reminds us of the profound role that personal circumstances play in shaping migration experience. It suggests that family relationships play a pivotal role in shaping migration experience for young and dependent migrants who migrate with their parents. Yet, Donat often found ways to generate agency in circumstances that were not of his choosing and he actively shaped his young life in Australia. By examining Donat's narrative through the analytical lens of age, intersecting with ethnicity and gender, this chapter has illuminated how Donat's age at the time of his migration mattered and has demonstrated the value of considering age and the life stage when interpreting memories of migration.[21]

NOTES

1. See, for example, Erik Erikson, *Childhood and Society* (New York: W.W. Norton, 1993); Chapter 7 "Eight Ages of Man" 247–274; George E. Vaillant, *Adaptation to Life* (Boston: Little, Brown, 1977); Martin A. Conway, "The Inventory of Experience: Memory and Identity", in *Collective Memory of Political Events: Social Psychology Perspectives*, ed. by James W. Pennebaker, Dario Paez, and Bernard Rimé (Mahwah, NJ: Lawrence Erlbaum Associates, 1997), 21–45.

2. For literature on how historians of childhood and youth have used age in analysis of life story interviews see Mary Jo Maynes, "Age as a Category of Historical Analysis: History, Agency, and Narratives of Childhood," *The Journal of the History of Childhood and Youth* 1, no. 1 (2008): 118–23; and Selina Todd and Hilary Young, "Baby-Boomers to 'Beanstalkers': Making the Modern Teenager in Post-War Britain," *Cultural and Social History* 9,

no. 3 (2012): 453–54. Contributions by historians of old age are also relevant: see Charlotte Greenhalgh, *Aging in Twentieth-Century Britain* (Oakland, CA: University of California Press, 2018).

3. Valerie Raleigh Yow, *Recording Oral History: A Guide for the Humanities and Social Sciences*, 2nd edition (Walnut Creek, CA: Altamira Press, 2005), 238.

4. Paul Thompson with Joanna Bornat, *The Voice of the Past: Oral History*, 4th edition (New York: Oxford University Press, 2017), 180. Katy Gardner's work is one exception: see Katy Gardner, *Age, Narrative and Migration: The Life Course and Life Histories of Bengali Elders in London* (Oxford and New York: Berg, 2002).

5. A. James Hammerton and Alistair Thomson, *Ten Pound Poms: Australia's Invisible Migrants* (Manchester and New York: Manchester University Press, 2005), 261.

6. Joy Damousi, *Memory and Migration in the Shadow of War: Australia's Greek Immigrants after World War II and the Greek Civil War* (Cambridge: Cambridge University Press 2015), 174.

7. See Jessica Stroja, "Settlement of Refugee Women and Children Following the Second World War: Challenges to the Family," *The History of the Family* 22, no. 4 (2017): 510–30; Niro Kandasamy, "Unravelling Memories of Family Separation Among Sri Lankan Tamils Resettled in Australia, 1983–2000," *Immigrants & Minorities* 36, no. 2 (2018): 143–60; Sarah Green, "'All Those Stories, All Those Stories': How Do Bosnian Former Child Refugees Maintain Connections to Bosnia and Community Groups in Australia?," *Immigrants & Minorities* 36, no. 2 (2018): 161–77.

8. Donat Santowiak interviewed by Alistair Thomson, 19–20 June 2014, Moe, Victoria, Australian Generations Oral History Project, National Library of Australia, TRC 6300/292. Unless otherwise stated, all quotations are from this interview.

9. Rob White and Johanna Wyn, *Youth and Society: Exploring the Social Dynamics of Youth Experience* (South Melbourne: Oxford University Press, 2004), 186.

10. For a discussion on this topic, see Rob White and Johanna Wyn, *Rethinking Youth* (London: Sage Publications, 1997); Chapter 1, "The Concept of Youth," 8–25.

11. Michelle Arrow, *Friday on Our Minds: Popular Culture in Australia since 1945* (Sydney: UNSW Press, 2009); Chapter 3, "The Rise of Youth Cultures," 44–73.

12. Conway, "The Inventory of Experience," 32–35.

13. L. Paszkowski, "Characteristics of Polish Immigrants," in James Jupp ed., *The Australian People: An Encyclopaedia of the Nation, Its People and Their*

Origins, 2nd edition (Cambridge: Cambridge University Press, 2001), 623.

14. Sev Ozdowski and Jan Lencznarowicz, "Post-War Polish Refugees," in *The Australian People*, 624.
15. Jerry Zubrzycki, *Settlers of the Latrobe Valley: A Sociological Study of Immigrants in the Brown Coal Industry in Australia* (Canberra: Australian National University, 1964), 12–13.
16. Maynes, "Age as a Category of Historical Analysis," 116.
17. See Isabelle Bertaux-Wiame, "The Life History Approach to the Study of Internal Migration," *Oral History* 7, no. 1 (1979): 26–32; and Mary Chamberlain, "Gender and the Narratives of Migration," *History Workshop Journal* 43 (1997): 87–108.
18. Graeme Davison with Sheryl Yelland, *Car Wars: How the Car Won Our Hearts and Conquered Our Cities* (Crows Nest, NSW: Allen and Unwin, 2004); Chapter 3, "Sex, Power and Speed," 48–73.
19. Kate Douglas, *Contesting Childhood: Autobiography, Trauma and Memory* (New Brunswick, NJ: Rutgers University Press, 2010), 60.
20. For composure theory, see Penny Summerfield, "Culture and Composure: Creating Narratives of the Gendered Self in Oral History Interviews," *Cultural and Social History* 1, no. 1 (2004): 65–93; and Alistair Thomson, "*Anzac Memories* Revisited: Trauma, Memory and Oral History," *Oral History Review* 42, no. 1 (2015): 22–23.
21. I wish to thank Alistair Thomson, Kate Murphy and the editors of this collection for their helpful comments on drafts of this chapter. Thanks also to Donat Santowiak for so generously sharing his experience with the Australian Generations Oral History Project. My research has been supported by an Australian Government Research Training Program Scholarship.

Bibliography

Arrow, Michelle. *Friday on Our Minds: Popular Culture in Australia since 1945.* Sydney: UNSW Press, 2009.

Bertaux-Wiame, Isabelle. "The Life History Approach to the Study of Internal Migration." *Oral History* 7, no. 1 (1979): 26–32.

Chamberlain, Mary. "Gender and the Narratives of Migration." *History Workshop Journal* 43 (1997): 87–108.

Conway, Martin A. "The Inventory of Experience: Memory and Identity." In *Collective Memory of Political Events: Social Psychology Perspectives*, edited by James W. Pennebaker, Dario Paez and Bernard Rimé, 21–45. Mahwah, NJ: Lawrence Erlbaum Associates, 1997.

Damousi, Joy. *Memory and Migration in the Shadow of War: Australia's Greek Immigrants after World War II and the Greek Civil War*. Cambridge: Cambridge University Press, 2015.

Davison, Graeme with Sheryl Yelland. *Car Wars: How the Car Won Our Hearts and Conquered Our Cities*. Crows Nest, NSW: Allen & Unwin, 2004.

Douglas, Kate. *Contesting Childhood: Autobiography, Trauma and Memory*. New Brunswick: Rutgers University Press, 2010.

Erikson, Erik. *Childhood and Society* (1964). New York: W. W. Norton, 1993.

Gardner, Katy. *Age, Narrative and Migration: The Life Course and Life Histories of Bengali Elders in London*. Oxford and New York: Berg, 2002.

Green, Sarah. "'All Those Stories, All Those Stories': How Do Bosnian Former Child Refugees Maintain Connections to Bosnia and Community Groups in Australia?" *Immigrants & Minorities* 36, no. 2 (2018): 161–77.

Greenhalgh, Charlotte. *Aging in Twentieth-Century Britain*. Oakland, CA: University of California Press, 2018.

Hammerton, A. James, and Alistair Thomson. *Ten Pound Poms: Australia's Invisible Migrants*. Manchester and New York: Manchester University Press, 2005.

Kandasamy, Niro. "Unravelling Memories of Family Separation Among Sri Lankan Tamils Resettled in Australia, 1983–2000." *Immigrants & Minorities* 36, no. 2 (2018): 143–60.

Maynes, Mary Jo. "Age as a Category of Historical Analysis: History, Agency, and Narratives of Childhood." *The Journal of the History of Childhood and Youth* 1, no. 1 (2008): 114–24.

Ozdowski, Sev, and Jan Lencznarowicz. "Post-War Polish Refugees". In *The Australian People: An Encyclopaedia of the Nation, Its People and Their Origins*, 2nd edition, edited by James Jupp, 623–25. Cambridge: Cambridge University Press, 2001.

Paszkowski, L. "Characteristics of Polish Immigrants". In *The Australian People: An Encyclopaedia of the Nation, Its People and Their Origins*, 2nd edition, edited by James Jupp, 623. Cambridge: Cambridge University Press, 2001.

Santowiak, Donat. Interviewed by Alistair Thomson, 19–20 June 2014, Moe, Victoria. Australian Generations Oral History Project. National Library of Australia, TRC 6300/292.

Stroja, Jessica. "Settlement of Refugee Women and Children Following the Second World War: Challenges to the Family." *The History of the Family* 22, no. 4 (2017): 510–30.

Summerfield, Penny. "Culture and Composure: Creating Narratives of the Gendered Self in Oral History Interviews." *Cultural and Social History* 1, no. 1 (2004): 65–93.

Todd, Selina, and Hilary Young. "Baby-Boomers to 'Beanstalkers': Making the Modern Teenager in Post-War Britain." *Cultural and Social History* 9, no. 3 (2012): 451–67.

Thompson, Paul with Joanna Bornat. *The Voice of the Past: Oral History*, 4th edition. New York: Oxford University Press, 2017.

Thomson, Alistair. "*Anzac Memories* Revisited: Trauma, Memory and Oral History." *Oral History Review* 42, no. 1 (2015): 1–29.

Vaillant, George E. *Adaptation to Life*. Boston: Little, Brown, 1977.

White, Rob, and Johanna Wyn. *Rethinking Youth*. London: Sage Publications, 1997.

White, Rob, and Johanna Wyn. *Youth and Society: Exploring the Social Dynamics of Youth Experience*. South Melbourne: Oxford University Press, 2004.

Yow, Valerie Raleigh. *Recording Oral History: A Guide for the Humanities and Social Sciences*, 2nd edition. Walnut Creek, CA: Altamira Press, 2005.

Zubrzycki, Jerry. *Settlers of the Latrobe Valley: A Sociological Study of Immigrants in the Brown Coal Industry in Australia*. Canberra: Australian National University, 1964.

CHAPTER 6

Memory, Migration and Television: National Stories of the Small Screen

Kate Darian-Smith and Kyle Harvey

The post-World War II era of mass migration to Australia coincided with the launch of television in 1956, enabling home viewing of the Melbourne Olympic Games. Yet despite the temporal convergence of these socially and culturally transformative processes for the nation, histories of television *and* of migration have generally been written in parallel rather than intricately linked together. This may be explained by the intimacy of television as a domestic medium, part of ordinary daily routines from the 1950s throughout the twentieth century, and as such disassociated from the defining historical and political narratives of nation-building. More recently, the focus of memory studies on questions of identity, emotion and affect has situated television as the creator and the repository—the *mediator*—of individual and collective memories of key moments within the public sphere and in family or private lives.[1] Indeed, popular studies of

K. Darian-Smith (✉) • K. Harvey
University of Tasmania, Hobart, TAS, Australia
e-mail: kate.dariansmith@utas.edu.au; kyle.harvey@utas.edu.au

© The Author(s) 2019
K. Darian-Smith, P. Hamilton (eds.), *Remembering Migration*,
Palgrave Macmillan Memory Studies,
https://doi.org/10.1007/978-3-030-17751-5_6

Australian television, often highly nostalgic in tone, emphasize the shared nature of viewing and remembering specific programmes on shaping the national psyche.[2]

Absent from histories of Australian television are the alternative voices of migrants, whose experiences of TV were diverse and often differed from those of the mainstream Anglo-Celtic population. Yet skilled migrant technicians, presenters and camera operators from Britain, Europe and the United States were essential to the establishment and growth of Australia's early television industry, and were recruited to employment in the expanding communications sector.[3] More broadly, migrants to Australia during the 1950s and 1960s brought varied knowledge of television from their countries of origin. For those from the UK, where television was established in the 1930s, some programming was familiar, and the popularity of imported British "soaps" like *Coronation Street* offered a point of conversational departure with new Australian friends. In contrast, those from Italy and Greece arrived with no or limited encounters with television and had to grapple with broadcasts in a new language. For all migrants, however, television news and current affairs provided insights into Australia's place in the world, while domestically produced drama and variety programmes shed light on local customs and values.

This chapter discusses new research that examines the conjoined histories of television, migration and cultural diversity in Australia.[4] Drawing upon oral histories and memoirs, we argue that migrants' memories differ substantially from a "public archive" of programmes at the core of mainstream television history.[5] Instead, migrant memories of watching television operated in social and cultural spaces that were intimately linked to settlement and adjustment to Australian life. In many cases, the *experience* of viewing television in certain contexts—with family members or neighbours—was equally if not more important than recollections of programmes. While migrants were, like the general Australian population, quick to purchase or rent a television, the materiality of a set displayed in the living room is often remembered as a symbol of economic success in a new land.[6]

For Australia's large post-war migrant population, arriving in successive waves from Europe, the Middle East and South-East Asia, the history of television is also one of absence. Migrants, especially from non-English speaking backgrounds, have historically comprised what Tom O'Regan and Stuart Cunningham call "marginal audiences," whose interests are "under-served or poorly represented within our television system."[7] Since the early 1990s, and despite Australia's official policy of multiculturalism, subsequent government and industry inquiries have reiterated that non-English speaking migrants, as well as Indigenous Australians, are under-represented in Australian media and often portrayed in ways that are racist or draw on ethnic stereotypes.[8] The distinctive memories of migrants and their Australian-born children of such representational absences often include a pivotal moment of finally "seeing me" on television. These narratives offer alternative cultural accounts of the everyday presence of an industry invested heavily in its contribution to national identity and an innate "Australian-ness."[9]

The records and archives of the television industry, its programming and reception, are generally incomplete or missing, although the institutional history of the national network, the Australian Broadcasting Corporation (ABC), is one exception. Collecting of television materials by the National Film and Sound Archive has also been highly selective. This has meant that oral histories and memoirs have been an essential source in capturing how migrant communities and individuals have experienced television as part of their new lives in Australia—not merely in charting the multiple dimension of their social interaction with television as a media form, but also as a transmitter of cultural representation and diversity. Indeed, our investigation of the relationship between television and migration has relied upon first-person narratives to address gaps in the records and to provide alternative histories. To illustrate this point, this chapter draws upon two groups of oral histories—of migrants to Australia across several decades and of migrant television producers and entrepreneurs—to tease out new and hitherto buried stories of the intersections between migration and television.[10]

Unsettling Television Histories

Early Australian television was dominated by imported programmes from the United States and Britain, alongside locally produced news, entertainment shows and advertisements. However, the dearth of locally made content, notably dramas, led to substantial industry agitation, with the federal government appointing a Senate Select Committee on the Encouragement of Australian Productions for Television in 1963. Its report pointed to the "undesirable sociological and cultural consequences" of television dominated by American imports.[11] By the late 1960s, the "TV: Make it Australian" campaign was launched, and in 1972 the Australian

Broadcasting Control Board directed commercial stations to screen 50 per cent of Australian content during prime time, a quota later measured by a "points system."[12] The system was overhauled in 1990, but the requirement for quality local content has remained a distinctive feature of Australia's highly regulated television industry.

The early years of Australian television offered little from mainstream production organizations, apart from some educational programming, for non-English speaking audiences. Nonetheless, the role of the broadcast media was widely recognized as key to the successful settlement of migrants. The Special Broadcasting Service (SBS) was formed in response the federal government's Review of Post-Arrival Programs and Services for Migrants in 1978, which advocated the development of a radio and television service to deliver content for migrants in their native languages.[13] SBS Television, broadcast in Sydney and Melbourne from 1980, screened imported programmes from across the globe, international sporting matches and its renowned *World News*. Its presenters were migrants themselves, while its subtitling department ensured English-speaking audiences were not alienated.[14] SBS Television enabled a means to engage with the full diversity of multicultural, Indigenous and minority cultures in a way that Gay Hawkins describes as "a bizarre and pleasurable heterogeneity."[15] Produced by migrants and aimed—if not exclusively—at migrant audiences, SBS provided greater linguistic and cultural diversity on Australian television. As viewer surveys have shown, many migrants of non-English speaking backgrounds watched SBS primarily for programmes in their native tongue, and for those migrants we interviewed, it did not play a major role in their television viewing habits.[16]

Nonetheless, the success of SBS has meant that its introduction in 1980 has been situated in mainstream media histories as the "first" television broadcasting aimed at non-English speaking migrants. This dominant narrative ignores other programmes made in the 1970s and 1980s that targeted specific ethnic groups such as *Variety, Italian Style* (1972–1986) or *Greek Variety Show* (1977–1986). These programmes are remembered as being significant in our oral histories, and at the time were rated highly with migrant audiences in surveys.[17] *Variety, Italian Style* was especially popular with viewers of Italian, but also Spanish, and Serbo-Croatian origin.[18] For migrants, especially those from non-English speaking countries, memories of television constitute different forms of belonging to the Australian nation. Sport, game shows, reality television, films and American sitcoms feature heavily in these migrant stories from the 1950s to the present. The role that "ordinary television" plays in migrants' everyday lives is an integral part of Australia's television history, and an equally integral part of the story of migration and how it is remembered.[19]

TELEVISION AND MIGRANT IDENTITY

In the 1970s, when nine-year old Dmetri Kakmi emigrated with his family from a remote Turkish island in the Aegean Sea to Melbourne, television enabled him to adjust to the city. "The fabulous invention was no mere abstraction," he later recalled, with "The images presented on screen were more real and contained more truth than reality." For Kakmi, discovering television "shifted the ground beneath my feet and changed my life."[20] This response is not unusual, as oral histories with migrants living in Australia between the 1950s and 1990s demonstrate. For Rita Price, born in Melbourne to Italian migrant parents, childhood in a café with her extended family was a world away from the location of quintessential Australian children's drama such as *Skippy the Bush Kangaroo*.[21] Instead, Price remembered being immersed in the American worlds of cartoons, sitcoms and films.[22] Anna Maria Dell'Oso recalled that

> It was asking for trouble to plant a Magic Box—stuffed full of American English-speaking fantasy culture, 1940s nostalgia and 1950s morality—into a home of rural immigrant Italians struggling to cope with a big city life in Melbourne, Australia.[23]

Television also highlighted the gulf between parents and children when it came to English-language proficiency. For Dell'Oso and her siblings during the 1960s, "The English language cut us apart like a knife. We kids understood the television programs, Mamma and Papa didn't."[24] This generational divide in the understanding of English-language television is a consistent theme in migrant memories across decades, although it is complicated in oral histories with the advent of satellite television and the proliferation of streaming services. In the 2000s, Salim Noorzai, born in Australia to Afghan refugee parents, often watched television alone as his parents did not understand English. They preferred to watch Afghan news and Indian, Pakistani and Turkish dramas received through a satellite dish installed in the family's backyard, which they recorded during the night and viewed later. Noorzai recalled his own evening "ritual" of watching typical fare on Australian free-to-air television, including imports such as

The Simpsons and the long-running Australian soap *Neighbours*.[25] Viewing *Neighbours* and other Australian programmes as a teenager amplified Salim's feelings of exclusion: "There's no Afghans in *Neighbours*. There's no Indians in *Neighbours*. There's no Asians in *Neighbours*. Nothing. It's just a bunch of white people in a street."[26]

Other non-English speaking migrants used television as a vehicle to learn English at the same time as their children. Cuc Lam, a refugee from Vietnam, "could speak English a little bit" on arrival in Australia in 1978, but would view *Play School* with her young children in the migrant hostel where they were first accommodated to improve her proficiency.[27] Lam found television "wonderful" and "very clear," reflecting many migrants' fascination with colour broadcasting, introduced in Australia in 1975 but unavailable in many countries of origin. When Lam and her family moved into their own apartment, they purchased a second-hand TV set which she recalled as "huge, very bulky, but we loved it."[28] When former teacher Tatek Menji arrived as a refugee from Ethiopia in the mid-1980s, he savoured the diversity available on Australian television, especially the "more realistic" news on ABC and SBS. He would use videocassette technology to record documentaries and watch them on weekends.[29]

The memoir of Serbian Australian Sofija Stefanovic, who with her family left the former Yugoslavia and war in the 1990s, explains her "cultural immersion" in English-language television:

> Not only did these shows provide me with the entertainment, joy and linguistic skills that I desperately needed, they also offered the beautiful and comforting formula of beginnings, middles and ends. … And even though I didn't know all the words, I could make predictions based on my knowledge of storytelling, and learning English became less of a chore, more of an adventure. Watching TV brought order into the chaos. I turned into a devoted couch potato; the screen became my most loved teacher.[30]

For children and young adults of migrant backgrounds, watching television programmes was essential for communicating with peers and fitting in at school. As a young girl in the 1960s, Dell'Oso "relied on TV for instruction about the world, about myself as a woman, about the values and morals I should adopt in life." She cast herself as "a kind of pioneer in Australian society with television as my only map and bowie knife."[31]

More recently, Erica Sun, a teenager of Chinese Australian heritage, admitted in an interview that while she mostly watched Chinese television programmes at home, she pretended to know about American television programmes, streamed on Netflix, when socializing with her school friends.[32] While contemporary viewing practices, relying on YouTube and access to digital streaming, differ in technology from older pre-digital forms of television watching, our analysis of migrant oral histories and memoirs reveal a constancy in the use of a shared knowledge of television programmes as contributing to social and cultural integration.

Some migrants found television's guide to "being Australian" resulted in the rejection of parental cultural values and even ethnicity. For others, television in the mid-twentieth century also offered some points of cultural affirmation. Barry York, of Maltese origin, recalled watching *World Championship Wrestling* because the wrestlers provided positive role models for ethnic communities.[33] Maria Doganieri, who migrated to regional Victoria from Italy, recalled her family's Sunday ritual of watching television over lunch, and their identification with the champion Italian wrestler Mario Milano.[34]

A group interview we conducted with Rita Price, Marina De Stefanis, Michelina D'Urbano and Ninette Cilia—all born to Italian migrant parents—revealed shared memories of Sundays dominated by church, family lunch and television viewing, mostly on commercial channels. Programmes included *World Championship Wrestling*, movies in the *Epic Theatre* slot and a televised ten-minute lecture by the conservative politician B. A. Santamaria.[35] Although Price's parents could not understand Santamaria, who spoke in English, "they felt that they needed to watch" because he was from an Italian background.[36] The women recalled how their family members would also point out Italian actors appearing in the credits of American films.

Simon Palomares, born in Germany to Spanish parents, migrated to Melbourne in the early 1970s. While he did not initially question the lack of cultural diversity on television, he remembered

> watching *Chico and the Man*, the American series, and seeing for the first time someone who spoke Spanish. I remember getting very excited when characters in *Sesame Street* spoke Spanish, because that was the only time that you saw anything like that.[37]

Imported material from the United States provided encounters with non-white characters and non-English languages, especially in the genres of comedy, drama and children's programmes. Indeed, American television embraced its migrant populations through representation on television much earlier than in Australia, as well as catering to immigrant communities through specialized programming in foreign languages.[38]

Variety Shows and Migrant Producers

In the early 1970s a new magazine-style programme, presented in English and Italian, was launched on commercial television. It featured music, documentary, travel and sporting segments imported from television stations in Italy, Switzerland and Yugoslavia. Initially known as *Tonight, Italian Style*, it was renamed *Variety, Italian Style* to reflect a scheduling shift to Sunday mornings. Joseph Pugliese recalled watching the first episode in October 1972:

> The whole family was glued to the TV. It was a powerful moment due to the fact that Italian culture and language (through song) were being aired on Australian television. It was a moment that entailed both cultural affirmation and recognition. I clearly remember that both my mother and father became quite emotional while watching the program.[39]

Pugliese's father telephoned the television station to thank them for the broadcast. In an oral interview, Doganieri remembered the travel segments screened on *Variety, Italian Style* were the first time her family had seen footage of Italy on television since they had left.[40] In the years before SBS Television offered Australian audiences a plethora of documentaries, music, film and sport from around the world, *Variety, Italian Style* occupied a crucial niche in the television viewing habits of Italian migrants, their children and many others.

Conventional histories of television in Australia during its first decades have ignored the production of programmes in languages other than English. The focus has been on the role of the ABC and commercial networks, and on the big production companies, such as Melbourne-based Crawford Productions, responsible for dozens of long-running Australian dramas, soaps and comedies.[41] There are very few records of small-scale production companies producing television for migrant communities. By the mid-1970s, those of Italian and Greek origin were Australia's largest non-English speaking migrant groups: some 445,000 people regularly spoke Italian, alongside around 262,000 regular Greek speakers.[42] As oral histories have highlighted, migrant television producers also worked in very different ways than the mainstream production companies. They relied on personal connections and self-financing to make a successful product that repackaged imported content from Europe, and then exported the programmes to other Italian and Greek diasporic communities around the globe.[43] They operated as successful ethnic entrepreneurs, whose small business models enabled them to survive in what has traditionally been a ruthless industry dominated by media moguls and international conglomerates.

In the early 1970s, Antonio (Tony) Luciano, born in Australia to an Italian father and Anglo-Australian mother, set up his own production company, Panorama Productions, to put together an Italian programme for the 0/10 Network (later Network Ten).[44] Luciano was enmeshed in Australia's Italian community through the Italian-language newspaper run by his father and uncle—*Il Corriere d'Australia*—from 1953 to 1961. Employed in advertising, the shift to television seemed logical, as he recalled:

> I thought, there's a career here in terms of putting together a national service that is good for the consumption of the community. I'm going to do it in [the] English language, even though the component is going to be Italian, so that it will also be of interest to Australians.[45]

The financial success of *Variety, Italian Style* owed much to its ability to be packaged and re-sold in different markets: to commercial stations in metropolitan and regional Australia, and since it operated as a "package" of segments, the programme was easily sold overseas, especially to television stations in the United States and Canada. Its value for audiences, Luciano felt, was broad. "The essence was entertainment and information. That was the whole philosophy behind it, with a cultural dimension." Music clips proved popular, since "even if you didn't understand the language there would be a visual appeal." Cooking segments formed the basis of a subsequent programme also produced by Luciano, *Anne's International Kitchen*, which ran on SBS Television into the mid-1990s.[46]

By the late 1970s there were other "ethnic" variety shows. *Greek Affair*, later renamed *Greek Variety Show*, was produced in Sydney from 1977 by Harry Michaels, a Greek Cypriot who had migrated to Australia in 1966 and risen to fame as an actor on popular soap *Number 96*. Michaels recalls severe obstacles to getting *Greek Affair* on air:

> The racism was so high in those days. It was an insult. ... I approached the then General Manager of Channel 10 who I [had] got to know and we got along very well. I asked whether I could produce a Greek variety show and he said to me: 'We have one. It's Italian. You're all the same aren't you?'[47]

Like Luciano, Michaels imported footage for the programme from Greece, especially Greek music clips, and also filmed cooking and music segments at the NBN television studios in Newcastle. Co-producer Ted Jobbins remembered attending "many Greek nightclubs around Sydney" to source, and to film, local Greek singers and musicians for the programme.[48] A competing Greek variety programme, *Let's Go Greek*, began broadcasting in 1979, also on the 0/10 Network. It was produced by Theo Skalkos, another self-made entrepreneur whose Media Press publishing company had been in operation since 1966, after Skalkos had worked stints in sugar-cane cutting, various factories, a driving school, a wedding car rental company and, finally, a printery.[49] Skalkos' good relationship with Rupert Murdoch, who purchased the 0/10 Network in 1979, ensured two Greek variety programmes were aired in Sydney. In a similar fashion, Greek music clips were imported, and segments filmed in rented studios and at cultural functions, alongside interviews with notable Greek Australians and visitors.[50] In Melbourne, yet another Greek variety programme entitled *Grecian Scene* ran for several years in the late 1970s. Produced by Anastasios Yiannopoulos (Stan Young), whose family had migrated in the 1930s, it was financed by members of the Melbourne Greek community, and comprised musical segments, interviews with community members and other items of interest to Greek Australians.[51]

The value of such programmes for audiences, as those involved in their production suggest, was immense, especially in the years before SBS Television offered migrant television viewers a broader sampling of content from their home countries. *Grecian Scene*, recalled screenwriter and musician Deborah Parsons, "was really important" for Greek Australians. Its value stemmed from "people wanting to see themselves on television. It was the first time they'd actually seen themselves, to hear their language. To just be mainstream."[52] This value would continue with the Greek programming screened on SBS Television from 1980, reflecting its mission to cater to minority television audiences. In oral interviews both Luciano and Michaels also attached similar cultural value to the screening of European soccer highlights on their variety programmes, as this was the first time that Italians, Greeks and others had been able to watch soccer matches from their home countries on Australian television.[53]

Conclusion

As this chapter has argued, with the dearth of written sources on the production and consumption of television programming by migrants to Australia during the twentieth century, first-person reflections in oral histories and memoirs may offer alternatives to mainstream media and television histories. Indeed, our research into the nexus between migration and television—as an industry, but also as an everyday experience—has been highly dependent on such accounts. Representations of migrants and multiculturalism have been limited on Australian television, and especially on the commercial networks, from its inception. This is still a contentious issue, despite a plethora of reports since the early 1990s critiquing the "monocultural nature" of mainstream television productions, and consequentially the low employment of Australians of non-English-speaking backgrounds in the industry.[54] As recently as 2016, a Screen Australia survey found that "minorities and marginalized communities are underrepresented in TV drama compared to the population," especially people of Asian, African or Middle Eastern origin.[55] Yet despite this, over several decades Australian television's mixture of imported programmes (with glimpses of ethnicity in *other* places) and local programmes (that barely acknowledged the demographic changes in Australian society), did provide models that enabled migrants and their children to adapt to their new home. For some young people, television allowed them to step away from their parents' world to adjust and fit in with their peers. Through oral histories, we can discover from the margins of Australian society new national stories of migrant television audiences and producers, and see how the experiences of migration and television are deeply connected.

Notes

1. Kate Darian-Smith and Sue Turnbull eds, *Remembering Television: Histories, Technologies, Memories* (Newcastle upon Tyne: Cambridge Scholars Publishing, 2012); Mottie Neiger, Oren Meyers and Eyal Zandberg eds, *On Media Memory: Collective Memory in a New Media Age* (Basingstoke: Palgrave Macmillan, 2011); Susan Bye, "TV Memories, the *Daily Telegraph* and TCN: 'First in Australia'," *Media International Australia*, no. 121 (2006) 159–73; Bridget Griffen-Foley, "Diary of a Television Viewer," *Media International Australia*, no. 162 (2017): 33–48.

2. Alan McKee, *Australian Television: A Genealogy of Great Moments* (Melbourne: Oxford University Press, 2001); Nigel Giles, *Number 96: Australian TV's Most Notorious Address* (Melbourne: Melbourne Books, 2017); Brendan Horgan, *Radio with Pictures: 50 Years of Australian Television* (Sydney: Lothian Books, 2006); and Nick Place and Michael Roberts eds, *50 Years of Television in Australia* (Prahran, VIC: Hardie Grant, 2006).
3. Kate Darian-Smith and Paula Hamilton, "Part of the Family: Australian Histories of Television, Migration and Memory," in Kate Darian-Smith and Sue Turnbull eds, *Remembering Television: Histories, Technologies, Memories* (Newcastle upon Tyne: Cambridge Scholars Publishing, 2012), 44–45.
4. This work is funded by the Australian Research Council: LP150100202 "Migration, Cultural Diversity and Television: Reflecting Modern Australia": Kate Darian-Smith (lead), Sukhmani Khorana, Sue Turnbull, Kyle Harvey, with Moya McFadzean and Michael Reason at Museums Victoria and Helen Simondson at the Australian Centre for the Moving Image.
5. McKee, *Australian Television*, 6.
6. Darian-Smith and Hamilton, "Part of the Family," 38–41; Derham Groves, *TV Houses: Television's Influence on the Australian Home* (Carlton North, VIC: Black Jack Press, 2004).
7. Tom O'Regan and Stuart Cunningham, "Marginalised Audiences," in Graeme Turner and Stuart Cunningham eds, *The Australian TV Book* (St Leonards, NSW: Allen & Unwin, 2000), 201.
8. Some early examples include Helen Carmichael ed., *Seeing Is Believing: Scriptwriting in a Multicultural Society: Report to the Office of Multicultural Affairs* (Canberra: Office of Multicultural Affairs, 1991); Bronwyn Coupe, Andrew Jakubowicz and Lois Randall, *Nextdoor Neighbours: A Report for the Office of Multicultural Affairs on Ethnic Group Discussions of the Australian Media* (Canberra: Office of Multicultural Affairs, 1993); and Stephen Nugent, Milica Loncar and Kate Aisbett, *The People We See on TV: Cultural Diversity on Television* (North Sydney: Australian Broadcasting Authority, 1993).
9. Andrew Jakubowicz et al., *Racism, Ethnicity and the Media* (St Leonards, NSW: Allen & Unwin, 1994), Chapter 14.
10. These interviews were undertaken for a project funded by the Australian Research Council LP150100202, and cover histories and memories of migration, television viewing and work in the television industry. They are supplemented by interviews held at the National Film and Sound Archive (NFSA) and National Library of Australia (NLA).

11. Vincent Report, 1963, quoted in Franco Papandrea, "Television Stations' Compliance with Australian Content Regulation," *Agenda* 2, no. 4 (1995): 468.
12. Papandrea, "Television Stations' Compliance," 468.
13. James Jupp, *From White Australia to Woomera: The Story of Australian Immigration*, 2nd edition (New York: Cambridge University Press, 2007), 83–86.
14. Adriaan van der Weel, "Subtitling and the SBS Audience," *Media Information Australia*, no. 56 (1990): 22–26.
15. Gay Hawkins, "SBS: Minority Television," *Culture and Policy* 7, no. 1 (1996): 47.
16. David Bednall, *Media and Immigrant Settlement* (Canberra: Commonwealth of Australia, 1992), 31–32.
17. Jonathan Bollen, "Here from There—Travel, Television and Touring Revues: Internationalism as Entertainment in the 1950s and 1960s," *Popular Entertainment Studies* 4, no. 1 (2013): 64–81; McKee, *Australian Television*, Chapter 1.
18. Pamela Williams, "Commercial TV Productions," *Media Information Australia*, no. 15 (1980): 49.
19. Frances Bonner, *Ordinary Television: Analyzing Popular TV* (London: Sage, 2003); John Fiske, "Everyday Quizzes, Everyday Life," in John Tulloch and Graeme Turner eds, *Australian Television: Programs, Pleasures & Politics* (Sydney: Allen & Unwin, 1989).
20. Dmetri Kakmi, "Night of the Living Wog," in Kent McCarter and Ali Lemer eds, *Joyful Strains: Making Australia Home* (Melbourne: Affirm Press, 2013), 22.
21. On the familiar aspects of viewing *Skippy* as an Anglo-Australian child, see Mark Gibson, "Tchk, Tchk, Tchk: *Skippy the Bush Kangaroo* and the Question of Australian Seriousness," *Continuum* 28, no. 5 (2014): 574–75.
22. Rita Price, "The Cafe at the Edge of the Bay," in Barbara Walsh ed., *Growing up Italian in Australia: Eleven Young Australian Women Talk About Their Childhood* (Sydney: State Library of New South Wales Press, 1993), 39.
23. Anna Maria Dell'Oso, "White Man's Dreaming," in David Watson and Denise Corrigan eds, *TV Times: 35 Years of Watching Television in Australia* (Sydney: Museum of Contemporary Art, 1991), 20–21.
24. Dell'Oso, "White Man's Dreaming," 21.
25. Salim Noorzai, interviewed by Sukhmani Khorana, 30 October 2016, Sydney, digital recording in interviewer's possession.
26. Salim Noorzai, interview, 30 October 2016.

27. Cuc Lam, Tuyet Lam, David Demant and Tatek Menji, interviewed by Kyle Harvey and Kate Darian-Smith, 23 November 2016, Melbourne, digital recording in interviewers' possession.
28. Cuc Lam, Tuyet Lam, David Demant and Tatek Menji, interview, 23 November 2016.
29. Cuc Lam, Tuyet Lam, David Demant and Tatek Menji, interview, 23 November 2016.
30. Sofija Stefanovic, *Miss Ex-Yugoslavia* (Melbourne: Viking, 2018), 65.
31. Dell'Oso, "White Man's Dreaming," 21.
32. Wanning and Erica Sun, interviewed by Sukhmani Khorana, 20 December 2016, Sydney, digital recording in interviewer's possession.
33. Barry York, interviewed by Sukhmani Khorana, 3 November 2017, by telephone, digital recording in interviewer's possession.
34. Maria Doganieri, interviewed by Kyle Harvey, 27 April 2018, Melbourne, digital recording in interviewer's possession.
35. See, for example, "Week-end TV," listings, *The Age*, 1 June 1968, 15.
36. Rita Price, Marina De Stefanis, Michelina D'Urbano, and Ninette Cilia, interviewed by Kyle Harvey and Kate Darian-Smith, 23 April 2017, Melbourne, digital recording in interviewers' possession.
37. Simon Palomares, interviewed by Kyle Harvey, 30 January 2018, Melbourne, digital recording in interviewer's possession.
38. David M. Reimers, *Other Immigrants: The Global Origins of the American People* (New York: New York University Press, 2005), 183, 214, 248, 290.
39. Email to Kyle Harvey, 18 April 2018.
40. Maria Doganieri, interview, 27 April 2018.
41. See Rozzi Bazzani, *Hector* (North Melbourne: Arcadia, 2015).
42. Michael Clyne, *Multilingual Australia* (Melbourne: River Seine, 1982), 12.
43. See K. W. Strahan and A. J. Williams, *Immigrant Entrepreneurs in Australia: A Report to the Office of Multicultural Affairs* (Canberra: Office of Multicultural Affairs, 1988), 4–5, 13.
44. Antonio Luciano, interviewed by Kyle Harvey, 13 September 2017, Sydney, digital recording in interviewer's possession; "Tonight Show with Italian Flavour," *Sun-Herald*, 13 August 1972, 136.
45. Antonio Luciano, interview, 13 September 2017.
46. Antonio Luciano, interview, 13 September 2017.
47. Harry Michaels, interviewed by Kyle Harvey, 15 September 2017, Sydney, digital recording in interviewer's possession.
48. Ted Jobbins, interviewed by Nigel Giles, 8 February 2007, Wentworth Falls, National Film and Sound Archive, Canberra, Tape 3, Title 720837.
49. Theo Skalkos, "The Differences of the Archdiocese with the Greek Herald," *Greek Herald*, 1 May 1991, 1, 8–9. English translation in Folder

"Stylianos Harkianakis," Box 3810, DAHD 05913, Dardalis Archives of Hellenic Diaspora, La Trobe University, Melbourne.

50. Theo Skalkos, interviewed by Frank Heimans, 9 March 2000, National Library of Australia, ORAL TRC 3996; Helen Zerefos, interviewed by Kyle Harvey, 20 August 2018, Sydney, digital recording in interviewer's possession.

51. Tim Barnett, informal conversation with Kyle Harvey, 28 February 2018, Melbourne; Episode of *Grecian Scene*, 28 November 1979, National Film and Sound Archive, Canberra, Title 57587.

52. Deborah Parsons, interviewed by Kyle Harvey and Kate Darian-Smith, 15 November 2017, Melbourne, digital recording in interviewers' possession.

53. Antonio Luciano, interview, 13 September 2017; Harry Michaels, interview, 15 September 2017.

54. Coupe, Jakubowicz and Randall, *Nextdoor Neighbours*, 29–30; Philip Bell, *Multicultural Australia in the Media: A Report to the Office of Multicultural Affairs* (Canberra: Office of Multicultural Affairs, 1993), 59–60; Santina Bertone, Clare Keating and Jenny Mullaly, *The Taxidriver, the Cook and the Greengrocer: The Representation of Non-English Speaking Background People in Theatre, Film and Television* (Surry Hills, NSW: Australian Council for the Arts, 2000).

55. Screen Australia, *Seeing Ourselves: Reflections on Diversity in Australian TV Drama* (2016), 2, http://www.screenaustralia.gov.au/fact-finders/reports-and-key-issues/reports-and-discussion-papers/seeing-ourselves.

BIBLIOGRAPHY

Barnett, Tim. Informal conversation with Kyle Harvey, 28 February 2018, Melbourne.

Bazzani, Rozzi. *Hector*. North Melbourne: Arcadia, 2015.

Bednall, David. *Media and Immigrant Settlement*. Canberra: Commonwealth of Australia, 1992.

Bell, Philip. *Multicultural Australia in the Media: A Report to the Office of Multicultural Affairs*. Canberra: Office of Multicultural Affairs, 1993.

Bertone, Santina, Clare Keating, and Jenny Mullaly. *The Taxidriver, the Cook and the Greengrocer: The Representation of Non-English Speaking Background People in Theatre, Film and Television*. Surry Hills, NSW: Australia Council for the Arts, 2000.

Bollen, Jonathan. "Here from There—Travel, Television and Touring Revues: Internationalism as Entertainment in the 1950s and 1960s." *Popular Entertainment Studies* 4, no. 1 (2013): 64–81.

Bonner, Frances. *Ordinary Television: Analyzing Popular TV*. London: Sage, 2003.

Bye, Susan. "TV Memories, *The Daily Telegraph* and TCN: 'First in Australia'." *Media International Australia* no. 121 (2006): 159–73.

Carmichael, Helen, ed. *Seeing Is Believing: Scriptwriting in a Multicultural Society: Report to the Office of Multicultural Affairs.* Canberra: Office of Multicultural Affairs, 1991.

Clyne, Michael. *Multilingual Australia.* Melbourne: River Seine, 1982.

Coupe, Bronwyn, Andrew Jakubowicz, and Lois Randall. *Nextdoor Neighbours: A Report for the Office of Multicultural Affairs on Ethnic Group Discussions of the Australian Media.* Canberra: Office of Multicultural Affairs, 1993.

Darian-Smith, Kate, and Paula Hamilton. "Part of the Family: Australian Histories of Television, Migration and Memory." In *Remembering Television: Histories, Technologies, Memories*, edited by Kate Darian-Smith and Sue Turnbull, 30–51. Newcastle upon Tyne: Cambridge Scholars Publishing, 2012.

Darian-Smith, Kate, and Sue Turnbull, eds. *Remembering Television: Histories, Technologies, Memories.* Newcastle upon Tyne: Cambridge Scholars Publishing, 2012.

Dell'Oso, Anna Maria. "White Man's Dreaming." In *TV Times: 35 Years of Watching Television in Australia*, edited by David Watson and Denise Corrigan, 18–22. Sydney: Museum of Contemporary Art, 1991.

Doganieri, Maria. Interviewed by Kyle Harvey, 27 April 2018, Melbourne. Digital recording in interviewer's possession.

Fiske, John. "Everyday Quizzes, Everyday Life." In *Australian Television: Programs, Pleasures & Politics*, edited by John Tulloch and Graeme Turner. Sydney: Allen & Unwin, 1989.

Gibson, Mark. "Tchk, Tchk, Tchk: *Skippy the Bush Kangaroo* and the Question of Australian Seriousness." *Continuum* 28, no. 5 (2014): 574–82.

Giles, Nigel. *Number 96: Australian TV's Most Notorious Address.* Melbourne: Melbourne Books, 2017.

Grecian Scene, 28 November 1979. Title 57587, National Film and Sound Archive, Canberra.

Griffen-Foley, Bridget. "Diary of a Television Viewer." *Media International Australia*, no. 162 (2017): 33–48.

Groves, Derham. *TV Houses: Television's Influence on the Australian Home.* Carlton North, VIC: Black Jack Press, 2004.

Hawkins, Gay. "SBS: Minority Television." *Culture and Policy* 7, no. 1 (1996): 45–63.

Horgan, Brendan. *Radio with Pictures: 50 Years of Australian Television.* Sydney: Lothian Books, 2006.

Jakubowicz, Andrew, Heather Goodall, Jeannie Martin, Tony Mitchell, Lois Randall, and Kalinga Seneviratne. *Racism, Ethnicity and the Media.* St Leonards, NSW: Allen & Unwin, 1994.

Jobbins, Ted. Interviewed by Nigel Giles, 8 February 2007, Wentworth Falls. National Film and Sound Archive, Canberra, Tape 3, Title 720837.

Jupp, James. *From White Australia to Woomera: The Story of Australian Immigration*, 2nd edition. New York: Cambridge University Press, 2007.

Kakmi, Dmetri. "Night of the Living Wog." In *Joyful Strains: Making Australia Home*, edited by Kent McCarter and Ali Lemer, 19–31. Melbourne: Affirm Press, 2013.

Lam, Cuc, Tuyet Lam, David Demant, and Tatek Menji. Interviewed by Kyle Harvey and Kate Darian-Smith, 23 November 2016, Melbourne. Digital recording in interviewer's possession.

Luciano, Antonio. Interviewed by Kyle Harvey, 13 September 2017, Sydney. Digital recording in interviewer's possession.

McKee, Alan. *Australian Television: A Genealogy of Great Moments*. Melbourne: Oxford University Press, 2001.

Michaels, Harry. Interviewed by Kyle Harvey, 15 September 2017, Sydney. Digital recording in interviewer's possession.

Neiger, Mottie, Oren Meyers, and Eyal Zandberg, eds. *On Media Memory: Collective Memory in a New Media Age*. Basingstoke: Palgrave Macmillan, 2011.

Noorzai, Salim. Interviewed by Sukhmani Khorana, 30 October 2016, Sydney. Digital recording in interviewer's possession.

Nugent, Stephen, Milica Loncar, and Kate Aisbett. *The People We See on TV: Cultural Diversity on Television*. North Sydney: Australian Broadcasting Authority, 1993.

O'Regan, Tom, and Stuart Cunningham. "Marginalised Audiences." In *The Australian TV Book*, edited by Graeme Turner and Stuart Cunningham, 201–12. St Leonards, NSW: Allen & Unwin, 2000.

Palomares, Simon. Interviewed by Kyle Harvey, 30 January 2018, Melbourne. Digital recording in interviewer's possession.

Papandrea, Franco. "Television Stations' Compliance with Australian Content Regulation." *Agenda* 2, no. 4 (1995): 467–78.

Parsons, Deborah. Interviewed by Kyle Harvey and Kate Darian-Smith, 15 November 2017, Melbourne. Digital recording in interviewer's possession.

Place, Nick, and Michael Roberts, eds. *50 Years of Television in Australia*. Prahran, VIC: Hardie Grant, 2006.

Price, Rita. "The Cafe at the Edge of the Bay." In *Growing up Italian in Australia: Eleven Young Australian Women Talk About Their Childhood*, edited by Barbara Walsh, 19–42. Sydney: State Library of New South Wales Press, 1993.

Price, Rita, Marina De Stefanis, Michelina D'Urbano, and Ninette Cilia. Interviewed by Kyle Harvey and Kate Darian-Smith, 23 April 2017, Melbourne. Digital recording in interviewer's possession.

Reimers, David M. *Other Immigrants: The Global Origins of the American People*. New York: New York University Press, 2005.

Screen Australia, *Seeing Ourselves: Reflections on Diversity in Australian TV Drama* (2016), http://www.screenaustralia.gov.au/fact-finders/reports-and-key-issues/reports-and-discussion-papers/seeing-ourselves.

Skalkos, Theo. Interviewed by Frank Heimans, 9 March 2000, Sydney. National Library of Australia, Canberra, ORAL TRC 3996.

Stefanovic, Sofija. *Miss Ex-Yugoslavia*. Melbourne: Viking, 2018.

Strahan, K. W. and A. J. Williams, *Immigrant Entrepreneurs in Australia: A Report to the Office of Multicultural Affairs*. Canberra: Office of Multicultural Affairs, 1988.

Sun, Wanning and Erica. Interviewed by Sukhmani Khorana, 20 December 2016, Sydney. Digital recording in interviewer's possession.

van der Weel, Adriaan. "Subtitling and the SBS Audience." *Media Information Australia*, 56 (1990): 22–26.

Williams, Pamela. "Commercial TV Productions." *Media Information Australia*, 15 (1980): 49–50.

York, Barry. Interviewed by Sukhmani Khorana, 3 November 2017, by telephone. Digital recording in interviewer's possession.

Zerefos, Helen. Interviewed by Kyle Harvey, 20 August 2018, Sydney. Digital recording in interviewer's possession.

CHAPTER 7

A Shared Social Identity: Oral Histories of an Urban Community of Italian Market Gardeners in Adelaide 1920s–1970s

Madeleine Regan

When the Australian Institute of Multicultural Affairs was established in 1979, one of its aims in deepening understanding of the cultural groups who had migrated to Australia was to develop repositories of knowledge, including oral histories, about the experience of migrants.[1] Institutions expanded their collections of oral histories, focusing the experiences of the nearly two and half million migrants who had settled in Australia between 1947 and 1972.[2] However, migrants who had arrived before World War II were generally not well-represented in these commissioned oral history projects because they were either very elderly or dead.

This chapter reviews the development over 12 years of a community oral history project that documents the settlement of Italian Australians who migrated in the 1920s. It draws on interviews with direct descendants to explore how the emigration of parents from the Veneto region of Italy, and belonging to migrant market gardening families in one geographical area, has shaped a "shared social identity."[3] It also examines the role of the project's website in preserving individual memories and transmitting the

M. Regan (✉)
Flinders Park, SA, Australia
e-mail: madeleine@ideasandwords.com.au

© The Author(s) 2019
K. Darian-Smith, P. Hamilton (eds.), *Remembering Migration*,
Palgrave Macmillan Memory Studies,
https://doi.org/10.1007/978-3-030-17751-5_7

history and identity of this small migrant community, reflecting the national aim espoused in the 1979 legislation of creating permanent collections of migrant memories.

The Veneto Market Gardeners

Although Italian migrants have arrived in Australia since initial European settlement, numbers were insignificant until after World War II. Of Australia's population of 5.4 million in 1921, approximately 8100 were born in Italy.[4] In contrast, Italians migrated in large numbers to South and North America from the late nineteenth century; in the United States, for instance, over a quarter of a million Italians had immigrated in the four years up to 1914.[5] Between the census dates of 1921 and 1933, the Italian population in South Australia increased from 344 to nearly 1500.[6] By late 1930s the small group from the Veneto region, comprising 17 men and 1 woman, had established market gardens on leaseholds in the urban periphery of Adelaide, living and working within an area of approximately one and a half square kilometres on neighbouring farms near a river, an easy eight-kilometre horse and cart trip to the wholesale vegetable market. These circumstances suggested a migration narrative outlining the initial migration, family life, work on the land and life within the community.

As Daniel James concluded in the discussion of his oral history with members of a meatpacking union in Argentina, I also found that "theory clearly followed practice."[7] I invited sons and daughters of the pioneer market gardeners as narrators to provide evidence of common experience across the Veneto migrant families. This approach differs from the methodological convention of selecting a range of narrators, including "outsiders," in community oral history projects.[8] The work is ongoing and builds on written studies of Italian migration and settlement in South Australia.[9] It differs, however, by focusing on a subgroup of a regional community with a single occupation, and taking a microhistory approach.[10]

Of 46 oral history narrators, 35 were direct descendants of the original migrants to South Australia. Ten represent the 1.5-generation who arrived as children in the 1930s; the second generation was born in Adelaide. Twenty-five narrators were women. Two community members received training and recorded four interviews in Italian to enable elderly women and men to speak in dialect. Involving the community in this way contributed to a relationship of "shared authority" and enabled the "broadening … [of] the participatory base in history-making."[11] A sense of urgency was a constant motivation because the majority of the children of the pioneers are over 80 years old, and several have died since the project commenced. Recruitment of narrators outside the Veneto community included those located in the wider network of families farming in the area, including three whose families emigrated from other regions of Italy and three whose parents were Anglo-Australian market gardeners. These six narrators represent the outsiders or "outliers."[12] They can point to "wider social forces that influence and shape individual lives," which Alistair Thomson suggests is a continuing challenge in a community oral history project.[13]

As the project developed, I became more conscious of the intersubjectivity created by my interactions with narrators.[14] I was not from the local community, nor was I of Italian origin. My "outsider" status; however, was modified through my formal and informal presence in the community over an extended period. In meetings with the narrators and relatives, it is clear they supported recording the oral histories of their families and community. Also evident was the sense of authority in the voices of narrators and pride in the identity of market gardeners. The strong feelings of belonging were tangible, what Jan Assmann describes as "affective ties" in the co-constructing of group memory and the fondness with which individuals remember the historical environment.[15]

The act of remembering opens new opportunities for individuals to reflect on and question their experience. Remembering can assist narrators in locating feelings, accessing imperfect and blurred memories and even forgetting, all part of the processes of oral history interviews. There are limitations, of course, when second-generation migrants speak about their parents' circumstances because some recollections are uncertain and there are gaps. However, through the large number of narrators in this project a community memory has been formed: of place, the market garden area in Adelaide's Western suburbs and the everyday work and relationships that existed within that space. All narrators, whether Veneto, Italian or Anglo Australian, recall specific geographical locations of market gardens, referring to physical features such as the river, positions of roads and tracks, ownership of land, boundaries and crops.

Shared Identity

The Veneto community narrators attribute particular meanings to their shared identity as children of migrants. Their parents settled and formed a close community of market gardeners, and their lives were bound by "the old peasant triangle of family, work and land."[16] Interviews provide vivid, detailed memories at each point of the triangle, sometimes with prompts of family photos to highlight the density of the Veneto community in the locality. Assunta, born in 1937, describes her mental map of the route to school across farms:

> We'd cross all the market gardens ... go down the dirt track and then we'd cross over the Ballestrin's land and they all had their land there, they were all market gardeners, the Zerella's and the Berno's, they were all there.[17]

To understand the importance of shared memory of place, it is instructive to turn to a framework for how Italian migrants remember their forebears in historical Italian space. Anne-Marie Fortier categorizes four ways in which the descendants of Italian migrants remember "Little Italy" in London in the nineteenth and twentieth centuries through reading contemporary written accounts of Italians who lived there. First, the area was recalled through the filter of a romantic nostalgia. Second, people appreciate acquiring knowledge about everyday life associated with the Italian-ness of the past. Third, people value learning about the historical period and the community of earlier times. A fourth way of remembering, however, refers to the constraints and restrictive family values in a narrow cultural environment.[18] Fortier's four ways of remembering place and community is evident in interviews recorded in the Veneto market gardeners project. Memories invoked in the interviews span the continuum of feelings from nostalgia to discomfort, while narrators recall the temporal features of place to trace their history in the present.[19]

For the 1.5- and second-generation Veneto Australians, the nostalgia associated with memory of the land is synonymous with community. A woman compresses the meanings of place when she explains how she met her Veneto market gardener husband in the 1940s:

> And what we were doing is—it was a community that we were all close together. His family used to live next to Bruno's father. ... It was all connected. ... And that's how we got to know each other.[20]

The description emphasizes links between geography, location of farms and intimacy of the community (Fig. 7.1).

Fig. 7.1 Johnny and Romano Marchioro, sons of pioneer Veneto market gardeners, Adelaide c. 1946. Courtesy of the Marchioro family

Narrators recollected extensive details of work, a mode equated with the second way of remembering where value is placed on knowing the everyday context. These interviews recall effortlessly the seasons, crops, cycle of labour, roles in families, dimensions of glasshouses, access to water and selling at market. The *minutiae* are provided as functions of the occupational identity communicated by all the narrators who grew up on the farms. Fortier's third category of remembering through historical knowledge is apparent when narrators provide information about the Veneto region before their parents emigrated or describe the effects of the Depression in the 1930s or World War II on the Italian community, the arrival of new Veneto migrants in the 1950s or the sub-division of land and progressive urbanization from the 1960s.

Difficult memories replicate Fortier's example of negative feelings about constraints of family and community. Several male narrators recall the loss of hope for employment and career outside the market gardens. Many parents wanted their sons to maintain the family business and some narrators express feelings of being trapped by familial expectations. One man remembers the lack of privacy as he grew up because the family home accommodated relatives, and also recalls the role of women like his mother "they were slaves to the garden, to be honest."[21] Women narrators in another family remember feeling "unlucky" or unhappy because they could not continue their education as their parents required them to contribute wages towards buying a market garden.

Nonetheless, for the 1.5 and second generations, negative memories never override their Veneto identity. When narrators speak about family origins and attachment to the home in the Veneto region, they embody the most profound meaning of shared social identity as *veneti*. In interviews, descriptions of family life are underscored by references to speaking dialect, food and wine traditions, bonds between families and across generations through marriages, choices of godparents and regular social activities within the group of Veneto market gardeners. Descendants of the pioneer Veneto migrants regarded the market garden locality, the site of permanent settlement, as a "second place of origin."[22] In this evocation, meaning is bestowed on the place where first-generation migrants establish a community.

Italian migration researchers have discussed approaches that successive generations use to maintain their Italian identity to conclude that the meaning is "a continuous process of transformation."[23] In this project, narrators provide a range of replies to questions about identity. In initial responses they describe being both Australian and Italian, although several reflected that at a younger age, they felt more ambivalence about their Italian identity. Using a finer classification and asking narrators about connection to the Veneto region elicit strong feelings of belonging to the place of family origin from both women and men. About 95 per cent of narrators report having visited the Veneto region at least once, strengthening connections to relatives and place.

Narrators in one family whose father emigrated from the Veneto region in 1928 and married an Irish Australian woman identify strongly as *veneti*. After the marriage in 1930, the woman's parents initially disowned her, reflecting wider racist attitudes towards Italians at that time. The family of nine children mixed almost entirely within the Veneto market gardener community. Six sisters in separate interviews claimed Italian identity and Veneto ties, reinforced by marriages to Veneto men. Only the father spoke Italian because he wanted the family to be proficient English speakers. Yet, they all sustained their Italian identity through adulthood. The eldest daughter, Milva, born in 1932, responds to a question about her Italian heritage:

> How do I feel about it? Well, they're my people, aren't they? They're—well, they are my heritage, more so than the Australian ones, well, let's face it, we've been brought up with it. … we were brought up with Italians. It's not that we don't know Australians, it's Italians and most of our ways are Italian.[24]

The Website and Community Cohesion

Since the development of the Internet, it has become increasingly possible to transmit oral history recordings in various forms including audio, visual and on websites, in combination with text and other digital items.[25] The project website features the family of each narrator with a brief biography, recordings of interviews, photos, maps and other documents. Some transcripts are available and are being translated progressively into Italian. Narrators have participated in processes of interviews, collecting historical information about their family, checking biographies, selecting family photos and documents, and participating in events. Using Alessandro Portelli's term, this approach is "co-created" oral history.[26]

Recording interviews with children of pioneer market gardeners who returned to live permanently in Italy and uploading them on the website is expanding the transnational relevance of the project. There is evidence that the Veneto market gardeners' oral history project has generated a sense of social cohesion within families, both in Adelaide and in the Veneto region of Italy. However, a question remains about relevance when later generations will not remember the individuals whose stories appear on the website.

Veneto families who returned to live in Italy reciprocate a sense of an enduring transnational Veneto-Australian identity.[27] In 2017, a narrator in Italy exemplified the cohesion fostered by this project. After his interview, Remo, a second-generation narrator whose family returned permanently in 1969, listened to online interviews with people from his childhood in Adelaide. He wrote his reflections:

> you opened up a drawer in my mind and out came the home of my youth. With Dad in the car we went down the path that leads from the Valetta Road entrance to our garage. Then from there I entered the old house. I could see the rooms and all of us that lived in them.
>
> After this recall I went to your website (or should I say our website) to listen to some other interviews, and I can see that the way you put simple questions to your interviewees creates the basis for flashbacks to specific moments of the past, in places that are no longer there and sharing these moments with those who were present then and probably are no longer.[28]

Although having lived in Italy for 45 years, Remo conveys a sense of social identity as an enduring member of the Veneto market gardening community. His memories bridge temporal and physical space and point to the past in the present through the website. Research into the use of information communication technologies and new media for developing transnational communication and connections and building "co-presence" provides evidence of new reciprocal relationships between relatives.[29]

The community identity of Veneto market gardeners in South Australia has been sharpened through the oral history project. The digital access makes the history of the Veneto market gardeners an accessible transnational resource with relevance for descendants in Australia and the Veneto, and more widely as a public history of an Australian migrant community that originated 90 years ago. This project has enabled individuals to contribute to the formation of a narrative of their migrant experience, with their recorded memories providing glimpses into family life in South Australia during the inter-war years—in a period of Italian migration history about which there has been limited documentation and few oral history accounts.

Notes

1. Michael D. Kirby, "Ethnic History in Australia," Speech, State Library of New South Wales Seminar on Ethnic, Oral and Local History (Sydney, 22 February 1982): 5.
2. Charles A. Price, "Australian Immigration: The Whitlam Government 1972–1975," in Charles. A. Price and Jean I. Martin eds, *Australian*

7 A SHARED SOCIAL IDENTITY: ORAL HISTORIES OF AN URBAN...   101

Immigration: A Bibliography and Digest, No. 3 (Canberra: Australian National University 1976), A1–A3.

3. Linda Shopes, "Oral History and the Study of Communities: Problems, Paradoxes and Possibilities," *The Journal of American History* 89, no. 2 (2002): 588–98.

4. Australian Bureau of Statistics, "Census of the Commonwealth of Australia Taken Between the Night of 3rd and 4th April 1911," in *Part II—Birthplaces*, cat. no. 2111.0, Australian Bureau of Statistics, Melbourne, 1921, 45–48.

5. Herbert S. Klein, "The Integration of Italian Immigrants into the United States and Argentina: A Comparative Analysis," *The American Historical Review* 88, no. 2 Apr. (1983): 307, 308.

6. Desmond O'Connor, *No Need to be Afraid: Italian Settlers in South Australia between 1839 and the Second World War* (Kent Town, SA: Wakefield Press, 1996), 3.

7. Daniel James. "Listening in the Cold: The Practice of Oral History in an Argentine Working-class Community," in Robert Perks and Alistair Thomson eds, *The Oral History Reader*, 2nd edition (New York: Routledge, 1998), 87.

8. See Shopes, "Oral History and the Study of Communities," 588–98; Paul Thompson with Joanna Bornat, *The Voice of the Past: Oral History*, 4th edition (New York: Oxford University Press, 2017); Alistair Thomson, "Oral History and Community History in Britain: Personal and Critical Reflections on Twenty-five years of Continuity and Change," *Oral History* 36, no. 1 (2008): 95–104.

9. Daniela Cosmini-Rose, *Caulonia in the Heart: The Settlement in Australia of Migrants from a Southern Italian Town* (Adelaide, SA: Lythrum Press, 2008); Don Longo, *Terra Lasci, Terra Trovi: From Molinara to Adelaide: The History of a Southern Italian Community in South Australia, 1927–2007* (Adelaide, SA: Molinara Social and Sports Club Inc. in association with Lythrum Press, 2010); Antonio Mercurio and Angela Scarino, *We Left: Narratives of the Sangiorgesi in South Australia* (Adelaide: San Giorgio la Molara Community Centre, 2004); Michael Peter Corrieri, *Italians of Port Pirie: A Social History* (Port Pirie, SA: Our Lady of Martyrs, Port Pirie Italian Community, 1992); Sara S. King, "Agriculture in South Australia: The Italian Contribution," PhD diss., Flinders University, 2007.

10. Ginzburg, Carlo (1993), "Microhistory—Two or Three Things that I Know About It," *Critical Inquiry* 20, no. 1 (1993): 10–35. In Australia Annamaria Davine has used microhistory to study Italians and Swiss Italians on the Walhalla goldfields, Annamaria Davine, "Italian Speakers on the Walhalla Goldfield: A Micro-History Approach," in *Provenance: The Journal of Public Record Office Victoria*, no. 7, 2008, https://prov.vic.gov.

au/explore-collection/provenance-journal/provenance-2008/italian-speakers-walhalla-goldfield.

11. Michael Frisch, *A Shared Authority: Essays on the Craft and Meaning of Oral and Public History* (Albany: State University of New York Press, 1990), 185.

12. Thompson with Bornat, *The Voice of the Past*, 290.

13. Thomson, "Oral History and Community History in Britain," 99.

14. Lynn Abrams, *Oral History Theory*, 2nd edition (Abingdon: Routledge, 2016), 58–63.

15. Jan Assmann, "Communicative and Cultural Memory," in Astril Eril and Ansgar Nünning eds, *A Companion to Cultural Memory Studies: An International and Interdisciplinary Handbook* (Berlin: Walter De Gruyter Inc. 2008), 114.

16. Robert Pascoe, "Place and Community: The Construction of an Italo-Australian space," in Stephen Castles et al., eds, *Australia's Italians: Culture and Community in a Changing Society* (Sydney: Allen & Unwin, 1992), 92.

17. Assunta Giovannini nee Tonellato, interviewed by Madeleine Regan, 15 July 2010, Adelaide, South Australia, J. D. Somerville Oral History Collection, State Library of South Australia, OH 872/6.

18. Anne-Marie Fortier, "Re-Membering Places," *Theory, Culture & Society*, 45, 46.

19. Gavin J. Andrews et al., "'Their Finest Hour': Older People, Oral Histories, and the Historical Geography of Social Life," *Social & Cultural Geography* 7, no. 2 (2006): 170–71.

20. Mary Tonellato nee Zoanetti, interviewed by Madeleine Regan, 3 October 2008, Adelaide, South Australia, J. D. Somerville Oral History Collection, State Library of South Australia, OH 872/3.

21. Lino Ballestrin, interviewed by Madeleine Regan, 22 November 2016, Adelaide, South Australia, J. D. Somerville Oral History Collection, State Library of South Australia, OH 872/40.

22. Fortier, "Re-Membering Places," *Theory, Culture & Society*, 47.

23. Loretta Baldassar and Ros Pesman, *From Paesani to Global Citizens: Veneto Migrants in Australia* (Crawley: University of Western Australia Press, 2005), 224, 225.

24. Milva Rebuli, interviewed by Madeleine Regan, 27 March 2016, Adelaide, South Australia, J. D. Somerville Oral History Collection, State Library of South Australia, OH 872/36.

25. See www.venetimarketgardeners1927.net.

26. Alessandro Portelli, "A Dialogical Relationship: An Approach to Oral History," In *Expressions Annual* 2005, http://www.swaraj.org/shikshantar/expressions_portelli.pdf, 5.

27. Kate Darian-Smith and Paula Hamilton, "Memory and History in Twenty-first Century Australia: A Survey of the Field," *Memory Studies* 6, no. 3 (2013): 370–83.
28. Remo Berno, email correspondence with the author, 1 July 2017.
29. Loretta Baldassar et al., "ICT-based Co-presence in Transnational Families and Communities: Challenging the Premise of Face-to-face Proximity in Sustaining Relationships," *Global Networks* 16, no. 2 (2016): 133–44.

BIBLIOGRAPHY

Abrams, Lynn. *Oral History Theory*, 2nd edition. Abingdon: Routledge, 2016.
Andrews, Gavin J., Robin A. Kearns, Pia Kontos, and Viv Wilson. "'Their Finest Hour': Older People, Oral Histories, and the Historical Geography of Social Life." *Social & Cultural Geography* 7, no. 2 (2006): 153–77.
Assmann, Jan. "Communicative and Cultural Memory." In *A Companion to Cultural Memory Studies: An International and Interdisciplinary Handbook*, edited by Astrid Eril and Ansgar Nünning, 109–18. Berlin: Walter De Gruyter Inc., 2008.
Australian Bureau of Statistics. "Census of the Commonwealth of Australia Taken Between the Night of 3rd and 4th April 1911." In *Part II—Birthplaces* cat. no. 2111.0. Australian Bureau of Statistics. Melbourne (1921), 45–48.
Baldassar, Loretta, Mihaela Nedelcu, Laura Merla, and Raelene Wilding. "ICT-based Co-presence in Transnational Families and Communities: Challenging the Premise of Face-to-face Proximity in Sustaining Relationships," *Global Networks* 16, no. 2 (2016): 133–44.
Baldassar, Loretta and Ros Pesman. *From Paesani to Global Italians: Veneto Migrants in Australia*. Crawley: University of Western Australia Press, 2005.
Ballestrin, Lino. Interviewed by Madeleine Regan, 22 November 2016, Adelaide, South Australia. J. D. Somerville Oral History Collection, State Library of South Australia, OH 872/40.
Corrieri, Michael P. *Italians of Port Pirie: A Social History*. Port Pirie, SA: Our Lady of Martyrs, Port Pirie Italian Community, 1992.
Cosmini-Rose, Daniela. *Caulonia in the Heart: The Settlement in Australia of Migrants from a Southern Italian Town*. Adelaide: Lythrum Press, 2008.
Darian-Smith, Kate and Hamilton, Paula. "Memory and History in Twenty-first Century Australia: A Survey of the Field." *Memory Studies* 6, no. 3 (2013): 370–83.
Davine, Annamaria. "Italian Speakers on the Walhalla Goldfield: A Micro-History Approach." In *Provenance: The Journal of Public Record Office Victoria* 7, 2008. https://prov.vic.gov.au/explore-collection/provenance-journal/provenance-2008/italian-speakers-walhalla-goldfield.

104 M. REGAN

Fortier, Anne-Marie. "Re-Membering Places and the Performance of Belonging(s)." *Theory, Culture & Society* 16, no. 2 (1999): 41–64.

Frisch, Michael. *A Shared Authority: Essays on the Craft and Meaning of Oral and Public History.* Albany: State University of New York Press, 1990.

Ginzburg, Carlo. "Microhistory—Two or Three Things that I Know About It." *Critical Inquiry* 20, no. 1 (1993): 10–35.

Ginzburg, Carlo. *The Cheese and the Worms: The Cosmos of a Sixteenth-century Miller.* London: Penguin Books, 1992.

Giovannini nee Tonellato, Assunta. Interviewed by Madeleine Regan, 15 July 2010, Adelaide, South Australia. J. D. Somerville Oral History Collection, State Library of South Australia, OH 872/6.

Hamilton, Paula, and Linda Shopes, eds. *Oral History and Public Memories.* Philadelphia: Temple University Press, 2008.

James, Daniel. "Listening in the Cold: The Practice of Oral History in an Argentine Working Class Community." In *The Oral History Reader,* 2nd edition, edited by Robert Perks and Alistair Thomson, 83–101. New York: Routledge, 1998.

King, Sara S. "Agriculture in South Australia: The Italian Contribution." PhD diss., Flinders University, 2007.

Kirby, Michael D. "Ethnic History in Australia," Speech to the State Library of New South Wales Seminar on Ethnic, Oral and Local History, 22 February 1982.

Klein, Herbert S. "The Integration of Italian Immigrants into the United States and Argentina: A Comparative Analysis." *The American Historical Review* 88, no. 2 (1983): 306–29.

Longo, Don. *Terra Lasci, Terra Trovi: From Molinara to Adelaide: The History of a Southern Italian Community in South Australia, 1927–2007 = La storia di una comunità italiana meridionale in Sud Australia, 1927–2007.* Adelaide, SA: Molinara Social and Sports Club Inc. in association with Lythrum Press, 2010.

Mercurio, Antonio, and Angela Scarino. *We Left: Narratives of the Sangiorgesi in South Australia = E partimmo: Narrazioni dei sangiorgesi sel Sud Australia.* Adelaide, SA: San Giorgio la Molara Community Centre, 2004.

O'Connor, Desmond. *No Need to be Afraid: Italian Settlers in South Australia between 1839 and the Second World War.* Kent Town, SA: Wakefield Press, 1996.

Pascoe, Robert. "Place and Community: The Construction of an Italo-Australian Space." In *Australia's Italians: Culture and Community in a Changing Society,* edited by Stephen Castles, Caroline Alcorso, Gaetano Rando and Ellie Vasta, 85–97. Sydney: Allen & Unwin, 1992.

Perks, Robert, and Alistair Thomson. *The Oral History Reader,* 3rd edition, Abingdon: Routledge, 2016.

Portelli, Alessandro. "A Dialogical Relationship: An Approach to Oral History." *Expressions Annual 2005.* http://www.swaraj.org/shikshantar/expressions_portelli.pdf.

Price, Charles A. "Australian Immigration: The Whitlam Government 1972–1975." In *Australian Immigration: A Bibliography and Digest, No. 3*, edited by Charles A. Price and Jean I. Martin, A1–A3. Canberra: Australian National University, 1976.

Rebuli, Milva. Interviewed by Madeleine Regan, 27 March 2016, Adelaide, South Australia. J. D. Somerville Oral History Collection, State Library of South Australia, OH 872/36.

Shopes, Linda. "Oral History and the Study of Communities: Problems, Paradoxes and Possibilities." *The Journal of American History* 89, no. 2 (2002): 588–98.

Thompson, Paul with Joanna Bornat. *The Voice of the Past: Oral History*, 4th edition. New York: Oxford University Press, 2017.

Thomson, Alistair. "Oral History and Community History in Britain: Personal and Critical Reflections on Twenty-five Years of Continuity and Change." *Oral History, The Journal of the Oral History Society* 36, no. 1 (2008): 95–104.

Tonellato nee Zoanetti, Mary. Interviewed by Madeleine Regan, 3 October 2008, Adelaide, South Australia. J. D. Somerville Oral History Collection, State Library of South Australia, OH 872/3.

CHAPTER 8

Forgotten Women: Remembering "Unsupported" Migrant Mothers in Post-World War II Australia

Karen Agutter and Catherine Kevin

Social historians have long understood the richness of oral history for accessing accounts of the lives of marginalized peoples, including women and migrants. However, for the task of historicizing those who have lived at the intersection of multiple forms of marginalization, who have been least visible and least able to record their stories, oral history has its limitations. By offering an account of unsupported mothers who arrived with their children in Australia as displaced persons (DP) after World War II, this chapter illustrates both the crucial and limited nature of oral history. We argue for the necessity of embedding the scant pearls of oral testimony available in a broader research project that draws on film, memoir, contemporary newspapers and government documents. We also look to the work of public historians seeking, through heritage projects, to expand the collective

---

K. Agutter (✉)
The University of Adelaide, Adelaide, SA, Australia
e-mail: karen.agutter@adelaide.edu.au

C. Kevin
Flinders University, Adelaide, SA, Australia
e-mail: catherine.kevin@flinders.edu.au

© The Author(s) 2019   107
K. Darian-Smith, P. Hamilton (eds.), *Remembering Migration*,
Palgrave Macmillan Memory Studies,
https://doi.org/10.1007/978-3-030-17751-5_8

memory of post-World War II migration to accommodate the stories of unsupported mothers and their children. The most fruitful investigations of this project have been in the reports of social workers and migrant hostel managers within the archive of the Australian Department of Immigration. In light of what we learned from very few oral testimonies, we mined this archive and other sources to document the dynamics of both marginalization and resistance in the lives of unsupported mothers and their children.

Despite the rise of social history in the 1960s, and although women migrate in equal or even greater numbers than men, it was not until the 1980s that migrant women started to be considered by historians of migration as individuals and their experiences examined through a "gender-sensitive lens."[1] Since then, scholars focused on female migration have shown the importance of this lens in understanding that both the process of migration and the acculturation that generally follows are very different for women and men. Similarly, the reasons for women's migration have often differed from men's. For example, the historiography of Australian migration includes studies of single women who were sought by colonial and federal governments to redress gender imbalances in Australian populations, and those who were trained to fill labour shortages, most notably in domestic service.[2] And, as Oliva Espin and Zora Simic have shown, women and men have confronted new hegemonic gendered identities in the host society that have demanded a degree of assimilation and been attended by gendered forms of discrimination.[3]

One of the greatest obstacles faced by historians of gender and migration is finding the migrant woman's voice, and this is especially the case for DP women who are significantly underrepresented in Australian life writing and oral testimony. Katarzyna Williams argues it was not until the 1970s, 1980s and 1990s, as Australia embraced multiculturalism, that "alternative voices and migrant writing" moved from the private to the public sphere, although the visibility of many groups of European writers did not noticeably increase.[4] As Gay Breyley notes, the public storytelling of female refugees has been absent, or at least significantly delayed for many reasons including the obstacles of language, the practical demands of resettling in a new nation, the expectations of the assimilation policy of the period and the subsequent lack of public interest in hearing "victims" voices.[5] Latvian-born author Elena Jonaitis recalls her own personal delay in writing about her migration experience:

> On arrival in Australia, for a long time there could be no writing. Every minute of the day and every ounce of energy were used to fitting in,

bringing up children, hurriedly learning English, working, studying, becoming Australian.[6]

Consequently, scholars have frequently turned to oral histories as a key historical source, although in relation to female DPs, this too has its difficulties in the twenty-first century. In the case of our research focus, many of the women we have written about were born in the period around World War I and have passed away.[7] The general lack of publicly available, published or recorded personal testimony from women about their experiences as DPs in Australia following World War II is further exacerbated by the difficulty of the subject matter for some, especially the unsupported mothers. These widows or unmarried mothers with children often suffered terribly as they tried to establish themselves and their young dependants. In addition to the material challenges of their migration experiences, the government agents' perceptions of this group as failing to contribute to the economic and social goals of the migration scheme, and their lack of suitability for illustrating the dominant celebratory tropes of migrant histories in the context of multiculturalism, suggest that shame and silence kept many of these women from sharing their stories. Indeed, those who remain, or whose voices we have found in oral history archives, have been reticent to speak publicly about experiences of unsupported motherhood that were painful and subject to moral judgement.

It is essential to gather information from multiple sources, extracting clues wherever possible in order to remember these women as part of Australia's larger immigration history. Sophia Turkiewicz's autobiographic film *Once My Mother* (2013) became an impetus to search the archival and newspaper sources to see how they support, extend or challenge the narrative of the film and the larger story of the impact of immigration policy on unsupported DP mothers and their children.

ONCE MY MOTHER: THE TIP OF A VERITABLE ICEBERG

Turkiewicz's film explores the life of her mother Helen, a Polish refugee, who arrived in Australia as a young single mother with baby Sophia. A film made in many stages, its earliest material was created when the filmmaker was practising her newly acquired skills on her mother. This is a work of love and forgiveness; it is predicated on an intimacy and mutual reckoning that is rare in oral history interviews, as is the oral history participant's capacity for filmmaking. At one point, the interviewer asks, "Why do you think Sophia is making this film?" Helen replies, "Because she loves me." Turkiewicz relates her mother's gruelling refugee journey from Poland to a Siberian gulag, then to Uzbekistan, Persia, Rhodesia and finally to Australia. As a single mother with a young child seeking to establish herself in her new homeland, she faced challenges: "I couldn't find a job when Sophia was small. They didn't like it in hotel or somewhere if you bring children." Helen was forced to temporarily relinquish Sophia to an Adelaide orphanage, an experience that left its mark on both the mother and the child. In coming to terms with the experience in middle-age, the daughter-turned-filmmaker seeks a detailed biography of Helen so that she might comprehend the reasons for her abandonment.

Working with the absence of this story from Australian histories of immigration in this period, she takes seriously Helen's memories and her own, showcasing those that have been recorded at a number of key moments over a period of many years. The memory loss plaguing Helen in the footage just months before her death is a reminder of the ephemerality of memory for the work of constructing historical narratives. It is also a reminder of the complex relationship between remembering and making history. Turkiewicz's earlier films, from a trip to the places of her mother's childhood, the footage from past projects and a handful of archival documents, provide the stitches that sew Helen's patchy recollections into a chronological narrative, in some cases prompting events to return to her memory. The deeply personal and painful nature of this process for both the mother and the daughter that is made visible in *Once My Mother* collapses private and public storytelling. In so doing, the film simultaneously undertakes the projects of individual healing[8] and bringing historical experiences into collective memory.[9]

ORAL HISTORIES AND GENDERED SILENCE

Such detailed and personal renderings of the experiences of unsupported DP mothers and their children are rare. Alexandra Dellios has shown that those who were the children have only recently begun to speak about their mothers. The painful nature of their mothers' memories, compounded by the shame many women felt for being unsupported mothers, contributed powerfully to the silencing of their voices.[10] For the mothers who relinquished their children permanently, or whose relationships with them in the aftermath of temporary relinquishment were strained or broken, one effect of their struggle has been silence. Anne Maree Payne has demonstrated that for Aboriginal mothers caught up in coercive removal of their children in twentieth-century Australia, the complexity of their loss, isolation and projected inferiority, meant that the Human Rights and Equal

Opportunity Commission was unable to persuade mothers to be interviewed for *The National Inquiry into the Separation of Aboriginal and Torres Strait Islander Children from Their Families*.[11] The images of violent separation of children from mothers that have come to characterize dominant narratives of the Stolen Generations have alienated mothers whose stories do not include this single dramatic point of crisis, but rather a process of diminishing options and coercion, what Payne refers to as the "choiceless choice."[12] Archival records reveal a different set of diminishing options were experienced by unsupported DP mothers who were pressured to relinquish their children.

The oral history component of this project, which originated in the Hostel Stories Project, offered little illumination of experiences of unsupported motherhood and other aspects of women's intersectional marginalization.[13] Interviewers found women reticent to examine gendered challenges in their migration stories. Similarly, Donna Kleiss' 1990–1991 oral history interviews specifically sought stories from women of intimacy, pregnancy and its consequences, including abortion, in the Wacol Holding Centre in Queensland.[14] Yet, participants were reluctant to share their own intimate histories. Where details were offered, they were about the lives of others and the accounts were generally unspecific and partial.

Beyond Oral Histories

Increasing the challenge for historians of earlier periods is that there are virtually no specific records dedicated to the experiences of female migrants in general and to these unsupported mothers in particular, unlike refugees and migrants who arrived in later periods,[15] or those who participated in immigration schemes designed especially to recruit women such as the Earl Grey Irish Scheme of the late 1840s[16] or those who trained and delivered Greek domestic servants to Australia's door in the 1960s.[17] Therefore, their story is pieced together from their children's stories and snippets of information contained within thousands of pages in records spread across many different reporting agencies.

The major turning point for our research was the discovery of the announcement in February 1949 that, unlike other nations, and given the grave and impossible situation unsupported mothers and their children faced in Europe, Australia was willing to accept widows, deserted wives and unmarried mothers with children as refugees.[18] Minister for Immigration Arthur Calwell stressed that this agreement was "surely one of the most humanitarian yet considered."[19] The actual number of unsupported mothers admitted to Australia with their children is unknown. After February 1949, ships' nominal rolls list widows and single mothers and their children, but to date no detailed study has been made of their number or countries of origin.[20] The best indication of the size of this cohort comes from various government reports which discuss the "problem" these women came to present to the Australian authorities. These reports provide individual snapshots at moments in time; for example, in March 1950 the Government Holding Centres, where the majority of these families lived, reported that there were 773 widows with a total of 1077 children in residence.[21] The Turkiewiczs' situation, while generally unreported, was not unique.

In fact, archival documents indicate that the institutional placement of the children of unsupported mothers was not uncommon. Department of Immigration social worker reports provide many examples of mothers placing their children in orphanages and other institutions either permanently or temporarily. While some of these examples are as a consequence of illness or injury that rendered women without other family members unable to care for their children, the vast majority are as a result of financial hardship and the inability to find work and provide a secure home outside of the initial Migrant Holding Centre.[22] This problem was exacerbated by the requirement of the two-year work contract which all DPs, including unsupported mothers, were expected to fulfil in return for their acceptance into Australia. As a 1951 government report states:

> widows who come to Australia are under Contract, the Commonwealth Employment Service is responsible for them and they are not permitted to take employment unless it is approved by the Regional Director ... it is almost impossible to place widows with more than one child.[23]

Therefore, many of these women, in order to fulfil their contractual obligations and move forward, had little option but to place their children in care.[24]

A second influential factor was that these women had to pay board for their accommodation in Holding Centres and many ran up very large debts that could not be repaid while they were unable to work. By November 1950, for example, one widow with five children had a debt of £230[25] and another with four children owed £615.19s.6d.[26]

Archival evidence indicates that by November 1950, less than two years after Australia signed the agreement with the International Refugee Organization to accept unsupported mothers and their children, the Secretary of the Department of Immigration, T. H. E. Heyes acknowledged that "[w]idows with children are amongst our greatest employment problems [and] [u]nless some appropriate action is taken, the majority of the widows and the younger children will be a charge on this Department for many years to come."[27] The solution to the "problem" was twofold: to find work with accommodation for these women and their children[28] or to encourage women to place their children so that they could work and become financially independent.

Archival evidence also indicates that women were strongly encouraged to place children or, in a more extreme and permanent solution, to give them up for adoption. In an annual report, July 1950–June 1951, an Immigration Department senior social worker in Western Australia stated:

> Besides 23 cases of child placement dealt with late last year by the Social Worker at Northam—twenty eight children were placed from the Perth Office in institutions or homes, either temporarily or permanently. ... Plans for child placement were discussed with a number of New Australians.[29]

Through social worker reports that regularly listed the number of adoptions facilitated per month, we know that adoption was generally limited to young children, or to those widows and single women who gave birth after arrival. For example, monthly reports might state "[t]wo babies have been adopted"[30] or that "the adoption for the newborn of an unmarried mother was finalised."[31] Often social worker reports combined the figures for placement and adoption, but an indication of the scale of this "solution" is evident in the New South Wales returns where, between 1949 and 1952, an average of 52 migrant babies/children in that state alone were placed or adopted per year.[32] Certainly the incidence was high enough that the Department of Immigration felt the need to issue instructions to those concerned (including Holding Centre directors, doctors and social workers), which outlined the legal requirements and procedures required to facilitate adoption for "New Australian" mothers.[33] The direct coercion of unmarried mothers was particularly evident in the case of an Estonian woman attending the Uranquinty Accommodation Centre Hospital and expecting her second child. Members of the Estonian community reported:

all kinds of efforts were made by the Australian Doctor and the Matron to arrange the adoption of the baby through an Organisation, and an official visited the hospital to complete the papers for ... to sign, this she would not do.[34]

The pressures placed on women to fulfil work contracts and to become financially independent may also have influenced some to seek abortions, and archival evidence indicates that illegal abortion was an option for some migrant mothers, including those who were unmarried or widowed. In 1951 a Polish-born unmarried mother of a five-year-old returned from her work allocation on a farm near Newcastle pregnant and required hospital care for three months after an abortion.[35] Information regarding abortions also surfaces in records related to the operation of Holding Centres; for example, the issue was discussed in a report concerning police attendance at the Woodside Centre in South Australia in March 1950.[36]

There is also evidence that the situation for some women, including a Latvian-born widow with two children housed at the Uranquinty Centre, was so untenable that attempted suicide occurred.[37] The situation for these unsupported mothers and their children is perhaps best summed up in a report by a senior Western Australian social worker. The social worker, Mr Vincent, and Catholic Migration Officer Father Stinson interviewed 30 single mothers, approximately six months after their arrival on the *Langfitt* in February 1950, and found:

> Placement of children of widows is still acute. ... Many of the widows from the 'Langfitt' seem prematurely old and have perhaps had the most difficult adjustments to make. ... Clontarf and St. Josephs Orphanage take most of the children but several placements have been arranged at Wanslea Home for Children ... [buses take the] children ... directly to the institutions and the mothers to Graylands from which Centre they are placed in employment. One wonders however, just how this second generation of young people are going to grow up in these places where there are too many children for any one individual to receive the adequate personal attention every child needs.[38]

Although these mothers are not named, it is no coincidence that the young Sophia and her mother Helen had arrived on this very ship. These comments mirror the experiences explored in *Once My Mother*.

Heritage and Generational Storytelling

What can be remembered publicly changes over time. Government inquiries and national apologies have brought the histories of single mothers, coercive child removal and child migration into national consciousness.[39] These incursions on Australia's historical consciousness have not yet included the stories of unsupported DP mothers and their children. For the children of unsupported DP mothers, the auto/biographies of their mothers have found a register and an audience in the wake of recognition extended to other mothers.

More fruitful oral histories have come from the children of unsupported DPs who have sought to tell their mothers' stories posthumously. In particular, those children who remained with their mothers at the Benalla Holding Centre, which became something of a depot, and then a home (to the chagrin of the Department of Immigration), for these single-parent families that refused to be separated. The heritage work undertaken by Sabine Smyth and Bruce Pennay at the site of the Benalla Holding Centre, by challenging the criteria for heritage listing, has given voice to and provided local recognition for the stories of the children of unsupported DP mothers who lived there.[40] Dellios has argued in relation to this work that

> former child migrants are actively engaging with instruments of cultural power … to push their site and its associated story into the public realm. In doing so, they have the potential to expand the boundaries of official memory cultures with alternative and sometimes subversive narratives about migration and settlement.[41]

In speaking of their life at Benalla, these children enacted a desire to bring their mothers' stories out from the shadows of immigration history, honouring and destigmatizing them in the process. For a fuller historical understanding of these stories, the rich archive of the Department of Immigration and print media of the time can provide context, a sense of scale and accounts of ways in which women were perceived to respond to the requirements of the government agents who sought their compliance.

Conclusion

Turkiewicz's story, as she tries to come to terms with her sense of betrayal and abandonment as the child of Helen, an unsupported displaced immigrant to Australia in 1950, provided significant clues to a larger story of widowed and unmarried mothers and their children and underlined the importance of its telling. Its emotional resonance was particularly poignant given the official record's negative construction of this cohort of women, which was referred to by the International Refugee Organization as "one of the greatest problems of the Hard Core" refugees remaining in Europe.[42]

Turkiewicz was fortunate to have her own memories to draw on and was also able, over the years, to interview her mother and piece together her story. However, towards the end of her quest to understand, her mother was already in the early stages of dementia, and the memories offered in oral accounts had to be set alongside other points of access to a lived past, to archived documents, photographs and footage of places and conversations, in order to construct a coherent narrative. Helen's gasps of recognition and demonstrative re-remembering when confronted with these clues reinforce the narrative offered by the film. Our study shows that many aspects of the history narrativized by Turkiewicz are discoverable in the archival record. Turkiewicz begins this process for her mother's story. We have applied it to a group of women who shared her status as an unsupported DP mother at the time of her arrival in Australia. Recent accounts from the adult children of unsupported DP mothers can echo and elaborate the historical understanding we have sought to discover and convey.

While we acknowledge the anecdotal view that the archival record has limitations in terms of presenting only the "official" side of the story, the richness of the record in this case has allowed us to understand not just the policies and procedures, but also the very personal, individual and collective stories of the people affected by them. The records we have examined, especially those of social workers and the reports into individual cases, often include the voices of officials and interested parties, such as community groups, charged with the women's care. In piecing together accounts of unsupported mothers who came to Australia as DPs in these records, we have demonstrated that by pursuing the meanings of an individual testimonial in the context of the archive and newspaper reports, and in some cases testimony provided for heritage projects, a fuller historicization of the impact of immigration policies on a particular cohort can be achieved.

The story of the unsupported mothers and their children has been hard to find; however, its telling benefits enormously from a multidimensional approach using all of the information sources at our disposal. Furthermore, remembering unsupported mothers and their children is particularly important, not just for the people involved but to add to, and correct, the historical record, which tends to gloss over this period of Australian immigration history as a success story and to celebrate this group of migrants, DPs in particular, as the precursors of multiculturalism.

NOTES

1. Debra L. DeLaet, "Introduction: The Invisibility of Women in Scholarship on International Migration," in Gregory A. Kelson and Debra L. De Laet eds, *Gender and Migration* (New York: New York University Press, 1999), 2.
2. Debra L DeLaet, "Introduction: The Invisibility of Women," 1–2; Srebrenka Kunek, "Brides, Wives, and Single Women: Gender and Immigration," *Lilith: A Feminist History Journal* 8 (1993): 99–100; Paula Hamilton and B. W. Higman, "Servants of Empire: The British Training of Domestics for Australia, 1926–31," *Social History* 28, no. 1 (2003): 67–82; and Alexandra Dellios, "'It Was Just You and Your Child': Single Migrant Mothers, Generational Storytelling and Australia's Migrant Heritage," *Memory Studies* (2018): 1–15.
3. Oliva M. Espin, "The Role of Gender and Emotion in Women's Experience of Migration," *Innovation* 10, no. 4 (1997): 445; Zora Simic, "Bachelors of Misery and Proxy Brides: Marriage, Migration and Assimilation, 1947–1973," *History Australia* 11, no. 1 (2014): 149–74.
4. Katarzyna Kwapisz Williams, "Displaced Women: Eastern European Post-War Narratives in Australia," *Life Writing* 11, no. 4 (2014): 375–87.
5. Gay Breyley, "Imagined Ancestral Communities of Displaced Australian Daughters," in Cynthia Anne Huff ed., *Women's Life Writing and Imagined Communities* (London: Routledge, 2005), 37.
6. Elena Jonaitis, *Elena Jonaitis*, http://www.slic.org.au/Culture/Elena.htm.
7. See "Hostel Stories: Toward a Richer Narrative of the Lived Experiences of Migrants," Australian Research Council Linkage Grant LP120100553. Over 100 interviews were conducted with migrants who arrived between 1948 and 1980.
8. See Sidonie Smith and Julia Watson, "Introduction," in Sidonie Smith and Julia Watson eds, *Getting a Life* (Minneapolis: University of Minnesota Press, 1996), 15.
9. Carol Gluck, "Operations of Memory: 'Comfort Women' and the World," in Shelia Miyposhi Jager and Rana Miatter eds, *Ruptured Histories: War, Memory, and the Post-Cold War in Asia* (Cambridge, MA: Harvard University Press, 2007), 74.

10. Dellios, "It Was Just You and Your Child."
11. Anne Marie Payne, *Untold Suffering?: Motherhood and the Stolen Generations*, PhD diss., University of Technology Sydney, 2016.
12. Payne, "Untold Suffering?," Chapter 3.
13. "Hostel Stories: Toward a Richer Narrative of the Lived Experiences of Migrants," ARC Linkage Grant LP120100553, University of Adelaide. These stories historicised the accommodation centres where many post-World War II migrants settled.
14. Donna Kleiss, *OH 24 Migrant Women Oral History* (Brisbane: John Oxley Library).
15. National Archives Australia (NAA): 1209, 1987/1114 Part 1—The Office of the Status of Women Report on Migrant Women in Women's Refuges.
16. Kay Maoloney Caball, *The Kerry Girls and the Earl Grey Scheme* (Dublin: The History Press, 2014).
17. Srebrenka Kunek, "Greek Female Migration in the Post War II Period in Australia," *Australian Studies* (London, England) 2 (1989): 36–58.
18. Diana Kay and Robert Miles, *Refugees or Migrant Workers? European Volunteer Workers in Britian 1946–1951* (London: Routledge, 1992).
19. NAA: CP815/1, 21.134; Immigration—Displaced Persons—General. See James Franklin, "Calwell, Catholicism and the Origins of Multicultural Australia," in *Proceedings of Catholics in Australian Public Life Since 1788* (Strathfield, NSW: Australian Catholic Historical Society, 2009) and Klaus Neumann, *Refuge Australia: Australia's Humanitarian Record* (Sydney: University of New South Wales Press, 2004).
20. *General W. C. Langfitt*, which departed Europe in December 1949, carried eleven widows and their twenty-five children. See NAA: J25, 1950/1123; General W. C. Langfitt—nominal passenger roll.
21. NAA: D1917, D15/50; Employment of Displaced Persons—Widows with Children.
22. NAA: A445, 276/2/11; Social Welfare Special Problems Financial.
23. NAA: A434, 1950/3/25969; Placement of Displaced Persons—Widows with Children—Policy.
24. Karen Agutter, "Fated to be Orphans: The Consequences of Australia's Post-War Resettlement Policy on Refugee Children," *Children Australia* 41, no. 3 (2016).
25. NAA: A434, 1950/3/27104; Widows with Dependent Children at Immigration Centres—Employment and Accommodation.
26. NAA: A446, 1962/65241; Immigration Advisory Council Committee on Hostels and Centres Part 1.
27. NAA: A434, 1950/3/25969. For more on these women as "problems" see Karen Agutter, and Catherine Kevin, "The 'Unwanteds' and 'Non-compliants': 'Unsupported Mothers' as 'Failures' and Agents in Australia's Migrant Holding Centres," *The History of the Family* 22, no. 4 (2017).

28. *The Cessnock Eagle and South Maitland Recorder*, "Plight of Migrant Widows," New South Wales, 23 June 1950, 7.
29. NAA: A445, 276/3/1; Senior Social Workers Annual Reports—All States.
30. NAA; A445, 276/3/1.
31. NAA: A437, 1949/6/385; Social Worker's Report, Uranquinty Centre, New South Wales.
32. NAA: A445, 276/3/2; Social Workers Annual Reports—New South Wales.
33. NAA: K403, W59/926 Part 1; [Immigration Department] Instructions—Migrant Centres—Numbers 1–100.
34. NAA: A434, 1950/3/22943; Irregular Practise of Child Adoption at Uranquinty. Karen Agutter and Catherine Kevin, "Lost In Translation: Managing Medicalised Motherhood in Post-World War Two Australian Migrant Accommodation Centres," *Women's History Review*, 2018.
35. NAA: A445, 276/2/10; Social Welfare. Widows and Unmarried Mothers with Dependent Children.
36. NAA: A1658, 556/9/1 Part 1; Immigration Reception and Training Centres—Woodside—Displaced Persons Centre—General.
37. *Daily Advertiser*, Wagga Wagga, New South Wales, 5 May 1949, "Quinty Migrant Found Unconscious," 2.
38. NAA: A445, 276/3/1.
39. Human Rights and Equal Opportunity Commission, *Bringing Them Home: The Report of the National Inquiry into the Forced Separation of Aboriginal and Torres Strait Islander Children from their Families*, 1997 and National Apology to the Stolen Generations, delivered by Prime Minister Kevin Rudd on 13 February 2008; Senate Community Affairs References Committee reports *Lost Innocents: Righting the Record—Report on Child Migration*, August 2001 and *Forgotten Australians—A Report on Australians Who Experienced Institutional or Out-of-home Care as Children*, August 2004 and the National Apology to the Forgotten Australians and Former Child Migrants delivered by Prime Minister Kevin Rudd, 16 November 2009; Australian Institute of Family Studies, *Past Adoption Experiences: National Research Study on the Service Response to Past Adoption Practices*, 2012 and National Apology for Forced Adoption, delivered by Prime Minister Julia Gillard, 21 March, 2013.
40. Bruce Pennay. "Remembering Benalla Migrant Camp," *The History of the Family* 22, no. 4 (2017): 575–96.
41. Dellios, "It Was Just You and Your Child," 3.
42. Australia was one of the only nations willing to accept unsupported mothers (widows and single mothers) and their children. National Archives Australia: CP815/1, 21.134.

Bibliography

Agutter, Karen. "Fated to Be Orphans: The Consequences of Australia's Post-War Resettlement Policy on Refugee Children." *Children Australia* 41, no. 3 (2016), 224–31.

Agutter, Karen, and Catherine Kevin. "The 'Unwanteds' and 'Non-Compliants': 'Unsupported Mothers' as 'Failures' and Agents in Australia's Migrant Holding Centres." *The History of the Family* 22, no. 4 (2017), 554–74.

Agutter, Karen, and Catherine Kevin. "Lost in Translation: Managing Medicalised Motherhood in Post-World War Two Australian Migrant Accommodation Centres." *Women's History Review* 27, no. 7 (2018a), 1065–1084.

Agutter, Karen, and Catherine Kevin. "Failing 'Abyan', 'Golestan' and 'the Estonian Mother': Refugee Women, Reproductive Coercion and the Australian State." *Immigrants and Minorities* 36, no. 2 (2018b), 87–104.

Breyley, Gay. "Imagined Ancestral Communities of Displaced Australian Daughters." In *Women's Life Writing and Imagined Communities*, edited by Cynthia Anne Huff, 17–42. London: Routledge, 2005.

Caball, Kay Maoloney. *The Kerry Girls and the Earl Grey Scheme.* Dublin: The History Press, 2014.

Daily Advertiser. "Quinty Migrant Found Unconscious." Wagga Wagga, New South Wales, 5 May 1949.

DeLaet, Debra L. "Introduction: The Invisibility of Women in Scholarship on International Migration." In *Gender and Immigration*, edited by Gregory A. Kelson and Debra L. De Laet, 1–20. New York: New York University Press, 1999.

Dellios, Alexandra, "'It Was Just You and Your Child': Single Migrant Mothers, Generational Storytelling and Australia's Migrant Heritage." *Memory Studies* (2018): 1–15.

Espin, Oliva M. "The Role of Gender and Emotion in Women's Experience of Migration." *Innovation* 10, no. 4 (1997), 445–55.

Gluck, Carol, "Operations of Memory: 'Comfort Women' and the World." In *Ruptured Histories: War, Memory, and the Post-Cold War in Asia*, edited by Shelia Miyposhi Jager and Rana Miatter, 47–77. Cambridge, MA: Harvard University Press, 2007.

Hamilton Paula, and B. W. Higman. "Servants of Empire: The British Training of Domestics for Australia, 1926–31." *Social History* 28, no. 1 (2003): 67–82.

Jonaitis, Elena. *Elena Jonaitis.* http://www.slic.org.au/Culture/Elena.htm.

Kay, Diana, and Robert Miles. *Refugees or Migrant Workers? European Volunteer Workers in Britian 1946–1951.* London and New York: Routledge, 1992.

Kleiss, Donna. *OH 24 Migrant Women Oral History.* Brisbane: John Oxley Library.

Kunek, Srebrenka. "Brides, Wives, and Single Women: Gender and Immigration." *Lilith: A Feminist History Journal* 8 (1993): 99–100.

Kunek, Srebrenka. "Greek Female Migration in the Post War II Period in Australia." *Australian Studies* (London, UK) 2 (1989): 36–58.

Lerner, Gerda. *The Majority Finds Its Past: Placing Women in History.* Chapel Hill: University of North Carolina Press, 2005.

Mahler, Sarah J., and Patricia R. Pessar. "Gender Matters: Ethnographers Bring Gender from the Periphery toward the Core of Migration Studies." *The International Migration Review* 40, no. 1 (2006): 27–63.

National Archives Australia: A1658; 556/9/1 Part 1, Immigration Reception and Training Centres—Woodside—Displaced Persons Centre—General.

National Archives Australia: A434; 1950/3/22943, Irregular Practise of Child Adoption at Uranquinty.

National Archives Australia: A434; 1950/3/25969, Placement of Displaced Persons—Widows with Children—Policy.

National Archives Australia: A434; 1950/3/27104, Widows with Dependent Children at Immigration Centres—Employment and Accommodation.

National Archives Australia: A437; 1949/6/385, Social Worker's Report, Uranquinty Centre, New South Wales.

National Archives Australia: A445; 276/2/10, Social Welfare. Widows and Unmarried Mothers with Dependent Children.

National Archives Australia: A445; 276/2/11, Social Welfare Special Problems Financial.

National Archives Australia: A445; 276/3/1, Senior Social Workers Annual Reports—All States.

National Archives Australia: A445; 276/3/2, Social Workers Annual Reports—New South Wales.

National Archives Australia: A446; 1962/65241, Immigration Advisory Council Committee on Hostels and Centres Part 1.

National Archives Australia: CP815/1; 21.134, Immigration—Displaced Persons—General.

National Archives Australia: D1917; D15/50, Employment of Displaced Persons—Widows with Children.

National Archives Australia: K403; W59/926 Part 1 [Immigration Department] Instructions—Migrant Centres—Numbers 1–100.

Payne, Anne Maree. *Untold Suffering?: Motherhood and the Stolen Generations.* PhD diss., University of Technology Sydney, 2016.

Pennay, Bruce. "Remembering Benalla Migrant Camp." *The History of the Family* 22, no. 4 (2017): 575–96.

Simic, Zora. "Bachelors of Misery and Proxy Brides: Marriage, Migration and Assimilation, 1947–1973." *History Australia* 11, no. 1 (2014): 149–74.

Smith, Sidonie, and Julia Watson. "Introduction." In *Getting a Life*, edited by Sidonie Smith and Julia Watson, 1–24. Minneapolis: University of Minnessota Press, 1996.

The Cessnock Eagle and South Maitland Recorder. "Plight of Migrant Widows." New South Wales, 23 June 1950.

Turkiewicz, Sophia (Director). *Once My Mother.* Change Focus Media, Australia, 2013.

Williams, Katarzyna Kwapisz. "Displaced Women: Eastern European Post-War Narratives in Australia." *Life Writing* 11, no. 4 (2014): 375–87.

CHAPTER 9

Years of Separation: Vietnamese Refugees and the Experience of Forced Migration After 1975

Nathalie Huynh Chau Nguyen

"I was here in 1982 but my wife and my two sons, they did not arrive until 1990. It was a hard time for me to live here alone … my younger son, the first time I saw him was when he arrived in Australia. He was nine years old."[1] These spare words by Vu Van Bao allude to the anguish of years of separation from his loved ones after he escaped from Vietnam by boat in 1981. His narrative conveys not only his experiences during the Vietnam War and in the war's aftermath but also his trajectory as a refugee. Although he reached Indonesia safely and resettled in Australia the following year, it took him another eight years to sponsor his family. These nine years of separation followed five years of internment in post-war communist re-education camps, also known as Vietnam's "bamboo gulag." In all, Bao was separated from his family for 14 years after the end of the Vietnam War. The story of Bao and his family reflects that of many Vietnamese refugees to Australia following the Vietnam War, for whom the experience of forced migration encompassed lengthy periods of separation from loved ones, even after successful resettlement in a second country of asylum.

N. H. C. Nguyen (✉)
Monash University, Melbourne, VIC, Australia
e-mail: nathalie.nguyen@monash.edu

© The Author(s) 2019
K. Darian-Smith, P. Hamilton (eds.), *Remembering Migration*,
Palgrave Macmillan Memory Studies,
https://doi.org/10.1007/978-3-030-17751-5_9

123

Oral history enables the articulation of these individual memories of migration and family separation from one of the most significant refugee movements of the late twentieth century. More than two million people left Vietnam in the wake of the fall of Saigon and the end of the Vietnam War in 1975.[2] The international response to this refugee movement was unprecedented in that it lasted 25 years (1975–2000)[3] and involved the resettlement of Vietnamese in 50 countries.[4] Bao's post-migration experiences are situated in the context of the implementation of the United Nations High Commissioner for Refugees' (UNHCR) Orderly Departure Program (ODP) in 1979. His story not only illustrates the difficulties associated with putting the ODP into practice in the 1980s, but also relates a relatively little-known aspect of Australian and international migration history.

While the broad outlines of the post-war Vietnamese exodus are well known, the extent of family separation for Vietnamese refugees post-resettlement is rather less so. Although the ODP was a remarkable emigration and resettlement programme, the experiences of Vietnamese involved in it reveal the gaps through which people could fall and the casualties that could ensue. The oral histories in this chapter add a little-known perspective on the experiences of first-generation Vietnamese refugees in Australia, and the effects of prolonged separation between husband and wife, and between parent and child post-migration. For these Vietnamese, surviving war, post-war internment, escape from Vietnam and finding acceptance in second-asylum countries represented only successive stages in the refugee experience. After resettlement, refugees faced another challenge: that of sponsoring family members from Vietnam.

As Bao's narrative reveals, this process could take years, with adverse impacts on refugees' mental health and wellbeing, and additional strains placed on intergenerational relationships in families. His account forms part of a wider intergenerational dialogue in the Vietnamese diaspora between first-generation Vietnamese who experienced war, post-war repression and the exodus directly, and second-generation Vietnamese who bear the legacy of their parents' experiences of forced migration. Vietnamese diasporic memories are often fragmented and ephemeral. They allude to experiences that are recalled through a prism of temporal and geographical distance, and to a country that exists only in memory. Many first-generation Vietnamese refugees are now in their 70s and 80s. Once they are gone, their stories and memories will fade with them.

Recording the oral histories of first-generation Vietnamese is therefore vital as a means of not only preserving transient refugee histories but also communicating these histories to later generations.

Historical Background

The end of the Vietnam War in 1975 and Vietnam's reunification under a communist regime were the catalysts for the post-war diaspora. The Vietnamese exodus was driven by widespread state repression including the internment of one million people in re-education camps,[5] the forced de-urbanization and displacement of another million to the New Economic Zones,[6] restriction of free speech and movement[7] and discrimination against three distinct groups in society: those associated with the former South Vietnamese government, ethnic Chinese and Amerasians.[8] By 1979, more than 700,000 people had left Vietnam.[9] The plight of refugees in overcrowded boats and accounts of deaths at sea were widely reported. The United Nations responded with a major conference on Indochinese refugees in Geneva in 1979. Its emotional tone was set by the United States Vice-President Walter Mondale, who referred to "the failure of the Evian conference forty-one years earlier to provide international sanctuary to the persecuted Jews of Germany and Austria."[10] Sixty-five governments participated in the conference, and there were two major outcomes: first, an increase in resettlement offers; and second, the ODP, which allowed Vietnamese to leave their country legally after they had been accepted for resettlement. The conference endorsed the general principles of asylum and *non-refoulement*, and paved the way for temporary refuge in first asylum countries, *prima facie* refugee status for the boat people and permanent resettlement in secondasylum countries.[11]

There were three central aspects to the ODP. First, it was an exceptional international emigration and resettlement programme, and the only time in the history of the UNHCR when the organization actively helped people to leave their country on such a large scale.[12] Second, initial implementation problems meant that there were few departures from Vietnam during the first eight years of the programme (1979–1987). Only 125,000 people were able to leave Vietnam under the ODP between 1979 and 1987[13]—a fraction of the number of those who fled by boat. Many more left in the following decade, however, with 623,509 people emigrating under the ODP in total, the majority to the United States.[14] Third, intake in second-asylum countries varied considerably in nature. In the United

States, the ODP had two distinct tracks: those who had relatives resettled in the United States, and those who had suffered persecution because of their prior association with the United States before 1975.[15]

Australia, on the other hand, like Canada and New Zealand, prioritized family reunion under the ODP. As with the other second-asylum countries, Australia experienced delays with the ODP. It was not until 1982 that an agreement was signed between the Australian and Vietnamese governments, an Australian Migration Officer posted to Hanoi and the names of 6000 Vietnamese handed over to the Vietnamese government.[16] Only 624 Vietnamese were admitted to Australia under this programme in 1982–1983, a very small number compared to the 54,397 Vietnamese refugees resettled in Australia until 30 June 1982.[17] By the time the ODP came to an end in 1997, however, 46,711 Vietnamese had resettled in Australia under the programme.[18]

The problem with the ODP was that the Vietnamese governmentcontrolled departures from Vietnam. Lists of names provided by resettlement countries differed considerably from lists provided by the Vietnamese government.[19] Although Vietnam signed a Memorandum of Understanding on Orderly Departure on 30 May 1979 and advised the UNHCR that it would not prevent people who wished to depart from leaving,[20] it proceeded to impede departures under the programme. Vietnamese applicants for the programme lost their jobs and ration cards.[21] If family members awaiting sponsorship could not bear repeated delays and obfuscations on the part of local authorities, they made the risky decision to organize their own escape by sea. What happened, therefore, to those who chose to do this? There were three possible outcomes for Vietnamese escapees: first, they tried and failed—as many boat escapes ended in failure—and faced either a fine or internment by the Vietnamese authorities[22]; second, they survived to reach a first asylum country; or third, they disappeared at sea. Survivors, however, then faced a further wait in a camp or detention centre while their case was assessed. The ODP could therefore be a fraught process for those who wanted to leave Vietnam—applicants either were confronted by lengthy processing delays or risked death at sea if they opted to escape.

The ODP was devised as a means of enabling Vietnamese to leave their country legally and safely. In practice, however, repressive measures adopted by the Vietnamese state towards applicants for the programme, such as the cancellation of family registration cards and rations and repeated obstructions or delays, led to many Vietnamese attempting to

9 YEARS OF SEPARATION: VIETNAMESE REFUGEES AND THE EXPERIENCE... **127**

escape by boat rather than wait for the outcome of their ODP application. As Robert Funseth stated in 1989, the ODP "did not become the truly viable alternative to clandestine departure its authors envisaged."[23] The following three oral narratives illustrate two different aspects of the refugee experience for Vietnamese in the 1980s: those who managed to escape, resettle successfully and sponsor relatives to Australia; and those who stayed behind in Vietnam and were sponsored by relatives in Australia.

THE NARRATIVES

The first two narratives are those of men, both war veterans who escaped Vietnam by boat in the early 1980s and sponsored family members after resettling in Australia. The first veteran, Vu Van Bao, was born in Hanoi in 1948.[24] His family joined the mass movement of one million refugees who left the communist North for the non-communist South after the signing of the 1954 Geneva Accords partitioned Vietnam into two halves at the 17th parallel. Bao served in the Vietnamese Air Force from 1968 to 1975. He was a Chinook pilot, and his squadron supplied munitions and transported troops. One of the highlights of his career was the successful evacuation of 120 emaciated women and children from the Battle of An Loc in his Chinook in 1972, when Chinooks normally carried up to 55 troops. When the war ended, Bao spent five years in the gulag. He notes that former South Vietnamese service personnel were labelled "*nguy*" (puppet) by the post-war state. Bao had married in 1972 and had a two-year-old son. After his release, he was not allowed to live in Saigon, and became one of the city's many illegal residents. In 1981, he escaped from Vietnam by boat, and reached Indonesia. He arrived in Melbourne in 1982. Bao relates how he "lost everything":

> When I escaped from Vietnam, my wife was two or three months pregnant. She tried to escape three or four times but was captured and failed each time. It was very hard for her and for my eldest son. He was too scared and the last time, he said, "No, no, I don't want to go, I don't want to go, I'll stay back." I tried to do the paperwork to sponsor her here but in Vietnam, you have to have a family certificate in order to apply to leave.
>
> My first son was born in 1973. When I went to the concentration camp, he was two years old. ... They allowed him to visit me once in the camp but when I came home, he looked at me like I was a stranger. And my younger son, the first time I saw him was when he arrived in Australia. He was nine years old.

Bao's narrative makes it clear that administrative delays were from the Vietnamese side and not from Australian immigration restrictions. As he notes:

> It was always money under the table when they [the Vietnamese authorities] did the paperwork. … money under the table to get that family certificate, then another year and more money to get her name on it. Then they stopped processing applications for two years. Then my wife had to apply again.

Although Vietnam chided resettlement countries including the United States, Australia and France for backlogs in processing ODP applications in 1985,[25] Bao lays the blame for delays in processing at the feet of Vietnamese authorities. Bureaucratic impediments and the necessary bribery of officials stretched the sponsorship process to eight years.

The second veteran, Nguyen Van Long, was born in Hanoi in 1945.[26] His family also escaped south after partition in 1954. He joined the armed forces in 1965 and the Airborne Division in 1968, serving as an Intelligence Officer. He was taking part in Operation Lam Son in Laos in 1971 when he was wounded and the only survivor after his bunker was hit. He spent seven years as a prisoner of war of the North Vietnamese during which he was transferred to several different camps, before his release in 1977. This is Long:

> When I got home, my family and friends were shocked when I walked in through the door. They believed that I was dead. I looked at the altar and saw my photo. My mother was weeping [he broke down]. Everyone was so happy and I was so glad to rejoin my family. I used the time to visit my friends, especially my girlfriend, who is now my wife. In 1978, I was told I had to move to the New Economic Zones and work on the land. We had to work, work and work.

Long had met his girlfriend in 1968, the year that he joined the Airborne Division. They did not see each other again until nearly ten years later, after his release from prison camp. He said, "We talked about the old times when we went out together as a man and a woman." Life was difficult under the communist regime, and he had to do forced labour in the New Economic Zones. Long escaped from Vietnam by boat in 1982 and reached Indonesia. He arrived in Melbourne in 1983 and lodged sponsorship papers for his fiancée in 1985. After four years of waiting, however, she made her own escape from Vietnam in 1989 and reached Pulau Bidong in Malaysia. She arrived in Melbourne in 1990. He relates:

Here is my wife on Valentine's Day, arriving in Australia [showed photographs]. I knew her in 1968 and in 1990 we organised the wedding. She was forty-four. Many veterans and community members attended our wedding. They were surprised that it was twenty-two years before we got married. She became pregnant and we had one child, our son, we were lucky.

Long does not detail the conditions that his fiancée experienced during those eight years in Vietnam after his departure, but the fact that she made the decision to escape by boat is an indication of how difficult things were, and how desperate she was to leave. Pirate attacks against boat people reached new heights in the 1980s, with UN High Commissioner for Refugees Poul Hartling referring to "cruelty, brutality and inhumanity that go beyond [his] imagination."[27] Long's fiancée was fortunate to survive the journey. Long notes that it was with the assistance of Bruce Ruxton, then President of the Victorian Returned and Services League (RSL), the Australian Department of Veterans' Affairs and the Australian Department of Immigration and Ethnic Affairs, that his fiancée was flown to Australia from Malaysia in 1990. After nearly 22 years of separation encompassing his wartime service, internment in prison camps, forced displacement to the New Economic Zones, and eight years post-migration in Australia, he feels lucky to have finally married the woman he had first met in 1968.

The third narrative is that of a woman, Hong.[28] Unlike those of Bao and Long, Hong's account reveals the experiences of those who were left behind in Vietnam when family members made their escape by sea. Hong was born in 1940 in Quang Tri, central Vietnam. A teacher by training, she married a civil servant, and the couple had five children. Her husband won a scholarship to undertake postgraduate studies in the United States for four years and returned to Vietnam in 1973 to become Director of the Department of Education and Research. In 1975, he was sent to re-education camps in northern Vietnam. Hong remembers,

The communist government considered that he owed a "blood debt" (*no mau*) to the people, since he had used the people's money to study in America, an imperialist country (*De quoc My*). He was imprisoned for five years. I had to look after our five children without any support. Neither of us had any extended family. It was terribly difficult. ... I was worried about the authorities carrying out their "Reform of the Bourgeoisie" and sending us to the New Economic Zone. ... Life was terribly hard. It was so hard that I just wanted to die. But I thought about my five children.

Hong details a visit to her husband in 1978 during which it took her ten days to make her way to the re-education camp and back, all for a visit that lasted 15 minutes. Hong and her family were labelled "*nguy*" (puppet) by the communist regime. After her husband was released in 1980, he escaped by boat. As she says, "We did not have any other choice. *Nguy* army and civil personnel could not do any work. It was either life or death in that society." Hong made the deliberate decision not to escape by boat with her children as she believed that less than 10 per cent of escapees survived the journey. She was fortunate in that she received news of her husband's survival after just one month. She was interrogated by Vietnamese officials after her husband's disappearance and subjected to harassment by local authorities and home inspections. As for the sponsorship process, she relates:

> I had to arrange the money and see the authorities at each level until I got to the top person [bribery of officials]. When I had enough supporting documentation, then I felt that I became another person, and they suddenly changed their attitude.
>
> We wanted to go because we hoped to be reunited as a family but no one here wanted us to go. ... When I visited my brother who was still interned, I had to use the permit to go overseas as an ID because I did not have any ID with me. They [the Vietnamese authorities] were envious when they saw my permit. Even the prison guards were envious. ... I was very nervous before coming here [to Australia] and during the time our application was being processed.

While Hong's experiences in some ways parallel those of Bao's wife—both had to bribe Vietnamese officials in order to have their applications processed—in her case, the process took four years instead of eight. She arrived in Melbourne with her children in 1984. Her narrative articulates the stress she experienced while the sponsorship process was underway but notes that once she had all the required documents, Vietnamese authorities "changed their attitude."

Forced Migration and Family Separation

Family separation constitutes one of the major life stressors for refugee and humanitarian entrants, with research consistently documenting its negative impacts on refugees' mental health and wellbeing.[29] Separation from a family member adversely affects conditions such as depression, anxiety and post-traumatic stress disorder, and can significantly impact on the resettlement process as well as perceptions of resettlement.[30] Post-migration factors have been found to be "significantly associated with adverse mental health outcomes over and above the impact of pre-migration trauma."[31] Refugees worry about family members who followed a different escape route, or were left behind and subjected to interrogation or harassment by local authorities. Vietnamese refugees either escaped as a family unit in the belief that they would survive or die together, or deliberately split up into several units in the hope that some family members would survive the journey. When post-migration family separation is preceded by pre-migration separation as well as personal, familial and communal exposure to nationwide events such as the collapse of a country and profound post-war social upheaval, as was the case with South Vietnam after 1975, the level of psychological and emotional trauma is compounded.

The narratives of Bao, Long and Hong reveal how successive traumas have shaped their memories and the telling of their stories. "When memories recall acts of violence against individuals or entire groups," note Paul Antze and Michael Lambek, "they carry additional burdens—as indictments or confessions, or as emblems of a victimized identity."[32] The memories of all three narrators refer to repressive acts by the Vietnamese state against *nguy* military and civil personnel and their families, and elucidate the political as well as the personal consequences of state policy. As such, these narratives not only convey the extent of personal loss and suffering experienced, but also include an implicit indictment of post-war Vietnam and the discriminatory measures that the state continued to direct against *nguy* families, even a decade or more after the end of the war. Measured as it is, Bao's narrative reveals the emotional cost of that long separation from his family. Intense grief punctuates Long's reconstruction of past events, while Hong's account is a powerful testimony of the post-war marginalization of *nguy* families.

The three narrators experienced family separation in three distinct contexts: first, during the war; second, during internment (either their own or that of their family members); and third, post-migration (either their own or that of their family members). Separation in wartime was difficult but to be expected, as was the case for Bao and Long, both of whom served in the Republic of Vietnam Armed Forces (RVNAF) as junior officers. Hong's husband had a unique opportunity to further his education and career overseas, and Hong does not recall his absence as a hardship. Separation due to internment, on the other hand, had a traumatic impact for internees as well as their family members. Political indoctrination, hard labour, malnutrition, isolation from their families and the absence of any timeframe for their incarceration were particularly damaging.[33] Bao notes that when he was released from the gulag and returned home, his eight-year-old son looked at him "like a stranger." As for Long, he was cut off from any news of family or friends for seven years while he was interned in a series of communist prison camps. For Hong, those five years when she and her children experienced discrimination as *ngụy* while her husband was incarcerated at the other end of the country were harrowing. She refers several times to wanting to kill herself, and states that it was only the thought of her children that stopped her from doing so.

Separation from his family post-migration was particularly difficult for the first narrator, Bao. While his words on this subject are few, the repetition of the adjective "hard" attests to the pain of that separation, particularly in light of all that he had already endured prior to migration. The reserved tone of his recollections of military service, internment and then the final hurdle of nearly a decade away from his loved ones post-resettlement signifies stoic resignation. His priority on arrival was to work so as to send money home to his family. The strain of that separation was also evident on his wife and sons, as they made "three to four" failed escape attempts, and finally stopped because their eldest son could no longer bear the stress of these attempts. It was fortunate that these escape attempts failed because at least his wife and sons remained alive to be sponsored.

The second narrator, Long, wept quietly throughout his account. His grief encompassed his service for his country, and his years as a prisoner of war. Like Bao's wife, Long's fiancée also decided not to wait any longer for the sponsorship process to take effect, and to escape by sea. She survived the journey, and they were reunited and married 22 years after they first met. Theirs is a story that comprises successive life stressors including loss, separation and internment, but that ends positively, with a late marriage, and a son born to them. As Long relates, they were "lucky."

For the third narrator, Hong, awaiting sponsorship to Australia was a relatively light burden to bear after the trauma of the immediate post-war years. She was separated from her husband for a total of nine years from 1975 to 1984, and although she remembers the anxiety of waiting for the sponsorship to go through, and having to bribe several levels of Vietnamese bureaucracy, she knew that she was going to be able to leave Vietnam with her children. In the case of all three narratives, the sponsorship process is only briefly alluded to within life histories that encompass war, post-war and post-migration experiences. None of the narrators refers to the terms "Orderly Departure Program" or "ODP," only to the sponsorship process. This process was out of their control, and pales in comparison to the narrators' other experiences. Once they had exerted their agency by applying to the relevant authorities, the matter was out of their hands.

From the timeline provided in all three narratives, the efforts of Bao and Long to sponsor family members to Australia in the 1980s coincided with the problematic first eight years of the ODP (1979–1987). There was a clear disjuncture between the number of names provided to the Australian Migration Officer in Hanoi in 1982 and the actual number of Vietnamese who were able to emigrate under the ODP in 1982–1983.[34] As was the case with Bao's wife and Long's fiancée, it can be surmised that others who were waiting to be sponsored by family members overseas during those years also gave up on the sponsorship process and attempted their own escapes by boat. Of those that did, some would have failed, others would have survived and others still would have disappeared at sea and died. The narratives of Bao and Long are a reminder of the casualties of the ODP. That Bao's wife and sons were finally able to emigrate legally in 1990 was the result of new procedures initiated in 1988. Vietnam agreed to provide substantial lists of eligible people to Australian authorities, and those wishing to leave could lodge their applications with Australian migration officials without seeking the permission of Vietnamese authorities.[35] The Vietnamese government, however, retained the right to grant exit permits.[36] While Hong and her children were able to emigrate four years after her husband lodged sponsorship papers, they were among the lucky few who were able to emigrate from Vietnam under the ODP in 1979–1987.

CONCLUSION

"The most distinctive contribution of oral history," suggest Robert Perks and Alistair Thomson, "has been to include within the historical record the experiences and perspectives of groups of people who might otherwise have been 'hidden from history'."[37] The narratives of Bao, Long and Hong convey the experiences of veterans and women of the Vietnamese diaspora—voices that remain marginal and largely unheard in Australian and international migration histories. Their stories not only relate specific examples of Australian ODP entries but also provide instances of family separation lasting between nine and 22 years. The stories of these three individuals and of their families highlight the impediments in the programme's implementation, particularly during the problematic first decade of the ODP. These accounts of ODP departures from Vietnam and resettlement in Australia were part of a larger international history of ODP departures from post-war Vietnam. As Australia privileged family reunion, it seems logical that these three accounts involved cases of family reunion.

For Bao and Long, both of whom were former soldiers and re-education camp detainees, this extended process was yet another challenge to their resilience and mental health. Their accounts also reveal the level of stress and pressure that these delays placed on their loved ones in Vietnam, which led to failed escape attempts by Bao's wife and sons, and to Long's fiancée escaping by boat. The gravity and risks of these decisions are highlighted by Hong's account where the option of a boat escape with her five children was only a measure of last resort. Their stories illustrate the individual, familial and communal costs of the refugee experience, the effects of family fragmentation on intergenerational relations and the potential secondary trauma of later generations born in Australia.

The Vietnamese community in Australia is well established and constitutes Australia's largest refugee community. Vietnamese refugees formed "the first and most difficult test case"[38] of the abolition of the White Australia Policy, with a high profile in the media and in national discourse.[39] Most Vietnamese arrived in Australia directly from first asylum camps, and many did so under the ODP. Within the larger story of the post-war Vietnamese exodus, and the success of the ODP and resettlement in Australia, the experiences of these three people and their families elucidate the delays and complexities involved in the experience of forced migration for Vietnamese refugees after 1975. While these narratives end well, they serve as a reminder of the casualties that could occur in even the most exceptional international emigration and resettlement programmes.

NOTES

1. Vu Van Bao, interviewed by Nathalie Huynh Chau Nguyen, 27 July 2013, Springvale South, Victoria, National Library of Australia, ORAL TRC 6525/11.
2. See W. Courtland Robinson, *Terms of Refuge: The Indochinese Exodus and the International Response* (London: Zed Books, 1998), 272 and 294–95. The number of exiled Vietnamese comes to 1.8 million, which includes

839,228 arrivals in UNHCR camps, 134,000 evacuated to the United States in 1975, 263,000 who fled to the People's Republic of China in 1978–1979, and 623,509 who left under the ODP. An estimated 100,000 to more than a million dead of the exodus need to be added to this total.

3. The last Vietnamese refugee camp, Pillar Point Vietnamese Refugees Centre in Hong Kong, closed on 31 May 2000.
4. Robinson, *Terms of Refuge*, 127.
5. United Nations High Commissioner for Refugees, *The State of the World's Refugees: Fifty Years of Humanitarian Action* (Oxford: Oxford University Press, 2000), 82.
6. Jacqueline Desbarats, "Human Rights: Two Steps Forward, One Step Backward?" in Thai Quang Trung ed., *Vietnam Today: Assessing the New Trends* (New York: Crane Russak, 1990), 60.
7. Desbarats, "Human Rights," 47–64: Linda Hitchcox, *Vietnamese Refugees in Southeast Asian Camps* (Basingstoke: Macmillan in association with St Antony's College, Oxford, 1990), 37–68; James M. Freeman and Nguyen Dinh Huu, *Voices from the Camps: Vietnamese Children Seeking Asylum* (Seattle: University of Washington Press, 2003), 7.
8. Desbarats, "Human Rights," 60–64; Hitchcox, *Vietnamese Refugees*, 37–68; Kieu-Linh Caroline Valverde, "From Dust to Gold: The Vietnamese Amerasian Experience," in Maria P. P. Root ed., *Racially Mixed People in America* (Newbury Park: Sage Publications, 1992), 144–61.
9. Robinson, *Terms of Refuge*, 50.
10. Quoted in Robinson, *Terms of Refuge*, 53.
11. United Nations High Commissioner for Refugees, *State of the World's Refugees*, 83–84.
12. Judith Kumin, "Orderly Departure from Vietnam: Cold War Anomaly or Humanitarian Innovation?" *Refugee Survey Quarterly* 27, no. 1 (2008): 104.
13. Kumin, "Orderly Departure," 105.
14. Robinson, *Terms of Refuge*, 272.
15. See US Department of State, "Fact Sheet: US Expands Orderly Departure for Vietnamese Refugees," *US Department of State Dispatch* (Washington: U.S. Government Printing Office, 1 April 1991), 225.
16. Barry York, *Australia and Refugees, 1901–2002: An Annotated Chronology Based on Official Sources* (Canberra: Parliament of Australia, Department of the Parliamentary Library, 2003), paragraph 1982.
17. York, *Australia and Refugees*, paragraph 1982.
18. Robinson, *Terms of Refuge*, 295.
19. Teresa Albor, "Very Heavy Going," *Far Eastern Economic Review*, 12 July 1990, 54–55; Robinson, *Terms of Refuge*, 173.
20. Kumin, "Orderly Departure," 114.

21. Ben Jr Bradlee, "A Plea for Indochina Refugees; Head of Aid Organization Calls on US to Admit More Immigrants," *Boston Globe*, 12 February 1984, 1.
22. Robinson, *Terms of Refuge*, 179–80.
23. Statement of Robert Funseth and David Lambertson, *Orderly Departure Program and U.S. Policy Regarding Vietnamese Boat People. Hearing before the Subcommittee on Immigration, Refugees, and International Law of the Committee on the Judiciary House of Representatives, One Hundred First Congress, First Session, June 28, 1989, Serial No. 29* (Washington: U.S. Government Printing Office, 1990), 7.
24. See Nathalie Huynh Chau Nguyen, *South Vietnamese Soldiers: Memories of the Vietnam War and After* (Santa Barbara: Praeger, 2016), 50–66.
25. Robinson, *Terms of Refuge*, 174.
26. Nguyen Van Long, interviewed by Nathalie Huynh Chau Nguyen, 20 August 2014, Keysborough, Victoria, National Library of Australia, ORAL TRC 6525/13.
27. Quoted in Robinson, *Terms of Refuge*, 169.
28. Hong, interviewed by Thao Ha, 13 October 2005, Melbourne, Victoria, Australian Research Council Project "Vietnamese Women: Voices and Narratives of the Diaspora," digital recording in author's possession. See Nathalie Huynh Chau Nguyen, *Voyage of Hope: Vietnamese Australian Women's Narratives* (Altona: Common Ground Publishing, 2005), 97–115.
29. See Cécile Rousseau et al., "Trauma and Extended Separation from Family among Latin American and African Refugees in Montreal," *Psychiatry* 64, no. 1 (2001): 40–59; Brooke Wilmsen, "Family Separation: The Policies, Procedures, and Consequences for Refugee Background Families," *Refugee Survey Quarterly* 30, no. 1 (2011): 44–64; Alexander Miller et al., "Understanding the Mental Health Consequences of Family Separation for Refugees: Implications for Policy and Practice," *American Journal of Orthopsychiatry* 88, no. 1 (2018): 26–37.
30. Alexander Miller et al., "Mental Health Consequences," 26–37.
31. Susan S. Y. Li et al., "The Relationship Between Post-Migration Stress and Psychological Disorders in Refugees and Asylum Seekers," *Current Psychiatry Reports* 18, no. 82 (2016): 1–9. It should be noted, however, that a 2002 study on the long-term effect of psychological trauma on Vietnamese refugees resettled in Australia noted that "trauma exposure was the most potent, and the only consistent, predictor of current mental illness, even when postmigration factors were taken into account." Zachary Steel et al., "Long-term Effect of Psychological Trauma on the Mental Health of Vietnamese Refugees Resettled in Australia: A Population-based Study," *The Lancet* 360 (5 October 2002), 1060–61.

32. Paul Antze and Michael Lambek, "Preface," in Paul Antze and Michael Lambek eds, *Tense Past: Cultural Essays in Trauma and Memory* (New York: Routledge, 1996), vii.
33. See Nguyen Van Canh, *Vietnam Under Communism 1975–1982* (Stanford: Hoover Institution Press, 1983), 188–225; Nghia M. Vo, *The Bamboo Gulag: Political Imprisonment in Communist Vietnam* (Jefferson: McFarland, 2004); and Nguyen, *South Vietnamese Soldiers*, 139–62.
34. York, *Australia and Refugees*, paragraph 1982.
35. York, paragraph 1988.
36. York, paragraph 1988.
37. Robert Perks and Alistair Thomson, "Introduction to Second Edition," in Robert Perks and Alistair Thomson eds, The *Oral History Reader: Second Edition* (London: Routledge, 2006), ix.
38. Nancy Viviani, *The Indochinese in Australia 1975–1995: From Burnt Boats to Barbecues* (Melbourne: Oxford University Press, 1996), 1.
39. Mandy Thomas, "The Vietnamese in Australia," in James E. Coughlan and Deborah J. McNamara eds, *Asians in Australia: Patterns of Migration and Settlement* (South Melbourne: Macmillan Education Australia, 1997), 275.

BIBLIOGRAPHY

Albor, Teresa. "Very Heavy Going." *Far Eastern Economic Review* (12 July 1990): 54–55.

Antze, Paul, and Michael Lambek. "Preface." In *Tense Past: Cultural Essays in Trauma and Memory*, edited by Paul Antze and Michael Lambek, vii–ix. New York: Routledge, 1996.

Bradlee, Ben Jr. "A Plea for Indochina Refugees; Head of Aid Organization Calls on US to Admit More Immigrants." *Boston Globe*, 12 February 1984, 1.

Desbarats, Jacqueline. "Human Rights: Two Steps Forward, One Step Backward?" In *Vietnam Today: Assessing the New Trends*, edited by Thai Quang Trung. 47–64. New York: Crane Russak, 1990.

Freeman, James M., and Nguyen Dinh Huu. *Voices from the Camps: Vietnamese Children Seeking Asylum*. Seattle: University of Washington Press, 2003.

Hitchcox, Linda. *Vietnamese Refugees in Southeast Asian Camps*. Oxford: Macmillan in association with St Antony's College, 1990.

Hong. Interviewed by Thao Ha, 13 October 2005, Melbourne, Victoria. Australian Research Council Project "Vietnamese Women: Voices and Narratives of the Diaspora," digital recording in author's possession.

Kumin, Judith. "Orderly Departure from Vietnam: Cold War Anomaly or Humanitarian Innovation?" *Refugee Survey Quarterly* 27, no. 1 (2008): 104–17.

Li, Susan S. Y., Belinda J. Liddell, and Angela Nickerson. "The Relationship between Post-Migration Stress and Psychological Disorders in Refugees and Asylum Seekers." *Current Psychiatry Reports* 18, no. 82 (2016): 1–9.

Miller, Alexander, Julia Meredith Hess, Deborah Bybee, and Jessica R. Goodkind. "Understanding the Mental Health Consequences of Family Separation for Refugees: Implications for Policy and Practice." *American Journal of Orthopsychiatry* 88, no. 1 (2018): 26–37.

Nguyen, Van Canh. *Vietnam Under Communism 1975–1982.* Stanford: Hoover Institution Press, 1983.

Nguyen, Nathalie Huynh Chau. *Voyage of Hope: Vietnamese Australian Women's Narratives.* Altona: Common Ground Publishing, 2005.

Nguyen, Nathalie Huynh Chau. *South Vietnamese Soldiers: Memories of the Vietnam War and After.* Santa Barbara, CA: Praeger, 2016.

Nguyen, Van Long. Interviewed by Nathalie Huynh Chau Nguyen, 20 August 2014, Keysborough, Victoria. National Library of Australia, ORAL TRC 6525/13.

Perks, Robert, and Alistair Thomson. "Introduction to Second Edition." In *The Oral History Reader: Second Edition,* edited by Robert Perks and Alistair Thomson, ix. London: Routledge, 2006.

Robinson, W. Courtland. *Terms of Refuge: The Indochinese Exodus and the International Response.* London: Zed Books, 1998.

Rousseau, Cécile, Abdelwahed Mekki-Berrada, and Sylvie Moreau. "Trauma and Extended Separation from Family among Latin American and African Refugees in Montreal." *Psychiatry* 64, no. 1 (2001): 40–59.

Steel, Zachary, Derrick Silove, Tuong Phan, and Adrian Bauman. "Long-term Effect of Psychological Trauma on the Mental Health of Vietnamese Refugees Resettled in Australia: A Population-based Study." *The Lancet* 360 (5 October 2002): 1056–62.

Thomas, Mandy. "The Vietnamese in Australia." In *Asians in Australia: Patterns of Migration and Settlement,* edited by James E. Coughlan and Deborah J. McNamara, 274–95. South Melbourne: Macmillan Education Australia, 1997.

United Nations High Commissioner for Refugees. *The State of the World's Refugees: Fifty Years of Humanitarian Action.* Oxford: Oxford University Press, 2000.

Valverde, Kieu-Linh Caroline. "From Dust to Gold: The Vietnamese Amerasian Experience." In *Racially Mixed People in America,* edited by Maria P. P. Root, 144–61. Newbury Park: Sage Publications, 1992.

Viviani, Nancy. *The Indochinese in Australia 1975–1995: From Burnt Boats to Barbecues.* Melbourne: Oxford University Press, 1996.

Vo, Nghia M. *The Bamboo Gulag: Political Imprisonment in Communist Vietnam.* Jefferson: McFarland, 2004.

Vu, Van Bao. Interviewed by Nathalie Huynh Chau Nguyen, 27 July 2013, Springvale South, Victoria. National Library of Australia, ORAL TRC 6525/11.

Wilmsen, Brooke. "Family Separation: The Policies, Procedures, and Consequences for Refugee Background Families." *Refugee Survey Quarterly* 30, no. 1 (2011): 44–64.

York, Barry. *Australia and Refugees, 1901–2002: An Annotated Chronology Based on Official Sources.* Canberra: Parliament of Australia, Department of the Parliamentary Library, 2003.

CHAPTER 10

The Pear Tree: Family Narratives of Post-War Greek Macedonian Migration

Andrea Cleland

When the pear tree was planted by my great-grandfather in 1901 to hon our the birth of his son, my father's small village was in Ottoman Macedonia when Florina was known by its Slavic name of *Lerin* and the village of Itea was known as *Vrbeni*. Over time, Florina has also been known by its Byzantine name *Chlorine*, and the Latinized name *Chlerina*, reflecting successive periods of occupation from the Romans to the Ottomans. Florina was a region of agricultural bounty, but landholdings were usually small and barely adequate to sustain even a small family. Migration became epidemic due to political instability, war and poor economic conditions.

A particularly contested region of the Balkans, with a diverse population, Florina was incorporated into Greece in 1912 following the First Balkan War. With the partitioning of Macedonia after the Second Balkan War in 1913, my father's village became part of the Macedonian region in Northern Greece, near the current borders of Albania to the west, and the Republic of Macedonia to the north. A Greek Macedonian identity was formed at the regional level after 1912, though in Florina social conditions and networks differed from other parts of the country, with family remaining a primary signifier of identification, along with faith and region.[1]

A. Cleland (✉)
University of Melbourne, Parkville, VIC, Australia
e-mail: andrea.cleland7@gmail.com

© The Author(s) 2019   141
K. Darian-Smith, P. Hamilton (eds.), *Remembering Migration*,
Palgrave Macmillan Memory Studies,
https://doi.org/10.1007/978-3-030-17751-5_10

The pear tree has been witness to the end of the Ottoman Empire, the painful process of Greek nation building and successive wars and—ultimately—my father and many in his village and region leaving Greece in a mass exodus to seek a better life elsewhere.

My research involves an oral history project over three genealogical generations and examines how the transmission and circulation of family stories about migration shape the identity of the grandchildren of migrants who left Florina for Australia during the 1950s and 1960s. Taking an ethno-regional approach, it is attentive to the formation of the Greek Macedonian identity as a result of the (non)circulation of migration stories within the family. How do families from a region with a troubled history collectively narrate and pass down stories about their experiences? What types of stories are kept alive through repetition across the generations and what stories have become lost? In the absence of stories of the homeland, what is remembered through the collective networks of family?

From the 1890s, Greeks have migrated to almost 150 countries.[2] The devastating impact of World War II (1939–1945) and the Greek Civil War (1946–1949) prompted large-scale emigration during the 1950s–1970s. This was particularly substantial in Northern Greece where the economic, social and political consequences of war, particularly the Greek Civil War, were acutely felt.[3] It was not unusual for whole villages from Florina to be transplanted to Canada and to Australia, where the developing economy needed migrant labour and offered government-assisted migration programmes.[4] Almost a quarter of a million arrivals from Greece came to Australia, with a concentration from the Macedonian region, including Florina.[5] Within this context, my father Theodoros' migration in 1960 was sponsored by his brother Pandos, who had migrated to Australia with his wife Olga and their two young children in 1954. He spoke of the hope in moving to what he called the "lucky country" after the fear and poverty he remembered in Florina, a place he "never" wanted to return to as a home.[6] This sentiment was echoed by Lazaros a third brother who arrived shortly after in 1960, and never returned to Greece; he saw life in Australia as a "holiday" compared to that in Greece.[7]

To understand how storytelling shapes intergenerational family memories about migration, oral history is a particularly useful technique as it recognizes the complex interconnections between migration and the formation of ethnic identities.[8] Memories can provide unique insights into the processes that shape migrant belonging over time, including into diasporic family life from the perspectives of men, women and children.[9] This space of social networks between people is crucial to the experience of migration, although often there is little written about these relations.[10] Despite some limitations, such as memory loss and ethical responsibilities, personal accounts are often the only way to fully understand migrant experiences.[11]

As a type of collective memory, family memory can mediate between national history and family history by keeping sites of memory alive, although it can also lead to their "decay."[12] The family is the key agent for the transmission of Greek identity in the migrant diaspora, followed by language.[13] For many Greek Australians, the affiliation with region has remained significant and is often strengthened through return visits by the second and third generations to connect with an idea of "homeland" fostered through family narratives. For example, for migrants and their descendants from Castellorizo to Australia, a distinct sense of belonging as "Cazzies" has been maintained through systematic socialization in the island culture within the family and transmission of positive stories associated with place.[14] Feelings of nostalgia for the homeland may also be transferred to the second and third generations.

Yet, the disruption of war in the Macedonian region of Greece has led to a very circumscribed circulation of migration stories within the family. For subsequent generations, this has meant that there is a greater sense of belonging to the family and to Australia rather than to the Greek homeland. Despite this, many in the second and third generations wish to acknowledge their Greek Macedonian heritage and so the use of family storytelling is a crucial tool of maintaining culture, identity and tradition. Family intergenerational memory is constituted through ongoing social interaction and communication between children, parents and grandchildren. It is through genealogy and kinship situated in historical context that I have framed my research on questions of belonging and change in Greek Macedonian families.[15]

Stories narrated by the first, second and third generations documented the lived *experiences* of Greek Macedonian families in Australia, including connections to Greece and the negotiation of cultural identity. Equally important was understanding the types of stories that were actively *transmitted* to subsequent generations about Greek Macedonian migration, as well noting what was not passed down. In my oral history interviews, migrants and their families narrated stories about war, trauma, hardship, separation of family and loss, all serving to balance national narratives of the celebratory aspects of post-war migration to Australia.[16] The interviews

144   A. CLELAND

also highlighted the complexity of mediating regional Greek Macedonian identity, which may sit at odds with broader notions of common Greek ancestry, cultural traditions and religion.[17]

The Pear Tree: Belonging Through the Memory of Family

My father intentionally narrated many stories about his life growing up in Greece and as a migrant in Australia to myself, my sisters and his grandchildren. Many of these stories were about surviving the terrifying experiences of war, including how my father would climb the pear tree to find solace as a young child by eating pears, and decades later remembered their sweet taste. Through my father's storytelling, I had my own "memory" of the pear tree, even before I had seen it, as a connection to my ancestral home and grandparents who I would never meet. I came to understand that family kept me connected to Greece rather than the soil that the pear tree was planted in. As I interviewed other extended family, it was the enduring power of family that lay at the heart of identification with the homeland. Such a focus limited the circulation of narratives of place, as has been the case for other Greek diasporic regional communities.

Memories of Greece for the second generation were often framed by stories about the trees and gardens of their grandparents as symbolic of their connection to the homeland. Second-generation participant Andreas recalled his favourite memory of Greece was being in the garden with his grandparents:

> I remember my grandfather in Florina would love sitting in the garden in summer. It was big open grass filled with flowers and a couple of overhanging trees providing shade. He loved sitting there with the Greek radio station on listening to news, right on his ear because he could hardly hear.[18]

While it was important for the first generation to narrate their premigration stories about place and diverse identity within their villages and their direct experiences of war, little of these experiences were mentioned by subsequent generations. By the third generation, a greater sense of being Australian accompanied the desire to understand Greek Macedonian migrant heritage and legacy, of which limited cultural understanding remained. The loss of the migration story occurred when grandparents did not consciously narrate stories to their grandchildren. Overall, the stories narrated by the first to the third generation reflected the opportunities in Australia, with the loss of migration explained by reference to family members who remained in Florina. These memories also referred to the breakdown of traditional life in the village as a result of war and migration, with the enduring memory of home located very locally rather than a broader attachment to Greece.

Recent studies have shown how the development of second- and third-generation diasporic identities has been forged through visits "home" to Greece, with such visits recreating connections to the idea of "homeland" through family narratives.[19] But what of those migrants from Florina whose sense of home and belonging is more complicated? The transformation of various Greek diasporic communities into transnational national communities based on Hellenism was not always a uniform or linear process, and for some, belonging remained incomplete, uneven and contested.[20]

Indeed, the meaning of the terms "Macedonia" and "Macedonian" has been, and continues to be, extensively debated. While the Greek community in Australia was relatively united in protesting against the Republic of Macedonia declaring its independence in 1991, in previous decades there were deep divisions within the Greek Macedonian community over language and claims to a genuine Greek identity.[21] The name dispute between Greece and Macedonia was settled in February 2019 as the "Republic of North Macedonia", albeit with sizeable protests in 2018 by the Greek community to oppose any name that includes the term "Macedonia" during United Nations negotiations to resolve the name issue.

While the development of Greek Macedonian communities in the diaspora can be judged as largely successful in terms of settlement, the cohesiveness of the community has been disrupted by a politics of identity. This has implications for how families negotiated intergenerational legacy, particularly the ability to transmit a collective narrative of place. It has been noted that a "double stigma" is attached to the questions of ethnicity and identity in Florina following the Greek Civil War.[22] This has had an impact on memories and their intergenerational transmission. With contestations over place for those originating from the Florina region, intergenerational stories have centred instead on the less political memories of the village and family structures.

Debate about Macedonian identity is often framed in terms of belonging exclusively to Greece or to Macedonia. All participants in my research confirmed that their idea of Macedonia was the territory that lay within Greek national boundaries. In my analysis, I have defined the terms

"Macedonia" and "Greek Macedonia" in a similar way. I also use the terms "Macedonians" and "Greek Macedonians" to describe the people within the region of Florina within Greek Macedonia. This local *and* regional identity is not mutually exclusive from Greek identity. While collective memories of migration are often framed within the national domain, the idea of "home" does not always fit comfortably into a national project nor does it engage with an official narrative of place.[23]

In addition, the trauma and violence experienced during World War II and the Greek Civil War in Florina also limited the transmission of family stories of "home" and belonging through to the third generation. This period in the Florina region was equated with memories of hunger, poverty and destruction. Not surprisingly, the migration narratives of Greek Macedonians were not anchored by a nostalgia to return to Greece, but the acknowledgement that home was wherever the family had put down its roots. With Macedonia described as the "most blood-soaked region of Greece," it is difficult to tell a story of connection to "home" if one does not wish to return.[24] For example, first-generation participant Eleni stated her feelings about Greece as a place of return: "No I never wanted to go home. I'm scared I would be hungry if I went back. This is our home [in Australia]."[25] Lazaros talked about the difficulties he experienced in Greece and how he later found comfort in Australia where he was able to identify as a local Macedonian: "We were scared in Greece because we were Macedonians. They didn't like us much and there was politics. They treated you as less. Here I never feel scared."[26]

GREEK MACEDONIAN IDENTITY AND BELONGING IN THE THIRD GENERATION

For families from Florina, migration stories can best be viewed as family memories within a more expansive collective memory. To paraphrase Michael Herzfeld, the goals of "historical streamlining" by the nation-state cannot quite conceal the sense of contradiction that occurs in identity formation at the level of family and kinship.[27] I do not seek to contest Macedonian identity *per se*, but rather to comprehend how a regional Greek Macedonian identity becomes possible in the context of migration, and how and why it remains relevant across generations. The transmission of family stories about "back home" are a significant element of second-generation Greek diasporic identity, providing a "roadmap" of connections to a symbolic homeland.[28]

Second-generation participant Peter stated that "every family has a different story," highlighting the complex issue of identity for families from Florina.[29] It also speaks to Loring M. Danforth's question of "how can a woman give birth to one Greek and one Macedonian?"[30] Of course, many factors influenced the process of identity formation for migrants from Florina to Australia, including Balkan history, village politics, family situation and individual biography. The official classifications that are often used to describe very complex ideas of identity are often projected into the past for those from Ottoman Macedonia.[31] As Peter explained:

> I was born under the Greek banner. Dad's dad's dad could have been Macedonian. The problem is every family has a different story to tell. I have a cousin who changed his name back to his Macedonian name. He was born two years after me but he believes he is Macedonian.[32]

The limited transmission of family stories about identity and place meant that in my interview sample it was difficult for many third-generation participants to understand what Macedonian identity and place meant to their grandparents or how it was expressed in terms of Greek national identity. For example, third-generation participant Sarah stated she knew little about the region and what the term "Macedonia" meant.[33] For Andrew, the complexity of Macedonian identity stemmed from how people from the same place could identify in distinctly different ways. Without any knowledge of the historical context, Andrew felt he was unable to understand why people who come from the same region of Florina could form a different sense of identity. Andrew also felt that "the only real understanding I have is that it gets very political."[34]

This gap in the transmission of memories occurred despite the willingness of first-generation participants to narrate their pre-migration experiences during the interviews. Third-generation participant John sensed his grandfather Pandos did not want to speak about the past: "My grandparents, especially grandpa, wanted to experience and be with us rather than just telling us where he'd came from. It almost felt like he never wanted to talk about it."[35]

Third-generation participant Belinda, John's sister, was unable to contextualize what migrant identity meant to her own family heritage, although it remained important to her. Belinda said, "I don't understand why we are Greek Macedonian but mum doesn't understand either and so I ask her questions, but she can't really explain."[36] Indeed, across the second and third generations, there was little understanding of the meaning of Greek Macedonian heritage and identity, aside from what was practised within the family household in terms of language, food and traditions. While John and Belinda knew little detail about where and when their grandparents Olga and Pandos migrated from Greece, they were aware of their mother's experiences growing up in between the Greek Macedonian and Australian cultures. This reframing of migration stories to centre the experiences of the second generation's living between two cultures was common. John's mother Kathy had narrated stories of post-settlement migration, when his grandparents first settled in inner-city Richmond in Melbourne, and the places the family visited became sites of family memory. John said:

> I do feel a connection to places like Richmond and where the family landed. Mum would always drive us around and say, this is where we first arrived and that were the areas we would go and visit. When I'm there I think back to all the immigrants that must have landed at the time, but no not to Greece itself.[37]

In contrast, my parents Theodoros and Zoi continually exposed their grandchildren to traditional notions of the Greek family through day-to-day activities, albeit reconstructed in an Australian setting. Andrew narrated the crucial role his grandparents played in his upbringing and felt his relationship with his grandparents was integral to shaping his development and this included the transmission of the "fundamentals" of Greek values.[38] The visibility of Greek Macedonian migration was extremely high for Andrew and his brother Michael as all four grandparents emigrated from villages in Florina, as did their father and many relatives on both sides of the family.

Yet both Andrew and Michael felt a greater identification with Australian culture despite their upbringing shaped by the maintenance of many elements of the traditional Greek family. Andrew felt that he did not feel any significant connection to Greece as the family had been settled so long in Australia. However, Andrew noted that family storytelling was a means to transmitting culture and Greek values. Andrew spoke about how stories about migration were circulated by both sets of grandparents, outlining the journey and how war disrupted opportunities in Greece. Post-migration stories were framed around employment and the values and ethics of hard work as a step to an improved future.

The third generation expressed a loss of many traditional aspects of their Greek cultural heritage, such as language. But their interviews also reflected hope and renewal through the reconnection with Greek culture and the continued importance placed on family. Thus the legacy of what it means to be the grandchildren of migrants may also come to occupy more significance in their own family story in the future. Belinda wanted to understand her place in the bigger picture of Greek Macedonian migration history in Australia:

> Upon reflection, I wish things were different. I want to identify more with it and I want to learn more so that's why this [study] will be really good because it would really help. I feel like I've got so much to learn.[39]

The sentiment to transmit stories about family migration is best summarized by Andrew:

> You don't want to forget what your roots are. It will be good for my grandchildren to know where they came from. I will tell them about my *pappou* [grandfather]. I will tell them about both of them. They may not care but I think it's good to educate them.[40]

Andrew's statement echoed the sentiments of his grandfather—my father Theodoros—who made a conscious effort to ensure that there was not a forgetting of what it meant to be a migrant from Florina.

This chapter demonstrates how family stories can further our understanding of the longer-term implication of how Greek Macedonian migration has reshaped the idea of family and cultural identity in the diaspora. In the absence of stories about the ancestral homeland of Greece, family memories were more closely associated at the localized level of the village and the family. Ongoing connections to Greece for the second and third generations were shaped by visits to Florina, through stories narrated by grandparents and parents about family villages, and by viewing photographs. The importance of family storytelling in maintaining culture, identity and tradition was recognized, with a continued desire by the third generation to not "forget your roots" in the face of changing family life, and limited transmission and knowledge about their ancestral region of Florina.

NOTES

1. Anastasia N. Karakasidou, *Fields of Wheat, Hills of Blood: Passages to Nationhood in Greek Macedonia 1870–1990* (Chicago: The University of Chicago Press, 1997).
2. Anastasios M. Tamis, *The Greeks in Australia* (Port Melbourne: Cambridge University Press, 2005).
3. Victor Roudometof, "From Greek Orthodox Diaspora to Transnational Hellenism: Greek Nationalism and the Identities of the Diaspora," in *The Call of the Homeland: Diaspora Nationalisms, Past and Present* (Leiden: Brill, 2010), 139–68.
4. Anastasios M. Tamis, *The Immigration and Settlement of Macedonian Greeks in Australia* (Bundoora: La Trobe University Press, 1994), 350.
5. Loring M. Danforth, "'How Can a Woman Give Birth to One Greek and One Macedonian?' The Construction of National Identity among Immigrants to Australia from Northern Greece," in Jane K. Cowan ed., *Macedonia: The Politics of Identity and Difference* (London: Pluto Press, 2000).
6. Theodoros (born 1935, Florina, Greece), interviewed by Andrea Cleland, 14 February 2011, Melbourne, digital recording in author's possession.
7. Lazaros (born 1928, Florina, Greece), interviewed by Andrea Cleland, 19 July 2010, Melbourne, digital recording in author's possession.
8. Alistair Thomson, "Moving Stories: Oral History and Migration Studies," *Oral History* 27, no. 1 (Spring 1999).
9. Mary Chamberlain and Selma Leydesdorff, "Transnational Families: Memories and Narratives," *Global Networks* 4, no. 3 (2004): 227–41.
10. Thomson, "Moving Stories: Oral History and Migration Studies," 28.
11. Lynn Abrams, "Memory as Both Source and Subject of Study: The Transformations of Oral History," in Stefan Berger and Bill Niven eds, *Writing the History of Memory* (London: Bloomsbury Academic, 2014), 89–109; Paula Hamilton, "The Knife Edge: Debates About Memory and History," in Kate Darian-Smith and Paula Hamilton eds, *Memory and History in Twenty-First Century Australia* (Melbourne: Melbourne Oxford University Press, 1994), 9–32.
12. Astri Erll, "Locating Family in Cultural Memory Studies," *Journal of Comparative Family Studies* 42, no. 3 (2011): 303–18; Maurice Halbwachs, *On Collective Memory* (Chicago and London: The University of Chicago Press, 1992), 63.
13. Georgina Tsolidis, "Greek-Australian Families," in Robyn Hartley ed., *Families and Cultural Diversity in Australia* (St Leonards: Allen & Unwin in Association with the Australian Institute of Family Studies, 1995).

14. Vassiliki Chryssanthopoulou, "Reclaiming the Homeland: Belonging among Diaspora Generations of Greek Australians from Castellorizo," *Diaspora: A Journal of Transnational Studies* 18, no. 1/2 (Spring/Summer 2009): 67–88.
15. David Kertzer, "Generation as a Sociological Problem," *Annual Review of Sociology* 9 (1983): 125–49.
16. This chapter forms part of a wider oral history PhD project over three genealogical generations that included interviews with 38 people invited to participate from my extended family networks. It examines how the transmission and circulation of family migration stories shape identity and belonging of the grandchildren of migrants who left Florina in Greece for Australia during the 1950s and 1960s (the third generation). Interviews with Greek Macedonian migrant families provided the key primary sources for the project. First names have been used to support the privacy of interviewees with recorded interviews privately held.
17. Anna Triandafyllidou, "National Identity and the 'Other'," *Ethnic and Racial Studies* 21, no. 4 (1998): 593–12.
18. Andreas (born 1971, Melbourne, Australia), interviewed by Andrea Cleland, 11 October 2015, Melbourne, digital recording in author's possession.
19. Dimitra Giorgas, "Transnationalism and Identity among Second Generation Greek-Australians," in *Ties to the Homeland: Second Generation Transnationalism*, 53–71.
20. Victor Roudometof, "From Greek Orthodox Diaspora to Transnational Hellenism," 146.
21. Anastasios M. Tamis, *The Immigration and Settlement of Macedonian Greeks in Australia*, 134; Nicholas Doumanis, "The Greeks in Australia," in Richard Clogg ed., *The Greek Diaspora in the Twentieth Century* (Oxford: Macmillan Press Ltd, 1999), 81.
22. Riki Van Boeschoten, "When Difference Matters: Sociopolitical Dimensions of Ethnicity in the District of Florina," in Jane K. Cowan ed., *Macedonia: The Politics of Identity and Difference* (London: Pluto Press, 2000).
23. Nergis Canefe, "Home in Exile: Politics of Refugeehood in the Canadian Muslim Diaspora," in Julia Creet and Andreas Kitzmann eds, *Memory and Migration: Multidisciplinary Approaches to Memory Studies* (Toronto: University of Toronto Press, 2011), 156–80.
24. Anastasios M. Tamis, *The Immigration and Settlement of Macedonian Greeks in Australia*, 354; Stuart Hall, "Culture, Community, Nation," *Cultural Studies* 7, no. 3 (1993): 349–63.
25. Eleni (born 1940, Florina, Greece), interviewed by Andrea Cleland, 6 April 2014, Melbourne, digital recording in author's possession.

26. Lazaros (born 1928, Florina, Greece), interview, 19 July 2010.
27. Michael Herzfeld, *Cultural Intimacy: Social Poetics in the Nation-State* (New York: Routledge, 1997).
28. Noula Papayiannis, "Identity and Belonging among Second-Generation Greek and Italian Canadian Women," in May Friedman and Silvia Shultermandl eds, *Growing up Transnational: Identity and Kinship in a Global Era* (Toronto: University of Toronto Press Incorporated, 2011), 69–83.
29. Peter (born 1961, Florina, Greece), interviewed by Andrea Cleland, 24 November 2013, digital recording in author's possession.
30. Danforth, "'How Can a Woman Give Birth to One Greek and One Macedonian?'"; Danforth, *The Macedonian Conflict: Ethnic Nationalism in a Transnational World* (Princeton, NJ: Princeton University Press, 1995).
31. Hans Vermeulen, *The Ethnic Identities of European Minorities: Theory and Case Studies*, Bruno Synak ed. (Gdanskiego: Wydawnictwo Uniwersytetu 1995).
32. Peter (born 1961, Florina, Greece), interview, 24 November 2013.
33. Sarah (born 1981, Sydney, Australia), interviewed by Andrea Cleland, 23 October 2010, Melbourne, digital recording in author's possession.
34. Andrew (born 1985, Melbourne, Australia), interviewed by Andrea Cleland, 29 October 2013, Melbourne, digital recording in author's possession.
35. John (born 1986, Melbourne, Australia), interviewed by Andrea Cleland, 21 August 2016, Melbourne, digital recording in author's possession.
36. Belinda (born 1989, Melbourne Australia), interviewed by Andrea Cleland, 21 August 2016, Melbourne, digital recording in author's possession.
37. John (born 1986, Melbourne, Australia), interview, 21 August 2016.
38. Andrew (born 1985, Melbourne, Australia), interview, 29 October 2013.
39. Belinda (born 1989, Melbourne, Australia), interview, 21 August 2016.
40. Andrew (born 1985, Melbourne, Australia), interview, 29 October 2013.

Bibliography

Abrams, Lynn. "Memory as Both Source and Subject of Study: The Transformations of Oral History." In *Writing the History of Memory*, edited by Stefan Berger and Bill Niven, 89–109. London: Bloomsbury Academic, 2014.

Andreas (born 1971, Melbourne, Australia). Interviewed by Andrea Cleland, 11 October 2015, Melbourne. Digital recording in author's possession.

Andrew (born 1985 Melbourne, Australia). Interviewed by Andrea Cleland, 29 October 2013, Melbourne. Digital recording in author's possession.

Belinda (born 1989, Melbourne, Australia). Interviewed by Andrea Cleland, 21 August 2016, Melbourne. Digital recording in author's possession.

Canefe, Nergis. "Home in Exile: Politics of Refugeehood in the Canadian Muslim Diaspora." In *Memory and Migration: Multidisciplinary Approaches to Memory Studies*, edited by Julia Creet and Andreas Kitzmann, 156–82. Toronto: University of Toronto Press, 2011.

Chamberlain, Mary, and Selma Leydesdorff. "Transnational Families: Memories and Narratives." *Global Networks* 4, no. 3 (2004): 227–41.

Chryssanthopoulou, Vassiliki. "Reclaiming the Homeland: Belonging among Diaspora Generations of Greek Australians from Castellorizo." *Diaspora: A Journal of Transnational Studies* 18, no. 1/2 (Spring/Summer 2009): 67–88.

Danforth, Loring M. *The Macedonian Conflict: Ethnic Nationalism in a Transnational World*. Princeton, NJ: Princeton University Press, 1995.

Danforth, Loring M. "'How Can a Woman Give Birth to One Greek and One Macedonian?' The Construction of National Identity among Immigrants to Australia from Northern Greece." In *Macedonia: The Politics of Identity and Difference*, edited by Jane K. Cowan. London: Pluto Press, 2000.

Doumanis, Nicholas. "The Greeks in Australia." In *The Greek Diaspora in the Twentieth Century*, edited by Richard Clogg. Oxford: Macmillan Press Ltd, 1999.

Eleni (born 1940, Florina, Greece). Interviewed by Andrea Cleland, 6 April 2014, Melbourne. Digital recording in author's possession.

Erll, Astri. "Locating Family in Cultural Memory Studies." *Journal of Comparative Family Studies* 42, no. 3 (2011): 303–18.

Giorgas, Dimitra. "Transnationalism and Identity among Second Generation Greek-Australians." In *Ties to the Homeland: Second Generation Transnationalism*, edited by Helen Lee. Newcastle upon Tyne: Cambridge Scholars Publishing, 2008.

Hall, Stuart. "Culture, Community, Nation." *Cultural Studies* 7, no. 3 (1993): 349–63.

Hamilton, Paula. "The Knife Edge: Debates About Memory and History." In *Memory and History in Twenty-First Century Australia* edited by Kate Darian-Smith and Paula Hamilton, 9–32. Melbourne: Melbourne Oxford University Press, 1994.

Herzfeld, Michael. *Cultural Intimacy: Social Poetics in the Nation-State*. New York: Routledge, 1997.

Hill, Peter. *The Macedonians in Australia*. Carlisle: Hesperian Press, 1989.

John (born 1986, Melbourne, Australia). Interviewed by Andrea Cleland, 21 August 2016. Digital recording in author's possession.

Karakasidou, Anastasia N. *Fields of Wheat, Hills of Blood: Passages to Nationhood in Greek Macedonia 1870–1990*. Chicago: The University of Chicago Press, 1997.

154 A. CLELAND

Kertzer, David. "Generation as a Sociological Problem." *Annual Review of Sociology* 9 (1983): 125–49.

Lazaros (born 1928, Florina, Greece). Interviewed by Andrea Cleland, 19 July 2010, Melbourne. Digital recording in author's possession.

Papayiannis, Noula. "Identity and Belonging Among Second-Generation Greek and Italian Canadian Women." In *Growing up Transnational: Identity and Kinship in a Global Era*, edited by May Friedman and Silvia Shultermandl, 69–83. Toronto: University of Toronto Press, 2011.

Peter (born 1961, Florina, Greece). Interviewed by Andrea Cleland, 24 November 2013, Melbourne. Digital recording in author's possession.

Roudometof, Victor. "From Greek Orthodox Diaspora to Transnational Hellenism: Greek Nationalism and the Identities of the Diaspora." In *The Call of the Homeland: Diaspora Nationalisms, Past and Present*, edited by Allon Gal, Athena S. Leoussi and Anthony D. Smith, 139–68. Leiden: Brill, 2010.

Sarah (born 1981, Sydney, Australia). Interviewed by Andrea Cleland, 23 October 2010, Melbourne. Digital recording in author's possession.

Tamis, Anastasios M. *The Immigration and Settlement of Macedonian Greeks in Australia*. Bundoora: La Trobe University Press, 1994.

Tamis, Anastasios M. *The Greeks in Australia*. Port Melbourne: Cambridge University Press, 2005.

Theodoros (born 1935, Florina, Greece). Interviewed by Andrea Cleland, 14 February 2011, Melbourne. Digital recording in author's possession.

Thomson, Alistair. "Moving Stories: Oral History and Migration Studies." *Oral History* 27, no. 1 (Spring 1999).

Triandafyllidou, Anna. "National Identity and the 'Other'." *Ethnic and Racial Studies* 21, no. 4 (1998): 593–612.

Tsolidis, Georgina. "Greek-Australian Families." In *Families and Cultural Diversity in Australia*, edited by Robyn Hartley. St Leonards: Allen & Unwin in Association with the Australian Institute of Family Studies, 1995.

Van Boeschoten, R. "When Difference Matters: Sociopolitical Dimensions of Ethnicity in the District of Florina." In *Macedonia: The Politics of Identity and Difference*, edited by Jane K. Cowan. London: Pluto Press, 2000.

Vermeulen, Hans. *The Ethnic Identities of European Minorities: Theory and Case Studies*, edited by Bruno Synak. Gdanskiego: Wydawnictwo Uniwersytetu 1995.

CHAPTER 11

Negotiating Trauma and Cultural Dislocation Through Memory: South Sudanese in Western Sydney

Atem Atem

In the preface of his book *On Collective Memory*, Maurice Halbwachs tells the story of a young girl found in a forest.[1] She was from an unknown, faraway place and she found herself in a strange country where people she came in contact with did not share her past, a past that she herself had to piece together from fragmentary recollections. The point Halbwachs is making is that memory is dependent on the social environment and context in which one remembers. He recognizes that migration has important implications on memory, especially if the new country is socially, culturally and linguistically different from that of the original country of migration. How do migrants, in migration nations like Australia, reconstruct the past? How is collective memory reconstructed, especially when migration is forced? How is such reconstructed memory used to navigate the new context?

South Sudanese migrated to Australia in the late 1990s and the early 2000s, with arrivals peaking in 2004.[2] Their migration was driven by civil

A. Atem (✉)
Australian National University, Canberra, ACT, Australia
e-mail: atem.atem@anu.edu.au

© The Author(s) 2019
K. Darian-Smith, P. Hamilton (eds.), *Remembering Migration*,
Palgrave Macmillan Memory Studies,
https://doi.org/10.1007/978-3-030-17751-5_11

155

war in Sudan that led to the displacement and cultural dislocation of millions of South Sudanese.[3] Prior to coming to Australia, South Sudanese lived in different parts of Sudan before crossing borders into neighbouring countries to seek refuge. The subjects I interviewed for this research, which was done as part of my doctoral thesis in 2011, told me that they lived in Khartoum and surrounding displaced camps in the northern part of Sudan; others lived in Egypt, Ethiopia, Uganda and Kenya, either as urban or camp refugees.[4] Many South Sudanese children, born just before or during this time of upheaval, are now adults living in Australia. They comprise the majority of Australia's small South Sudanese community of more than 20,000 people, and most now have their own families.

Here I explore how South Sudanese migrants in western Sydney who experienced forced migration actively engage with the past to make sense of the present. These South Sudanese came to Australia between 1996 and 2007 through Australia's generous humanitarian programme.[5] Humanitarian entrants to Australia are generally seen as traumatized and helpless people who must be looked after through settlement support services to help them adjust to life during the first five years of their settlement.[6] In addition, while Australia is a multicultural society, it requires all migrants from non-English-speaking backgrounds (NESB) to learn to speak English and to adopt Australian "core values" that are predominantly Anglo-Celtic in nature.[7] While all migrants have to deal with institutions that are British in origin, they are also expected to conform to multicultural policies which encourage migrant communities to maintain their cultural identities. Current equality policies require agencies receiving funding from the government to address barriers based on culture, religion or language to enable access to migrants.[8] However, this is within a broader Anglo-conformity, as defined by Milton Gordon, which assumes that British institutions and culture are maintained, including the use of the English language and culture as the dominant standard.[9]

To investigate the way South Sudanese migrants in Australia deploy memory, I draw on Aleida Assmann's thesis that memory is a social but dynamic process.[10] I also keep in mind Michael Rothberg's notion that memory in a multicultural society is multidirectional, and a process that is influenced not only by its social context but by the major political events and narratives that seem to have no relation to it. At the same time, narratives based on memory influence the way other historical events are memorized and constructed.[11] In this sense, memory, like identity, is malleable and borrows, reacts to and interacts with its current context. In addition to the interviews, I employed participant observation as a method of data collection.[12] Given that I was a South Sudanese man myself, the participant observation approach allowed me to take part in community activities as a member of the community, and as a researcher. My analysis follows grounded theory analytical techniques as suggested by Juliet Corbin and Anselm Strauss.[13]

The Dynamics of Memory and South Sudanese Stories

Assmann argues that the dynamics of memory can be understood by identifying the dimensions of memory and fleshing out their components. The first dimension of memory is neural memory, which is dominated by the nervous system and operates at the individual level. The prevailing social setting provides the environment in which memory operates. Individuals support memory through deploying strategies such as repetition, anecdotalization and media recording. The second dimension is social memory, carried by social groups. The group is thus the site where such memory is archived. Individual members of the social group constitute the environment through which memories of collective experience are shared, with symbolic media supporting such social memory. The final dimension of memory in Assmann's schema is cultural memory, transmitted through the practices passed down from one generation to another, including symbols, artefacts, practices, rituals and institutions. Group identity is crafted through these elements that are passed on intergenerationally, with individuals engaging in these practices in creative ways, and changing them for a new generation's purpose.

Assmann's approach underpinned my fieldwork with the South Sudanese. I was already familiar with members of this community, and many of the people I interacted with during my fieldwork were relatives, friends or family friends. The fieldwork was conducted within a community where I was well known through family networks and active engagement as an advocate for South Sudanese over the years. I was interested in critically observing community processes that I would otherwise take for granted. I wanted to make the familiar strange and to problematize these processes through continuous participation, observation and questioning.

I asked how South Sudanese migrants in Sydney talk about their experiences of living in the western suburbs of Sydney, in particular how they see the past and link it to the present. One of the avenues that allowed me to do this was to attend various social events, focusing on the stories that my peers told as they socialized. I was also interested in how these stories were reflected in more formal settings, such as when South Sudanese community leaders speak to authorities on behalf of their constituency. Finally, I wanted to find out how these ideas were institutionalized in the South Sudanese community. Most of my interlocutors were men who have a dominant position in the Sudanese culture, so these were largely masculine stories. Some South Sudanese women also took on these narratives as part of their ethnic identity and matched them with stories of their own experiences. At other times, they shared stories which came from their female ancestors with other women.

I started fieldwork just a few weeks after South Sudan gained independence, on 11 July 2011. At the events I attended in celebration of this momentous occasion, stories of struggle for independence dominated. Individuals spoke proudly of the role they played supporting the liberation movement. For many men, the stories revolved around their participation in war as freedom fighters, sacrificing their youth and losing their families, and of their own suffering. South Sudanese women spoke about their contribution to the liberation movement through their invaluable work that supported the war. They carried ammunitions on their heads and backs. They cooked and carried food supplies for long distances, sometimes over many days. However, they were most proud of the role they played in bringing up children in displaced persons and refugee camps while the men were away in war.

Not all South Sudanese migrants in Australia participated in the war. Indeed, as a result of the conflict, a large proportion came to Australia without direct involvement in the war or time spent in the bush. Instead, they lived in the northern part of Sudan, sought refuge in Egypt and finally migrated to Australia. South Sudanese who went to the bush sometime viewed this cohort as being not "authentic" South Sudanese.[14] The experience of suffering and trauma as a result of direct participation in the war and living in the bush had become important components of South Sudanese identity. Those who did not experience the war and the bush directly, although they suffered in different ways, were expected to compensate for this absence in their life stories. The independence of South Sudan and the accompanying celebration events provided an opportunity for the telling of stories of trauma and suffering. Those who did not share these experiences were given the opportunity to learn about them, and in turn to internalize them and retell them as if they themselves had been there.

The memories also provided the opportunity for groups in private settings to reflect on being South Sudanese and belonging to South Sudanese culture. My peers almost always told stories of life before the war, and this became an important temporal marker of "before" and "after" in their identity and storytelling. The free, but difficult, life on cattle camps was narrated with a passion. Other South Sudanese told stories of villages where crops were grown, an equally challenging experience. Even those who were children at the time told of significant events, such as cattle camp moves. They also told stories about the great wrestling contests that took place in the camps, and named the heroes who won them. They invoked the names of other significant figures, recalled verses of traditional songs and put on show their language skills in their mother tongue.

South Sudanese who did not have experiences of war, of cattle camps, or did not possess traditional language skills were perceived as lost and without credibility in the community. To combat this perception, such individuals learnt stories of the war and of the cattle camps, and retold them as if they had first-hand experience of these times. This was the means by which the community formed a collective memory which was openly or silently agreed to by all, even though not all had experienced the events which were narrated.

In South Sudanese community events cultural knowledge was displayed to make a claim on identity as being collectively crafted. The idea of authenticity of cultural knowledge was strongly competitive between members of the group. Mastery of the mother tongue is strong proof that one's identity is firmly South Sudanese. Those who could remember stories from the past and could tell them were seen as authentic South Sudanese, and cultural custodians. At some events it was critical for speakers to demonstrate their knowledge of family genealogies and explain who was related to whom and how. At fund-raising events, songs were sung which displayed that the depth of cultural knowledge was still maintained. Negotiating marriages was another significant occasion during which cultural credibility was displayed. This required both cultural knowledge and linguistic skills, and a greater understanding of genealogical frameworks. This is the ultimate event for proving oneself as a custodian of traditional knowledge, and the ultimate model of South Sudanese identity.

The stories of suffering and the significance of cultural knowledge also form the basis on which South Sudanese humanitarian entrants received settlement support in Australia from the mid-1990s to the mid-2000s. Settlement services were driven by a trauma discourse that seeks trauma and suffering stories as the basis for support. South Sudanese were conceived of by the Australian settlement agencies as traumatized and helpless due to their pre-migration experiences of war, displacement and suffering. In addition, settlement support services were expected to demonstrate that they were culturally appropriate and had a good understanding of the culture of their traumatized clients. Members of the South Sudanese community were, therefore, employed by settlement support services as bicultural workers who were able to work directly with their own community in a culturally appropriate way. During my fieldwork, I was employed in such a role.

The trauma discourse and the emphasis on cultural appropriateness in settlement support delivery by the Australian government thus reinforce a particular South Sudanese collective memory based on war experiences. However, this emergent South Sudanese collective memory is subverted by the multicultural narrative of Australia that emphasizes Anglo-conformity. South Sudanese were expected to speak English and adopt Australian values as soon as possible. The former Immigration Minister Kevin Andrews explicitly made this point when he announced the reduction in the intake of African humanitarian entrants in 2007, and there has been more recent commentary on the supposed "failure" of the South Sudanese to integrate completely into Australian society.[15] Settlement support services were expected to enable South Sudanese to pick up the English language and Australian values within the first five years of arrival.[16] They were then expected to navigate mainstream systems in child protection, health care system, housing and employment. My interview data, however, indicated that South Sudanese struggle with the Anglo-centric nature of these institutions.

In this wider context, South Sudanese community leaders, by default, played the role of gatekeeping for the South Sudanese community. South Sudanese migrants in western Sydney expected their community leaders to protect their identity through sustaining the previously described trauma and cultural narratives, and they used these narratives to resist Anglo-conformity. This is a strategy learnt from other migrant communities that have settled in Australia. South Sudanese community leaders therefore insist that Australia is a multicultural society, and that their identity narratives had to take a central place in their engagement with authorities and institutions. This enabled them to access Australian government funding streams available to support the settlement of communities which base their vulnerability on trauma histories and cultural difference.

As a result of these contradictions in the Australian settlement policy—whereby humanitarian migrants are expected to assimilate while also receiving additional support based on their pre-migration trauma—there is an interplay between conforming to Australian values and resisting them in order to sustain a Sudanese identity. South Sudanese narratives are thus destabilized, and have begun to change and adapt to prevent the risk of identity loss. South Sudanese collective memory is being shaped and reshaped by more powerful forces beyond its control. Individual experiences of discrimination and exclusion in the Australian society fuel a post-migration collective narrative of identity, which re-enforces the South Sudanese sense of victimhood through trauma.

Memories and Identity

Unlike the little girl or the migrant children Halbwachs refers to, South Sudanese migrants in western Sydney find themselves living together in a group. Consequently, they embark on reconstructing a common collective memory. How do South Sudanese migrants do this? And how do they use this shared constructed collective memory to navigate life in western Sydney as they settle?

According to Halbwachs, memory survives in a social environment that nurtures it. South Sudanese, as shown, used independence celebration events and private group settings to communicate their experiences of war, suffering, trauma and life before the war. Assmann's social memory dimension suggests that the social group thus becomes an archive for memories. For South Sudanese, some of these memories come from different sources, including from abroad. South Sudanese migrants hear the stories, cross reference them and incorporate pieces of information in a process reflecting Assmann's third dimension of memory—cultural memory. Cultural memory involves a group adopting a collectively-agreed upon general memory so that particular narrative of events and their meaning is available to members of the group who have no connection to the events or settings that are being remembered. A large proportion of South Sudanese who have never experienced the bush or the village before the war were able to internalize them as if they were there in person.

The result of this is that South Sudanese collective memory is based on two themes. One is that trauma and suffering became the hallmarks of South Sudanese identity in western Sydney, and the experience of war, life in the bush as freedom fighters, displacement and extended anguish as the war years dragged on became firmly established. The other theme which became a significant element in the South Sudanese memory that signified cultural purity is related to remembering life before the war, especially village life. One also had to communicate effectively in the mother tongue, in order to tell stories about village life and culture. These stories were verified through communicating with South Sudanese who still lived in South Sudan or in other parts of the world. Thus, the evolving South Sudanese identity in western Sydney has a transnational character.

The themes of trauma and cultural identity that underpin collective memory for South Sudanese migrants in western Sydney coincide with Australian settlement support and multicultural narratives. They use the trauma and cultural identity narratives to challenge Anglo-conformity within multicultural Australia, and to maintain their own legitimacy as a distinctive cultural group. Through the reconstruction of collective memory, South Sudanese are able to gain some control over the settlement process that generally disempowers them.

The settlement process has thus become a struggle between maintaining a conservative, internally constructed and idealized identity which seeks to keep control within the community, and the outward orientation that conforms to the pressures of social integration. The struggle between older generation of South Sudanese and the younger generation is a symptom of this. For the older generation, maintaining South Sudanese cultural identity means upholding the integrity of the family, including the place of the male as the head of the family. Young people are expected to show respect, if not reverence, to their elders and honour their parents by accepting that they have ultimate control over them. For young South Sudanese, the situation is much more complex. They find themselves representing their community as they go out and about. They learn English faster than their parents' generation. They know very little about the civil war in Sudan and the associated traumas, and have no traditional knowledge or enough mother tongue skills to assert their cultural place in the community. They are also more likely to make use of institutions such as the police and child protection services to challenge the control of their parents over them.

The internal dynamics between the generations in the South Sudanese community are complex. Nonetheless, an evolving South Sudanese reconstructed collective memory, based on trauma and cultural identity narratives, still provides an opportunity for South Sudanese to navigate the settlement process in a way that works for them and allows them to make a unique contribution to the Australian multicultural society.

Conclusion

The reconstruction of collective memory is significantly influenced by its context. In the case of South Sudanese in western Sydney, the trauma and cultural sensitivity narratives incorporated in Australia's multicultural framework through the provision of settlement support services have enabled South Sudanese to reconstruct their collective community memory. The independence of South Sudan in 2011 provided a key moment in which trauma and cultural identity were revisited. South Sudanese who did not experience the war were given the opportunity to learn the narratives and reclaim their place in the community as authentic members.

For younger members of the community, constructed collective memory is problematic since they lack the necessary background knowledge and cultural skills. Rothberg argues that memory is multidirectional, borrowing and incorporating prevailing social, cultural and political ideals. Reconstructed collective memory for the South Sudanese is flexible enough to incorporate some aspects of the dominant Anglo-Australian culture. Over time, collective memory can become more open to the dominant culture, most particularly within the next generation of South Sudanese whose role and influence within the community are becoming more significant. At the same time, young people can also utilize collective memory as a way of resisting racism and discrimination, regaining some pride and taking control of their lives.

Notes

1. Maurice Halbwachs, *On Collective Memory*, trans. Lewis A. Coser (Chicago: University of Chicago Press, 1994), 37; for discussion on "collective memory" see Amy Corning and Howard Schuman, *Generations and Collective Memory* (Chicago and London: The University of Chicago Press, 2015), 1, 6.
2. David Lucas, Monica Jamali and Barbara Edgar, "South Sudanese in Australia: A Statistical Profile," *Australian Review of African Studies* 32, no. 2 (2011): 10–24.
3. Jay Marlowe, "South Sudanese Diaspora in Australasia," *Australian Review of African Studies* 32, no. 2 (2011): 3–9.
4. The fieldwork with the South Sudanese community in Sydney which forms the basis of this study was conducted between July and December 2011, and included community social gatherings, meetings and other events. I took audio recordings and made written notes. The records are currently

privately held. The PhD research titled "Settlement Experiences of Sudanese Community in Western Sydney" at the Australian National University is current.

5. Commonwealth Department of Social Services, *Sudanese Community Profile* (Canberra: Commonwealth Department of Social Services, 2007). https://www.dss.gov.au/sites/default/files/documents/11_2013/community-profile-sudan.pdf.

6. Mary Hutchinson and Pat Dorsett, "What Does the Literature Say about Resilience in Refugee People? Implications for Practice," *Journal of Social Inclusion* 3, no. 2 (2012): 55–78. Jay Marlowe, "Using a Narrative Approach of Double-listening in Research Contexts," *International Journal of Narrative Therapy and Community Work* 3 (2010): 41–51.

7. Gavin Jones, 2003. "White Australia, National Identity and Population Change," in Laksiri Jayasuriya, David Walker and Jan Gothard eds, *Legacies of White Australia: Race, Culture and Nation* (Sydney: University of NSW Press), 124–25.

8. See Andrew Theophanous, *Access and Equity in the Role of Commonwealth Government* (Canberra: Department of Social Services, 2014); Department of Immigration and Citizenship, *2012 Access and Equity Enquiry Report* (Canberra: Department of Immigration and Citizenship, 2012).

9. Gordon Milton, *Assimilation in American Life: The Role of Race, Religion, and National Origins* (New York: Oxford University Press, 1964), 88; for historic context see Jean Martin, *The Migrant Presence: Australian Response 1947–1977* (Sydney: George Allen & Unwin, 1978).

10. Aleida Assmann, *Shadows of Trauma: Memory and the Politics of Postwar Identity*, trans. Sarah Clift (New York: Fordham University Press, 2016), 9–23.

11. Michael Rothberg, *Multidirectional Memory: Remembering the Holocaust in the Age of Decolonization* (California: Stanford University Press, 2009).

12. Chava Frankfort-Nachmias and David Nachmias, *Research Methods in the Social Sciences*, 5th edition (London: Arnold, 1997), 282.

13. See Juliet Corbin, and Anselm Strauss, *Basics of Qualitative Research: Techniques and Procedures for Developing Grounded Theory* (Los Angeles: SAGE Publications, 2008).

14. Liisa Malkki makes similar observations about Burundi refugees in Tanzania. See Liisa Malkki, *Purity and Exile: Violence, Memory and National Cosmology among Hutu Refugees in Tanzania* (Chicago: University of Chicago Press, 1995).

15. Cath Hart, and Samantha Maiden, "Race to Point Finger of Blame," *The Australian*, https://www.theaustralian.com.au/news/inquirer/race-to-point-finger-of-blame/news-story/1e49ed9ad27f5240ebac8c9d5b7ee311; Andrew Bolt, "Who Let In the Sudanese? Amanda Vanstone,"

The *Herald Sun*, 22 December 2016, http://www.heraldsun.com.au/blogs/andrew-bolt/who-let-in-the-sudanese-amanda-vanstone/news-story/9497646aaac16f3fdfa11673d2a12ea4.

16. See Parliamentary Joint committee on Migration, *No One Teaches You How to Become an Australian: Report into Migrant Settlement Outcomes* (Canberra: Commonwealth of Australia, 2017).

BIBLIOGRAPHY

Assmann, Aleida. *Shadows of Trauma: Memory and the Politics of Postwar Identity*, trans. Sarah Clift. New York: Fordham University Press, 2016.

Bolt, Andrew. "Who Let In the Sudanese? Amanda Vanstone." *The Herald Sun*, 22 December 2016, http://www.heraldsun.com.au/blogs/andrew-bolt/who-let-in-the-sudanese-amanda-vanstone/news-story/9497646aaac16f3fdfa11673d2a12ea4.

Commonwealth Department of Social Services. *Sudanese Community Profile*. Canberra: Commonwealth Department of Social Services, 2007. https://www.dss.gov.au/sites/default/files/documents/11_2013/community-profile-sudan.pdf.

Corbin, Juliet, and Anselm Strauss. *Basics of Qualitative Research: Techniques and Procedures for Developing Grounded Theory*. Los Angeles: SAGE Publications, 2008.

Corning, Amy, and Howard Schuman. *Generations and Collective Memory*. Chicago and London: Chicago University Press, 2015.

Department of Immigration and Citizenship. *Access and Equity Enquiry Report*. Canberra: Department of immigration and Citizenship, 2012.

Frankfort-Nachmias, Chava, and David Nachmias. *Research Methods in the Social Sciences*, 5th edition. London: Arnold, 1997.

Gordon, Milton. *Assimilation in American Life: The Role of Race, Religion, and National Origins*. New York: Oxford University Press, 1964.

Halbwachs, Maurice. *On Collective Memory*, trans. Lewis A. Coser. Chicago: University of Chicago Press, 1994.

Hart, Cath, and Samantha Maiden. "Race to Point Finger of Blame." *The Australian*. 2007. https://www.theaustralian.com.au/news/inquirer/race-to-point-finger-of-blame/news-story/1e49ed9ad27f5240ebac8c9d5b7ee311.

Hutchinson, Mary, and Pat Dorsett. "What Does the Literature Say about Resilience in Refugee People? Implications for Practice." *Journal of Social Inclusion* 3, no. 2 (2012): 55–78.

Jones, Gavin. "White Australia, National Identity and Population Change." In *Legacies of White Australia: Race, Culture and Nation*, edited by Laksiri Jayasuriya, David Walker and Jan Gothard. Sydney: University of NSW Press, 2003.

Lucas, David, Monica Jamali, and Barbara Edgar. "South Sudanese in Australia: A Statistical Profile." *Australian Review of African Studies* 32, no. 2 (2011): 10–24.

Malkki, Liisa. *Purity and Exile: Violence, Memory and National Cosmology among Hutu Refugees in Tanzania.* Chicago: University of Chicago Press, 1995.

Marlowe, Jay. "South Sudanese Diaspora in Australasia." *Australian Review of African Studies* 32, no. 2 (2011): 3–9.

Marlowe, Jay. "Using a Narrative Approach of Double-listening in Research Contexts." *International Journal of Narrative Therapy and Community Work* 3 (2010): 41–51.

Martin, Jean. *The Migrant Presence: Australian Response 1947–1977.* Sydney: George Allen & Unwin, 1978.

Parliamentary Joint Committee on Migration. *No One Teaches You to Become an Australian: Report into Migrant Settlement Outcomes.* Canberra: Commonwealth of Australia, 2017.

Rothberg, Michael. *Multidirectional Memory: Remembering the Holocaust in the Age of Decolonization.* Stanford, CA: Stanford University Press, 2009.

Theophanous, Andrew. *Access and Equity in the Role of Commonwealth Government.* Canberra: Department of Social Services, 2014.

CHAPTER 12

"I Leave *Everything*": Encountering Grief with an Hazara Refugee

Denise Phillips

Abdul is an Hazara refugee who fled Afghanistan. He is one of 64,422 asylum seekers whose arrival in Australia since 1999 has sparked bitter political controversy.[1] Hostile responses from some Australians to the arrival of asylum seekers are arguably shaping public memories across both refugee communities and the wider host population. Australian scholars and journalists have been interrogating current refugee issues,[2] and historians are now contextualizing these events within longer and broader migration histories.[3] Internationally, there have also been calls for refugees to be brought to the heart of historical studies and for their human experiences to be fully recognized. A key concern is that refugees are frequently cast not as individuals but as voiceless victims or a threatening mass.[4] There is a need, as Klaus Neumann argues, to foster social inclusion by including "the histories and memories of resettled refugees" within our understanding of Australia's diverse heritage.[5] The stories of some refugees and asylum seekers in Australia have been told in important biographical, creative or documentary formats, but often without analysis of their memories.[6] Additionally, loss—frequently

D. Phillips (✉)
University of New England, Armidale, NSW, Australia
e-mail: dphilli3@myune.edu.au

© The Author(s) 2019
K. Darian-Smith, P. Hamilton (eds.), *Remembering Migration*,
Palgrave Macmillan Memory Studies,
https://doi.org/10.1007/978-3-030-17751-5_12

167

168 D. PHILLIPS

traumatic in nature— is a core element of displacement, but historians have given little scholarly attention to refugee grief, nor to the relationships between memory and such emotions.

This chapter addresses these gaps, and in doing so brings to the fore the little-known history of the Hazara community in Australia. Firstly, it tells parts of Abdul's story. It locates Abdul's experiences in the long history of warfare in Afghanistan, and then traces the loss of loved ones and personal aspirations that he suffered as a result of persecution and conflict, and discusses his experiences of flight and resettlement. Secondly, through analysing oral history interviews conducted with Abdul, it shares the difficult process of encountering his grief and examines his use of silence, metaphor and existential reflections to communicate his story and manage his sorrow.

I have discussed elsewhere how trauma and a persecuted identity shape remembering, forgetting and particular emphases in the memories of Hazara refugees.[7] Here, I am engaging with Hazaras' memories of forced migration in a different form, through that of the single story. Traumatic experiences can be difficult to form into coherent or chronological narratives,[8] and Abdul and I worked collaboratively to reflect on and record his life story for historical purposes. While the hardships suffered by Abdul resonate with those expressed by other Hazara refugees, I recognize the limitations of a single story and this exploration does not claim to be representative of all. This chapter invites empathetic imagining of the lived experience, and seeks a role in countering or adding to Australia's understanding of its recent refugee arrivals. Abdul's testimony is part of a larger study of Hazara refugees' experiences of loss and hope. Oral history enables in-depth and sensitive engagement with such stories, and provides interdisciplinary concepts to examine the ways memory is subjectively constructed.

To deepen understanding of the dialogic tensions at play in Abdul's interview, I have adapted a concept described as "breaking the frame" from oral historian Yvette J. Kopijn.[9] She argues that Western research frameworks often dominate communication styles when non-Western groups are being studied, and the interviewer may instead need to yield to the narrator's social conventions for speaking.[10] Other frameworks come into play for individuals relating painful memories. Terrence Des Pres identifies one of these mechanisms as "detachment" which enables trauma survivors to remain "at a distance from self-pity."[11] Abdul manages his memories which inflict pain by giving whatever details he can bear to speak of—and these are usually minimal—and then retreating from a linear narrative. He turns to existential reflections and places his experiences in broader contexts.

About Abdul

Abdul belongs to the ethnic Hazaras, a group suffering more than a century of ethnic and religious persecution.[12] As most are Shiite Muslims, Hazaras are a significant minority among the Sunni Muslim population of Afghanistan and have been targeted as infidels by militant groups particularly since the 1990s. Abdul was born in the Hazarajat, and during Afghanistan's Soviet-backed rule, his family began experiencing intimidation. His brother and father were killed in separate incidents. Warned that his life was also endangered, Abdul escaped with people smugglers through Iran, Malaysia and Indonesia. His journey from Indonesia to Australia in 2001 ended in tragedy at sea. From 2001 to 2004, he was detained in Australia's offshore immigration processing centre on Nauru. When resettled in Australia, he spent three years on a Temporary Protection Visa (TPV) before gaining permanent protection and then citizenship in 2008.

I conducted three interviews with Abdul: two in 2005 and a third in 2012.[13] In the 2005 interviews, he feared speaking and gave only a collective account of Hazaras' persecution. Although I came to know Abdul well over seven years, in that time he barely spoke about his family. I listened closely when we talked informally, but refrained from questions, as his memories were shrouded in sorrow. Gaining newfound security as a citizen, Abdul then publicly commented on Australia's refugee policies and chose to tell his life story in the third interview with me. The boundaries around parts of his story loosened: he revisited childhood memories, discussed his life as a refugee and revealed glimpses of his inwardly-held trauma.

Political upheaval forms the backdrop to Abdul's youth. The 1978 overthrow of Afghanistan's president and the 1979 Soviet invasion plunged the nation into turmoil. Existing power structures fell and Mujahideen rallied against the occupying Russians and the new communist regime. While communism brought the prospect of greater equity for Hazaras, many in the Hazarajat came to abhor its radical reforms and were mistreated by the regime's party members.[14] Hazaras rebelled and reclaimed most of the Hazarajat by mid-1979, and established a *shura*, a council, to transform the region into a proto-state. But deep divisions saw Hazaras form rival Mujahideen factions and engage in internecine power struggles.[15]

Abdul's narrative sketches out how this conflict disrupted his youth. Excelling in science, mathematics and geography, Abdul dreamt of becoming a doctor or an electrical engineer. However, while declining to discuss his family's political views, Abdul recalls that his family were given "terrible problem[s]" because some deemed his school communist.[16] Public schools were especially condemned as tools of "Marxist indoctrination."[17] Abdul was captured and held in a mountain jail. When rescued, he relocated to Mazar-e Sharif in northern Afghanistan for almost two years. Harassment of his family continued, and they were accused of working for the communist regime and suspicions were raised about Abdul's absence. Fearful, Abdul's father summoned his return. Later, Abdul worked as a panel beater in Kabul, but warfare again saw him return home, where he helped his family grow food to survive. His brothers and uncles had held jobs which would have given the extended family "a good life," but he says "war destroyed everything, for, not just us, for all people around the country." Abdul also declined marriage prospects, asking how he could protect a wife and children with his own life endangered, and now sadly expresses that life alone is "not easy." The derailment of Abdul's education and early adulthood had lasting consequences, and he says, "I leave *everything* ... unfortunately I wasn't a lucky man."[18]

Abdul's father, after surviving several attacks on his life, was killed in 1996. Details are not given. Instead Abdul only says, "It was a lots of issues," and a mixture of sorrow, injustice and anger frames his memory. He reveals a private worry that the motive for the killing was "because I'm ... his son." There is little opportunity for me to ask more about his father. Abdul's voice weakens momentarily, and then he swiftly expands the discussion to vocalize disgust in those who justify crimes in the name of Islam, to condemn the lack of accountability for Hazara deaths and to speak of seeing a mass grave in his district's mountains. Abdul also raises the prospect of institutionalized persecution as he recalls the death of his brother while serving in the Afghan Army in the 1980s as it fought the broader Mujahideen resistance. Abdul tells that a fatal wound to his brother's head was consistent with being shot at close range rather than on a battlefield engaging an enemy.[19] The army was plagued by internal problems[20] and, although he cannot be sure, Abdul suspects his brother might have been shot by a fellow soldier because of his Hazara ethnicity. Abdul remembers his brother with admiration as a "very intelligent man." He recalls how an Hazara teacher working for the government in his district was shot and left to die alone after being asked "to fight with the Mujahideen." He laments that if someone could gain the trust of Hazaras in remote regions, they may begin to "open their mouth and they tell you what's happened to them."[21] The memories of his father and brother's deaths are marked by feelings of powerlessness. Abdul's seamless shift from the personal to broader injustices casts these topics as inseparable for him.

Breaking the Frame

The tragedy of his brother's death also includes the devastating effects on their mother—later compounded by Abdul's flight. In a snapshot of village life, Abdul uses a childhood memory as a metaphor to convey his sorrow in witnessing his mother's decline. He recalls the family's cow giving birth to a sickly calf, which did not survive. Worried that the cow would now not produce their much-needed milk, his family skinned the calf, then filled the skin with "wet grass." They returned this to the cow, propping it up like a calf, in the hope of stimulating lactation. But the cow gained the scent of her dead calf and repeatedly raised her head to the sky, exhaling in distress. Abdul's mother tended the cow. The cow finally put her head to Abdul's mother's "head [and] shoulder and cried." Abdul says, when "I saw that condition, I couldn't control myself. I start crying, crying, crying." Abdul told his mother he was "crying for the feeling of life" and for a mother's hardship when losing her baby.[22]

This memory has merged with that of leaving Afghanistan. After his father's death, growing threats to Abdul's life placed him "under pressure." In seeking his mother's permission to leave, she faced losing him through either his possible murder if he remained or his permanent relocation abroad. He "cannot forget that condition" of his mother and his words dissolve as he remembers her unassailable grief when parting.[23] The harsh significance of loss within Afghani society is likely to compound Abdul's distress. As Robert Canfield shows, losing a loved one can lead to extreme poverty and a fall in social status. A son ensures financial security, care and companionship for ageing parents, along with the esteem of having offspring.[24] Widows also face difficulties in going out into the community without a male chaperone.[25] Abdul's forced flight prevents him from caring for his mother in the traditional manner, leaving him anguished and wounding his sense of honour.[26]

While Abdul and I both wished to record his memories in order to shed light on Hazaras' experiences, speaking directly sometimes proved too confronting for him. The following excerpt reveals his attempt to talk about his mother and then his need to retreat. His voice tone drops and, with rhythm slowing, he says:

> When my brother has been killed, I saw my mum condition ...

> *And, and how was your mum? Was she, was she ever okay again or—?*
> No.

> *What happened with your mum?*
> She get skinny, very—

> *Hmm.*
> Not easy. ... when I left country to come to Australia, I cannot forget that condition when I see my mum. Because ... I wasn't safe on there and I *had* to leave the country. And when I said, "Mum, can you give me permission to go?," she just look at me ... and then she said, "I don't have another choice to say to you, if I say no, I may lose you. But I have to say yes." And when I said bye, goodbye to her, she couldn't stop. And just she fall back to the wall.

> *Abdul.*
> [Long pause.] Life have a challenge like this. ... not easy.[27]

Still distancing himself, he says some people enjoy life—laughing, pursuing money and being free of problems. But for those sensitive to human feelings, he repeats that life is "not easy." He re-positions his own tragedy as representative of many who have suffered: "There's not *a* story like myself in Afghanistan about Hazara people. There is a million, a billion, million story like this."[28] When we try to resume talking about his mother, his grief intensifies, he can no longer speak and he requests in a whisper that I refrain from this topic.

My questions, in spite of being gently asked, had broken the protective framework that Abdul implements in both the interviews and life. Abdul wept bitterly in silence. Tears streamed quietly down my own face. He chose to pause the interview and left the room to regain his composure; he had done the same during his earlier interview when remembering the 1993 massacre of Hazaras in Afshar, West Kabul.[29] The pattern of physically removing himself when distressed typifies his solitary management of grief. He also asserted *his* communication framework by rendering his mother a taboo topic, her fate remaining unspoken.

Smuggled: Confined Spaces and Tragedy at Sea

Abdul describes fleeing Afghanistan through a hazardous people-smuggling network. Abdul notes the moral dichotomy in the use of people smugglers, saying the smugglers are breaking international laws, yet without them, "hundred per cent I would have been killed." Sent from Iran to Malaysia, Abdul and others were then smuggled to Indonesia on a "tiny boat," imprisoned below deck. Finally, a smuggler took Abdul and others to board the *Sumber Lestari*, "an old Indonesian coastal trader."[30] Detailed reports of this boat's fate are given elsewhere, most notably in David Marr and Marian Wilkinson's *Dark Victory*.[31] Abdul recalls many coming on board, reportedly around 160.[32]

After the September 11, 2001, terror attacks, Australia's national security intensified. Both major political parties knew that angst within the Australian community over the arrival of boats, carrying mostly Muslim asylum seekers, could determine votes in the pending 2001 federal election.[33] The *Tampa* incident in August 2001 had seen the Howard federal government implement a policy that became known as the Pacific Solution, where asylum seekers who arrived on boats were sent to detention centres on regional island nations to have their status determined offshore. Operation Relex was underway too, with the Royal Australian Navy instructed to intercept and turn asylum seeker boats back, contrary to time-honoured maritime laws of aiding and protecting life on the high seas. In turn, some asylum seekers disabled their boats in a bid to be rescued and landed in safety.[34]

Over seven days, Abdul's boat encountered "crazy seas" and the captain abandoned the boat and its passengers as it neared Australia.[35] On November 8, two days before the federal election, the Australian Customs vessel *Arnhem Bay* intercepted the *Sumber Lestari* near Ashmore Reef and warned it "to turn back."[36] When it failed to comply, Abdul recalls that Navy personnel boarded the boat, ordering men below deck, and women and children to stay above. He did not know what occurred next, but recalls women crying and suddenly calling, "Fire. Fire."[37] That Abdul recounts this in a flat tone, with little dramatic inflection, shows the numbing effects of trauma.[38] Marr and Wilkinson report that an explosion came from the engine room, the boat was alight, and panic erupted. Navy personnel ordered passengers "to jump overboard," pushing those too afraid, while others grasped at them in terror.[39] Abdul was among those who jumped. The

174   D. PHILLIPS

asylum seekers were publicly accused of sabotaging the boat, but police investigations later found there was no consensus about the cause of the fire.[40]

The life and death experience he faced in the sea dominates Abdul's narrative. HMAS *Wollongong,* the Navy patrol boat, now faced a large-scale rescue with more than "a hundred people" floundering in the ocean. "Survivors ... clung to anything that floated" and some wore "cheap life jackets" which actually prevented them from "stay[ing] upright in the water."[41] Abdul describes his helplessness: "I wasn't good in the swimming. Just I had ... a small life jacket, and just I lied down like this and I said, '*God*. I cannot do anything, if you want to save my life or if you want me to die, that's everything in your hand.'"[42] He was rescued around sunset. His voice becomes soft as he recounts the trauma. Tragically, two asylum seekers died. Fifty-five-year-old mother, Nurjan Husseini, drowned. Twenty-year-old Fatima, wife of Sayyed Shahi Husseini, was retrieved from the water. Fatima and Sayyed had jumped from the burning boat, holding hands, but "the waves carried her away from Sayyed almost immediately." Searching for her, Sayyed later learnt she was dead, in spite of Navy personnel having desperately tried to resuscitate her.[43]

Abdul grieves Fatima's death. In the television documentary *Leaky Boat* Abdul says, "she was—," but grapples with emotion. When continuing, he says, "She was next to me and she was pregnant."[44] In my interview, he repeats with heaviness, "she was pregnant, she was very young" and "she was in front of me." He recalls Fatima crying and "screaming." Her proximity to him personalizes her death, and his emphasis on her nearness suggests he is troubled by being unable to help Fatima. At this point in our interview, a facsimile machine suddenly beeped in the room, breaking the intensity of our discussion. Abdul took this opportunity to turn to existential reflections, saying, "Denise, that's the life challenge ... what can we do?"[45]

NEWLY ARRIVED IN AUSTRALIA

After three years on Nauru, Abdul was resettled in Australia on a TPV. Those who arrived onshore without authorization, such as Abdul were denied full access to Australian resettlement services, an arguably punitive measure designed to deter more arrivals. These refugees faced hardships and possible removal from Australia when their visas expired.[46] Abdul gives insights into the lived experience of this policy. Significant in Abdul's memory is being destitute in a foreign land and the immediate need to find shelter. Community groups, churches and various state and local governments, although often under-resourced, stepped in to assist TPV holders.[47] Staff at the Romero Centre helped Abdul and others find short-term accommodation and hosted a welcoming barbeque which Abdul says made them feel "freedom" and happiness.[48] In his dire circumstances, it was the Australian community which provided hope and support.

Finding stable employment and learning English proved challenging for Abdul. TPV holders were denied access to federally supported English language programmes[49] so Abdul attended local centres to study English. In Afghanistan, Abdul had excelled in Dari language and wrote poetry, but struggled to resume his craft in Australia, unable to concentrate and feeling "all broken down from the life."[50] He mourned his homeland too, explaining an abiding sadness because a person's "country ... is like a mother for him," but now lost.[51] He redirected his grief into assisting those around him, often the vulnerable, and admonished others to care especially for their mothers. After several short-term jobs, he found steady factory work—a far cry from his earlier career hopes. Temporary protection also makes a sense of belonging elusive. Abdul confides that he was always feeling "nervous in the bottom of my heart" until receiving his Australian citizenship in 2008. The citizenship ceremony brought a turning point, with, "One of the best time in my life ... and happiest day," and allowing him to then share in the "freedom of human being ... [and] country," with the reassurance of security.[52]

SUFFERING, SILENCE AND SPEAKING

Hazaras in Australia regularly hear of the deaths of Hazaras abroad. At the time of our 2012 interview, a suicide bombing at the Abul Fazal Abbas shrine in Afghanistan had recently killed at least 56 people, mostly Hazaras.[53] I asked how Abdul copes with such news. He responds by recalling one of the few poems he wrote earlier in Australia, in which he says, "I'm smiling to the people" outwardly, and explains that, "I'm not showing my sadness" because he does not want to "make *them* sad." However, he reveals the angst expressed in private: "Many time ... I'm just inside my room, or ... I'm going away, you know, I'm just putting it out ... crying by myself. ..."[54]

The enormity of Hazara suffering overwhelms him. He asks what "crime" have Hazaras committed. His reliance on faith falters briefly as he questions why God has not intervened. Neither religion, nor history nor reason, can quiet Abdul's despair and he emphasizes that true humanity does not ignore the pain of others.[55] While I sometimes wanted to bring Abdul back from his philosophical reflections to details of his life, I learnt that digressions not only help him manage his distress, but they are also his story, revealing the moral codes by which he lives and the events that have shaped him.

Abdul had moved from silence to sharing personal memories. In 2005, Abdul said, "those hard memories ... stopped me to speak."[56] In 2012, he says his mental health is "okay" and he acknowledges the difficulty of "remembering," but adds, "if I can, I will tell you, doesn't matter for me." To explain further, Abdul cites a culturally familiar Hazaragi proverb which translates as: "When you're drowning, doesn't matter ... [whether] there's a metre of water or hundred metres water ... You're drowned already."[57] Abdul's life is already characterized by trauma, a type of drowning, and talking, he feels, would not worsen his circumstances. When I checked on his wellbeing after the interview, he reminded me of the aforementioned proverb and maintained his pattern of contextualizing his difficult life as one of many. Abdul had implored Australians to learn about Hazaras' persecution history[58] and reiterated that, "I want to say that much as I can."[59] Some silences remained. His purpose in sharing parts of his life story was to more broadly illustrate the plight of Hazaras. Although suggesting with good humour that he might lose memories with age, he recognizes the historical value of recording his story.[60] While Abdul and I shared a commitment to documenting experiences of injustice, his interview also prompts reflection on the process of gathering such memories. Encountering Abdul's grief deepened my awareness of the need to recognize the narrator's authority to recount their life story in their own way and, as Sean Field says, "to respect the speaker's right to silence and understand the reasons for and 'content' of these silences" when they occur.[61]

Conclusion

Abdul's story reveals a personal experience of flight from Afghanistan to Australia. Decades of warfare and persecution derailed his aspirations, brought family tragedies and saw him leave all he held dear to seek refuge. His life-changing losses are keenly felt in the present, and past traumas continue to haunt. Abdul's childhood memory of the cow losing her calf takes on renewed significance within the later context of his mother's catastrophic bereavement, becoming a metaphor for anguish he cannot directly articulate. The deaths at sea assume particular meaning, with grief for his mother possibly conflated with feelings of being unable to protect the young asylum seeker, Fatima, who died. While feelings of vulnerability under Australia's refugee policies and multiple traumas affected Abdul's wellbeing, he found support within the community and surety through citizenship.

I came to recognize Abdul's digressions, cultural metaphors, silence and contextualizing of his suffering as a protective framework in which he asserts himself and as a means of emphasizing that his story is but one among many. Abdul's hopes are now bound up in living peacefully and contributing to society, with the safety of his fellow Hazaras a constant but elusive wish. Finally, building oral history collections of the narratives of refugees like Abdul ensures that experiences of this phase of Australia's refugee history are recorded for present and future references, and helps bring refugee memories more centrally into Australian national histories.[62]

NOTES

1. Janet Phillips, *Boat Arrivals and Boat "Turnbacks" in Australia since 1976: A Quick Guide to the Statistics*, Parliamentary Library, Canberra (17 January 2017), 2. This number is an estimate based on arrivals from 1999 to 2016.
2. See Madeline Gleeson, *Offshore: Behind the Wire on Manus and Nauru* (Sydney: NewSouth Publishing, 2016); and David Marr and Marian Wilkinson, *Dark Victory*, updated edn (Crows Nest: Allen & Unwin, 2004).
3. See Claire Higgins, *Asylum by Boat: Origins of Australia's Refugee Policy* (Sydney: NewSouth Publishing, 2017); Klaus Neumann, *Across the Seas: Australia's Response to Refugees: A History* (Melbourne: Black Inc., 2015); and the special issue "'Boat People': The Long History of Immigration in Australia," *Journal of Australian Studies* 40, no. 4 (2016).
4. Jérôme Elie, "Histories of Refugee and Forced Migration Studies," in Elena Fiddian-Qasmiyeh et al. eds, *The Oxford Handbook of Refugee and Forced Migration Studies* (Oxford: Oxford University Press, 2014), 30; Tony Kushner and Katharine Knox, *Refugees in an Age of Genocide: Global, National and Local Perspectives during the Twentieth Century* (London: Frank Cass, 1999), 1; Arnold Zable, "Foreword," in Neumann, *Across the Seas*, vii.
5. Klaus Neumann, *Historians to the Fore, Or How to Inform a Much-needed Debate about Australia's Response to Refugees*, Australian Policy and History (October 2010), 9.

6. See Michael Green et al. eds, *They Cannot Take the Sky: Stories from Detention* (Crows Nest: Allen & Unwin, 2017); *Mary Meets Mohammad*, directed and produced by Heather Kirkpatrick (Hobart: Waratah Films, 2013); and Najaf Mazari and Robert Hillman, *The Rugmaker of Mazar-e-Sharif* (Elsternwick: Insight Publications, 2008).
7. Denise Phillips, "Wounded Memory of Hazara Refugees from Afghanistan: Remembering and Forgetting Persecution," *History Australia* 8, no. 2 (August 2011): 177–98.
8. Selma Leydesdorff, "When All is Lost: Metanarrative in the Oral History of Hanifa, Survivor of Srebrenica," in Mark Cave and Stephen M. Sloan eds, *Listening on the Edge: Oral History in the Aftermath of Crisis* (New York: Oxford University Press, 2014), 24, 26.
9. Yvette J. Kopijn, "The Oral History Interview in a Cross-cultural Setting: An Analysis of its Linguistic, Social and Ideological Structure," in Mary Chamberlain and Paul Thompson eds, *Narrative and Genre* (London: Routledge, 1998), 149.
10. Kopijn, "The Oral History Interview," 142–59.
11. Terrence Des Pres, "Holocaust *Laughter?*," in Berel Lang ed., *Writing and the Holocaust* (New York: Holmes & Meier, 1988), 229–30.
12. See Sayed Askar Mousavi, *The Hazaras of Afghanistan: An Historical, Cultural, Economic and Political Study* (Richmond: Curzon, 1998), 155–74, 111–38.
13. Abdul (with translator Chaman Shah Nasiri), interviewed by Denise Phillips, 14 May 2005, digital recording in author's possession; Abdul (with translator Chaman Shah Nasiri), interviewed by Denise Phillips, 25 May 2005, digital recording in author's possession; Abdul, interviewed by Denise Phillips, 5 February 2012, digital recording in author's possession. Location of interviews is suppressed. Abdul spoke in Hazaragi, a dialect of the Dari language, in the 2005 interviews and in English in the 2012 interview.
14. Brian Glyn Williams, "Afghanistan," in Assaf Moghadam ed., *Militancy and Political Violence in Shiism: Trends and Patterns* (New York: Routledge, 2012), 184; Niamatullah Ibrahimi, *The Hazaras and the Afghan State: Rebellion, Exclusion and the Struggle for Recognition* (London: Hurst, 2017), 117–18.
15. Ibrahimi, *Hazaras*, 117–75.
16. Abdul, interview, 5 February 2012.
17. Ibrahimi, *Hazaras*, 118.
18. Abdul, interview, 5 February 2012.
19. Abdul, interview, 5 February 2012.
20. Jerry Meyerle et al., *Conscription in the Afghan Army: Compulsory Service Versus an All Volunteer Force*, CNA Strategic Studies (April 2011), v–vi, 25–28.

21. Abdul, interview, 5 February 2012.
22. Abdul, interview, 5 February 2012.
23. Abdul, interview, 5 February 2012.
24. Robert L. Canfield, "Suffering as a Religious Imperative in Afghanistan," in Thomas R. Williams ed., *Psychological Anthropology* (The Hague: Mouton, 1975), 465–66.
25. Mark Eggerman and Catherine Panter-Brick, "Suffering, Hope, and Entrapment: Resilience and Cultural Values in Afghanistan," *Social Science & Medicine* 71 (2010): 75.
26. See Eggerman and Panter-Brick, "Suffering, Hope, and Entrapment," 78, 81.
27. Abdul, interview, 5 February 2012.
28. Abdul, interview, 5 February 2012.
29. Abdul, interview, 14 May 2005.
30. Abdul, interview, 5 February 2012; Marr and Wilkinson, *Dark Victory*, 350. Australian authorities recorded the *Sumber Lestari* as SIEV (Suspected Illegal Entry Vessel) 10. The SIEV 10 should not be confused with the SIEV X (the 'X' denoting unknown) which sank in October 2001, resulting in the deaths of an estimated 353 asylum seekers.
31. Marr and Wilkinson, "The Burning Issue," in their *Dark Victory*, 350–64. Also see *Leaky Boat*, directed and written by Victoria Midwinter Pitt, aired 7 July 2011 on Australian Broadcasting Corporation; Mary Edmunds, *A Good Life: Human Rights and Encounters with Modernity* (Canberra: ANU E Press, 2013), 10–16; and Susan Metcalfe, *The Pacific Solution* (North Melbourne: Australian Scholarly Publisher, 2010), 53–55.
32. Abdul, interview, 5 February 2012; Edmunds, *Good Life*, 10.
33. Dennis Shanahan, "Pandering to Basest Instincts," *The Australian*, 9 November 2001, 13.
34. Tony Kevin, "Remember SIEV X Before Waging War on Boat People," *Eureka Street* 20, no. 13 (16 July 2010): 35; Marr and Wilkinson, *Dark Victory*, 302.
35. Abdul, interview, 5 February 2012.
36. Marr and Wilkinson, *Dark Victory*, 350–51. Also see Abdul, interview, 5 February 2012.
37. Abdul, interview, 5 February 2012.
38. See Gadi BenEzer, "Trauma Signals in Life Stories," in Kim Lacy Rogers and Selma Leydesdorff eds, with Graham Dawson, *Trauma: Life Stories of Survivors* (New Brunswick: Transaction Publishers, 2004), 34–35.
39. Marr and Wilkinson, *Dark Victory*, 352–53.
40. Marr and Wilkinson, *Dark Victory*, 358–60. See Steve Gee and Malcolm Farr, "Boat Set Alight—Asylum Seekers Killed on Eve of Federal Poll," *Daily Telegraph*, 9 November 2001, 3rd edn, 1; and Michael Madigan, "Two Asylum Seekers Die as Vessel Torn Apart," *Advertiser*, 10 November 2001, 8.

180   D. PHILLIPS

41. Marr and Wilkinson, *Dark Victory*, 350, 353–54.
42. Abdul, interview, 5 February 2012.
43. Marr and Wilkinson, *Dark Victory*, 354–56, 363–64.
44. Pitt, *Leaky Boat*.
45. Abdul, interview, 5 February 2012.
46. Peter Mares, *Borderline: Australia's Response to Refugees and Asylum Seekers in the Wake of the Tampa*, 2nd edn (Sydney: UNSW Press, 2002), 4–8, 104–05; Refugee Council of Australia, "Temporary Protection Visas," *Policy Brief: Analysing Critical Issues in Refugee and Asylum Policy*, 24 September 2013.
47. Mares, *Borderline*, 194–95.
48. Abdul, interview, 5 February 2012.
49. Mares, *Borderline*, 193.
50. Abdul, interview, 5 February 2012.
51. Abdul, interview, 25 May 2005.
52. Abdul, interview, 5 February 2012.
53. Ernesto Londoño, "Pakistani Group Claims Role in Kabul Attack," *Washington Post*, 7 December 2011, A.1.
54. Abdul, interview, 5 February 2012.
55. Abdul, interview, 5 February 2012.
56. Abdul, interview, 25 May 2005.
57. Abdul, interview, 5 February 2012.
58. Abdul, interview, 25 May 2005.
59. Abdul, interview, 5 February 2012.
60. Abdul, interview, 5 February 2012.
61. Sean Field, "Beyond 'Healing': Trauma, Oral History and Regeneration," *Oral History* 34, no. 1 (Spring 2006): 33.
62. I sincerely thank Abdul for his courage to share his story and Janis Wilton for comments on an earlier draft.

Bibliography

Abdul (with translator Chaman Shah Nasiri). Interviewed by Denise Phillips, 14 May 2005. Digital recording in author's possession.

Abdul (with translator Chaman Shah Nasiri). Interviewed by Denise Phillips, 25 May 2005. Digital recording in author's possession.

Abdul. Interviewed by Denise Phillips, 5 February 2012. Digital recording in author's possession.

BenEzer, Gadi. "Trauma Signals in Life Stories." In *Trauma: Life Stories of Survivors*, edited by Kim Lacy Rogers and Selma Leydesdorff, with Graham Dawson, 29–44. New Brunswick: Transaction Publishers, 2004.

"'Boat People': The Long History of Immigration in Australia." *Journal of Australian Studies* 40, no. 4 (2016).

Canfield, Robert L. "Suffering as a Religious Imperative in Afghanistan." In *Psychological Anthropology,* edited by Thomas R. Williams, 465–86. The Hague: Mouton, 1975.

Des Pres, Terrence. "Holocaust *Laughter?*" In *Writing and the Holocaust,* edited by Berel Lang, 216–33. New York: Holmes & Meier, 1988.

Edmunds, Mary. *A Good Life: Human Rights and Encounters with Modernity.* Canberra: ANU E Press, 2013.

Eggerman, Mark, and Catherine Panter-Brick. "Suffering, Hope, and Entrapment: Resilience and Cultural Values in Afghanistan." *Social Science & Medicine* 71 (2010): 71–83.

Elie, Jérôme. "Histories of Refugee and Forced Migration Studies." In *The Oxford Handbook of Refugee and Forced Migration Studies,* edited by Elena Fiddian-Qasmiyeh, Gil Loescher, Katy Long and Nando Sigona, 23–35. Oxford: Oxford University Press, 2014.

Field, Sean. "Beyond 'Healing': Trauma, Oral History and Regeneration." *Oral History* 34, no. 1 (Spring 2006): 31–42.

Gee, Steve, and Malcolm Farr. "Boat Set Alight—Asylum Seekers Killed on Eve of Federal Poll." *Daily Telegraph,* 9 November 2001, 3rd edition.

Gleeson, Madeline. *Offshore: Behind the Wire on Manus and Nauru.* Sydney: NewSouth Publishing, 2016.

Green, Michael, André Dao, Angelica Neville, Dana Affleck, and Sienna Merope eds. *They Cannot Take the Sky: Stories from Detention.* Crows Nest: Allen & Unwin, 2017.

Higgins, Claire. *Asylum by Boat: Origins of Australia's Refugee Policy.* Sydney: NewSouth Publishing, 2017.

Ibrahimi, Niamatullah. *The Hazaras and the Afghan State: Rebellion, Exclusion and the Struggle for Recognition.* London: Hurst, 2017.

Kevin, Tony. "Remember SIEV X Before Waging War on Boat People." *Eureka Street* 20, no. 13 (16 July 2010): 35–37.

Kirkpatrick, Heather (Director and Producer). *Mary Meets Mohammad.* Hobart: Waratah Films, 2013.

Kopijn, Yvette J. "The Oral History Interview in a Cross-cultural Setting: An Analysis of Its Linguistic, Social and Ideological Structure." In *Narrative and Genre,* edited by Mary Chamberlain and Paul Thompson, 142–59. London: Routledge, 1998.

Kushner, Tony, and Katharine Knox. *Refugees in an Age of Genocide: Global, National and Local Perspectives during the Twentieth Century.* London: Frank Cass, 1999.

Leydesdorff, Selma. "When All is Lost: Metanarrative in the Oral History of Hanifa, Survivor of Srebrenica." In *Listening on the Edge: Oral History in the Aftermath of Crisis,* edited by Mark Cave and Stephen M. Sloan, 17–32. New York: Oxford University Press, 2014.

Londoño, Ernesto. "Pakistani Group Claims Role in Kabul Attack." *Washington Post*, 7 December 2011.

Madigan, Michael. "Two Asylum Seekers Die as Vessel Torn Apart." *Advertiser*, 10 November 2001.

Mares, Peter. *Borderline: Australia's Response to Refugees and Asylum Seekers in the Wake of the Tampa*, 2nd edition. Sydney: UNSW Press, 2002.

Marr, David, and Marian Wilkinson. *Dark Victory*, updated edition. Crows Nest: Allen & Unwin, 2004.

Mazari, Najaf, and Robert Hillman. *The Rugmaker of Mazar-e-Sharif*. Elsternwick: Insight Publications, 2008.

Metcalfe, Susan. *The Pacific Solution*. North Melbourne: Australian Scholarly Publishing, 2010.

Meyerle, Jerry, Nilanthi Samaranayake, Mike Markowitz, Lonn Waters, Hilary Zarin, Brian Ellison, Chris Jehn, and Bill Rosenau. *Conscription in the Afghan Army: Compulsory Service Versus an All Volunteer Force*. CNA Strategic Studies, April 2011.

Mousavi, Sayed Askar. *The Hazaras of Afghanistan: An Historical, Cultural, Economic and Political Study*. Richmond: Curzon, 1998.

Neumann, Klaus. *Across the Seas: Australia's Response to Refugees: A History*. Melbourne: Black Inc., 2015.

Neumann, Klaus. *Historians to the Fore, or How to Inform a Much-needed Debate about Australia's Response to Refugees*. Australian Policy and History, October 2010.

Phillips, Denise. "Wounded Memory of Hazara Refugees from Afghanistan: Remembering and Forgetting Persecution." *History Australia* 8, no. 2 (August 2011): 177–98.

Phillips, Janet. *Boat Arrivals and Boat "Turnbacks" in Australia since 1976: A Quick Guide to the Statistics*. Parliamentary Library, Canberra, 17 January 2017.

Pitt, Victoria Midwinter (Director and Writer). *Leaky Boat*. Aired 7 July 2011 on Australian Broadcasting Corporation.

Refugee Council of Australia. "Temporary Protection Visas." *Policy Brief: Analysing Critical Issues in Refugee and Asylum Policy*, 24 September 2013.

Shanahan, Dennis. "Pandering to Basest Instincts." *The Australian*, 9 November 2001.

Williams, Brian Glyn. "Afghanistan." In *Militancy and Political Violence in Shiism: Trends and Patterns*, edited by Assaf Moghadam, 181–200. New York: Routledge, 2012.

Zable, Arnold. "Foreword." In *Across the Seas: Australia's Response to Refugees: A History*, Klaus Neumann, v–x. Melbourne: Black Inc., 2015.

PART II

Migrant Heritage: Representation, Sources and Genres of Memory

CHAPTER 13

The Voices of Diversity in Multicultural Societies: Using Multimedia to Communicate Authenticity and Insight

Andrew Jakubowicz

Oral testimony and evidence have particularly important roles to play in exploring the history of multicultural societies, and enabling them to hear the voices of their diversity. While documentary and archival materials continue to provide extremely important evidence for historical interpretations, and these may be held in state collections, the majority culture rarely collects and preserves the perspectives of its minority cultures from their points of view.[1] Thus, in order to understand how colonizing and migrant societies such as Australia have evolved historically and how relations between its multiple communities have taken shape, the voices of its diverse peoples and their ways of framing the events and relationships they have experienced need to be foregrounded.[2]

Moreover, in the development of public history approaches to the communication of historical and sociological research, orally communicated accounts provide an accessible and emotionally nuanced contribution to capturing the dynamics under examination.[3] The standpoint that different

---

A. Jakubowicz (✉)
University of Technology Sydney, Ultimo, NSW, Australia
e-mail: Andrew.Jakubowicz@uts.edu.au

© The Author(s) 2019   185
K. Darian-Smith, P. Hamilton (eds.), *Remembering Migration*,
Palgrave Macmillan Memory Studies,
https://doi.org/10.1007/978-3-030-17751-5_13

186   A. JAKUBOWICZ

people with different experiences bring to their telling of the stories of which they have been a part disturbs the more taken-for-granted supposedly "objective" voice in which much history still tends to be told.

When the Australian continent was claimed for the British crown in the late eighteenth century, it became the location for a colonial and postcolonial society that had reached 25 million in population by 2018. Despite expectations among many European settlers that they would in time totally replace the Indigenous population, the original owners of the land remain and continue to demand recognition and rights. With the federation of the original British colonies in 1901 into the Commonwealth of Australia, the new national government swiftly passed the racially prescribed Immigration Restriction Act. The White Australia Policy, as it was known, continued for over seven decades, crumbling in 1972 as new values of egalitarian non-racism spread widely. In the wake of White Australia the national governments adopted a non-racial immigration policy and a multicultural settlement policy. Multiculturalism became bi-partisan policy at the national and state levels throughout Australia, despite many political struggles both to remove it and to protect its legacy.

As the child of Holocaust survivors, I grew up in the post-war enclave of Bondi in eastern Sydney during the 1950s.[4] Australia was a major receiver of Holocaust survivors, even though government policies became increasingly anti-Semitic through the late 1940s, with restrictive quota on Jewish immigrants reminiscent of the quotas against Chinese arrivals during the nineteenth century. Over 17,000 Jewish immigrants arrived in Australia from Europe and China by 1954, and another 10,000 by 1961, especially from Hungary. Bondi, about eight kilometres east of the city, with its many apartment blocks available for rent, became a centre for Jewish refugee residence in Sydney. Living in this environment, I was aware from an early stage that my experience differed substantially from that of my Anglo-Australian peers in a society where Jews were "not quite white". This was true, though affected by class issues both at my local state primary school and later at the more elite-focused primary and secondary school of Sydney Grammar. I was aware that in my Jewish religion class in primary school nearly all the children were from Holocaust survivor families, most with fractured kin networks. We shared the silences with which our parents often shrouded their answers to our queries about their pasts and our relatives.[5]

We were our community's first Australian-born generation; elsewhere in the school the children could narrate generations of settlement in

Australia, nannas and pops, cousins and relatives spread into the distances of far rural towns, other states or into the mainstream Anglo or Irish Australian heritage. While older Australian-born children might have lost fathers in World War II, we were born just a few years later—though for most of us most of our families had been lost in Europe. Just across the road at the Benevolent Society's Scarba House orphanage were other children without parents or other relatives. Our teachers, who were mainly older Australian-born women, had no real sense of our European Jewish families and their trajectories. Our Australian friends similarly had no sense of reference to our experiences, except later the "exciting" adventures retold in the line drawings of World War II battle comic books shared among pre-teen boys.[6]

My interest in the telling of stories and the building of mind pictures of the lives of others flourished in these circumstances. There is a photo from 1957 of my primary school third year class (Fig. 13.1), with our Chinese

Fig. 13.1 Changing faces of White Australia: Miss Jessie Wong's third grade class, Sydney Grammar Edgecliff, 1957 (author rear row second from left). Courtesy of Andrew Jakubowicz

Australian teacher Jessie Wong. Seven of the twenty boys are Jewish, with three or four being the children of refugee survivors. This photograph exemplifies a curious point of intersection, with the Jewish children sent to a non-denominational private school with the sons of landed families, military officers and senior public servants. I am squeezed between a boy who went on to be a security consultant and another who became a conservative rabbi.

From 1966, as an undergraduate at the University of Sydney I chose to study politics, economics and law, probably drawn by my mother's stories of studying business and politics in pre-World War II Poland, and the resource this provided as she assessed how the family might move to escape the Nazis and then escape Europe. When the opportunity arose in my politics study to use oral interviews to generate research data, I was immediately hooked. I began with a series of interviews about the Australian Labor Party (ALP), a realm of being and knowing that I had never encountered. I had just joined the ALP in Bondi, a fiefdom dominated by the Irish Catholic right wing faction, and a cluster of pre-war Jewish members. My research explored the working class industrial suburb of Balmain on the other side of the city, where new class activists (the so-called gentrifiers) were challenging the old guard ALP Right and forming alliances with working class radicals. My first interviewees were Nick Origlass and Izzy Wyner, two former Trotskyist ("Trot") unionists who had become leaders in internecine ALP struggles between the forward-looking advocates of the gentrification of Balmain in the 1960s, and the old Irish Catholic stalwarts of the ALP.[7] Their interviews were balanced for me by a meandering conversation with former Depression-era Labor state Premier Jack Lang, who sketched out the way in which the ALP had responded to the challenges from radical leftist groups and conservative parties.

From Balmain I moved into a research project exploring the run-down and definitely then ungentrified inner-city suburb of Redfern. My interviewees were local residents, members of the local Aboriginal football team, local politicians, community professionals and activists in the mainly Southern and Eastern European refugee and immigrant communities.[8] Redfern was adjacent to the University of Sydney, and many students also lived there among the decaying terraces and receding industrial sites.

For the first time I used video to record some interviews, then editing the video with my interviewees to produce a conjointly composed narrative. Like my fellow university students involved in struggles over the removal of local populations and the demolition of older suburbs like Redfern, I used the then new technology produced by Sony, the half inch reel-to-reel black and white videotape, which was cumbersome but mobile enough. This was soon supplanted by the more mobile Portapak, which had been used in Canada in the National Film Board's "Challenge for Change" project, our inspiration.[9] Based on the skills developed in these political contexts, I used the technology to document the lives and perspectives of local inner-city residents. The idea was to use these interviews to help the process of community development, and as a way of opening communication between Indigenous, migrant and old Australian families.

In the late 1960s, the planning and political discourses of the state presented the inner urban areas of Sydney as slums that needed clearance, with those living there as inert or criminal.[10] The personal stories of these residents were either by-passed or presented in terms of inevitable consequences of modernity and change. However, as I collected the stories, with only a few on video, and interacted with the people who lived in Redfern, I began to understand the landscape as a terrain peopled with thousands of intertwined though separate narratives of self, each trailing a trajectory that provided an explanation and an account of their lives. There were men who had escaped across the border from Yugoslavia, coming as loners to Sydney's overcrowded boarding houses, gambling clubs and encounters with mental health workers; women from Lebanon keeping house for husbands never home and children often ill; young Aboriginal men down from the country finding comfort among kin and searching for respect and status in a racist milieu. The well-established tenants of the often run-down houses had lived through decades of economic depression, war, recovery, redevelopment and now waves of new immigration.

While I did not speak Serbo-Croatian, Greek or Arabic, the broken English of my interviewees and the occasional support from bilingual welfare workers helped to flesh out a deeper account of their lives than that put together by the clichéd tabloid press, or documentarists driven by the dramatic turn designed to awe their distant suburban audiences. As a sociologist, I used survey and statistical data, but these methods seemed dry and thin without their accompanying oral narrative. The interviews that I collected in Redfern at the time, and indeed for many decades of research thereafter, both generated hard evidence about particular "social facts"— housing, employment, social interaction, well-being—and provided a range of individual and collective world views that were silenced in standard descriptions in sociological texts and the mainstream news media.

190   A. JAKUBOWICZ

Increasingly, I grasped how "reality" was a mental construct fed by the process of selection, while boosted by the appetites of the researcher for complex and nuanced layers of telling.[11]

The Digital Turn: *Making Multicultural Australia*

The advent of digital media opened up ways of both recording and using oral historical material, and led to my work on *Making Multicultural Australia* (MMA), a social documentary project,[12] which I steered from the late 1980s for over thirty years. The recording of oral accounts in MMA exemplifies how memory can be elicited and retained, while also being processed and utilized to propose and challenge the mainstream writing of history. The project became possible with the widespread utilization of digital recording (especially the CD-ROM), which meant that the now smaller digital video cameras, the move from analogue to digital sound and digital photography could be used to create quite dense databases and multi-pathway search engines.

Multiculturalism as public policy had become institutionalized in Australia in the late 1970s, through the auspices opened up by the recommendations of the "Report into Post-Arrival Programs for Migrants", known by the name of its chairperson, as "The Galbally Report".[13] While reflecting on the first post-World War II generational wave of immigrants from Europe, the Report was released as large numbers of refugees from Indochina sought settlement at the end of the Vietnam War, while Muslim Arabs from the Middle East also sought sanctuary.[14] Even so, race and religion were barely discussed by Frank Galbally or examined as social questions, and were completely marginalized in his proposals, although the policy of multiculturalism would soon have to grapple with these issues. The MMA project was able in the 1990s to interview the politician who had commissioned Galbally's team, Prime Minister Malcolm Fraser, Committee chair Galbally and Committee member Francesca Merenda.[15]

With the uploading of the interviews, the MMA audience was able to listen to the tonal and intonal components of their narratives, responding to the stresses the narrators placed on words and phrases, understanding also thereby how hindsight had helped shape their accounts.[16] These personal stories explained the reasons why the Report was important for Fraser, Galbally and Merenda, and their imagined and real communities. Indeed, the oral histories revealed much about the different layers of perspective held by a prime minister from an elitist and privileged background with an empathy for the outsider, the Irish lawyer from the inner city who had grown up with immigrant children and became their advocate and an Italian woman from rural Queensland, interned as an enemy alien through World War II, who went on to become a voice for immigrant women.

The Galbally Report soon became the symbolic marker of the abandonment of the White Australia immigration restriction policy that had dominated Australian population politics from Federation until the early 1970s. However, the launch of the Report, and the implementation of its recommendations, faced increasing resistance from racial and religious conflict. The race question exploded when the large-scale immigration of Indo-Chinese refugees to Australia coincided with a period of economic contraction and rising unemployment, creating the circumstances in which racist populist ideology gained force. The well-known and conservative history academic Geoffrey Blainey argued in a public speech in 1984 (explored in an interview with him in 1986) that in effect multiculturalism was an elitist self-indulgence, producing a racially unrestricted immigration policy that accelerated the arrival of poor Asians to compete with unprepared poorer Australians in a contracting job market.[17]

By the late 1970s, these mainly Vietnamese arrivals were joined by poor Muslim and Orthodox refugees from the Arab world, particularly Lebanon.[18] Australia had received a continuing flow of refugees after World War II, including European Jews from China, Eastern Europeans fleeing the expansion of the Soviet Union, Hungarians, Czechs, Chileans and other South Americans, and would later receive Timorese, Bosnians, Africans and Rohingyas.[19] The MMA project sought to understand the experience of the earlier refugees, especially as increasing religious diversity had to be managed within the political discourses of the state. For the next thirty years or more some of these refugee communities encountered growing prejudice, often spreading from initial hostility to minorities within the groups who became involved in criminal activities ranging from drug dealing to sexual violence and murder.

Multiculturalism as public policy developed in lock step with the refugee arrivals from Indochina and the Middle East.[20] By the end of the 2000s discourses of criminality and social threat overlaid nearly all Australian media accounts of these communities. By that time too the MMA project had collected hundreds of oral interviews, produced a major three-disc CD-ROM interactive account of the development of Australia as a multicultural society and had translated its material from interactive disc to online database. While supported by the New South Wales

Education Department for fifteen years, it became the victim of a general streamlining of educational websites undertaken after that time by the conservative New South Wales state government. At the time of writing, *Making Multicultural Australia* remains an openly accessible online public compilation in Australia of the oral narratives generated by the multicultural innovations and the political challenges to them that followed. It continued to collect new interviews and documentation until 2012, and now exists as both archive through the National Library of Australia PANDORA Archive service and online through an Amazon server.

ONCE UPON A TIME ...: RESEARCHING, RECORDING AND BROADCASTING THE VOICES OF DIVERSITY

For a short period from 2010 to 2014, I became involved in a series of television documentary productions built on a pitch I had developed when first approached by the producers. One of their researchers had found on the MMA website my 2004[21] paper exploring the first generation of Vietnamese settlement in Australia, which I referred to as "quintessential cultures in collision". This became the skeleton on which the publicly funded Special Broadcasting Service (SBS) television series *Once Upon a Time in Cabramatta* (OUATIC) would be built.[22] The pitch proposed that in all immigrant settlement processes the beginning was a situation of chaos, and the first thing to get organized was crime (to which I would now add religion). It examined four dimensions of Vietnamese settlement in the western Sydney suburb of Cabramatta: the growth of the heroin trade and the role of young Vietnamese in it; the exploitation of Vietnamese women in the clothing outwork industry; the rise and fall of politician, gangster and murderer Phuong Ngo; and the emerging second generation of Australian-born Vietnamese, whose sights and capacities were focused on Australian society and its pathways to success.

The television series was to be built from interviews that were collected after extensive initial research. From oral histories provided by Asian Australian politicians such as Helen Sham-Ho and Thang Ngo, a world emerged of a community abandoned by police and government where the young criminal gangs, street smart, aspiring to power and consumer goods, had become exploiters of their own communities. The authorities it appeared had abandoned the local population to their fate, using the Cabramatta area as a dumping ground for heroin addicts and their suppliers.

The pattern of early immigrant poverty, exclusion and racism became evident from oral histories collected from some of the young people, survivors of the street gangs who had moved on. Their aspiration to have power not offered by the mainstream society provided motivation for the immersion in the rapidly expanding drug world. Their ethnicity, especially the Chinese Vietnamese youth who either had been members of triads in Saigon or were recruited into triads in Sydney, gave them advantages over some of the Anglo-Australian criminal networks, and even the Lebanese networks growing in nearby suburbs (covered in the second television series *Once Upon a Time in Punchbowl*). Often the young people, mainly men, had arrived in Australia without families and had to find their feet quickly in a society where they did not speak the language, for which they had little previous education, and in which violence and their capacity to use it stood them in good stead.[23]

In the 2004 article I had written on Vietnamese settlement, the key theoretical elements brought together research from the United States on migration with Australian data. Robert Park in Chicago in the 1920s had developed a model for the stages of settlement of new groups in immigrant areas, theorizing how assimilation might occur and what barriers could emerge.[24] The work of Robert Merton on *anomie* demonstrated the ways in which exclusion from socially sanctioned pathways for mobility drove some immigrants into developing alternative ways of defending identity and creating wealth to give access to consumer goods, ostentatious consumption and social status.[25]

Thus, when the SBS television series was starting to take shape, there was a subterranean narrative, described as "the multicultural theme", onto which the interviews were laid. We proposed that the Vietnamese were a community under attack from its own margins, unprotected by the "host" state, its ostensible older leadership still caught up in the post-war émigré politics of now communist Vietnam. This leadership had fled the new communist regime, against which their emotional attention was often focused, leaving them aghast but inert in the face of what they saw happening around them. Singular players like Phuong Ngo, owner of the Mekong Club, who had soon learned his way through the patterns of local corruption, police bribery and ways of extorting support from the local people, also had links into other political networks of influence and protection. His aspirations were for political power, achieved at the local government level, but thwarted in state politics. He was convicted of arranging the murder of the sitting member of the New South Wales state parliament,

194   A. JAKUBOWICZ

John Newman (born Johann Grauenig, later changed to Naumenko), a former trade union official, who had risen on the support of a previous generation of mainly Eastern European immigrants in the area. Newman had been a major opponent of the Asian organized crime gangs that had emerged.

Some Vietnamese, especially the new generation, refused to accept their abandonment by the state and organized politically to secure police attention and speak out against the media hyperbole and political corruption. The oral histories informed the television narrative and provided a significant component of personal insight and emotional impact into the conditions in Cabramatta. The interviewees were sourced by "mainstream" and local Vietnamese researchers. There was also a significant archival record to be utilized, particularly news footage of political and other players, also of police raids and the local area as documented during its height as a drug centre.

Using standpoint theory as a background to thinking about how Australian audiences could best approach the television material, I mapped a topology of the narrative arc.[26] The producers were anxious to connect with each of the major sectors of the audience, in ways that respected their perspectives but forced through divergent views. Authority would come from the authenticity of the speakers, not their official roles. Senior police, the local Anglo-Australian publican, the key politicians (Helen Sham-Ho and Thang Ngo), a former youth gang member, a former heroin addict and his parents, and other local residents were chosen as key subjects. They were interviewed a number of times, sometimes in Vietnamese, with the producers revisiting the interviews with me to test the narrative and look at how my commentary would be shaped by their contributions. The interviewees' use of language, summaries of events and perceptions, and reflections on their own experiences gave these oral histories an immediacy even a decade or more after the events being described.

The mass-audience television context for the OUATIC series determined that there would be an introduction of dramatic tension and a "resolution" to the crises analysed in the programmes. Even so, the Vietnamese participants all spoke in Vietnamese if they preferred, and there was a Vietnamese subtitled version of the series made available for those parts of the audience who did not speak English. This was the first documentary about the Vietnamese community in Australia that incorporated a sensibility of their presence as participants, through language and the employment of some Vietnamese "creatives".[27] Feedback from the Vietnamese communities was overwhelmingly positive, and many noted that the programme was the first time their story had been told with both comprehension and compassion. Moreover, OUATIC positioned the Vietnamese subjects in their own lives, and as "winners" when confronted by and pushing back against racist or indifferent "white" bystanders or officialdom.[28]

The most powerful segment in OUATIC series emerged from a sustained interview with a Vietnamese father whose son had been a heroin user in the late 1990s. The father describes cycle after cycle of trying to get his son off the drug, and the way in which his son was excluded from the few support and addiction programmes that then existed. He told how he tried to force his son into "cold turkey", by tying him to a bed, how impossibly traumatizing it was as a parent to watch his son's pain and how finally he bought illegal heroin that he administered in ever smaller doses to wean his son from the drug. This father relived his anguish, and these emotions were only relieved by the knowledge that he was in the end successful. The son fully recovered, but this was only when his heroin supply dried as a result of police action that broke up the triads and drug sellers in Cabramatta.

The personal experience of that world provided very moving oral testimony. For years, locals believed that the police had willingly left Cabramatta as a sink-hole where drugs could be sold, with the railway station a centre for heroin users coming and going from across the city. They also believed that because the suburb was mainly populated by Asian Australians, the government would not defend them from gangsterism. Government intervention was finally developed by the advocacy of Asian politicians. In the NSW Parliament, Helen Sham-Ho conducted an inquiry into the lack of effective policing in Cabramatta, while at the local Council level Thang Ngo rallied people to provide evidence and confront the gangs and their protectors. In the interviews with these two politicians, the slow and difficult process of gaining government revealed the self-serving and racist perspectives that underpinned years of political and law-enforcement inaction.[29]

LIGHTING UP THE DARK SIDE OF THE ROAD

The role of a documentary series that uses oral history to examine public events and their impact on private experiences builds viewer awareness and empathy.[30] Where the events under scrutiny are criminal, violent and painful, these stories and their resolution can reveal much about social power.[31] In a multicultural society, social cohesion depends on the social capital, its "glue" being made from trust.[32] Typically, multicultural societies demonstrate low levels of trust between neighbours who come from different ethnic groups and have limited capacity and opportunity to interact.[33] A multicultural and empathetic documentary consequently helps to build trust with mainstream audiences through the personalizing and deepening of existing stereotypical representations, demonstrating the sharing of values and anxieties, desires and aspirations between the interviewees and the television audience. By the end of the OUATIC series the audience has potentially moved from the distanced observers of a strange and threatening transformation of their putative neighbourhood, to engaged neighbours anxious for positive outcomes and understanding of the contradictory pressures that the refugees have experienced.

Oral historians who develop skills in audio-visual storytelling can contribute enormously to the impact of their research. Meanwhile, other series in which I have been involved which draw on similar insights into the value of oral history have included *Once Upon a Time in Punchbowl* and *Vietnam: The War that Made Australia*, and the produced but not released *Once Upon a Time in Carlton* (the story of Italian criminal communities in inner Melbourne and the Riverina district in rural New South Wales).

Two of the most widely respected historians who have worked on audio-visual histories, Americans Ken Burns and Lynn Novick, have long demonstrated through their intertwining of oral histories, archival materials and cinematographic excellence how effective such an approach can be. Reflecting on Burns and Novick's Vietnam War series, Michael Foley has concluded that it significantly misled its audience, by simplifying the analysis of the war and leaving the resolution only in an emotional vein, where the past should be allowed to "rest".[34] However, ultimately, there can be no rest, only consequences moving through time.

In developing histories in multicultural societies the voices of diversity are greatly enhanced through audio-visual approaches, be they broadcast documentaries or online interactive databases. Enabling those voices to be heard surely remains within the charge of sociologists and historians, where the audiences and the subjects are equally enabled to grapple with complexity, varied emotions and the demands of intellectual interpretation. In *Making Multicultural Australia* only two of the many hundreds of people interviewed have sought to remove or change interviews that we have used and made public. Down they came, however much we felt that they were valuable and should remain for the historical record. Our team did not have the "on the record" protection of journalists; rather, we are scholars, and the ethics of scholarly research gives subjects the freedom to remove themselves from the research up to the final point of irreversible publication, and sometimes even after that.

Over fifty years of researching cultural diversity in Australia, much of it using "new technologies" of the time, suggests to me that the richness of lived realities can be grasped more closely and transmitted very powerfully through authorizing research subjects to retain some control over their presentation of selves. Where we straddle that line, as in the *Once Upon a Time in Cabramatta* series, much remains hidden. But, that is for another chapter.

NOTES

1. Carol McKirdy, *Practicing Oral History with Immigrant Narrators* (New York: Routledge, 2015).
2. James Jupp, *An Immigrant Nation Seeks Cohesion: Australia from 1788* (London: Anthem Press, 2018).
3. Tim Carroll, "The Bankstown Oral History Project, a Multicultural Perspective," *The Oral History of Australia Journal*, no. 25 (2003): 53–55.
4. Suzanne D. Rutland, "Australian Responses to Jewish Refugee Migration Before and After World War Two," *Australian Journal of Politics and History* 31, no. 1 (1985): 29–48.
5. Ruth Wajnryb, *The Silence: How Tragedy Shapes Talk* (Sydney: Allen & Unwin, 2001).
6. Kathy Grinblat ed., *Children of the Shadows: Voices of the Second Generation* (Crawley: University of Western Australia Press, 2002).
7. Tony Harris, *Making and Unmaking the Labor Left in Leichhardt Municipality 1970–1991* (Newtown: Left Bank Publishing, 2007, 1969); Andrew Jakubowicz, "A New Politics of Suburbia," *Current Affairs Bulletin*, April (1972): 538–51.
8. Andrew Jakubowicz, "Changing Patterns of Community Organization" (Sydney University, 1969).
9. James Spigelman, "Film as a Social Action Tool," *Australian Quarterly* 41, no. 2 (1969): 74–80.
10. Peter Spearritt, "The Australian Slum Stigma," *Australian and New Zealand Journal of Sociology* (now *Journal of Sociology*) 9, no. 2 (1973): 41–45.
11. Hayden P. Smith, and Robert M. Bohm, "Beyond Anomie: Alienation and Crime," *Critical Criminology* 16 (2008), 1–15.

12. Jakubowicz, Andrew, "Making Multicultural Australia in the 21st Century," http://multiculturalaustralia.edu.au.
13. Alan Borowski, "Creating a Virtuous Society: Immigration and Australia's Policies of Multiculturalism," *Journal of Social Policy* 29, no. 3 (2000): 459–75; Australia. "Review of Post-arrival Programs and Services to Migrants, Chairman: F. Galbally," *Migrant Services and Programs: Report of the Review of Post-Arrival Programs and Services for Migrants* (Canberra: A.G.P.S., 1978).
14. Andrew Jakubowicz, Commentary On: The Galbally Strategy for Migrant Settlement, *Making Multicultural Australia*, http://www.multiculturalaustralia.edu.au/library/media/Timeline-Commentary/id/107.The-Galbally-Strategy-for-migrant-settlement.
15. Malcolm Fraser, "The Galbally Strategy for Migrant Settlement," audio recording, created 1994, *Making Multicultural Australia*, http://www.multiculturalaustralia.edu.au/library/media/Audio/id/396; "Migrant Services and Programs—Statement by the Prime Minister," *Making Multicultural Australia*, http://www.multiculturalaustralia.edu.au/doc/fraser_2.pdf; Frank Galbally, "Migrant Settlement," video recording, created 1994, *Making Multicultural Australia*, http://www.multiculturalaustralia.edu.au/library/media/Video/id/336.Migrant-Settlement; Francesca Merenda, "The Experience of Wartime Internment," video recording, created 2005, *Making Multicultural Australia*, http://www.multiculturalaustralia.edu.au/library/media/Video/id/814.The-experience-of-wartime-internment.
16. Andrew Jakubowicz, "The Galbally Strategy for Migrant Settlement: A Timeline Commentary," *Making Multicultural Australia*, 2004, http://www.multiculturalaustralia.edu.au/history/timeline/period/Multiculturalism-in-Practice/screen/2.The-Galbally-Strategy-for-migrant-settlement.
17. Andrew Jakubowicz, "The Blainey Debate on Immigration," *Making Multicultural Australia*, n.d, http://www.multiculturalaustralia.edu.au/history/timeline/period/Multiculturalism-in-Practice/screen/12.The-Blainey-debate-on-immigration; Frank Lewins, "'The Blainey Debate' in Hindsight," *Journal of Sociology* 23, no. 2 (1987): 261–73.
18. Frank Lewins, "The Significance of Factors Influencing Early Vietnamese Settlement in Australia," *Journal of Intercultural Studies* 5, no. 2 (1984): 29–48.
19. Klaus Neumann, *Across the Seas: Australia's Response to Refugees—A History* (Melbourne: Black Inc., 2015).
20. Hal Colebatch, "The Left Rewrites Its History on Refugees," *Quadrant* (October, 2010).

21. Andrew Jakubowicz, "Vietnamese in Australia: A Generation of Settlement and Adaptation/A Quintessential Collision: Vietnamese Identities in Modern Australia," *Making Multicultural Australia in the 21st Century* (2004), http://www.multiculturalaustralia.edu.au/doc/viet_aust.doc.

22. Thang Ngo, "Once Upon a Time in Cabramatta, SBS, 8th January 2012," *Noodlies.com* 2016, no. 15 (October 2011).

23. Paul Sheehan, "How the Politics of Sheer Populism Led to Racial Riots," *The Sydney Morning Herald*, 16 January 2006.

24. Robert Ezra Park, *Race and Culture* (New York: Free Press, 1950).

25. Robert K. Merton, "Social Structure and Anomie," *American Sociological Review* 3, no. 5 (1932): 672–82; Hayden P. Smith and Robert M. Bohm, "Beyond Anomie: Alienation and Crime."

26. Mark Orbe, "From the Standpoint(s) of Traditionally Muted Groups: Explicating a Co-Cultural Communication Theoretical Model," *Communication Theory* 8, no. 1 (1998): 1–26.

27. Karen Ross and Virginia Nightingale, *Media and Audience: New Perspectives* (Maidenhead: Open University Press, 2003).

28. Ghassan Hage, "Multiculturalism and White Paranoia in Australia," *Journal of International Migration and Integration* 3, no. 3 (2002): 417–37.

29. Thang Ngo, "Once Upon a Time in Cabramatta, SBS, 8th January 2012," *Noodlies.com* 2016, no. 15 (October 2011); Andrew Jakubowicz, "Empires of the Sun: Towards a Post-Multicultural Australian Politics," *Cosmopolitan Civil Societies: An Interdisciplinary Journal* 3, no. 1 (2011): 65–86.

30. Alistair Thomson, "Four Paradigm Transformations in Oral History," *The Oral History Review* 34 (2007): 49–70.

31. Diane Sivasubramaniam and Jane Goodman-Delahunty, "Ethnicity and Trust: Perceptions of Police Bias," *International Journal of Police Science & Management* 10, no. 4 (2008).

32. Michael Norton and Samuel Sommers, "Whites See Racism as a Zero-Sum Game That They Are Now Losing," *Perspectives on Psychological Science* 6, no. 3 (2011): 215–18.

33. Andrew Markus, *Mapping Social Cohesion: The Scanlon Foundation Surveys 2015* (ACJC, Faculty of Arts, Monash University, 2015). http://scanlon-foundation.org.au/wp-content/uploads/2015/10/2015-Mapping-Social-Cohesion-Report.pdf.

34. Michael Stewart Foley, "There Is No Single Lie in War (Films): Ken Burns, Lynn Novick, and the Vietnam War," *The Sixties: A Journal of History, Politics and Culture* 11, no. 1 (2018): 93–104.

200 A. JAKUBOWICZ

BIBLIOGRAPHY

Australia. "Review of Post-arrival Programs and Services to Migrants, Chairman: F. Galbally." *Migrant Services and Programs: Report of the Review of Post-Arrival Programs and Services for Migrants* (Canberra: A.G.P.S., 1978).

Borowski, Alan. "Creating a Virtuous Society: Immigration and Australia's Policies of Multiculturalism." *Journal of Social Policy* 29, no. 3 (2000): 459–75.

Carroll, Tim. "The Bankstown Oral History Project, a Multicultural Perspective." *The Oral History of Australia Journal*, no. 25 (2003): 53–55.

Colebatch, Hal. "The Left Rewrites Its History on Refugees." *Quadrant*, October (2010).

Foley, Michael Stewart. "There Is No Single Lie in War (Films): Ken Burns, Lynn Novick, and the Vietnam War." *The Sixties: A Journal of History, Politics and Culture* 11, no. 1 (2018): 93–104.

Fraser, Malcolm. "The Galbally Strategy for Migrant Settlement." Audio recording, created 1994. *Making Multicultural Australia*. http://www.multiculturalaustralia.edu.au/library/media/Audio/id/396

Galbally, Frank. "Migrant Settlement." Video recording, created 1994. *Making Multicultural Australia*. http://www.multiculturalaustralia.edu.au/library/media/Video/id/336.Migrant-Settlement.

Grinblat, Kathy, ed. *Children of the Shadows: Voices of the Second Generation*. Crawley: University of Western Australia Press, 2002.

Hage, Ghassan. "Multiculturalism and White Paranoia in Australia." *Journal of International Migration and Integration* 3, no. 3 (2002): 417–37.

Harris, Tony. *Making and Unmaking the Labor Left in Leichhardt Municipality 1970–1991*. Newtown: Left Bank Publishing, 2007; 1969.

Jakubowicz, Andrew. "Changing Patterns of Community Organization." Sydney University, 1969.

Jakubowicz, Andrew. "A New Politics of Suburbia." *Current Affairs Bulletin*, April (1972): 538–51.

Jakubowicz, Andrew. "The Galbally Strategy for Migrant Settlement." *Making Multicultural Australia*, 2004. http://www.multiculturalaustralia.edu.au/history/timeline/period/Multiculturalism-in-Practice/screen/2.The-Galbally-Strategy-for-migrant-settlement.

Jakubowicz, Andrew. "Vietnamese in Australia: A Generation of Settlement and Adaptation/a Quintessential Collision: Vietnamese Identities in Modern Australia." *Making Multicultural Australia in the 21st Century*, 2011a. http://www.multiculturalaustralia.edu.au/doc/viet_aust.doc.

Jakubowicz, Andrew. "Empires of the Sun: Towards a Post-Multicultural Australian Politics." *Cosmopolitan Civil Societies: An Interdisciplinary Journal* 3, no. 1 (2011b): 65–86.

Jakubowicz, Andrew. "Making Multicultural Australia in the 21st Century." n.d.-a. http://multiculturalaustralia.edu.au.

Jakubowicz, Andrew. "The Blainey Debate on Immigration." *Making Multicultural Australia*, n.d.-b. http://www.multiculturalaustralia.edu.au/history/timeline/period/Multiculturalism-in-Practice/screen/12.The-Blainey-debate-on-immigration.

Jupp, James. *An Immigrant Nation Seeks Cohesion: Australia from 1788.* London: Anthem Press, 2018.

Lewins, Frank. "'The Blainey Debate' in Hindsight." *Journal of Sociology* 23, no. 2 (1987): 261–73.

Lewins, Frank. "The Significance of Factors Influencing Early Vietnamese Settlement in Australia." *Journal of Intercultural Studies* 5, no. 2 (1984): 29–48.

Markus, Andrew. *Mapping Social Cohesion: The Scanlon Foundation Surveys 2015.* ACJC, Faculty of Arts, Monash University, 2015. http://scanlonfoundation.org.au/wp-content/uploads/2015/10/2015-Mapping-Social-Cohesion-Report.pdf.

McKirdy, Carol. *Practicing Oral History with Immigrant Narrators.* New York: Routledge, 2015.

Merenda, Francesca. "The Experience of Wartime Internment." Video recording, created 2005. *Making Multicultural Australia.* http://www.multiculturalaustralia.edu.au/library/media/Video/id/814.The-experience-of-wartime-internment.

Merton, Robert K. "Social Structure and Anomie." *American Sociological Review* 3, no. 5 (1932): 672–82.

Neumann, Klaus. *Across the Seas: Australia's Response to Refugees—A History.* Melbourne: Black Inc., 2015.

Ngo, Thang. "Once Upon a Time in Cabramatta, SBS, 8th January 2012." *Noodlies.com* 2016, 15 October 2011.

Norton, Michael, and Samuel Sommers. "Whites See Racism as a Zero-Sum Game That They Are Now Losing." *Perspectives on Psychological Science* 6, no. 3 (2011): 215–18.

Orbe, Mark. "From the Standpoint(s) of Traditionally Muted Groups: Explicating a Co-Cultural Communication Theoretical Model." *Communication Theory* 8, no. 1 (1998): 1–26.

Park, Robert Ezra. *Race and Culture.* New York: Free Press, 1950.

Ross, Karen, and Virginia Nightingale. *Media and Audience: New Perspectives.* Maidenhead: Open University Press, 2003.

Rutland, Suzanne D. "Australian Responses to Jewish Refugee Migration Before and After World War Two." *Australian Journal of Politics and History*, 31, no. 1 (1985): 29–48.

Sheehan, Paul. "How the Politics of Sheer Populism Led to Racial Riots." *The Sydney Morning Herald*, 16 January 2006.

Sivasubramaniam, Diane, and Jane Goodman-Delahunty. "Ethnicity and Trust: Perceptions of Police Bias." *International Journal of Police Science & Management* 10, no. 4 (2008).

Smith, Hayden P., and Robert M. Bohm. "Beyond Anomie: Alienation and Crime." *Critical Criminology* 16 (2008), 1–15.

Spearritt, Peter. "The Australian Slum Stigma." *Australian and New Zealand Journal of Sociology* (now *Journal of Sociology*) 9, no. 2 (1973): 41–45.

Spigelman, James. "Film as a Social Action Tool." *Australian Quarterly* 41, no. 2 (1969): 74–80.

Thomson, Alistair. "Four Paradigm Transformations in Oral History." *The Oral History Review* 34 (2007): 49–70.

Wajnryb, Ruth. *The Silence: How Tragedy Shapes Talk.* Sydney: Allen & Unwin, 2001.

CHAPTER 14

Oral History and First-Person Narratives in Migration Exhibitions: Tracking Relations Between "Us" and "Them"

Andrea Witcomb

This chapter charts the contours of how Australian museums have used oral history to represent the history of migration to Australia by tracing the intersections of oral history in museum collecting and documentation practices with the history of its presentation within exhibition practices.[1] Tracking the relations between these two distinct histories generates an understanding of the ways in which the increasing importance of personal narratives in the representation of migration histories has impacted upon the politics of the narrative structures of migration exhibitions. These impacts are also about the increasing importance of first-person narratives in exhibitions about migration which reflect a changing landscape in the ways relations between "us" and "them" or between successive waves of migrants are embodied. I term these different ways of capturing such relations a *pedagogy of reading*, a *pedagogy of looking*, a *pedagogy of listening* and a *pedagogy of feeling*, to characterize the different modes of communication in which oral history is embedded in exhibition practices.[2] In

A. Witcomb (✉)
Alfred Deakin Institute for Citizenship and Globalisation, Deakin University, Geelong, VIC, Australia
e-mail: andrea.witcomb@deakin.edu.au

© The Author(s) 2019
K. Darian-Smith, P. Hamilton (eds.), *Remembering Migration*, Palgrave Macmillan Memory Studies,
https://doi.org/10.1007/978-3-030-17751-5_14

203

analysing these, it is possible to discern a shift in interest leading towards an ethical environment in which difficult histories are shaped as issues that need addressing in the present. The practice of oral history at this point opens up ways in which the production of memory landscapes can be used for critical effect rather than simply for memorializing purposes, or democratizing and pluralizing the representation of the past.

Museum archives are surprisingly thin when documenting the use of oral histories. The sources of oral histories are not always clear in curatorial folders relating to particular exhibitions, in files relating to object acquisitions and recordings, or when oral history notes are not easily accessible. Many are not accessioned into collections or transcribed, being regarded instead as working tools. We can reconstruct some of the practices, however, by combining a review of discussions of oral history practices in social history museums with archival research in museums that represent migration history.

The literature on the use of social history in museums begins in the 1980s, a time when social history was gaining in popularity and many were arguing for its benefits. In the museum literature, these benefits included four dominant themes. First, that oral history enabled social history curators to get at histories not represented in material culture, particularly those histories associated with marginalized groups, such as the working class, women, LGBT (lesbian, gay, bisexual and transgender) groups and migrants.[3] In the process, oral history enabled museums to be more democratic in their representations of people's lives, giving them the agency to narrate their own stories and construct their own memory landscapes. The second benefit was that oral history enabled museums to develop closer relationships with the communities they served.[4] Third, oral history enabled first-person narratives to be included in exhibitions, giving a greater sense of immediacy and emotional connection for audiences. Finally, oral history enabled an engagement with difficult themes,[5] with the potential to deal with complex and difficult histories. Rob Perks, looking back over the 1980s and 1990s, recognized this tension when he suggested that "At its best, oral history is subversive, challenging and moving. At its worst it can be unsurprising nostalgia."[6] Using the examples of District Six Museum in Cape Town, the Genocide Museum in Rwanda and the human rights organization Memória Abierta (Open Memory), he went on to say that:

> Oral history works well at the extremes of human experience because it is so good at capturing and conveying emotions. In former totalitarian societies,

museum curators have played a crucial role in creating new civil societies; employing oral history to reconstruct a past that has been destroyed, denied or manipulated.[7]

Oral history, for Perks, "is a reminder that history is as much, if not more, about people than it is about objects."[8] He was arguing that oral history was key to constructing a landscape of memory that sought to memorialize those erased from history.

As Perks and Thomson summarize, museums have seen oral history as

merely a means of gathering information about material culture; for others it has underpinned community/'outreach' work in which the museum ventures outside its hallowed building. ... For a few major museums oral history has ... been used not merely as sound, explicitly seeking an emphatic response from visitors and encouraging interactivity between objects and experiences.[9]

In other words, oral history gave access to intimate issues and the emotional lives of people, helping to build empathetic connections with the subjects of history for museum audiences and fostered a sense of inclusivity.

Many of those arguing for the relevance of oral history to social history museums also pointed out it was an extra-curricular activity, with the result that material was not properly transcribed, catalogued or indexed, making it relatively inaccessible.[10] Oral history was an addition to the central activity of collecting material culture rather than either a collecting practice in its own right or a practice that was seen as central to the research practices surrounding the activity of collecting. As Stuart Davies put it:

Despite the ample evidence that oral history has made a positive contribution to museums over the past fifteen years or so, it still seems to lack the resources, respect and attention given to the more traditional curatorial disciplines. In some ways this is understandable. Museums were obviously not established as centres for oral history research and archives. Their first propriety will always tend to be the traditional artefacts and pictures which form the bulk of the collections.[11]

If we take these general comments on oral history practices to museums that engage with migration history, we can look more closely at the actual practice of getting first-hand insights into the significance of particular objects for their owners, or their accounts of personal experiences that connect with the history of migration. The documentation of Australia's migration history has frequently gone hand in hand with a privileging of first-person narratives, a function of the association between the history of migration and the role of museums in documenting and celebrating multiculturalism. As Ian McShane argued in relation to the migrant heritage collecting programme at the National Museum of Australia, "This program favoured a historiography of first-hand testimony and recognised the interpretive asset of oral history."[12] This was not an unusual situation. The National Maritime Museum, too, sought to combine the documentation of personal objects held within migrant families with oral history, a practice that made it possible to render the heterogeneity of individual experiences more explicit and which allowed for human emotions to shine through.[13]

If we look into museum archives it becomes evident that these practices have their beginnings in the more general curatorial practice performed by social history curators, of interviewing donors and taking notes of what they say which go on file. This is a practice which the Migration Museum in Adelaide explains to potential donors: "As part of the process of accepting items from donors, the Museum also collects the 'story' of the item and any relevant material such as photographs and oral histories."[14] These notes become the basis for label writing in which potted histories of the person and the object's significance to them are related to the visitor. While the focus is on a person, communication is not in the first person. This practice has a long history, as one particular example from curator Kate Walsh at the Migration Museum in 1995 illustrates. In a letter to a donor of material for *Chops and Changes*, an exhibition dealing with the contribution of migrants to Australia's culinary culture, Walsh asked the donor to check the text she had written for the labels. Walsh wanted to make sure the donor was happy with how he was represented in the places where he "had been mentioned or quoted."[15] The accompanying paperwork provides an insight into the ways in which first-person narrative is produced from the notes of the conversation. Under the heading "Quotes from our conversation," Walsh records the following points:

> It is hard for the Growers Market to be competitive with the big supermarkets, like Woolworths. Woolworths is able to promote its specials. Woolworths generally has a high standard of fruit and veg. Quality control is there. Leading fruit and veg sellers—fresh food, not necessarily cheaper.[16]

As with the rest of the notes, the writing is all in the third person. In the attached label that Walsh asks her informant to check, this information becomes a quote in the first person:

14 ORAL HISTORY AND FIRST-PERSON NARRATIVES IN MIGRATION... 207

The larger supermarkets can even undercut the growers who sell direct to the public. It is hard to be competitive.

Sam Makeas, co-ordinator, Norwood Growers Market[17]

Exhibition archives are full of examples such as these. When the time comes to turn that information, originally arrived at through conversation, into a label, a story which moves between third and first person is composed.

A second strategy for inserting a first-person narrative alongside the third-person narrative produced by the curator is that of taking extracts from oral histories done by others, or those presented in other media, such as books. While this practice does provide a first-person narrative, it does so without presenting the person themselves, as there is no voice recording and no photograph. An example is this label which presents three different voices through quotation:

What's good about Australia is that it's a multicultural country. The ingredients we use at home, you can find in Australia. But you have to search a bit.

Magdi Eltahir who came from Sudan, 1981

Australians are willing to try new foods because we have no real food culture of our own. Our Anglo-Saxon background isn't exactly enriched in a culinary sense. We have no pre-conceived barriers to overcome.

Graeme Andrews, *Market Adventures* tours, Adelaide Central Market
For bookings: phone 018 842 242

Migrants are involved in the food industry here in South Australia because they have a very strong food ethos of their own. There are 38 groups represented just in the market. A small population with a large degree of diversity, a good climate and low costs compared with other cities all assist people in developing their own little bit of home.

Graeme Andrews, *Market Adventures* tours, Adelaide Central Market[18]

The use of individual quotations, either real or made up from notes based on conversations, is most often used in the production of two key modes of interpretation, which I call, respectively, a *pedagogy of reading* and a *pedagogy of looking*. Both of these strategies were highly popular in the 1980s and 1990s. A *pedagogy of reading*, so called because this form of interpretation requires significant amounts of reading from visitors, involves a heavy use of graphic design panels with a lot of text, written mostly in the third person with small excerpts in the first person to give the story a personal colour. A slightly different example is the exhibition *A New Australia: Post-War Immigration to Western Australia* at the Fremantle Museum which also opened in 1995. The exhibition was largely designed as a flowing book on walls with images to break up the text. The two-dimensional feel of the exhibition was broken up by mounting objects, particular framed images on the walls, as well as by exhibition cases and dioramas, or installations that sought to recreate particular environments, such as a tent in one of the migrant camps. Small quotes were used to personalize and punctuate the larger narrative within these graphic panels, drawing out the main points. For example, in a section titled "Reasons for Leaving," the narrative began at the top left-hand corner with the following quotation: "My husband had been told we would be able to make it big. That is why we came to Australia." Below it were four photographs, two of which were of two families arriving in Western Australia, originally published by West Australian newspapers. These are publicity images, not private photographs. They show hopeful, smiling faces. Below them are two other photographs showing different migrants in their original town, and further to the right are two framed photographs—one of a destroyed town where all the eye can see lies in rubble, while beneath it the other image is of a mother and two children peering out of a barbed wire fence with a displaced people's camp behind them. The author of the quotation, however, is not named. They are simply a type: "Latvian Displaced Person, arrived 1951."[19] Their individual story or testimony of events does not matter, as they stand in for a much wider phenomenon—the idea that those who came were displaced people from countries that could not support them. Such a practice points to the ways in which oral history is used to produce a collective memory landscape, in which particular narrative tropes are repeated again and again—such as the idea that Europe was in a state of disarray and Australia was the land of milk and honey able to look after people. Individual memories are not the point here, though they are used to construct a collective memory that frames the post-war migration period as an act of generosity on Australia's part.

This practice of not treating first-person quotations as belonging to a particular person, but as scenes that are constructed for the visitor to conjure up the past, points to a second mode of display I term a *pedagogy of looking.* In the section that dealt with the migrant camps, it is clear that one of the points of this display was to show the shattering of hope. In front of an installation containing a large black and white photograph, showing an unlined tin shed with hessian curtains dividing up the space into "bedrooms," a simple metal frame bed and wooden chair, a wooden trunk serving as the table with a few plates, bowls, two tin mugs and a few pieces of cutlery, all given depth by the placement of a wire fence in front of the image, was the following label:

TENT CAMPS—HOPES SHATTERED

From the Northam Military camp we were sent to Lomos on the Brookton-Corrigin line. That's where we started off. It doesn't exist anymore. We lived in a couple of tents and an old tin shed with a wood stove in it. The boys in the gang got some old railway sleepers and made an enclosure and lined it with cardboard to keep the wind out. They roofed it with rusty tins they found in the paddocks, and that was our accommodation. We had cyclone beds and our mattresses were filled with straw. Dad was out there working on the gang. It was sledge hammers and shovels out in the sun. It was hard for Mum too: she had us two children and she couldn't speak any English.

Polish migrant, arrived 1951[20]

Immediately after this quotation, the text shifts to third person, changing gear towards a more authoritative account of the history of migrant accommodation. The first couple of paragraphs were bolded for emphasis:

The conditions facing post-war immigrants were grim indeed when compared to current immigration practice. This first generation of mass migrants were very much pioneers for those who followed.

In rural areas all over the State families were housed in temporary shelters alongside work locations. These were usually tents or canvas-covered wooden structures. Basic provisions such as cooking utensils, camp stretchers, straw-filled mattresses and army blankets were supplied at a fee. Rent was even charged on the tents.

Women and children could stay in the holding centres until private accommodation was found, but many chose to live in tent camps to keep families together. Although very basic, they provided a degree of privacy not available in the holding centres. Some migrants spent up to ten years in refugee camps in Europe and then faced up to a further eight years, without assistance, in tent camps in Australia.

These strategies for inserting small amounts of first-person narrative through a written mode of presentation operate through certain well-established tropes in the way the migration experience came to be understood during this period. There is always the pain of leaving, the passage, impressions on arrival, trials and tribulations, hope and cultural maintenance, building a collective memory of the period both for migrants and for the Anglo-Celtic mainstream. While the function of such narrative tropes is to actively support a narrative of multiculturalism, their other effect is to maintain a separation between "us" and "them." Migrants remain "other" to "Australians." The effect is particularly strong in exhibitions where the majority of the text is in third person, creating a distancing effect and the particulars of the individuals whose words are quoted, whose identity is not revealed. Their story is an archetypal one, and it is the third-person narrative provided by the curatorial voice that drives the interpretation. While the curatorial aim is to encourage an understanding of the harsh conditions migrants faced, the lack of an individual human story, of a person with a name, a face and a voice, disables visitors from identifying with those whose words are quoted. They remain an "other" because we are following types rather than a specific person or family. The story is representative, rather than specific and individual, even though much of it comes from oral history interviews. Its organizational structure is top down, with the quotations inserted into a standard narrative determined from above—a narrative that shapes a collective memory which determines how this period can be remembered.

A different strategy emerges when oral histories are embodied in exhibitions as an object in their own right, and as informing the interpretation strategy itself. I call this a *pedagogy of listening*, as the priority is to highlight different voices in order to represent history "from below." The themes are made to emerge from the quotations and the choice of images and objects, rather than these being an illustration of a theme which is presented in a way that prioritizes the institutional voice. An example is the oral history project for the Bonegilla stories component of the *Crossing Place* permanent exhibition at the Albury Museum and Library, developed in 2005.

In a hand-written note,[21] curator Mara (surname not given) expressed her opinion that the subjects of the interviews should be local, within a 150 kilometre radius of Bonegilla, as this would give the project a "great resource of human experiences and cross-section of nationalities." The list of questions was thorough and covered the usual topics, being divided around issues to do with leaving, the journey, arriving at Bonegilla, the facilities at the camp, language acquisition and cultural maintenance, responses from local people to the migrants, and the migrants' own responses to the local area and its people, as well as issues around work. This list in itself indicates the power of established tropes produced by the collective memory developed in the exhibitions discussed previously. The final section was more reflective, exploring the migrants' memories of Bonegilla, of their hopes in coming to Australia and whether or not they "had been back home and what was it like."[22] The instructions were quite specific in stressing to take each question slowly, the importance of listening to the interviewee and taking notes to enable the possibility of following up on particular points. In this way, a complete story was the focus of the interview, to enable comparisons and contrasts between different people's experiences to emerge, as well as to allow enough space and confidence for the surfacing of emotional responses. A number of questions were quite pointed in wanting to explore feelings. Under the heading "Leaving," for example, the list of questions finished with this one: "I'm wondering how did you feel about leaving your own country?," while under "Arriving," interviewees were asked "How did you feel" as part of a set of questions about arriving at Bonegilla. Under "Facilities" they were asked how they felt about their new home. Other questions were much more factual in their orientation, seeking to establish the detail of everyday life.

While each interview resulted in a detailed biography of a personal experience of migration, the exhibition broke the individual stories up into the same themes as the questions, grouping material culture with a representative sample of the range of experiences people had under that theme. This included both positive and negative experiences. However, this strategy did not provide an opportunity to experience a face-to-face encounter with an individual person. Thus, while the concern to personalize stories, to introduce individual voices through oral history, was about pluralizing the representation, the people nevertheless remained a container for particular kinds of narrative tropes. An example of the tensions embodied in this approach is a display under the general theme of life at Bonegilla in which a small number of items is laid out in a "drawer." The display is dominated by a reproduction of a black and white photograph of a toddler in a small plastic bath tub in the middle of the grass. To its right is a brass razor and various shaving utensils, and then a chamber pot to the far right. Underneath the photograph is the following label:

Migrants recall the long distances from the huts to the bathroom facilities and impatient early morning toilet queues, especially when the toilets became blocked. Children in particular were unable to wait, and did not want to venture out on cold nights—so chamber pots were often used. Many recall juggling the streams of hot and cold water when two or more residents were showering at the same time. Communal living had many disadvantages.

The toilets were long lines of holes in a wooden bench above a giant hole. Behind the timber wall behind you was another row of holes for women, same pit. Surrounding walls [were] made of hessian.
                    Barry John Hartnell, United Kingdom, 1951

The pit toilets that made me vomit ...
                    Valery Dalley (nee Raveil) United Kingdom, 1951

Green enameled chamber pot, typical of those used at Bonegilla, 1950s.
     Brass razor, blades and shaving cream brush used by Peter Holovka at Bonegilla, 1970.
     Photograph of Andreas Schymitzek as a toddler bathing at Bonegilla, 1958[23]

As is evident, there is no relation between the objects on display and the people who are quoted in the narrative part of the label. The quotes are there to pull out a particularly unpleasant aspect of life at Bonegilla that everyone could relate to or imagine. The focus, though, is on people's memories, pointing to the curator's recognition that giving colour relied on oral history's ability to generate an emotional landscape from the production of individual memories. However, we know little of each individual's biographies and we are not really meeting them. We are just learning about different kinds of experiences at the camps. This time the names are given, but the faces (other than that of Andreas Schymitzek who stands in for all small children) and the voices are not present. While more personal than the erasure of individual identities in the earlier examples, the effect is still to create a distance between those who did not experience the camps from those who did. It is someone else's history, not our own. For those who did, however, these strategies would have encouraged the recognition of their own experiences, thus building a "Bonegilla" community. In terms of how memory was produced in this exhibition, life histories are broken into thematic excerpts that reinforced established collective memories, both for the broader population and migrant communities themselves. As Paula Hamilton has argued, oral histories in exhibitions are more often than not "utilised more in the service of illuminating already established historical themes or questions than for its own sake."[24]

The question of distance between "us" and "them," however, changes when oral history is used to stage an encounter across difference in ways that implicate "us" in the "other." When this occurs, the interpretative strategy and the mode of communication are no longer a *pedagogy of listening*, aiming only at embodying as many voices as possible. It becomes what I call a *pedagogy of feeling*, where the intensity of personal encounters is aimed at "touching" us in ways that change relations between "us" and "them." For this to occur, oral histories need to be presented in ways that stage an encounter with both the voice and face of the person giving the oral history, rather than through a written quote. This is because of the importance of mimetic communication which establishes infectious connections between people and which demands attention.[25] A second method for staging an encounter across difference is when the content of the oral history speaks to the world of the viewer, not just the world of those on display. For example, in the exhibition *Identity: Yours, Mine, Ours* at the Immigration Museum in Melbourne, a filmed interview with a number of participants is broken up into a series of clips. Visitors encounter the participants' faces on a touch table that enables them to ask a series of pre-determined questions. The surprise is when the answer does not confirm expectations based on stereotypes. In other words, the excerpts are not aimed at generating a collective memory that is already well-engrained, but at disrupting it, turning it into a form of curatorial activism, into what some oral historians have always argued—that oral histories are sources for understanding how people remember, as much as what they remember.[26] In this case, what the audience remembers is used as the unspoken backdrop to be disrupted by specific accounts of individual people's complex backgrounds. Rather than producing memory, oral history is used to disrupt it. This is an unusual use of an oral history approach; the visitors are not learning about a specific moment in history, but are being challenged to engage critically with collective understandings of people's identities. The staging of these oral histories also requires a more complex mediation, usually through some form of multimedia—at a minimum a voice recording, more often a film presentation, either on large screens or more private settings. The effect is to move away from representative stories towards increased personalization. In the context of difficult histories, such as, for example, histories of forced migration or refugee experiences,

214   A. WITCOMB

there is a question as to whether oral histories become testimony, in the sense that they become requests to become involved in the lives of others by bearing witness.[27] At this point, the aim becomes that of producing a collective memory from the repetition of many voices on the same theme to a landscape of memory in which the aim is to disrupt easy identification. To do that, forms of collective memory which erase difference and power relations have to be opened up and challenged.

As this chapter has argued, understanding how oral history has been used in the representation of migration histories in museums involves recognizing a variety of oral history practices in museum contexts, as well as a variety of modes of display. Both of these have a complex relationship to the ways in which oral history has helped to shape relations between "us" and "them," relations which are embedded into the question of how oral history is used to either produce or challenge established tropes of collective memory.

Notes

1. I thank the Australian Research Council for its support of DP 120100594, "Collecting Institutions: Cultural Diversity and the Making of Australian Citizenship Since the 1970s," the fieldwork for which underpins this chapter.
2. Andrea Witcomb, "Curating Relations Between 'Us' and 'Them': The Changing Roles of Migration Museums in Australia," in Conal McCarthy and Philipp Schorch eds, *Curatopia: Museums and the Future of Curatorship* (Manchester: Manchester University Press, 2018), 262–278.
3. Helen Clark, "The People's Story," *Museum Management and Curatorship* 10, no. 1 (1991): 37–44; Annette Day, "Listening Galleries: Putting Oral History on Display," *Oral History* 27, no. 1 (Migration, Spring 1999): 91–96; Stuart Frost, "Secret Museums: Hidden Histories of Sex and Sexuality," *Museums and Social Issues* 3, no. 1 (2008): 29–40; Sian Jones and Carl Major, "Reaching the Public: Oral History as a Survival Strategy for Museums," *Oral History* 14, no. 2 (Museums and Oral History, Autumn 1986): 31–38; Campbell McMurray, "Oral History and Museums: An Overview and Critique," *Oral History* 14, no. 2 (Museums and Oral History, Autumn 1986): 26–30; April Whincop, "Using Oral History in Museum Displays," *Oral History*, 14, no. 2 (Museums and Oral History, Autumn 1986): 46–50.
4. Whincop, "Using Oral History in Museum Displays," 46–50.
5. Brenda Factor, "Making an Exhibition of Yourself: Museums and Oral History," *Oral History Association of Australia Journal* 13 (1991): 44–48;

Tony Kushner, "Oral History at the Extremes of Human Experience: Holocaust Testimony in a Museum Setting," *Oral History* 29, no. 2 (Hidden Histories, Autumn 2001): 83–94.

6. Robert Perks, "The Power of Oral History," *Museum Practice* 25 (Spring 2004): 44–47. https://www.museumsassociation.org/museum-practice/9215.

7. Perks, "The Power of Oral History."

8. Perks, "The Power of Oral History."

9. Robert Perks and Alistair Thomson, "Making Histories: Introduction," in Robert Perks and Alistair Thomson eds, *The Oral History Reader*, 2nd edition (London and New York: Routledge, 2006), 336–37.

10. Stuart Davies, "Falling on Deaf Ears? Oral History and Strategy in Museums," *Oral History* 22, no. 2 (25th Anniversary Issue, Autumn 1994): 74–84; Anna Green, "The Exhibition that Speaks for Itself: Oral History and Museums," in Robert Perks and Alistair Thomson eds, *The Oral History Reader*, 2nd edition, 416–24 (London and New York: Routledge, 2006); Donald Hyslop, "From Oral Historians to Community Historians: Some Ways Forward for the Use and Development of Oral Testimony in Public Institutions," *Oral History Association of Australia Journal* 17 (1995): 8; Whincop, "Using Oral History in Museum Displays."

11. Davies, "Falling on Deaf Ears?," 81.

12. Ian McShane, "Museology and Public Policy: Rereading the Development of the National Museum of Australia's Collection," Recollections 2, no. 2 (2007). http://recollections.nma.gov.au/issues/vol_2_no2/papers/museology_and_public_policy.

13. Chiara O'Reilly and Nina Parish, "Suitcases, Keys and Handkerchiefs: How are Objects Being Used to Collect and Tell Migrant Stories in Australian Museums?," *Museums and Social Issues* 12, no. 2 (2017): 99–114.

14. Migration Museum, n.d., "A Keeping Place: The Migration Museum and Cultural Diversity," Migration Museum, Adelaide, 1.

15. Kate Walsh, Letter to Sam Makeas, 18 July 1995, Ref. E36/Kw in File Gallery 8 *Chops and Changes* Working File for D.I.Y. Dairy Olive Oil Fish/ Poultry Rice Pulses Fruit & Veg, '95–'97. Migration Museum, History Trust of South Australia.

16. Notes accompanying Letter to Sam Makeas, page 2.

17. Copy of label in letter to Sam Makeas.

18. This label in *Chops and Changes* Gallery 8 Bread Sweets Meat Towers Folder, '95–'97, Migration Museum, History Trust of South Australia.

19. Description developed from a photograph of the display sent to author by Anne Delroy, former Head of the History Department that developed the exhibition at the Western Australian Museum.

216   A. WITCOMB

20. Panel 19 "Tent Camps—Hopes Shattered," page 10 of final copy of labels for Gallery 17 of the Fremantle History Museum, a branch of the Western Australian Museum. Electronic copy provided to author by Anne Delroy, former Head of the History Department, Western Australian Museum on 7 November 2016 via email.

21. Bonegilla Interviews—31/5/05 Mara's thoughts in Permanent Exhibition Resource Material 8c Bonegilla—Looking Back, Albury City, New Library Museum 2007, Folder.

22. List of interviewer questions and instructions for Oral History project for *Crossing Places* exhibition in Permanent Exhibition Resource Material 8c Bonegilla—Looking Back, Albury City, New Library Museum 2007, Folder.

23. Individual display under the *First Impressions of Bonegilla* display within the *Crossing Places* exhibition at the Albury City Museum, as seen on 9 February 2017.

24. Paula Hamilton, "Speak, Memory: Issues in Oral and Public History," in Paul Ashton and Alex Trapeznik eds, *What is Public History Globally? Working with the Past in the Present* (London and New York: Bloomsbury, 2019), 214.

25. See Witcomb, "Curating Relations Between 'Us' and 'Them.'"

26. Frisch, *A Shared Authority*; Portelli, *The Order Has Been Carried*.

27. Witcomb, "Xenophobia: Museums, Refugees and Fear of the Other," 74–87.

BIBLIOGRAPHY

Clark, Helen. "The People's Story." *Museum Management and Curatorship* 10, no. 1 (1991): 37–44.

Davies, Stuart. "Falling on Deaf Ears? Oral History and Strategy in Museums." *Oral History* 22, no. 2 (25th Anniversary Issue, Autumn 1994): 74–84.

Day, Annette. "Listening Galleries: Putting Oral History on Display." *Oral History* 27, no. 1 (Migration, Spring 1999): 91–96.

Factor, Brenda. "Making an Exhibition of Yourself: Museums and Oral History." *Oral History Association of Australia Journal* 13 (1991): 44–48.

Frisch, Michael. *A Shared Authority: Essays on the Craft and Meaning of Oral and Public History.* Albany: State University of New York Press, 1990.

Frost, Stuart. "Secret Museums: Hidden Histories of Sex and Sexuality." *Museums and Social Issues* 3, no. 1 (2008): 29–40.

Green, Anna. "The Exhibitions that Speaks for Itself: Oral History and Museums." In *The Oral History Reader*, edited by Robert Perks and Alistair Thomson, 2nd edition, 416–24. London and New York: Routledge, 2006.

Hamilton, Paula. "Speak, Memory: Issues in Oral and Public History." In *What is Public History Globally? Working with the Past in the Present*, edited by Paul Ashton and Alex Trapeznik, 213–224. London and New York: Bloomsbury, 2019.

Hamilton, Paula, and Linda Shopes, eds. *Oral History and Public Memories*. Philadelphia: Temple University Press, 2009.

Hyslop, Donald. "From Oral Historians to Community Historians: Some Ways Forward for the Use and Development of Oral Testimony in Public Institutions." *Oral History Association of Australia Journal* 17 (1995): 1–8.

Jones, Sian, and Carl Major. "Reaching the Public: Oral History as a Survival Strategy for Museums." *Oral History* 14, no. 2 (Museums and Oral History, Autumn 1986): 31–38.

Kushner, Tony. "Oral History at the Extremes of Human Experience: Holocaust Testimony in a Museum Setting." *Oral History* 29, no. 2 (Hidden Histories, Autumn 2001): 83–94.

McMurray, Campbell. "Oral History and Museums: An Overview and Critique." *Oral History* 14, no. 2 (Museums and Oral History, Autumn 1986): 26–30.

McShane, Ian. "Museology and Public Policy: Rereading the Development of the National Museum of Australia's Collection." *Recollections* 2, no. 2 (2007). http://recollections.nma.gov.au/issues/vol_2_no2/papers/museology_and_public_policy.

O'Reilly, Chiara, and Nina Parish. "Suitcases, Keys and Handkerchiefs: How Are Objects Being Used to Collect and Tell Migrant Stories in Australian Museums?" *Museums and Social Issues* 12, no. 2 (2017): 99–114.

Perks, Robert. "The Power of Oral History." *Museum Practice* 25 (Spring 2004): 44–47. https://www.museumsassociation.org/museum-practice/9215 (no page numbers).

Perks, Robert, and Alistair Thomson. "Making Histories: Introduction." In *The Oral History Reader*, edited by Robert Perks and Alistair Thomson, 2nd edition, 333–42. London and New York: Routledge, 2006.

Portelli, Alessandro. *The Order Has Been Carried Out: History, Memory and the Meaning of a Nazi Massacre in Rome*. New York: Palgrave Macmillan, 2003.

Whincop, April. "Using Oral History in Museum Displays." *Oral History* 14, no. 2 (Museums and Oral History, Autumn 1986): 46–50.

Witcomb, Andrea. "Curating Relations Between 'Us' and 'Them': The Changing Role of Migration Museums in Australia." In *Curatopia: Museums and the Future of Curatorship*, edited by Conal McCarthy and Philipp Schorch, 262–278. Manchester: Manchester University Press, 2018a.

Witcomb, Andrea. "Xenophobia: Museums, Refugees and Fear of the Other." In *The Contemporary Museum: Shaping Museums for the Global Now*, edited by Simon Knell, 74–87. London: Routledge, 2018b.

CHAPTER 15

Personal, Public Pasts: Negotiating Migrant Heritage—Heritage Practice and Migration History in Australia

Alexandra Dellios

Despite a pervasive and celebratory multicultural rhetoric, migrant community heritage in Australia has only in recent times become visible. It remains a low priority on heritage lists and registers. The heritage industry—and its state-funded agencies that determine what is recognized as "significant"—has demonstrated an institutional indifference to the tangible and intangible heritage associated with post-World War II migration and settlement experiences. The use of oral histories as a form of memory work in the identification, management and interpretation of migration heritage is scattered across various projects and agencies with no coherent schema for its practice in this field.

Over the last decade, interdisciplinary scholars in the field of "critical heritage studies" have emphasized the need for heritage practices and processes to change and integrate understandings of new sets of values: those that emphasize open dialogue with local community groups and collaborative practice, and, most importantly, a criterion that recognizes and privileges "social value,"

A. Dellios (✉)
Australian National University, Canberra, ACT, Australia
e-mail: alexandra.dellios@anu.edu.au

© The Author(s) 2019   219
K. Darian-Smith, P. Hamilton (eds.), *Remembering Migration*,
Palgrave Macmillan Memory Studies,
https://doi.org/10.1007/978-3-030-17751-5_15

rather than the built fabric and its (often Eurocentric and elite) aesthetic value.[1] Oral history has an important part to play in identifying and sharing these values and their associated histories. The collaborative and empowering processes of oral history become especially important when considering the sharing of previously marginalized histories.

Examining the ways in which migrant heritage is made public, in an official environment that sometimes constrains or nullifies (structural and lived) difference, can reveal the boundaries and limits of authorized heritage discourses and multicultural rhetoric. The case studies explored herein offer alternative models of public history practice at the grassroots level, in which personal memories made public challenge the limits of a multicultural heritage discourse.

Heritage is here theorized as a present-centred cultural practice and process and an instrument of cultural power, as it is approached in the heritage studies literature.[2] This can include the tangible but only as it is understood and interpreted through the intangible: the values and stories that people give it. The role of heritage in building community identity is well recognized.[3] For institutional heritage to resist its function as an "authorized heritage discourse"—disconnected from local and intersectional identities and histories, and imposed from above by "experts" on "what is often assumed to be a generally uninformed audience"—it needs to shift how assessments are undertaken and by whom.[4] Non-expert perceptions of the meaning and value of heritage, as Laurajane Smith asserts, are not readily accommodated by current discourses in the heritage industry. Celmara Pocock, David Collett and Linda Baulch argue that methodology is an issue: the institutional division between tangible and intangible heritage is artificial, a Western construct that obscures how communities create meaning in and about place.[5] Similar arguments have been made by Denis Byrne, Helen Brayshaw and Tracy Ireland, who argue that "social value" need not be conceptualized as distinct from historic, aesthetic or scientific value when assessing heritage "significance"—as is the current practice under the stipulations of Australia ICOMOS Burra Charter, which has also shaped heritage practice in the United Kingdom, North America and, more recently, China.[6]

The Australian heritage industry has a long way to go before it can achieve this "fundamental shift" in its view of heritage significance.[7] Although Australia ratified in 2009 the *Convention on the Protection and UNESCO Promotion of the Diversity of Cultural Expressions*, it has not yet ratified the 2003 *UNESCO Convention for the Safeguarding of the*

Intangible Cultural Heritage. In 2017, Australia ICOMOS drafted a new "Practice Note" on intangible heritage based on the UNESCO Convention. The practice note intends to help heritage practitioners become more confident in assessing intangible heritage by encouraging them to work with communities and de-centre their expertise. But changing practice to incorporate community values will take time.[8]

MULTICULTURALISM AND HERITAGE DISCOURSES

On a descriptive level, and beyond its framing as a settlement or welfare policy, the popular and political discourse of Australian multiculturalism forms part of a "success story" that begins in the post-war era of mass immigration. This story explicitly lends agency and foresight to government policy and Australian (conceived as the Anglo-Celtic "core") acceptance of cultural difference, especially if it comes in the palatable and politically neutral form of food and folklore.[9] The migrant success story, a trope explored in Ian McShane's classification of multiculturalism's representation in Australian museums since the 1980s, still informs heritage practice.[10] In the English-speaking world, museums moved away from "separate community histories to the collective shared experience of a postmodern and messy urban condition"—especially in cities like London and Melbourne.

Throughout the 1980s and 1990s, right-wing politicians and public intellectuals voiced their concerns over the perceived "special privileges" granted to "minorities" under the government's multicultural policy, which they also tied closely to immigration policy and the so-called Asianization of Australia.[11] Similar critiques were made in the United Kingdom, following assisted migration from former British colonies in Africa, the Caribbean, and Asia. In Australia, these critics were roundly condemned by both Labor and Liberal politicians, who argued: immigration was skills-based, not race-based, and Australia's settlement policy of multiculturalism ensured that these migrants made an economic contribution to the nation.[12] In political rhetoric, the previously contentious debates over the intersections between ethnicity and class were sidelined, in favour of a multiculturalism that promoted "diversity," which has been derided by scholars like Ghassan Hage as "pluralism without the substance."[13]

John Howard's Liberal prime ministership from 1996 to 2007 slowly untangled discussions of immigration from discussions of multicultural-

222   A. DELLIOS

ism, and again from debates around refugee policy, which continued to enforce racially discriminatory practice. The portfolio of "multicultural affairs", previously a part of the Department of Immigration, was shifted around various Departments until it finally came to rest in social services. Howard avoided using the term multiculturalism, in preference for a rhetoric that emphasized citizenship, social cohesion and integration—such words now dominate European and British discussions.

In Australia, in 2011, the Labor Government attempted to reintroduce the word multiculturalism into political rhetoric, with a policy document that emphasized multiculturalism "for all of us"—rather than a set of policies aiming to provide culturally sensitive services to new and older arrivals.[14] Malcolm Turnbull's Liberal government's 2017 document, *Multicultural Australia: United, Strong, Successful*, adopts a similar approach, offering a "managerial multiculturalism" that maintains the dominance of existing (and largely Anglo-Australian) power structures. It promotes a civic nationalism that permits certain expressions of cultural difference.[15] Political leaders continue to refer to Australia as "the most successful multicultural society in the world."[16] Such statements are uttered in contradistinction to other Western leaders, in Germany, France and the United Kingdom, who denounce multiculturalism as a failure—focusing instead on "social inclusion" measures that implicitly blame religious difference, and Muslim migrants in particular, for social alienation and political discontent. Alternatively, Australian multiculturalism is tempered by an emphasis on the "privileges" of Australian citizenship and the civic responsibilities that apparently "unify" those lucky enough to be counted in the multicultural state.[17]

Australian examples of state-sanctioned "migrant heritage sites" include Block 19, the remnants of the post-war Bonegilla Migration Reception and Training Centre (listed on the National Heritage Register [NHR] in 2007) and the Snowy Mountains Hydro Electric Scheme (listed on the NHR in 2016). These rare examples of migration heritage in the built landscape celebrate migrant contributions to Australian multiculturalism and civic nationalism while nullifying ethnic or cultural difference. They also ignore a history of migrant protest and the demands made by respective groups on a system that did not always provide for them.[18] Both listings emphasize contributions to national development and industry, and retrospectively locate the beginnings of a multicultural Australia in the post-World War II era.[19] This, according to the framework developed by Hamilton and Ashton, is an attempt at "retrospective commemoration".[20]

It conceals histories of state neglect or coercion, and continued structural inequality and difference in favor of promoting a "phantasmatic diversity".[21]

In Australia, official migration heritage is bound by a national historiography that stresses a linear and progressive journey from migration to settlement, and ultimately "becoming Australian." This "becoming" leaves room for the creation of a hyphenated identity (i.e. Greek-Australian), but its limits lie in its "methodological nationalism," reflecting the nation-bounded approach to identifying and preserving migration heritage.[22] This may not accord with the transnational experience and heritage record of some groups, as Byrne demonstrates regarding Chinese migration, the built environment and the "heritage corridor" that extends from China, through to South-East Asia and Australia.[23] The reality of non-linear and unsettled ways of being (or belonging) struggles to be accommodated in current heritage practice.

HISTORY OF MIGRATION HERITAGE PRACTICE IN AUSTRALIA

The conceptual and rhetorical constraints of multicultural heritage discourses in Australia have also shaped institutional responses to migration heritage. Since the early 1990s, various state and nationally funded heritage bodies have launched reports and projects into "migrant heritage places" in Australia. The first of these, led by Helen Armstrong and commissioned by the then Australian Heritage Commission, attempted to identify migrant heritage places and social values in the built fabric of major cities.[24] They offered a "handbook" for communities hoping to identify their sites for heritage protection. Much of the research stemming from this project found that migrant heritage places (which the researchers associated with work and recreation) were destroyed throughout the 1970s and 1980s due to urban redevelopment.[25] In one instance, Armstrong identified oral history methods as a means to identify migrant places with "heritage value"—but this value had to accord with grand narratives of national progress. Historically, few oral history projects have been attached to heritage nomination or conservation efforts.

Despite Australia's "wonderfully diverse cultural heritage," the reports and guides stemming from this Australian Heritage Commission project did not permit expressions of *in*visibility: the admission that heritage important to migrant groups flourished internally and was concealed within or behind an outwardly Anglo-Celtic built fabric because of the strictures of assimilation and structural discrimination. The old inner-city businesses, market gardens and places of worship identified as part of this project also contained stories of transnational political investment, of inter-generational tensions over cultural practice and translation, and the explicit or implicit fight for citizenship rights and better work conditions in a pre-multicultural Australia. Such stories are not easily contained in a nationalist historiography and heritage industry that until recently stressed progress and achievement.

The NSW Migration Heritage Centre at the Powerhouse Museum, funded by the New South Wales Labor Government, was established in the early 2000s. As a virtual immigration museum, which also staged exhibitions within communities, the NSW Migration Heritage Centre operated on a partnership model, working with local migrant communities in Sydney and regional New South Wales. They focused on migration memories, "belongings" (objects) and their association to places. They especially focused on *ageing* migrant communities, those who arrived in Australia from 1947 to the 1970s. Adopting proactive research based on interviewing community members proved an effective means of identifying the material history of postwar migration. The Centre generated new and previously marginal histories in their virtual exhibitions, which addressed: women, faith, fashion, hidden places of reception and rural communities, among other things.[26] Unfortunately, the Centre was defunded by the NSW Liberal Government and the website was archived in 2010. The Centre's projects offered successful models of collaborative migrant heritage-making that drew heavily on oral history. The wider institutional indifference to the results of these projects is perhaps due to their lack of tangible collections and sites. Like similar cultural institutions across the country, they found it difficult to secure ongoing funding for research projects on communities that are perceived as "marginal" to Australia's heritage.

The 2011 federally funded "Australian Heritage Strategy" attempted to take stock of the issues and shortcomings in heritage practice and legislation. Museum curator Susan Tonkin, in her submission to the Strategy, suggested that heritage bodies ignore migrant communities and their histories.[27] Tonkin also made a wider point about the need to enhance oral histories, family history and storytelling in recognition that personal or local connections are key to community interest and broader understandings of heritage. While the Burra Charter insists that heritage should reflect the "diversity of our communities, telling us about who we are and the past that has formed us," Tonkin points to Heritage Week 2011's programme and the lack of immigrant community stories to argue that "public understanding seems blind to the rich heritage of the non-British immigrant communities."[28] The 2013 revisions to the Burra Charter recognized the importance of *engaging* communities in conservation, interpretation and management, but practices enabling these types of engagements have not focused on migrant histories, beyond featuring token "multicultural" events as part of heritage weeks. Furthermore, "significance" remains something usually defined by authorities and experts within the industry, rather than in close consultation with community groups, though there are some more progressive heritage consultancies, particularly in Victoria, which are working to effect change utilizing oral histories.

Grassroots migrant heritage-making occurs beyond the purview of heritage agencies, but there are moments of encounter, or a contact zone, especially when community groups seek institutional funding or heritage listing. In this contact zone, intimate histories are made public, propelled into a setting in which they may cause disruption to established modes of discussing migration history in Australia.

Remnants of Built Structures

This was the case for the Royal Australian Air Force (RAAF) huts that formed part of Benalla Migrant Camp, in rural Victoria. Over 60,000 migrants, mostly from Eastern Europe, passed through the centre from 1949 to 1967. Approximately 500 lived in the camp for up to ten years. A high proportion of so-called problem cases, meaning "unsupported" mothers, were shunted to Benalla; they were expected to work off their two-year work contracts with the Australian Commonwealth at either of two nearby factories—Latoof and Callil clothing or Renolds Chains.[29] The cost of housing and childcare made it impossible for them to save enough money to leave the centre and find private accommodation. Single women with children, it was said, were accruing debt to the Commonwealth and "staying indefinitely in Centres in poverty."[30] Nonetheless, these isolated and Spartan surrounds became a familiar and contained space for the families who lived there—especially for those who spent most of their childhoods in the centre. This generation is behind the recent push to have the remaining huts listed on the Victorian Heritage Register (VHR) and the social values of the site preserved and promoted through public history projects.[31] Benalla's history as a discriminatory space and contradictory haven for single working migrant mothers has been excluded from popular histories of post-war immigration. The effort of Benalla children to insert these marginalized narratives into the national story has therefore posed a challenge to existing modes of heritage classification for state heritage.

For example, the Executive Director of Heritage Victoria originally rejected the inclusion of Benalla on the VHR in 2015, arguing that the place did not satisfy any of the criteria at a state level. He cited Criterion A: "importance to the course or pattern of Victoria's cultural history," and referred to the built fabric and physical changes to the place. He also argued that remnants of Bonegilla Migrant Camp (a reception centre, rather than a Holding Centre like Benalla) were already listed on the VHR to document post-World War II migration. These statements ignored the deep and ongoing social values ascribed to this place by a generation of Eastern European refugee families, many of them headed by single parents, and the particular function that Benalla played in the wider system of housing disadvantaged migrants throughout the 1950s and 1960s. Its role in housing "unsupported" women and their children for long periods is integral to its social value and the oral histories it contains.[32] The women who lived at Benalla migrant camp had experienced or witnessed the violence of war, many had been prisoners of war in German labour camps, or lost family members in the great population shifts of World War II. They also bore witness to the beginning of the Cold War, and through migration were cut off from family remaining behind the iron curtain. Their family histories in Australia—and the histories of their children in the migrant camp—have not been widely studied or disseminated until recently.[33]

Questions about the built fabric's "integrity," while still important to the community, were not as important as capturing the meanings and stories associated with the place. In this way, the Benalla group directly challenged the limits of heritage practice at the state level—especially in drawing attention to how few places on the VHR address the histories of marginalized peoples, and the limits of legislation in assessing "social value." Heritage scholar Deirdre Prinsen, when looking at the role of oral history in boosting heritage assessments, found "from a broad survey of heritage reports, including environmental impact statements and conservation management plans, social significance rarely appears to be investigated in depth."[34] When the Executive Director made his recommendation in 2015, neither he nor any member of Heritage Victoria visited the site containing the huts, the temporary museum on the migrant camp established by volunteers, or spoke to former residents of Benalla camp.

During a well-attended 2016 hearing in response to Heritage Victoria's rejection, former child residents of Benalla offered personal and collective memories of the place. One respondent spoke of "the role of widowed and single mothers who were significant players in the larger story of migration and the decentralisation of industry in Victoria's cultural history."[35] Their testimonies stressed the agency of their migrant mothers, using narratives of progress (their contributions of the economic and industrial history of Victoria) to consciously insert their previously marginalized mothers into an accepted heritage industry narrative. They spoke directly to the criteria of Heritage Council of Victoria. Drawing on archival research and personal histories to highlight "the different challenges and experiences of widowed or single migrant mothers with children [that] deserve recognition," the community around Benalla Migrant Camp successfully challenged the limits of authorized heritage discourses and multicultural rhetoric.

The format of a nomination for heritage listing, however, offered limited space in which to explore "social value" beyond the set criteria, which stresses a relationship to Victoria's history and progress. The group has subsequently gained funding from the Public Records Office of Victoria to conduct a digital storytelling project, which will amass oral histories of former residents that may be shared onsite and online. Some of the oral history and memory work occurring around this previously invisible migrant heritage site challenges a conservative multicultural rhetoric by making public the structural inequalities faced by their working migrant mothers. The project speaks to community values by privileging the voices of former residents, rather than the interpretations offered by heritage practitioners.

COMMUNITY-INITIATED MONUMENTS

Across Australia, community groups have erected monuments to migrant groups. One of the few monuments that pertain to post-World War II migrants is Gippsland Immigration Park and Wall of Recognition in Morwell, South-Eastern Victoria. It was launched in 2007 by a group of local residents, all of whom were volunteers and had a connection to Morewell's Italian community. The group made the decision that the eventual park would speak to "all migrants in the region," all but

Indigenous peoples, and not just the Italian community. They successfully obtained hundreds of thousands of dollars in state, national and Commonwealth heritage funding to launch and maintain the Park. Ultimately, the group was motivated by a vaguely multicultural rhetoric—"unity in diversity." In their grant applications, the group were enamored with the idea that the Park should celebrate the migrants who "made a significant and enduring contribution to the development of Gippsland."[36] However, the Committee was also conscious that not all migrants "settled," and that this monument should reveal and speak to the specific structural constraints of the migrant trajectory. In this way, the monument challenged the officially favoured mode of discussing migration as a linear progression towards "settlement" and belonging.

The realist bronze statue at the centre of the Park is of a male migrant clutching a bag and shielding his eyes from the sun with his passport. A series of walls listing migrants who passed through Gippsland hedge the statue. Despite the group's attempts to make this single, young male the "every migrant", I think he does speak to a specific historical context—his garb is 1950s vintage, for one. He speaks to the Department of Immigration's recruitment push for able-bodied young, single men, and their precarious situation in a post-war Australia suffering from a housing shortage and unaccustomed to difference. The male "breadwinner" (migrants from Italy, Greece and the Netherlands) often arrived ahead of other family. In this way, the statue does have something very specific to say about the situation facing single migrant men in this era, the uncertainty of their journey, and the isolation of their experiences in rural areas. Historian Karen Agutter describes the work contract that assisted migrants signed with the Commonwealth as creating an "endless parade of people being shifted from place to place" throughout the 1950s and well into the 1960s. Her description of postwar settlement under the contract system as a "continuum of mobility" is important to bear in mind. [37]

The Committee behind the Gippsland Immigration Park was particularly sensitive to the continued mobility assisted migrants experienced under their two-year work contracts with the Australian Commonwealth. This was the experience of Don Di Fabrizio, the President of the Committee, as well as the fathers of other members. Some of the names that appear on the walls are also of individuals who did not "settle" in Gippsland but moved on, some even returning to their countries of departure. Unlike guest-worker programmes in post-war Germany, migrants to Australia were encouraged to take up citizenship and "settle"—but this was not a universal experience.[38]

In other ways, too, the Park speaks to the history of the region: the bronze plaques featured on some of the walls depict the influence of the coal industry and power stations on migration and Gippsland's progress. The family migration stories of members of the Committee are intimately tied to the fortunes of the local power stations—like Morewell, Hazelwood, Yallourn—and other large public works commissioned by the State Electricity Commission that employed hundreds of thousands post-war migrants under often arduous working conditions. This aspect of the Park is not to be confused with a "fetishized site of the state," a monument to the state-sponsored coal industry or the State Electricity Commission.[39] The theme "Working Life," for example, warrants a whole wall, while "Major Projects" features on one plaque, but one which is placed alongside a longer history of all European (i.e., post-contact) migration to Australia.

In summary, the Park is a monument to failed industry and migrant uncertainty, which sidelines token expression of "ethnic contributions" in favour of depicting material conditions. The Park offers a highly visual heritage platform from which others could consider the intersections between industry, labour, migration and family settlement. It also opened up more storytelling spaces online and in print, for the dissemination of intimate pasts collected through oral histories.[40]

How does this example represent a challenge to authorized migration heritage and multicultural rhetoric? The Park offered a highly visual heritage platform from which to consider the intersections between industry, labour and migration. The celebratory and nostalgic depiction of power stations in the La Trobe Valley also spoke to the deleterious effects of privatization on the region (while ignoring the initial and ongoing environmental effects of the coal industry). The monument is therefore a mode through which elements of the migrant community mediated and made sense of these drastic social and economic changes to their region—in addition to implicitly commenting on how structural inequalities and government stipulations could contain the mobility and experiences of migrant others. Foregrounding the unsettled or uncertain status of "the migrant," blending, personal, familial and communal experiences of mobility in an ambiguous and porous visual representation, also undermined the linear and progressive narrative of settlement upon which the myth of harmonious multiculturalism (as adopting "Australian values") relies. This is a generous reading of the Park, in which I consciously search for progressive narratives that challenge the limits of heritage discourses. But this analysis of the Gippsland Immigration Park highlights the role of familial and intimate memories in public mediations of migration heritage, for which more official migration heritage discourses and practices do not currently account or foster.

CONCLUSION

The case studies in this chapter demonstrate how community-initiated or collaborative projects may challenge and expand existing heritage discourses around migration history and multicultural rhetoric. And while personal or community memories and officially sanctioned public memories are rarely as dichotomous as some categorizations would suggest, there remains a need to challenge the heritage industry to more enthusiastically consider the validity and meaning of oral histories in heritage nomination, management and promotion. Heritage making occurring within some community groups works against (and within) these legislative and official constraints—both the positivist nation-bound framework that limits expressions of their migration and settlement histories, and the criteria and management framework that values fabric over social meaning. Migration stories and sites of diasporic heritage are less easily accommodated in a heritage discourse that is bound by a national historiography and a linear view of the past. Moving towards a heritage practice that privileges "social value" and the collecting of community oral histories may offer us a migration heritage that works against reductive and conservative multicultural discourses.

NOTES

1. Leidulf Mydland and Wera Grahn, "Identifying Heritage Values in Local Communities," *International Journal of Heritage Studies* 18, no. 6 (2012): 564–87.
2. David C Harvey, "Heritage Pasts and Heritage Presents: Temporality, Meaning and the Scope of Heritage Studies," *International Journal of Heritage Studies* 7, no. 4 (2001): 337.
3. Emma Waterton and Laurajane Smith, "The Recognition and Misrecognition of Community Heritage," *International Journal of Heritage Studies* 16, no. 1–2 (2010): 4–15.
4. Laurajane Smith, *Uses of Heritage* (London: Routledge, 2006), 4, 22.

5. Celmara Pocock, David Collett, and Linda Baulch, "Assessing Stories before Sites: Identifying the Tangible from the Intangible," *International Journal of Heritage Studies* 21, no. 10 (2015): 963.
6. Denis Byrne, Helen Brayshaw and Tracy Ireland, *Social Significance: A Discussion Paper* (NSW National Parks and Wildlife Service, 2003).
7. Annie Clarke and Chris Johnston, "Time, Memory, Place and Land: Social Meaning and Heritage Conservation in Australia," Paper Presented at the Scientific Symposium, ICOMOS 14th General Assembly, 2003 in Zimbabwe, 4.
8. Chris Johnston, "Reshaping Practice: The Challenge of Intangible Cultural Heritage," at ICOMOS workshop on Practice Note, Intangible and invisible: Recognising intangible cultural heritage in place, 20 October 2017, Old Parliament House.
9. Stephen Castles et al., *Immigration and Australia: Myths and Realities*, (Sydney: Allen & Unwin in conjunction with the Housing Industry Association, 1998), 54.
10. Ian McShane, "Challenging or Conventional? Migration History in Australian Museums," in Darryl McIntyre and Kirsten Wehner eds, *Negotiating Histories: National Museums Conference Proceedings* (Canberra: National Museum of Australia, 2001), 122–33.
11. Geoffrey Blainey, "The Asianisation of Australia," *The Age*, 20 March 1984; Jock Collins, "Do We Want Geoffrey Blainey's Australia?," *The Australian Quarterly* 57, no. 1/2 (1985): 47–56.
12. Committee to Advise on Australia's Immigration Policies, and FitzGerald, *Immigration: A Commitment to Australia: Consultants' Reports* (Canberra: Australian Government Publishing Service, 1988).
13. Ghassan Hage, *White Nation: Fantasies of White Supremacy in a Multicultural Society* (London: Routledge, 2012).
14. Australian Government and the Australian Multicultural Advisory Council, "The People of Australia: Australia's Multicultural Policy," Canberra, 2011.
15. Hage, *White Nation*, 46–74.
16. See "Multicultural Statement," launched in March 2017, Department of Social Services, *Multicultural Australia: United, Strong, Successful: Australia's Multicultural Statement*, 7.
17. Tim Soutphommasane, *Don't Go Back to Where You Came From* (UNSW Press, 2012).
18. Alexandra Dellios, *Histories of Controversy: Bonegilla Migrant Centre* (Melbourne: Melbourne University Publishing, 2017).
19. See Australian Heritage Database, National Heritage List, Bonegilla Migrant Camp—Block 19, 76 Bonegilla Rd, Bonegilla, Victoria, Australia,

Place ID 105845, Place File no.2/08/246/0004; Commonwealth of Australia Gazette No. S257, Inclusion of a place in the National Heritage List—Bonegilla, Block 19 (7 December 2007); Minister for the Environment and Energy, Josh Frydenberg MP, Media Release, "National Heritage Listing for Snowy Mountains Scheme," 14 October 2016; Australian Heritage Database, National Heritage List, Snowy Mountains Scheme, Snowy Mountains Hwy, Cabramurra, New South Wales, Australia, Place ID105919, Place File no.1/08/284/0006; Commonwealth of Australia Gazette—C2016G01361, Inclusion of a place in the National Heritage List—Snowy Mountains Scheme (14 October 2016).

20. Paula Hamilton, Paul Ashton, and Rose Searby, *Places of the Heart: Memorials in Australia* (Melbourne: Australian Scholarly Publishing, 2012).

21. Cristóbal Gnecco, "Heritage in Multicultural Times," in *The Palgrave Handbook of Contemporary Heritage Research* (London: Palgrave Macmillan, 2015), 266–7.

22. Denis Byrne, "Heritage Corridors: Transnational Flows and the Built Environment of Migration," *Journal of Ethnic and Migration Studies* 42, no. 14 (2016): 2360–78.

23. Byrne, "Heritage Corridors," 2360.

24. Australian Heritage Commission and Helen Armstrong, *Migrant Heritage Places In Australia [A Handbook for Group Coordinators and How to Find your Heritage Places—A Guide]*, 1993.

25. Helen Armstrong, "Migrant Heritage Places in Australia," *Historic Environment* 13, no. 2 (1997): 12–23; Helen Armstrong, "Mapping Migrant Memories: Crossing Cultural Borders," *The Oral History Association of Australia Journal* 19 (1997): 59.

26. NSW Migration Heritage Centre, "Exhibitions," 2010. http://www.migrationheritage.nsw.gov.au/online-exhibitions/index.html.

27. Susan Tonkin, "Essay: What is Heritage?," Australian Heritage Strategy, Commissioned Essay, Department of Sustainability, Environment, Water, Population and Communities (2012), http://www.environment.gov.au/topics/heritage/australian-heritage-strategy/commissioned-essays.

28. Australia ICOMOS, *The Burra Charter: The Australia ICOMOS Charter for Places of Cultural Significance 1999: With Associated Guidelines and Code on the Ethics of Co-existence*, 2000; Tonkin, "Essay: What is Heritage?," 6.

29. National Archives of Australia (NAA), A445/1, 276/2/10, 276/1/6, Dobson, Hazel, "Social Welfare. Widows and Unmarried Mothers with Dependent Children," March 1951.

30. NAA, A437 1950/6/173, Dobson, 1951.

31. Bruce Pennay, *Benalla Migrant Camp: A Difficult Heritage* (Benalla Migrant Camp Incorporated, 2015).

32. Ann-Marie Jordens, *Alien to Citizens: Settling Migrants in Australia, 1945–1975* (Sydney: Allen & Unwin, 1997), 64–65.
33. Jayne Persian, *Beautiful Balts: From Displaced Persons to New Australians* (Sydney: NewSouth Books, 2017).
34. Deirdre Prinsen, "Oral History and Attachment to Place in Cultural Heritage Management: A Case Study of the Shack Community at Era, Royal National Park, NSW," *Oral History Association of Australia Journal* 35 (2013): 79.
35. Anonymized submission from Benalla resident to Heritage Victoria, 18 August 2015.
36. Gippsland Immigration Park Inc., Application Form: Victorian Community Support Grants, Department for Victorian Communities, 2006.
37. Karen Agutter, "Displaced Persons and the 'Continuum of Mobility' in the South Australian Hostel System," in Margrette Kleinig and Eric Richards eds, *On the Wing: Mobility Before and After Emigration to Australia, Visible Immigrants Vol 7* (Anchor Books: 2013), 147.
38. Rates of emigration exceeded immigration to Australia in the 1960s— mainly Dutch and Italian people returning to their countries of origin. Some groups were also more reluctant than others to take up citizenship, including those from Soviet-controlled Baltic States, who harboured a hope that their nations would escape Soviet rule and they'd be able to return.
39. Michael Rothberg, *Multidirectional Memory: Remembering the Holocaust in the Age of Decolonization* (Stanford: Stanford University Press, 2009).
40. Gippsland Immigration Park Inc., *Stories from the Gippsland Immigration Wall of Recognition*, 2012.

BIBLIOGRAPHY

Agutter, Karen. "Displaced Persons and the 'Continuum of Mobility' in the South Australian Hostel System." In *On the Wing: Mobility Before and After Emigration to Australia, Visible Immigrants Volume 7*, edited by Margrette Kleinig and Eric Richards, 136–52. Spit Junction, NSW: Anchor Books Australia, 2013.

Armstrong, Helen. "Mapping Migrant Memories: Crossing Cultural Borders." *The Oral History Association of Australia Journal* 19 (1997a): 59–65.

Armstrong, Helen. "Migrant Heritage Places in Australia." *Historic Environment* 13, no. 2 (1997b): 12–23.

Australian Government and the Australian Multicultural Advisory Council "The People of Australia: Australia's Multicultural Policy." Canberra, 2011.

Australian Government and the Department of Social Services. *Multicultural Australia: United, Strong, Successful: Australia's Multicultural Statement*. Canberra, March 2017.

Australian Heritage Commission and Helen Armstrong. *Migrant Heritage Places in Australia: A Handbook for Group Coordinators and How to Find your Heritage Places, A Guide*, 1993.

Australian Heritage Database, National Heritage List, Bonegilla Migrant Camp— Block 19, 76 Bonegilla Rd, Bonegilla, Victoria, Australia, Place ID 105845, Place File no.2/08/246/0004.

Australian Heritage Database, National Heritage List, Snowy Mountains Scheme, Snowy Mountains Hwy, Cabramurra, New South Wales, Australia, Place ID105919, Place File no.1/08/284/0006.

Blainey, Geoffrey. "The Asianisation of Australia." *The Age*, 20 March 1984.

Borin, Vladimir. "Australian Bachelors of Misery." *Quadrant* 5, no. 3 (1961): 3–7.

Byrne, Denis. "Heritage Corridors: Transnational Flows and the Built Environment of Migration." *Journal of Ethnic and Migration Studies* 42, no. 14 (2016): 2360–78.

Byrne, Denis, Helen Brayshaw, and Tracy Ireland. *Social Significance: A Discussion Paper*. NSW National Parks and Wildlife Service, 2003.

Castles, Stephen et al., *Immigration and Australia: Myths and Realities*. Sydney: Allen & Unwin in conjunction with the Housing Industry Association, 1998.

Clarke, Annie, and Chris Johnston. "Time, Memory, Place and Land: Social Meaning and Heritage Conservation in Australia." Paper Presented at the Scientific Symposium, ICOMOS 14th General Assembly, in Zimbabwe, 1–6, 2003.

Collins, Jock. "Do We Want Geoffrey Blainey's Australia?" *The Australian Quarterly* 57, no. 1/2 (1985): 47–56.

Committee to Advise on Australia's Immigration Policies, and Stephen FitzGerald. *Immigration: A Commitment to Australia: Consultants' Reports*. Canberra: Australian Government Publishing Service, 1988.

Commonwealth of Australia Gazette—C2016G01361, Inclusion of a place in the National Heritage List—Snowy Mountains Scheme (14 October 2016).

Commonwealth of Australia Gazette No. S257, Inclusion of a Place in the National Heritage List—Bonegilla, Block 19 (7 December 2007).

Dellios, Alexandra. *Histories of Controversy: Bonegilla Migrant Centre*. Melbourne: Melbourne University Publishing, 2017.

Gippsland Immigration Park Inc., Application Form: Victorian Community Support Grants, Department for Victorian Communities, 2006.

Gippsland Immigration Park Inc., *Stories from the Gippsland Immigration Wall of Recognition*. Victoria: Gippsland, 2012.

Hage, Ghassan. *White Nation: Fantasies of White Supremacy in a Multicultural Society*. London: Routledge, 2012.

Hamilton, Paula, Paul Ashton, and Rose Searby. *Places of the Heart: Memorials in Australia*. Melbourne: Australian Scholarly Publishing, 2012.

ICOMOS, Australia. *The Burra Charter: The Australia ICOMOS Charter for Places of Cultural Significance 1999: With Associated Guidelines and Code on the Ethics of Co-existence*. Australia ICOMOS, 2000.

Jordens, Ann-Marie. *Alien to Citizen: Settling Migrants in Australia, 1945–1975*. Sydney: Allen & Unwin, 1997.

McShane, Ian. "Challenging or Conventional? Migration History in Australian Museums." In *Negotiating Histories: National Museums Conference Proceedings*, edited by Darryl McIntyre, and Kirsten Wehner, 122–33. Canberra: National Museum of Australia, 2001.

Minister for the Environment and Energy, Josh Frydenberg MP, Media Release, "National Heritage Listing for Snowy Mountains Scheme," 14 October 2016.

Mydland, Leidulf, and Wera Grahn. "Identifying Heritage Values in Local Communities." *International Journal of Heritage Studies* 18, no. 6 (2012): 564–87.

National Archives of Australia (NAA), A445/1, 276/2/10, 276/1/6, Dobson, Hazel. "Social Welfare. Widows and Unmarried Mothers with Dependent Children," March 1951, and NAA, A437 1950/6/173, Dobson, 1951.

NSW Migration Heritage Centre. "Exhibitions." (2010). http://www.migrationheritage.nsw.gov.au/online-exhibitions/index.html.

Pennay, Bruce. *Benalla Migrant Camp: A Difficult Heritage*. Benalla Migrant Camp Incorporated, 2015.

Persian, Jayne. *Beautiful Balts: From Displaced Persons to New Australians*. Sydney: NewSouth Books, 2017.

Prinsen, Deirdre. "Oral History and Attachment to Place in Cultural Heritage Management: A Case Study of the Shack Community at Era, Royal National Park, NSW." *Oral History Association of Australia Journal* 35 (2013): 77–85.

Reeves, Keir, Erik Eklund, Andrew Reeves, Bruce Scates, and Vicki Peel. "Broken Hill: Rethinking the Significance of the Material Culture and Intangible Heritage of the Australian Labour Movement." *International Journal of Heritage Studies* 17, no. 4 (2011): 301–17.

Ross, Cathy. "From Migration to Diversity and Beyond: The Museum of London Approach." In *Museums, Migration and Identity in Europe: People, Places and Identities*, edited by Christopher Whitehead, Katherine Lloyd, Susannah Eckersley and Rhiannon Mason, 61–80. London: Routledge, 2015.

Rothberg, Michael. *Multidirectional memory: Remembering the Holocaust in the Age of Decolonization*. Stanford University Press, 2009.

Smith, Laurajane. *Uses of Heritage*. London: Routledge, 2006.

Tonkin, Susan. "Essay: What is Heritage?" *Australian Heritage Strategy, Commissioned Essay, Department of Sustainability, Environment, Water, Population and Communities* (2012). http://www.environment.gov.au/topics/heritage/australian-heritage-strategy/commissioned-essays.

Waterton, Emma, and Laurajane Smith. "The Recognition and Misrecognition of Community Heritage." *International Journal of Heritage Studies* 16, no. 1–2 (2010): 4–15.

CHAPTER 16

Hard Landings: Memory, Place and Migration

Susannah Radstone

In the chapter that follows, I use some insights from cultural memory studies to shed light on my own migration and its relation with memory—an exercise that has involved grappling with "[t]he enigma of arrival"—an experience Eva Hoffman has found "more difficult to analyse than the drama of departure."[1]

In writing this chapter—for what follows constitutes, in part, a particular kind of memory *writing*—I have drawn from the theories and methods that have informed my thinking about memory and, in particular, the psychoanalytic writings of Jean Laplanche and practiced a method or process of memory work and writing pioneered in Annette Kuhn's book *Family Secrets*.[2] Explaining the category to which her own memory texts belong, Kuhn writes that:

> they tread a line between cultural criticism and cultural production. ... As such, they are driven by two sets of concerns. The first has to do with the ways memory shapes the stories we tell, in the present, about the past—especially stories about our own lives. The second has to do with what it is

S. Radstone (✉)
Monash University, Melbourne, VIC, Australia
e-mail: Susannah.Radstone@monash.edu.au

© The Author(s) 2019
K. Darian-Smith, P. Hamilton (eds.), *Remembering Migration*,
Palgrave Macmillan Memory Studies,
https://doi.org/10.1007/978-3-030-17751-5_16

that makes us remember: the prompts, the pretexts of memory; the reminders of the past in the present.[3]

Kuhn's memory work involves following "clues ... [that] are traces of my own past: for the most part images and the memories associated with them" and tracing "a radiating web of associations, reflections and interpretations."[4] The chapter of *Family Secrets* that has most inspired me involves, like the essay that follows, the writing up of a walk.[5] "A Phantasmagoria of Memory" follows the clues that Kuhn finds in "a reverie: a view from below of trees, light filtering down through the leaves," that she experiences as she "tread[s] the pavement outside the British Museum's main entrance."[6] In reflecting on that walk, Kuhn traces the paths that lead through her reverie's associations to a complex network of cultural texts and contexts, revealing not only the part played by those remembered scenes, in the shaping of her own identity—and belonging to London—but also the agency of her inner world in the mediation of those remembered scenes.

If the starting point for my own excursion into memory and migration sits closer to memory's relations with unbelonging than with belonging, it nevertheless follows Kuhn's example by taking as its raw materials the clues provided by hard to categorize experiences and feelings prompted by place. As Kuhn points out elsewhere, the act of bringing these feelings into focus and making them available for reflection involves a kind of "inner speech" and "secondary revision."[7] The committal of these reflections to *actual* writing produces a written "memory text" informed by memory's associational logic and formal conventions, all of which position the memory text somewhere between creative practice and scholarly writing.[8] As Kuhn explains, the formal conventions of the memory text include repetitive or cyclical events: "[t]he memory text is typically a montage of vignettes, anecdotes, fragments, 'snapshots,' flashes ... memory texts are metaphorical rather than analogical."[9]

The text that follows is marked, therefore, by the conventions of scholarly writing and—if only to an extent—by those of the memory text, the formal attributes of which are perhaps most evident in its vignette-like structure. Starting out from inchoate feelings to which I give inner voice, the written text that follows seeks to share insights gathered as I tried to do memory work with the particularity of my own experiences of memory and migration.

STARTING OUT

A long time ago now, and several years before I migrated to Australia, I took a walk along the pedestrian path that skirts Melbourne's St Kilda beach. The inner-city seaside suburb St Kilda has a rich, colourful and unstable history. From its mid-nineteenth-century flowering as "'the place to be' for wealthy settlers,"[10] the 1890s depression saw it hit harder times until, by the 1890s, St Kilda was becoming home to a fair smattering of the less than law-abiding, and the suburb began to gain a reputation for prostitution and drugs. During the twentieth century, the area's fortunes rose again as it became home to migrant groups, including a substantial Jewish community who contributed to St Kilda's cosmopolitanism and, not least, to Acland Street's much-frequented and now dwindling string of continental cake shops. By the 1960s, St Kilda—like my birthplace of Chelsea, in London—had begun to draw a bohemian crowd of artists and musicians. It is thanks to this period of history that I came to be taking the walk through St Kilda with which I begin, for during my first visit to Melbourne in the early 2000s, I was staying near a new friend (now my partner) who had been attracted to St Kilda in the 1980s—like many others then and before her—by the suburb's liveliness and cultural vibrancy. Today, a little of that does remain, but St Kilda's bigger picture reveals a more recent history of deepening inequalities. Wealthy homeowners now live alongside homeless people; a grand church hall has been re-purposed as a mission for the destitute and rows of vacant shopfronts bear testimony to the damage wreaked by impossibly high rents. Within this streetscape sits *Café di Stasio*, the last remaining smart restaurant along Fitzroy Street's most southerly block, its windows protected by hoardings. Celebrating Australia's permanent pavilion at the Venice Biennale,[11] and etched with the artist Barrie Marshall's chalky scrawl, the marks on the hoardings fuse architectural notation with graffiti.

With its embrace of St Kilda's cosmopolitan, artistic and edgy heritage and its pragmatic bow to the tensions played out on its streets today, *Di Stasio*'s frontage speaks of St Kilda's past and present in its own terms. But when I walk past *Di Stasio*, it's not this eloquence that arrests me, but a sense of the impenetrable hardness of those boards. Looking at those hoardings, instead of through glass, I feel like something in me has been arrested; I feel like I'm looking into—or is it also out of?—dead eyes.[12]

The stresses of the twenty-first century have led many to take up meditation and mindfulness. Likening feelings and their fluctuations to the weather's ebbs and flows, these practices enjoin us to observe the waves of feeling that might otherwise overwhelm us, or throw us—metaphorically speaking—off-course. In some cases, however—pre-eminently those of the asylum-seeker, the refugee and the forced migrant—people may find themselves thrown actually, as well as figuratively, off-course. Unexpectedly, and due to what I can now recognize as sheer lack of foresight, I found that my own privileged voluntary migration brought with it aspects of this doubled "off-courseness", as I travelled myopically, if not blindly, through unfamiliar territory assailed all the while by powerful, "chaotic"[13] and unusual feelings.

The position of voluntary migrant permits no comparison with the rigours of those forced to leave their homes and loved ones. Permitted—or prescribed, even—however, by my position as voluntary migrant and memory researcher, is an enquiry into memory's relations with that unsettling fusion of actual and psychical "off-courseness" that has accompanied my own migration. As I start out on this investigation, I set aside the advice offered by meditation and mindfulness in favour of re-evoking and entering into rather than distantly observing the feelings that have accompanied my unmooring. Setting out to explore what migration might have to teach us about memory and its vicissitudes, I will let myself be led by the disturbances that have assailed me—specifically a sense of things in my new surroundings feeling—like the hoardings protecting *Di Stasio*'s windows—harder, less porous and less permeable, or in other cases, harder, thinner and shallower than they should or once did.

A Walk by the Sea

Perhaps it was in 2004 or 2005 that I took my first walk along the curve of St Kilda's seafront. A range of attractions await the foreshore's many visitors, including the Luna Park funfair, a string of cafés and bars fringed by outdoor terraces for balmy summer days, an indoor seawater swimming baths, multiply demolished and rebuilt since the nineteenth century and, stretching out into the bay for more than half a kilometre, a Victorian-era stone and timber pier. A breezy stroll along the pier rewards sightseers with panoramic vistas of Melbourne's rapidly developing twenty-first century skyline of gleaming skyscrapers and for those who make it to the end, there's also a lovely Edwardian-style pavilion café, reconstructed after fire damage in 2003. Beyond the pier, a wave-splattered breakwater built for the 1956 Olympic Games extends out into Port Phillip Bay. For those venturing furthest from shore, St Kilda's final reward might be a glimpse of a little penguin belonging to the colony that has—maybe since the 1950s—made its perilous home there amongst the breakwater's crevices, in the place where the land and then the rocks finally abandon themselves to the sea.

It is easy to see, now, that the landscape through which I took my walk is thick with evidence of its past. Stretching back to the 1840s, St Kilda's history of British colonial settlement is inscribed into the pier, the sea baths and the pavilion. In recalling my walk along the St Kilda foreshore, however, I am struck by my seeming obliviousness to the teeming presence of this past. In place of, and even in contradiction to any such apprehension, I recall my perturbing sense of the depthlessness of the environment, coupled with the hardness and thinness of the path beneath my feet. Looking back, I'm surprised that I didn't link that feeling with those academic writings on the depthlessness of postmodernity and its associated culture[14] that had played their part in the development of my own field of cultural memory studies, or with Walter Benjamin's writings on the impact of modernity on tradition and memory.[15] Yet it seemed that my response drew neither from my pre-migration academic knowledge and ways of thinking, nor from the evidence of the past—albeit dating back only to the 1840s—that was all around me. Instead, at the time, I made sense of my experience on the path in terms of my having felt, there on the shoreline, something that I was barely beginning to glimpse—the relatively short span of Australia's British settler colonial history, a history that had barely scratched the land's surface—as it seemed to me, then, particularly when set against the more than 65,000 year history of Australia's occupation by its Indigenous peoples.

Perhaps, by the time I took my walk, I had already read and been moved by Kate Grenville's historical novel *The Secret River*—a powerful work that confronts its readers with the violence perpetrated on Australia's Indigenous peoples by settlers who, bent on claiming acreage for themselves, made their homes on those peoples' ancestral lands.[16] My disturbing sense of the shallowness, the thinness of the path below my feet, accompanied, as it was, by a feeling that something important was somehow missing, might have been linked to that novel's distressing ending. In *The Secret River*'s final chapter, Australia's settler occupation is seen to do little more than thinly cover over the almost entirely vacated, yet haunted landscape bequeathed by this earlier violence to Australia's future generations. Even if I had yet to read *The Secret River*, since arriving in Melbourne

I had spent my time with people who, attuned to the presence of this past, continue to wrestle with its implications for all of those settlers—including newly arrived migrants—who call Australia home, today.

Memory studies offers more than one framework within which my disturbing experience might conceivably belong. Theories of the transgenerational transmission of trauma propose, for instance, that traumas suffered in the past may be passed on across generations, leaving their traces in symptoms including gaps and absences in memory. Within this paradigm,[17] and following the logic of trauma's pathologies of memory, my sense of the path's thinness—of something missing below my feet—could be linked with a pressing and disturbing absence of memory for what might have been perpetrated on this land, as well as with an apprehension of the thinness of the present's covering over of that past. Theories of transgenerational trauma refer, however, to the transmission of trauma among generations linked through shared history, experience and most usually through kinship. Where memory studies does conceive of the possibility that transgenerational trauma transmission might be extended beyond ties of history and kinship, such transmission is understood to require a cultural conduit. On Marianne Hirsch's account, it is experimental photography's capacity to call up the spectator's familial gaze that has facilitated its deployment as an instrument for the transmission of what she terms "postmemory."[18] On my walk through St Kilda, my scant knowledge of settler violence provided no such conduit for the transmission of the traumatic memories of past generations of Australia's Indigenous peoples and specifically of the Kulin people whose land included St Kilda. I am therefore led to conclude that though it might be possible to argue, albeit weakly, that my disturbance on the St Kilda foreshore was related to the transmission of past traumas suffered by Australia's Indigenous peoples, such an argument ought not to be made and cannot be substantiated. All I had with me on that walk—not untypically, perhaps, for the newly arrived visitor from overseas—were the merest scraps of information about Australia, its history and the history of Indigenous settler relations, in particular—and even if the extent of my knowledge had been greater, there is a world of difference between information and memory.[19]

If the model of transgenerational transmission of trauma can shed little light on the cause of the disturbance that I felt on the path, its focus on transmission may yet prove helpful—for it pushes me to pose the question of whether another kind of memory-related transmission might have been in play on the foreshore and, if so, whether that transmission was linked in any way to my dearth of knowledge and lack of memories of the place where I was, and to my feelings about what lay—or didn't lie—under my feet. After all, over dinner in Melbourne, a colleague from the UK told me that he simply could not move to Australia because of what wouldn't then be there, under his feet. Beneath the streets of the old world, but missing in Australia, he said, are the vestiges and remains laid down by the centuries; layers that somehow make their presence felt, even if they are glimpsed only rarely, when the streets are dug up. Perplexed, and yet reaching for an explanation about why he felt that these invisible layers were so essential to him, my colleague said that all he knew was that they somehow sustained him and enabled him to live. To my objection that Australia was, by virtue of its having been populated for more than 65,000 years by its Indigenous peoples, the longest-inhabited region on Earth,[20] my dinner companion responded that it was the sparseness of the traces left by that inhabitation (rather than, I inferred, the extent of their decipherability) that would make it impossible for him to live in Australia.

Hard Realities

To begin with, it seemed to me that this shared dinner conversation might shed light on the origin of the apparently irrational feelings that had been accompanying my excursions into St Kilda and beyond. I was born in London and had lived there for almost my entire life. Perhaps it was, indeed, a half-conscious awareness of the comparative absence of the past's material deposits in the ground under my feet that had been registered in those disturbing feelings of the thinness and shallowness of the path. Yet even if that were the case, my colleague couldn't explain what it was about his intimations of those buried deposits that somehow sustained his capacity to live. A second question left hanging, also, after that conversation concerned another aspect of my St Kilda experience, a response related not—or so it seemed—to the absence of buried deposits, but to what felt like the all too present materials of the city's surface—a city that I was visiting and to which I would eventually migrate. For, during my visit to Melbourne and as it turned out, after I migrated there, too, it wasn't just *Di Stasio*'s hoardings that felt harder and more unyielding than they somehow should. Wherever I went, the cement, asphalt and tarmac of Melbourne's streets and the glass, concrete and steel of its buildings seemed to assault me with their sheer, forbidding materiality. It might be just about plausible to suggest that my sense of the "too thinness" of the

St Kilda path and my colleague's apprehension of there not being "deep enough" remains and traces below ground to sustain his life in Australia both express—through a projection[21] made possible by the actual relative absence of material remains in Australia compared to, say, beneath the streets of London—something of the migrant's predicament. After all, the migrant's experience can be perceived as dominated by loss— not just of home, but of home's entanglement with memory's props and prompts.[22] Yet although it seems persuasive to link those apprehensions of thinness below the feet and of absent remains with a loss or absence of memory's supports and triggers, this explanation can't explain that other feeling with which I was being assailed—the sense of the sheer, hard materiality of Melbourne. To make sense of these experiences and to reach a better understanding of their relations with memory and migration requires a shift of focus. For as it turns out, we can make better sense of a path that feels depthless and a city that seems reduced to its sheer, hard materiality by linking these apprehensions not with the loss or absence of a known and familiar home, with all of its memory-rich resonances, but with migration's impact on the ability to access something unknowable and yet essential for life to feel alive.

On the account of the psychoanalyst Jean Laplanche, the unconscious is formed as the infant strives to translate messages implanted in it by its caretaker that contain an untranslatable element constituted by an enigmatic kernel.[23] Laplanche explains this process, which he terms seduction, by reference to the example of the child, who, while feeding at its mother's breast, passively receives messages containing untranslatable elements from the mother's unconscious related to her sexuality. These enigmatic signifiers—opaque to the mother, as well as to the child[24]—become implanted in the child, forming the basis of its unconscious and setting the scene for a life that feels alive. If we follow this Laplanchian path, encounters with life's everyday realities including with places, people or cultural experiences, bring with them a "something more," or supplement, constituted from what we bring to, "find" and seek to translate in them: the traces of enigmatic signifiers as they come to us in the forms of life's protean scenes.

Laplanche developed his theory of enigmatic signification by critically revising and combining Freud's early seduction theory of hysteria with his account of the failures of translation that occur between memory's successive psychical "inscriptions, translations or transcriptions"[25] —a connection that invites memory research to consider the relations between processes of remembering and Laplanchian translation. The connections or correspondences[26] of memory's associative logic work through encounters with the material of everyday life including smells, sounds, touch and sight. So when I walk from my new Melbourne home, down the railway path and across the little park to our local market, as I so often do, the sight of Prahran's town hall clock might call up memories of the clock tower that I would see every time I walked to the shops in my old London home of Crouch End. Seizing on such correspondences between familiar and strange places constitutes that "mysterious joining of old and new"[27] that animates what Roger Kennedy has termed "the living soul,"[28] and helps migrants to make homes in new worlds.[29] But if we follow Laplanche, those connections may not alone provide that vital tissue of connection required for life to feel truly life-full. For this, those correspondences would need to connect the new not just with the remembered known, but with the unknown or untranslatable signifier transmitted through memories prompted by new realities. It is this enigmatic dimension carried to us through every encounter that—if all goes well enough—we spend our lives trying to translate. But all does not always go well enough. Sometimes, as has been my experience, the ground feels thin and depthless under our feet, and the environment impingingly unyielding. These experiences have remained opaque to my earlier attempts to map their relations with memory and migration, but the path offered by Laplanche promises illumination, for, in the case of migration, it seems that experiencing the environment as unyielding, hard and impenetrable may be related to the blocking of the capacity to touch into the enigmatic dimension of correspondences between the old and new worlds.

Laplanche's expositor Dominique Scarfone offers the following account of implantation's pathological variant, intromission: "Implantation is a process," Scarfone explains, "which is common, everyday, normal or neurotic. Beside it, as its violent variant, a place must be given to intromission. While implantation allows the individual to take things up actively, at once translating and repressing, one must try to conceive of a process which blocks this … and puts into the interior an element resistant to all metabolizations."[30] As described by Scarfone, the normal process of transmission and translation of the enigmatic message relies on a number of compromises on the part of the adult and child. Intromission differs from this normal process suggests Scarfone, since it refers to the transmission of the enigmatic message without compromise:

no longer a violence of the message itself, but a violence of the transmitter of the message. No longer the enigma in itself, but rather the prohibition on translation that it carries in parallel, and which would be perhaps the essence, in this case, of the message coming from the adult.[31]

Elsewhere, Scarfone explains that: "[b]y putting 'into the interior' elements that are 'resistant to all metabolization' and thus fundamentally resistant to all translation, intromission performs a kind of hijacking, crippling the apparatus of translation itself."[32] The enigmatic message blocked by intromission, in the voice of the receiving child, "is what is beyond my mother; it is what makes in my mother a hollow, which makes her other, which gives her a complexity, a thickness or a depth; what makes her psychically *real*, a reality I cannot flee."[33]

The Laplanchian concept of intromission most often refers to the impact on the developing child of a process that blocks the active taking up, translation and repression of the enigmatic message. But psychoanalysis stresses that the temporality of psychical life is anything but linear; developmental processes are continually recapitulated and revised under new conditions. Likewise, it is axiomatic to psychoanalysis that psychical ease and unease are best construed as belonging on a spectrum, rather than within the binary categories of normal and pathological. Bearing both of these principles in mind allows an appreciation of the congruity between Laplanchian intromission and my own—and perhaps others'—experience of immigration, where, as I'm proposing, the unmitigated impingement of the new environment may impact similarly to intromission: the violent transmission of a message without compromise. Those experiences that I have described in terms of the impinging hardness of material reality—the glass, the steel the asphalt—constitute, on this reading, projections into place of the violent imposition of elements resistant to metabolization, and that unnerving sense of depthlessness that my colleague and I discussed over dinner becomes, on this reading, a projection into place of the utter inaccessibility of that enigmatic dimension that was, in its primary iteration, "what ma[de] my mother hollow, which g[ave] her ... a thickness, a depth."[34]

As other accounts confirm, there's nothing unique about the experience of unpliability and hardness that I've been describing. In an account suggestive of intromission, one (non-Laplanchian) psychiatrist writes that "[f]or the immigrant, the new immediate cultural surround is no longer materially pliable, will not bend to intention and creative impulse. ... The gestural idiom ... the temporal pace and interpersonal distance, the food, the words themselves are not as malleable as they were back home."[35] But if the uncompromising new environment's dearth of correspondences blocks access to the transmission and attempted translation of the enigmatic message, can there be light at the end of this tunnel?

A World Regained

Not so long after I had migrated to Melbourne, I was walking up Nicholson Street in Melbourne on my way to meet my adopted niece Ali at a bookstore where the Jewish lesbian New York writer Joan Nestle was to read from her work. On the stretch where Nicholson Street runs parallel to Carlton Gardens and the magnificent late nineteenth-century Great Exhibition Building I found myself arrested by what lay under my feet—an expanse of worn paving stones.

There, alongside the dwellings that I now know to be Nicholson Street's Royal Terrace (Fig. 16.1), the oldest remaining early terrace in Melbourne, I was standing on what the Heritage Council of Victoria's website tells me is pavement "probably contemporary to the terrace. Remnant original red sandstone paving is possibly from Arbroath, Scotland and the grey sandstone from Caithness."[36] Looking back at the passage I've just written, I note that the adjectives I've used in association with my encounter with that pavement—the *stretch* of Nicholson Street; the *expanse* of worn paving stones—touch on the feelings that pavement evoked in me—an intense sense of opening, expanding, taking in, almost to the point of coming alive. Did I sense that the paving I was walking on was familiar to my feet—imported from the UK and identical to many of the older paving stones of London? And was it this unexpected encounter with something so familiar—with finding something of home abroad—that provoked feelings powerful enough to bring tears to my eyes? Or, *en route* to a reading in a bookshop, did those paving stones transport me back to London, to memories of bookstores where I'd worked, bookstores and poetry centres where my mother had worked and readings I'd attended in those places? Or are all of these possible correspondences insufficient to explain the power of my response?

Marcel Proust describes a startlingly similar response to an encounter with paving stones in the following terms:

Fig. 16.1 Royal Terrace, Nicholson Street, Fitzroy. Photograph by Susannah Radstone

> I stood … repeating the movement of a moment since, one foot upon the higher flagstone, the other on the lower one. Merely repeating the movement was useless; but if … I succeeded in recapturing the sensation which accompanied the movement, again the intoxicating and elusive vision softly pervaded me as though it said 'Grasp me as I float by you, if you can, and try to solve the *enigma* of happiness I offer you.'[37]

In its final volume, Proust writes that it was in "stumbl[ing] against some unevenly placed paving stones" that he finally achieved some understanding of those moments of ecstasy that have punctuated *In Search of Lost*

Time's multiple volumes. Proust's insight into this happiness hinges on memory's relations with place and time. In that moment of mnemonic correspondence between his present act of stepping across uneven paving stones in the Guermantes' courtyard and his memory of doing so in the Baptistery of St Mark's Basilica in Venice, Proust identifies an experience released from time and distilled to its essence, releasing its bearer—fleetingly, yet ecstatically—from the burdens of time and death.

As Proust's epic work *and* Laplanchian psychoanalytic theory propose and as migration experiences confirm, being alive does not always equate to feeling alive. Migration may block the capacity to find correspondences of the order described by Proust—correspondences that, if we follow Laplanche, constitute the conduits not just of experiences distilled to their essence, but of an enigmatic dimension that, in calling for translation, calls their receiver into life. Proust's retrospectively Laplanchian references to the "enigma of happiness" and to his experience of "a newer scene which yet was penetrable by the past,"[38] show me that it was in the moment on Royal Crescent's pavement that I—as a relatively new migrant and after a long period of intromissive experience—became attuned once more to that endlessly enigmatic dimension of that message that lends depth and pliability to our worlds.

Perhaps, for the migrant, it simply takes time for the enigmatic to be restored as it is transmitted to us through the correspondences of memory. Conversely, there might have been something specific about that moment on Royal Terrace that allowed memory to return the pliability and mystery of the world to me—perhaps my mother's connections with literary events calling up echoes of the messages I first received from her, or the sight of Royal Terrace's paving stones re-evoking an enigma transposed from my much-loved London streets. But in the end, the quest to distinguish between these two possibilities would only serve to obscure their connectedness, for from a Laplanchian perspective, the places that surround us reverberate with the ever-renewed echoes of a message transposed *from* mother *to* place.

Worlds Gained and Lost

For Australia's Indigenous peoples, country is suffused with messages, myth and ancestral memory and land is inseparably connected to ancestors and the mother. As the Indigenous scholar Dennis Foley puts it, "[t]he land is the mother and we are of the land." Tempting as it might be to conclude my Laplanchian thoughts about memory and migrating to Australia by claiming Australia's Indigenous culture as Laplanchian *avant la lettre*, I will end by circling back to where I began, on a walk through what felt like a hard and depthless St Kilda. As I followed the foreshore path, it came to me that the feelings that were troubling me might have been aroused by my nascent understanding of the violent impact that settler-colonialism had wreaked on Australia's Indigenous communities; those feelings of depthlessness and of the absence of something important being associated, on this account, with the sheer absence of the Indigenous communities who had once been inseparably connected to this land. As it turned out, my migration experiences couldn't be fully explained in these terms, but it can hardly be lost on me that it was while walking along Royal Terrace, across Nicholson Street from the magnificence of Melbourne's Royal Exhibition Building that I became attuned once more to the enigmatic dimension of memory's correspondences. The setting for my epiphany could hardly have tied me more closely—or less enigmatically—to the mother country and to the part that London and England played in the "removal" of Indigenous people during the establishment of this nation that I am now able to call home, but at costs beyond measure.

Notes

1. Eva Hoffman, "Out of Exile: Some Thoughts on Exile as a Dynamic Condition," in Julia Beltsiou ed., *Immigration in Psychoanalysis: Locating Ourselves* (Abingdon: Routledge, 2016), 213.
2. Annette Kuhn, *Family Secrets: Acts of Memory and Imagination* (London: Verso, 1995).
3. Kuhn, *Family Secrets*, 3.
4. Kuhn, *Family Secrets*, 4.
5. Annette Kuhn, "A Phantasmagoria of Memory," in Annette Kuhn ed., *Family Secrets*, 104–21.
6. Kuhn, "A Phantasmagoria," 113.
7. Annette Kuhn, "A Journey Through Memory," in Susannah Radstone ed., *Memory and Methodology* (Oxford and New York: Berg, 2000), 189.
8. Kuhn, "A Journey Through Memory," 189–91.
9. Kuhn, "A Journey Through Memory," 189–90.
10. "St. Kilda's History Ain't No Mystery!" https://www.aclandstreetvillage.com.au/st-kildas-history-aint-no-mystery.
11. Debbie Cuthbertson, "Australia's First Venice Biennale Pavilion Finds Second Life as New Building Progresses," *Sydney Morning Herald*, 18

October 2014, https://www.smh.com.au/entertainment/art-and-design/australias-first-venice-biennale-pavilion-finds-second-life-as-new-building-progresses-20141017-117imr.html.

12. Roger Kennedy, *The Psychic Home: Psychoanalysis, Consciousness and the Human Soul* (Hove: Routledge, 2014), 5–6. In his study of the psychical resonances of home, Kennedy suggests that the sense of home resides primarily within us and has its origins in relations with others—relations that fall away as the other dies and the light of their gaze is exstinguished.

13. Leon and Rebeca Grinberg, *Psychoanalytic Perspectives on Migration and Exile*, trans. Nancy Festinger (New Haven: Yale University Press, 1989), 78. Leon and Rebeca Grinberg state that the new immigrant "may feel 'invaded' by what are for him 'chaotic messages'…"

14. Fredric Jameson, *Postmodernism, or, the Cultural Logic of Late Capitalism* (Durham, NC: Duke University Press, 1991).

15. Walter Benjamin, *Illuminations*, Hannah Arendt ed. (New York: Schocken Books, 1968).

16. Kate Grenville, *The Secret River* (Melbourne: Text Publishing, 2005).

17. Gabriele Schwab, *Haunting Legacies: Violent Histories and Transgenerational Trauma* (New York: Columbia University Press, 2010).

18. Marianne Hirsch, *Family Frames: Photography, Narrative and Postmemory* (Cambridge: Harvard University Press, 1997).

19. Benjamin, *Illuminations*.

20. Genelle Weule and Felicity James, "Indigenous Rock Shelter in Top End Pushes Australia's Human History Back to 65,000 years," *ABC News*, 20 July 2017, http://www.abc.net.au/news/science/2017-07-20/aboriginal-shelter-pushes-human-history-back-to-65,000-years/8719314.

21. Jean Laplanche and J. B. Pontalis, "Projection," in *The Language of Psychoanalysis* (London: Karnac Books, 1988), 349. Projection refers, here, to a psychical operation where aspects of the inner world that are hard to acknowledge are "expelled from the self and located in another person or thing." My hypothesis here is that an apprehension of there being too few buried remains under the ground may refer, in displaced form to memory's attenuation under the conditions of migration.

22. Sabine Marschall, "'Homesick Tourism': Memory, Identity and Be-longing," *Current Issues in Tourism* 18, no. 9 (2015): 876–92.

23. For a clear introduction to Laplanche's writings on enigmatic signification, see John Fletcher and Martin Stanton eds, *Jean Laplanche: Seduction, Translation and the Drives*, trans. Martin Stanton (London: Psychoanalytic Forum, Institute of Contemporary Arts, 1992) and John Fletcher, "Introduction: Psychoanalysis and the question of the Other," in John Fletcher ed., *Jean Laplanche: Essays on Otherness*, 1–52, Warwick Studies in European Philosophy (London and New York: Routledge, 1999).

24. Dominique Scarfone, "A Brief Introduction to the Work of Jean Laplanche," *International Journal of Psychoanalysis* 94 (2013), 554. The enigmatic kernel remains opaque to the adult since "'the adult is equally unable to integrate the unconscious dimension of communication inherent in the nurturer's attuned care."
25. Scarfone, "A Brief Introduction," 554.
26. Walter Benjamin, "On Some Motifs in Baudelaire," in Benjamin, *Illuminations*; see particularly 181–82.
27. Kennedy, *The Psychic Home*, 44.
28. Kennedy, *The Psychic Home*, 44.
29. These defensive manoeuvres can also give rise to confusion; see Grinberg and Grinberg, *Psychoanalytic Perspectives*, 88.
30. Scarfone, "A Brief Introduction," 556.
31. Dominique Scarfone, "'It Was *Not* My Mother': From Seduction to Negation," in trans. John Fletcher, "Jean Laplanche and the Theory of Seduction," John Fletcher ed., *New Formations* Number 48 (Winter 2003): 74.
32. Scarfone, "A Brief Introduction," 561.
33. Scarfone, "It Was *Not* My Mother," 72.
34. See note 22.
35. Francisco J. Gonzáles, "Only What Is Human Can Truly Be Foreign: The Trope of Immigration as a Creative Force in Psychoanalysis," in Julia Beltsiou ed., *Locating Ourselves* (Abingdon: Routledge, 2016), 29–30.
36. Heritage Council Victoria, Royal Terrace, https://vhd.heritagecouncil.vic.gov.au/places/481.
37. This quote is taken from Stephen Hudson's completion of K. Scott Moncrieff's translation of "Le Temps Retrouvé," Volume 12 of Marcel Proust's *A La Recherche Du Temps Perdu, In Search of Lost Time*, originally published in 1931 by Chatto & Windus, London, available at https://ebooks.adelaide.edu.au/p/proust/marcel/p96t/index.html.

    In this version, Proust's original term "l'énigme" is faithfully translated as "enigma"; see https://ebooks.adelaide.edu.au/p/proust/marcel/p96t/chapter3.html. In the later and more accessible English version, the term is translated as "riddle"; see Marcel Proust, *In Search of Lost Time*, Volume 6, *Time Regained*, trans. Andreas Mayor and Terence Kilmartin and revised by D. J. Enright (London: Vintage, 1996), 217. The original French language version of Proust's *In Search of Lost Time* is available at http://beq.ebooksgratuits.com/auteurs/Proust/proust.htm. The passage discussed can be found in section 15, "Le temps retrouvé," *Deuxième partie*, 7.
38. This quote is also taken from Chapter 3 of Stephen Hudson's translation of Marcel Proust's "Time Regained." Marcel Proust, "Time Regained," trans. Stephen Hudson, Chapter 3, see note 37.

BIBLIOGRAPHY

Benjamin, Walter. *Illuminations*, edited by Hannah Arendt. New York: Schocken Books, 1968a.

Benjamin, Walter. "On Some Motifs in Baudelaire." In Walter Benjamin, *Illuminations*, edited by Hannah Arendt, 155–200. New York: Schocken Books, 1968b.

Cuthbertson, Debbie. "Australia's First Venice Biennale Pavilion Finds Second Life as New Building Progresses." *Sydney Morning Herald*, 18 October 2014. https://www.smh.com.au/entertainment/art-and-design/australias-first-venice-biennale-pavilion-finds-second-life-as-new-building-progresses-20141017-117imr.html.

Fletcher, John. "Introduction: Psychoanalysis and the Question of the Other." In *Jean Laplanche: Essays on Otherness*, edited by John Fletcher, 1–52. Warwick Studies in European Philosophy. London and New York: Routledge, 1999.

Fletcher, John, and Martin Stanton eds. *Jean Laplanche: Seduction, Translation and the Drives*, translated by Martin Stanton. London: Psychoanalytic Forum, Institute of Contemporary Arts, 1992.

Gonzáles, Francisco J. "Only What Is Human Can Truly Be Foreign: The Trope of Immigration as a Creative Force in Psychoanalysis." In *Immigration in Psychoanalysis: Locating Ourselves*, edited by Julia Beltsiou, 15–38. Abingdon: Routledge, 2016.

Grenville, Kate. *The Secret River*. Melbourne: Text Publishing, 2005.

Grinberg, Leon, and Rebeca Grinberg. *Psychoanalytic Perspectives on Migration and Exile*, translated by Nancy Festinger. New Haven and London: Yale University Press, 1989.

Hirsch, Marianne. *Family Frames: Photography, Narrative and Postmemory*. Cambridge: Harvard University Press, 1997.

Hoffman, Eva. "Out of Exile: Some Thoughts on Exile as a Dynamic Condition." In *Immigration in Psychoanalysis: Locating Ourselves*, edited by Julia Beltsiou, 211–15. Abingdon: Routledge, 2016.

Jameson, Fredric. *Postmodernism, or, the Cultural Logic of Late Capitalism*. Durham, NC: Duke University Press, 1991.

Kennedy, Roger. *The Psychic Home: Psychoanalysis, Consciousness and the Human Soul*. Hove: Routledge, 2014.

Kuhn, Annette. *Family Secrets: Acts of Memory and Imagination*. London: Verso, 1995a.

Kuhn, Annette. "A Phantasmagoria of Memory." In *Family Secrets: Acts of Memory and Imagination*, edited by Annette Kuhn, 104–21. London: Verso, 1995b.

Kuhn, Annette. "A Journey Through Memory." In *Memory and Methodology*, edited by Susannah Radstone, 179–96. Oxford and New York: Berg, 2000.

Laplanche, Jean, and J. B. Pontalis. "Projection." In *The Language of Psychoanalysis*, 349–56. London: Karnac Books, 1988.

Marschall, Sabine. "'Homesick Tourism': Memory, Identity and Belonging." *Current Issues in Tourism* 18, no. 9 (2015): 876–92.

Proust, Marcel. *In Search of Lost Time*. Volume 6. *Time Regained*. Translated by Andreas Mayor and Terence Kilmartin. Revised by D. J. Enright. London: Vintage, 1996.

Proust, Marcel. *Remembrance of Things Past: Time Regained*. Translated by Stephen Hudson. https://ebooks.adelaide.edu.au/p/proust/marcel/p96t/index.html.

Scarfone, Dominique. "A Brief Introduction to the Work of Jean Laplanche." *International Journal of Psychoanalysis* 94 (2013): 545–66.

Scarfone, Dominique. "'It Was *Not* My Mother': From Seduction to Negation." Translated by John Fletcher. "Jean Laplanche and the Theory of Seduction," edited by John Fletcher, 69–76. *New Formations* Number 48 (Winter 2003).

Schwab, Gabriele. *Haunting Legacies: Violent Histories and Transgenerational Trauma*. New York: Columbia University Press, 2010.

"St. Kilda's History Ain't no Mystery!". https://www.aclandstreetvillage.com.au/st-kildas-history-aint-no-mystery.

Weule, Genelle, and Felicity James. "Indigenous Rock Shelter in Top End Pushes Australia's Human History Back to 65,000 years." *ABC News*, 20 July 2017. https://www.abc.net.au/news/science/2017-07-20/aboriginal-shelter-pushes-human-history-back-to-65,000-years/8719314.

CHAPTER 17

Purposeful Memory-Making: Personal Narratives of Migration at Melbourne's Immigration Museum

Moya McFadzean

Individuals, families and communities who engage with museums—whether as visitors, collection donors and lenders, public programme participants or storytellers—are all to varying degrees suppliers, producers and consumers of personal narratives. This chapter examines the collection, production and consumption of migrant memories in the public domain through the prism of the Immigration Museum and its collections. Since it opened in 1998, the Immigration Museum has related stories of migration experiences across time, but these also intersect with a breadth of life experiences through stories of identity, family inheritance, belonging and difference. The Museum's objective has been to develop narrative approaches in exhibitions which are diverse, multi-layered, embrace multiple voices and enable opportunities for narrative agency within and beyond its institutional boundaries. Telling these stories has involved brokering the complex politics of individuals, communities and governments as the Museum's focus on immigration negotiates an emotionally charged public space for its audiences and stakeholders.

M. McFadzean (✉)
Museums Victoria, Melbourne, VIC, Australia
e-mail: mmcfadzean@museum.vic.gov.au

© The Author(s) 2019
K. Darian-Smith, P. Hamilton (eds.), *Remembering Migration*,
Palgrave Macmillan Memory Studies,
https://doi.org/10.1007/978-3-030-17751-5_17

The Immigration Museum has been a significant heritage site of migration memory-making in Australia, and over time has experienced changes in the methodologies of collection development, exhibition interpretation and community engagement. It must be constantly engaged in the "dialogic encounter of narratives"[1] to avoid the binary assumption of a relationship that positions the Museum as the producer and its public audience as the consumer, with all the implications of power and single authoritative voice that this implies. Multiple voices no longer just focus on conventional narratives of a linear journey of migration and settlement but reflect on larger questions of personal identity formation, individual and collective belonging and prejudice, transient experiences and mobilities. In addition, the Immigration Museum's use of new technologies enables more sophisticated memory enactments to engage and even transform the world view of visitors—while highlighting the challenges for curators in preserving the authenticity of memories of migrations.

A MIGRATION COLLECTION AND MUSEUM FOR VICTORIA

The Migration Collection at Museums Victoria was founded in 1990 in the flush of the social history directions in Australian museums, and on the cusp of a burgeoning institutional research focus on migration and settlement histories.[2] The Migration and Cultural Diversity Collection documents and interprets the cross-cultural individual, family and community migration and settlement experiences of Victorians since the 1830s and, consequently, the political, social and cultural histories of Victoria and Australia as they relate to migration, cultural diversity, identity and multiculturalism.[3]

The scope of the collection (over 8000 objects, photographs, film and oral histories) has broadened to reflect the evolution of immigration policies, public protest and debate and notions of personal, national and cultural identities, reflecting also the evolution of museums and exhibitions of migration from a more pluralistic, ethnicity-oriented focus.[4] Establishing and documenting provenance underpins most acquisitions, enabling objects to speak through the voice of the people that owned, used and made them, while also providing insights into the broader narratives of migration and Australian society.

The Immigration Museum is situated in the Old Customs House in Melbourne. It is a two-storey, 1870s heritage-listed building which has created a challenging physical and ambient framework for museum exhibitions and programmes ever since. The colonial building and its neo-classical architecture provide interesting tensions for migration content that is frequently intimate and personal while addressing histories of White Australia that in actuality occurred within its very walls. A series of core exhibitions have evolved which explore people's motivations for leaving homeland, the voyages, the evolution of Victorian and Australian immigration policies and processes, shifts in community demographics and the evolving notions of personal identity in contemporary Australia.

Memory sharing and shaping is at the heart of the Immigration Museum's interpretative methodology. Individual and collective stories are told through objects, images and multi-voice text labels, video stories are edited to provide focused personal perspectives on specific themes and interactives engage in dialogue between storyteller and visitor. The nature of storytelling, its various forms, authors and potential uses, demands a multi-layered approach to presenting personal narratives, which attempts to meet the objectives of the Museum, its audiences and the memory-bearers themselves.

Museum as Storyteller: First-Person Voices

Memory offers validity, authenticity, and in combination with its associated material culture, it has the power to offer affecting visitor experiences. The Immigration Museum has presented a constant and changing stream of personal stories in its long-term exhibitions, which cover historical and thematic content. Some stories have been object-rich, some augmented by multimedia, and set dressing, all narrated via text labels. The living memory stories are based on oral history interviews, with those of migration in the nineteenth century drawing on personal diaries and letters where possible.

This is familiar museum narrative methodology, whereby the individual story personalizes, enhances and illustrates the larger historical narrative. When the stories are finally presented, they have gone through many processes of reinvention—by the natural processes of memory, by the storytellers in the editing and approval process and by the curators in the retelling of the stories. The installations involve consultation with families, collection acquisition and loans, film and audio interviews, research and external expert advice from historians and communities. The interpretation incorporates first-person voice wherever possible, in graphic or audio-visual form, and it validates the seemingly ordinary artefact—a knitting machine, a clay pot steamer, some wood carving tools—by connecting them to the personal experiences.

Objects can also be used to explore one concept, such as ancestry, and juxtapose different experiences through single artefacts and first-person voice in textual form. On display in the Museum's *Identity: Yours, Mine, Ours* exhibition (2011 to present) is a wedding veil imported from Ireland and worn by a young Scottish migrant at her wedding in Bendigo in 1865, and by subsequent generations until it was donated to the Museum by a great great granddaughter:

> This veil originally belonged to my great great grandmother Janet Srimgeour, who migrated to Victoria from Scotland in 1854. It connects me to her, such a special person during my early childhood years, and to many women in my family. I wore the veil at my own wedding in 1958 so I too am part of its long tradition.[5]

Next to the veil is an entry permit belonging to Nguyen Hong Duc, one of 200 children airlifted from Vietnam to Australia during Operation Babylift in 1975. Renamed Dominic, he was raised by the Golding family on a farm in South Australia:

> I was a four-month old orphan when I was given this permit in 1975. Bundled up, I was handed to strangers in Melbourne. This new family gave me a new home, name and a better future. But I'll never find my first mother and father. It's as though the passport erased a family to create a family.[6]

These objects reveal different and moving insights into the enduring impact of family ancestry. They also demonstrate how families seek connections across generations through objects, particularly when the object is the only tangible thing remaining when people are gone.

There exist significant ethical issues for museums in presenting the stories of real people and their objects. These stories are being inserted into a formal, public, museum environment. They are being placed adjacent to other stories, contemporary or from another time, similar in nature or completely different. They are related to objects, owned by the storytellers, or an object is used in a symbolic, collective way, to give tangibility to multiple connected stories. They are supplemented by images, film, props and dressing, often presented in text label form, to be read rather than spoken, usually in English rather than language of origin. The challenge is not to lose sight of the individuals in the presentation of the broader immigration narrative. Stories and objects illustrate historical contexts and connecting and diverging patterns. Yet the risk is the loss of the inherent value of the personal story, the humanity of the people themselves, in the quest for establishing a collective history. Is this an unresolvable tension? Perhaps. But while one voice, perspective or experience cannot represent or speak for an entire community, country or event, it can trigger visitor understandings about broad experiences of forced displacement, fear for life and loved ones, and alienation in a new country.

Here are the narrative dichotomies that confront museums—whether they acknowledge and engage with them or not—between personal and collective, public and private, local and national, diverging and intersecting. The Immigration Museum has been negotiating this territory for 20 years. When developing migration-related collections and exhibitions, the Museum privileges memory testimony as the lens through which migration history is understood. Memory offers validity, authenticity, and in combination with its associated material culture, it has the power to affect people. It is a balance of both representation and context which can be difficult to achieve.

The Museum requires a degree of detachment in how it presents these stories as part of the broader collective narrative of migration. Public expectations can be deeply personal, and frequently motivated by a need to find one's own ethnicity, country of origin or specific experience reflected in the stories told. This visitor imperative can lead to diversity for its own sake, even with the very best intentions.

In more recent years, the important emphasis placed by the Immigration Museum on representing diverse ethnicities to represent migration narratives has expanded and changed, with ethnicity becoming one of many forms of representation and migration stories exploring more nuanced themes, such as identity. But the challenges of representation do not end there. Sheila Watson has argued that community engagement requires a "consensus" view of the past, giving people ownership as they participate in the process of history-making through fostering cohesion, sense of place and belonging. But Watson also suggests that it is necessary to go beyond the consensus model to develop collections and exhibitions that at times may be seen to subvert and challenge the inclusivity message of the museum.[7] These two objectives of both consensus and disruption can be complicated when, for example, both inter- and intra-community approaches to self-representation can frequently conflict. The Immigration

260 M. MCFADZEAN

Museum's approach to storytelling is still grappling with how to effectively provide space for community viewpoints, which can disrupt as well as unify. Can it exhibit discordant memories of the same event, while at the same time fulfilling its political agenda as a place that champions social cohesion? That will demand a robust community and a bold museum.

AFFECTIVE STORYTELLING: VISITOR AS PERFORMER

The narrative form at the Immigration Museum has also taken a more expansive definition in certain exhibitions, a form of personal storytelling which is to varying degrees scripted, theatrical and aiming to affect visitors through enactment. One of the earliest examples of this approach was evident in the immersive immigrant ship environments (1998–2017).

This is where the museum experience becomes a form of visitor enactment, with visitors reliving the sights, sounds and emotions of voyage experiences, and commenting on the authenticity of the re-created post-World War II ocean liner cabin. It is a flood of nostalgic memory, what David Anderson et al. have described as how "people give unity to their lives by building thematically integrated narratives of experience within the context of their life histories."[8] In the context of the ship installation, it also validates memory by accurately re-creating an environment that can be remembered and shared with others.

Oral testimony can also be manipulated to create moments of emotional interaction for visitors in order to deliver specific messages about identity, belonging and prejudice. In 2011, the Immigration Museum launched *Identity: Yours, Mine, Ours*, shifting beyond the migration narrative paradigm to a focus on how ethnicity, language, spirituality, ancestry and citizenship have informed our inherited and adopted individual and collective identities. There are intimate spaces, close encounters with video stories and objects and seated opportunities for interaction. Diverse voices aim to do more than simply remind and inform visitors that Australia is a multicultural country; they also enable visitors to feel intimate connections with the people with whom they are engaging.

One central installation is a large multi-touch table which aims to challenge the visitor's assumptions by discovering more about the ten people who appear on the screen. Visitors can select the people they would like to "meet" and ask them prescribed questions about food, family, appearance, clothing, name and language, uncovering both apparent and hidden identities beneath the surface. This includes surprises and challenges to assumptions visitors might have had about an First Peoples Warlpiri lawyer, an Afrikaans speaker of Chinese descent, a second-generation Lebanese hip hop performer and a same-sex identifying Malaysian academic. These stories provided the opportunity to demonstrate the complexity of individual identity, as well as instances of stereotyping even within one's own culture.

The effectiveness of visitor interaction with personal voices was strongly demonstrated in the findings of a federally funded project between Deakin and Melbourne Universities, Museums Victoria and the Victorian Health Foundation.[9] The study used the *Identity* exhibition to test the public role of museums in countering racism and promoting positive attitudes and acceptance of diversity by focusing on secondary school students and teachers. The powerful qualitative data illustrated the affective power of personal stories, with its affective dimension providing an entry point through which students could connect to the individual people and their stories. In this way, the exhibition content was enlivened by the interaction between students' emotions and perspectives, and the way the audio-visual presentations brought people to life through their individual voices and expressions. As one senior secondary school student reflected after visiting *Identity*:

> It wasn't just like an overview of what people go through it was a specific person talking to you about what had happened to them and it just made it a whole lot more real when you could see their face and you could ... hear their voice ... it still felt like a one-on-one experience with them. [10]

Taking this a step further, the presentation of stories of a wide range of people has provided a vehicle via which students could begin to challenge their thinking and interactions with people from diverse backgrounds. The immersive and interpersonal interpretative methodology is critical to engendering this impact, with real stories demanding direct engagement. Creating affective experiences that engender emotional, sympathetic and even empathetic responses is a core objective of the Immigration Museum. It is a museological methodology discussed by academics and practitioners such as Andrea Witcomb, who has observed that such engagement opportunities result in "a deeply affective, sensorial form of experience which is palpable while also belonging to the poetic rather than the realist or positivist realm."[11]

Paul Williams points to the danger in this personalizing approach being offered at only a superficial level that results in encouraging visitors to find relatability to an extent that they lose sight of understanding the genuine, possibly deeply traumatic, experience. "In the act of making suffering meaningful most of all to visitors, museums may allow us to enjoy an unconscious sense of entitlement to the centrality of our experience."[12] In the effort to elicit the sharing of "similar" experiences, museum visitors may be unintentionally de-historicizing, normalizing and even trivializing the experiences of others, and at times a sympathetic rather than an empathetic response to a personal story is a more appropriate approach.

Storytelling Through Creative Visualization

In 2017, the Immigration Museum opened *British Migrants: Instant Australians?*, exploring the history of post-World War II British migration to Australia. This subject matter is challenging for a variety of reasons in terms of representation. This cohort of migrants were by far the largest migration wave in Australian history, with almost 1.5 million Britons migrating to Australia, most English and most on assisted passages, between 1947 and 1981. Yet, in part due to their numbers, their inextricable connection to Empire, Britain and Australia, and the seeming absence of a separate identity, they have become simultaneously visible and invisible, all-pervasive and yet rarely identified.

Personal narratives provided the bedrock of the exhibition, having intrinsic, emotional value and validity. They were carefully selected to demonstrate diversity and to deliberately complicate a migration metanarrative which has been frequently over-simplified. The personal stories were vehicles for challenging conventional understandings about British migration, and to assist visitors to extrapolate from real and relatable individuals to broader historical and contemporary contexts—such as white, British, nation-building in Australia, preference and entitlement, and notions of a British identity.

The challenge for memory presentation in this case was how to take visitors back in time, to the moment the memory was made, while still enabling the owner of the memory to own and share their story in the present. One approach was the creation of a table of tea cups which in style represented the 1950s–1970s period. A number of raised cups contained speakers from which a soundscape of voices could be listened to, and quotes were selected from written testimonies submitted by former British migrants to the project's online community crowd-sourcing website which were then enacted by actors with accurate regional accents (Fig. 17.1).

Fig. 17.1 Tea cup soundscape and story projection, *British Migrants: Instant Australians?* Exhibition, 2017–2018. Photograph by Jon Augier. Courtesy of Museums Victoria

First-person voices provided the primary overlay for immersive visual presentations through animation, objects, images and film. This heightened the presence and authenticity of the storytellers, and while curators had played an active role in the editing and selection process, the storytellers retained a strong degree of ownership of their narratives.

The sympathetic, highly accessible animations located visitors in the 1950s and 1960s, in urban and rural landscapes, as children, teenagers, young adults and within a complex family group. Suddenly the excitement of a child running down a gangplank, a teenager's horror at being dragged away from Liverpool and the Beatles and the homesickness witnessed in a woman waiting by a letterbox were writ large on wide screens which also embedded photographs and personal artefacts.

The exhibition provoked a range of visitor responses, which varied according to their degree of direct connection with post-war British migration history. It was a multi-faceted visitor engagement with a primarily historical narrative presentation. Some visitors took the opportunity to share their own first-person narrative with their companions, Museum staff or other visitors as a way of enriching the Museum narrative or presenting themselves as an expert witness to the history presented. Others used it as a platform to challenge the narrative as presented by the Museum, where their own experience did not match that of the story presented. Other visitors with no direct association with the subject have described themselves as absorbed in it through empathetic engagement with the storytellers.[13]

Undoubtedly, these responses were triggered by moments of nostalgic connection or interaction with the objects, images and stories on display. Through the objects, and the visualized stories connected to them, visitors often have visceral emotional responses: rediscovering a collective identity and values perceived to be lost; or rediscovering a memory or person from childhood triggered by a familiar item.[14] Thus, the display of a child's dress made in 1945 in Coventry to celebrate the end of World War II on Victory Day in Europe evoked strong memories of the end of the war, as well as the rubble ruins of English towns such as Coventry. The essential counter-balance to these safe, if emotional, memory triggers, was the final section of the exhibition which presented responses to contemporary questions about Australian and British identity, notions of privilege, colonization and prejudice by migrants, historians, cultural commentators and Indigenous Australians. The British migrants, whose stories had been animated and performed, became part of a broader cohort of Australians reflecting on national questions. Memories shifted from personal storytelling to contributing to social analysis.

Short Memories for Making Meaning

The production of oral histories for a public consumption heightens the challenges of the processes of consultation, approval, editing and immediate and future public access. Improved, more affordable and accessible technologies have expanded the opportunities for public engagement with oral history beyond text-based presentations. These include localized sound delivery for individual and collective listening, audio guides, small screen video presentations, touch tables, touch screens and large-scale projections.

However, does this mean, as Paula Hamilton has asked, that we focus too much on the production (how testimony is recorded, interpreted and turned into a public output) and not enough on "how to listen and who should listen."[15] This is both in terms of practice during the project (such as an exhibition) and sustaining its use, relevance and access after the project is completed. Perhaps public historians and curators have lost the ability to offer "deep listening" opportunities, to immerse visitors in long and complex stories in the need to meet expectations of visitors with short attention spans. An exhibition entitled *Love* at the Immigration Museum (December 2018–April 2019) featured 36 personal stories, 31 of which were presented through approximately three-minute audio clips delivered through hand-held digital devices. This equates to 90 minutes of listening content which is an ambitious demand of most visitors. One-hour interviews were conducted with the people representing diverse ages, genders, sexualities, ethnicities and experiences, and they focused on a set of questions exploring a particular emotion (such as grief or devotion) through an experience, event and/or object. Edited down to a couple of minutes, these audio experiences placed an "authentic" voice in the visitor's ear and provided moments of intimate connection and even empathy.

But there was no opportunity in the exhibition for visitors to explore the extended story. Are we then completely honouring the individual narrative, when the pressure is to count the seconds and contain the experience to what is believed to be an average visitor's total time commitment? In actuality, this interpretative methodology worked effectively for this project. Exhibition participants understood the nature of the storytelling methodology from the outset. Certainly, the contract with the storytellers was clear and the process of producing the story was transparent and consultative.

However, not all exhibitions should present voices as "shards of personhood."[16] As Stephen Sloan has argued, "The long form of oral history matters … as oral history is segmented and excerpted, it moves further away from the co-authored piece build by investigator and narrator."[17] There are times when the Museum has undertaken long form life testimony interviews, which are edited for subsequent projects. This can be problematic, where testimony is taken for one purpose and then utilized for another. For example, curators sought a Stolen Generations story for the Immigration Museum's *Love* exhibition and requested permission from First Peoples' colleagues to explore the possibility of re-purposing an interview presented in Melbourne Museum's *First Peoples* exhibition. However, the advice given (and accepted) was that even with storyteller's permission, this relocation of the story would remove it from the context for which it was created and result in it being inappropriately presented

266 M. MCFADZEAN

outside an environment which had been set up for deep listening audience engagement.

We need more opportunities for extended storytelling that can take visitors deep into whole-life narratives and allow them to go further into a story if they are willing. *They Cannot Take the Sky: Stories from Detention*, an exhibition developed by the Immigration Museum in 2017 in partnership with Behind the Wire, an asylum seeker advocacy group and online story repository, is an excellent example of such an approach. It is also an example of genuine community engagement methodology, whereby the storytellers were co-creators of the exhibition and had self-determination in the exhibition conception and development. The exhibition featured 22 audio and video presentations of edited extended interviews with former and current asylum seekers. An exit survey report of 100 visitors found that the average exhibition visit was half an hour with nearly ten per cent spending over one hour. Further findings include 86 per cent of visitors reported increased awareness or knowledge of asylum seeker issues, 25 per cent reported changed perceptions of asylum seekers and 63 per cent reported being motivated to investigate the issues further.[18] Nevertheless, it is unlikely that this longer form memory presentation would have been possible without the community collaboration which demanded the Museum's commitment to creating a deep listening environment.

Museums are in the business of public engagement, creating immersive experiences in lively and compelling spaces. What is critical is our adherence to the integrity of the story, the authenticity of the voice, the collaborative relationships with the storytellers and how we archive the long form for posterity, where that is indeed appropriate. Many interviews are conducted for very specific outcomes and are not necessarily of public value in an uninterpreted form. With the ever-increasing production of personal testimony in exhibitions in response to audience demand for authentic voices, it is unlikely that there will be an appetite, requirement or resourcing for the archiving of all interviews for future access and use. Not every memory-making activity must come with a "for posterity" caveat—they simply have not been created with this outcome in mind.

CONCLUSION

Museums must constantly re-evaluate who is doing the remembering and how that memory is being presented. People are willing to trust museums to tell their stories and to preserve the material culture of their experiences:

when the subject is migration, this often involves emotion, painful memories and precious objects. Interpretation which draws upon a creative and shifting amalgam of memory and material culture helps to humanize the past. During focus group testing by Museums Victoria for the *British Migrants* exhibition, one participant provocatively remarked that "suddenly you have a white person's story being told in the brown space."[19] Creating an exhibition about a large, predominantly white, privileged migrant group was an act of surrendering a public space, which has always striven to give voice to formerly silenced communities, to the already voiced and empowered. However, the exhibition wished to challenge incorrect assumptions that this was a story already told, as well as maintain the Museum as a democratic narrative space for all. If the Immigration Museum confined itself to "brown stories," it could be argued that instead of equalizing histories it was entrenching a divide.

Curators select, interpret and use stories to make broader connections and reflect on history and contemporary society. Museums can be storyhouses, but the stories need to be nuanced and purposeful—questioning, reflecting, framing and interpreting. Museums can speak for people, as well as stand back and enable them to speak for themselves. They can interpret a story, or let it stand, as valuable in its own right. Museums can embrace alternative storytellers who can offer innovative storytelling approaches that will challenge not just visitors but the museum itself, and thereby opening itself to moments of letting go. Museums can legitimize, give voice and even authority to the silent and the absent wherever possible, and do this in ways that truly affect both the storytellers and the story receivers: "To share my story with the other twelve people, to know that my feelings and experiences weren't isolated ones, was a wonderful cathartic and liberating feeling."[20]

NOTES

1. Rowe et al., "Linking Little Narratives to Big Ones: Narrative and Public Memory in History Museums," *Culture & Psychology* 8, no. 1 (2012): 97.
2. Viv Szekeres, "Museums and Multiculturalism: Too Vague to Understand, Too Important to Ignore," in Des Griffin and Leon Paroissien eds, *Understanding Museums: Australian Museums and Museology* (Canberra: National Museum of Australia, 2011).
3. Museums Victoria, Collection Plans, 1994, 2001, 2005 and 2013.

4. Eureka Heinrich, "Museums, History and Migration in Australia," *History Compass* 11, no. 10 (October 2013): 796.
5. Jean Billington, email correspondence with the author, 2010, for *Identity: Yours, Mine, Ours* exhibition (Melbourne: Immigration Museum, 2010).
6. Hong Duc Nguyen, email correspondence with the author, 2010, for *Identity: Yours, Mine, Ours* exhibition (Melbourne: Immigration Museum, 2010).
7. Sheila Watson, "History Museums, Community Identities and a Sense of Place: Rewriting Histories," in Simon J. Knell et al. eds, *Museum Revolutions: How Museums Change and Are Changed* (New York: Routledge, 2007), 160.
8. Anderson et al., "Insights on How Museum Objects Mediate Recall of Nostalgic Life Episodes at a Showa Era Museum in Japan," *Curator: The Museum Journal* 59, no. 1 (2016): 5–26.
9. Walton et al., *Identity: Yours, Mine, Ours Exhibition Evaluation Report* (Melbourne: Museums Victoria, 2016).
10. Walton et al., *Identity*, 129.
11. Andrea Witcomb, "Understanding the Role of Affect in Producing a Critical Pedagogy for History Museums," *Museum Management and Curatorship* 28, no. 3 (2013): 267.
12. Paul Williams, "The Personalization of Loss in Memorial Museums," in James B. Gardner and Paula Hamilton eds, *The Oxford Handbook of Public History* (Oxford: Oxford University Press, 2017), 382.
13. Refer to Rowe et al., "Linking Little Narratives to Big Ones," 108.
14. Anderson et al., "Insights on How Museum Objects Mediate Recall of Nostalgic Life Episodes at a Showa Era Museum in Japan," 10.
15. Paula Hamilton, "Speak, Memory: Issues in Oral and Public History," in Paul Ashton and Alex Trapeznik eds, *What is Public History Globally? Working with the Past in the Present* (London and New York: Bloomsbury, 2019) In Press.
16. Paul Williams, "The Personalization of Loss in Memorial Museums," 370.
17. Stephen Sloan, "Swimming in the Exaflood: Oral History as Information in the Digital Age," in Mary Larson and Doug Boyd eds, *Oral History and Digital Humanities. Voice, Access and Engagement* (New York: Palgrave Macmillan, 2014), 180–81.
18. Bonnie Temple, *Research Report. They Cannot Take the Sky: Stories from Detention* (Melbourne: University of Melbourne and Museums Victoria, 2017), 3.
19. Museums Victoria, *Ten Pound Poms Focus Group Evaluation*, Report no. 995 (April 2016): 7.
20. Jan Coolen, email correspondence with the author, 27 November 2017, after launch of *British Migrants: Instant Australians?* Exhibition (Melbourne: Immigration Museum, 2017).

BIBLIOGRAPHY

Anderson, David, Hiroyuki Shmizu, and Chris Campbell. "Insights on How Museum Objects Mediate Recall of Nostalgic Life Episodes at a Showa Era Museum in Japan." *Curator: The Museum Journal* 59, no. 1 (2016): 5–26.

Billington, Jean. Email correspondence with the author, 2010. *Identity: Yours, Mine, Ours* exhibition (Melbourne: Immigration Museum, 2010).

Coolen, Jan. Email correspondence with the author, 27 November 2017. *British Migrants: Instant Australians?* Exhibition (Melbourne: Immigration Museum, 2017).

Hamilton, Paula. "Speak, Memory: Issues in Oral and Public History." In *What is Public History Globally? Working with the Past in the Present*, edited by Paul Ashton and Alex Trapeznik. London and New York: Bloomsbury, 2019 (In Press).

Heinrich, Eureka. "Museums, History and Migration in Australia." *History Compass* 11, no. 10 (October 2013): 783–800.

Museums Victoria. "Migration & Settlement Collection Policy." *Social History Collection Policies* (1994): 25–31.

Museums Victoria. "Immigration & Cultural Diversity Collection Development Plan." *Australian Society Program Collection Policies* (2001): 6–9.

Museums Victoria. "Migration Collection Development Plan." *History & Technology Collection Development Plans* (2005).

Museums Victoria. "Migration & Cultural Diversity Collection Plan." *Museum Victoria Humanities Collection Plans 2013–18* (2013): 115–21.

Museums Victoria. *Ten Pound Poms Focus Group Evaluation*, Report no. 995 (April 2016): 7.

Nguyen, Hong Duc. Email correspondence with the author, 2010. *Identity: Yours, Mine, Ours* exhibition (Melbourne: Immigration Museum, 2010).

Rowe, Shawn M., James V. Wertsch, and Tatyana Y. Kosyaeva. "Linking Little Narratives to Big Ones: Narrative and Public Memory in History Museums." *Culture & Psychology* 8, no. 1 (2012): 96–112.

Sloan, Stephen. "Swimming in the Exaflood: Oral History as Information in the Digital Age." In *Oral History and Digital Humanities. Voice, Access and Engagement*, edited by Mary Larson and Doug Boyd, 175–86. New York: Palgrave Macmillan, 2014.

Szekeres, Viv. "Museums and Multiculturalism: Too Vague to Understand, Too Important to Ignore." In *Understanding Museums: Australian Museums and Museology*, edited by Des Griffin and Leon Paroissien. Canberra: National Museum of Australia, 2011. http://nma.gov.au/research/understanding-museums/VSzekeres_2011.html.

Temple, Bonnie. *Research Report. They Cannot Take the Sky: Stories from Detention.* Melbourne: University of Melbourne and Museums Victoria, 2017.

Walton, Jessica, Yin Paradies, Moya McFadzean, Jan Molloy, Linda Sproul, Naomi Priest, Emma Kowal, Fethi Mansouri, Margaret Kelaher, and Carolyn Meehan. *Identity: Yours, Mine, Ours. Exhibition Evaluation Report.* Melbourne: Museums Victoria, 2016.

Watson, Sheila. "History Museums, Community Identities and a Sense of Place: Rewriting Histories." In *Museum Revolutions: How Museums Change and Are Changed*, edited by Simon J. Knell, Suzanne MacLeod and Sheila E. R. Watson, 160–72. New York: Routledge, 2007.

Williams, Paul. "The Personalization of Loss in Memorial Museums." In *The Oxford Handbook of Public History*, edited by James B. Gardner and Paula Hamilton, 369–86. Oxford: Oxford University Press, 2017.

Witcomb, Andrea. "Understanding the Role of Affect in Producing a Critical Pedagogy for History Museums." *Museum Management and Curatorship* 28, no. 3 (2013): 255–71.

CHAPTER 18

Settled and Unsettled: The Spirit of Enterprise Project as (Post)Settler-Colonial Memory Activism

Alison Atkinson-Phillips

The Enterprise Migrant Hostel was a government-run reception centre for migrants and newly arrived refugees, located in the south-eastern Melbourne suburb of Springvale. The two decades of the Enterprise Hostel's operation, 1970–1991, marked a transitional period in Australia's migration history. The post-war boom of nation building was at an end, but migrants were still able to make use of government-run temporary accommodation on arrival. "The Spirit of Enterprise" is the umbrella term for a range of memory work related to the Enterprise Hostel. It has its genesis in the development of an exhibition for the community gallery of the Immigration Museum in Melbourne in the late 2000s. In this chapter, I offer a brief history of the Enterprise Hostel and of the Spirit of Enterprise memory work. I then consider the ways memory of the Enterprise Hostel has been mobilized politically, in response to a sense that something important has been lost, and in contrast with Australia's asylum seeker policy in the present. Like much memory work connected

A. Atkinson-Phillips (✉)
Faculty of Humanities and Social Sciences, School of History, Classics and Archaeology, Newcastle University, Newcastle upon Tyne, UK
e-mail: alison.atkinson-phillips@newcastle.ac.uk

© The Author(s) 2019
K. Darian-Smith, P. Hamilton (eds.), *Remembering Migration*,
Palgrave Macmillan Memory Studies,
https://doi.org/10.1007/978-3-030-17751-5_18

271

with Australia's post-war migration, the Spirit of Enterprise's focus on the moment of arrival risks continuing a settler-colonial celebratory narrative that smooths out the rough edges of history. Nonetheless, those involved have worked hard to create spaces where unexpected meanings can emerge.

This research draws on the digital archive of *The Spirit of Enterprise* website,[1] and materials provided by the Enterprise Migrant Hostel History Project committee, including the exhibition catalogue of the *Worthwhile Enterprise* exhibition,[2] the "*I'm Home!*" consultation report by Sinatra Murphy[3] and a wide range of ephemeral materials including postcards, greeting cards and launch event programmes. I conducted oral history interviews with three of the original members of the Enterprise Migrant Hostel History Project committee, Merle Mitchell, Betty Wilderman and Heather Duggan, at the site of the Enterprise Tribute Garden, and with Grissel Walmaggia from the City of Greater Dandenong Council. I have also had the opportunity to speak informally with a wider group of project participants over lunch in what was once the Enterprise Hostel dining room, and to follow the heritage trail through Springvale.

The Enterprise Hostel was announced by the Australian Government in 1967 as a "new era" of migrant support.[4] Migrants were to be housed in motel-style accommodation, in contrast to the post-war accommodation that was often converted army barracks or prefabricated huts.[5] However, despite this aesthetic break with the past, there were many continuities. Australia's post-World War II migration policy was driven by a need for workers, and this continued to drive policy decisions. The Enterprise Hostel was constructed in Springvale to be near work opportunities in Melbourne's south-eastern manufacturing corridor. Migrants were offered English classes and support to transition into the local community while this need for labour continued. Those arriving at the Enterprise Hostel during the first decade of its existence rarely stayed long, often quickly securing jobs in the local manufacturing industry and making use of the hostel accommodation as they settled into a new life. The last assisted passage schemes ended in 1975 and, from the mid-1970s until its closure, many of those who came through the Enterprise Hostel were refugees from South American or Asian countries. By 1983, a drop in demand for migrant labour led to policy change, so that only refugees were able to use the facilities.

This period is something of an anomaly in Australia's migration history, in which refugees were given a higher level of support than any time before

18 SETTLED AND UNSETTLED: THE SPIRIT OF ENTERPRISE PROJECT... 273

or since. Post-war refugees and displaced persons (DPs) in the 1940s and 1950s had been accepted as indentured labourers, rather than under a true humanitarian programme.[6] Indeed, as Klaus Neumann has argued, Australia's post-war intake of DPs was not driven by humanitarian ideals, but by a desire to increase the population of "white" Australia to mitigate the perceived threat of Asia from the north.[7] There was not, therefore, a tradition of offering hospitality to refugees as a "gift." In other words, Australia's history of accepting refugees has never been without self-interest, nor without the expectation that any support offered would be repaid in kind; except, arguably, for this brief period from the mid-1970s until the early 1990s. The length of time refugees were allowed to stay in the Enterprise Hostel was gradually reduced, and government support in the form of funded services was limited and then withdrawn. In the late 1980s, the Enterprise Hostel closed as a reception centre, but was used to house a group of Cambodian asylum seekers. However, in August 1991, some of the asylum seekers breached the terms of their detention, resulting in a dawn raid during which the whole group was removed to Villawood Detention Centre, Sydney.[8] The closure of the Enterprise Hostel in 1992 coincided with the introduction of mandatory detention policy for asylum seekers.

The Enterprise Migrant Hostel History Project began in the mid-2000s in response to a call for expressions of interest by the Immigration Museum in the city of Melbourne. A committee was formed by local people who had been involved with the hostel while it was in operation, with the aim of developing what became *A Worthwhile Enterprise* exhibition, and went on to become the Spirit of Enterprise project. At the heart of this memory work was Merle Mitchell, a formidable character recognized as a "Greater Dandenong living treasure."[9] Mitchell was already living in Springvale when the Enterprise Hostel was first announced, and immediately became involved in a community response project. She later became the first director of the Springvale Community Aide and Advice Bureau (SCAAB), now known as South East Community Links. In the 1980s, Mitchell also served for four years as director of the Australian Council of Social Services, so she has been involved in community work much more widely than Springvale, and was able to use her connections to build the profile of the Spirit of Enterprise project, as it developed.

Other members of the initial committee are predominantly long-term residents of the area who, like Mitchell, had good connections with civil society and government. A number of them had been previously involved with the hostel through the provision of services to migrants, rather than as migrants themselves. For example, two of the founding members of the group were Betty Wilderman, who had worked with Mitchell at SCAAB, and Heather Duggan, who had been coordinator of the Springvale Neighbourhood House. As retirees, Wilderman and Duggan have both been part of the Neighbourhood House committee of management, alongside a number of the Enterprise Hostel's ex-residents. Another member of the group, the late Joyce Rebeiro, worked as the access and equity officer, while other members taught in the local area. Jan Trezise also served on the Springvale council in the 1980s, becoming its first female Mayor in 1983. This demonstrates not only Springvale's relatively progressive character as a local government area, but the close and potentially blurred relationships between local government and civil society that characterize this project.

In gathering material for the exhibition, the committee set out to collect as many stories as they could from ex-residents and volunteers. They attended community events, conducting oral history interviews.[10] The primary aim was to collect material for the exhibition, rather than to create an oral history archive, so the method and style of collection varies widely. Over 100 people, including former residents, volunteers and workers, participated in the exhibition in various ways, by contributing display material and sharing their stories. This high level of engagement indicates that the memory work was valued by a wide range of people.

A Worthwhile Enterprise: The Migrant Hostel in Springvale ran at the Community Gallery of the Immigration Museum in Melbourne from 24 November 2008 to 13 April 2009. The display was then moved for a short time to the Springvale Historical Society. The exhibition catalogue acknowledges the variety of emotions migrants might go through on arrival in Australia. There is a strong emphasis, in the storytelling, of the effort made by the Springvale (and wider Australian) community to support and welcome new migrants. Stories about misunderstandings are told as humorous "getting to know you" anecdotes, but also as important challenges to be overcome. A section of the catalogue titled "Closure and lost opportunity" outlines reasons for the closure of the hostel, including the diminished employment options in the area and a reduction in the federal government support offered to refugee arrivals. While the catalogue ends on a positive note, outlining the "legacy" of the Enterprise Hostel, there is the subtle message that this is in contrast to the current government policy.

Following the closure of the exhibition, a grant from the Victorian Multicultural Commission allowed for further material to be gathered and digitized for a permanent online display as part of the *Spirit of Enterprise* website. Over 50 individual and collective testimonies from migrants who spent time at Enterprise Hostel are gathered on the website, in alphabetical order by continent, alongside stories from volunteers and paid workers (there is some overlap between these two groups). The oral histories gathered for the exhibition are included alongside other narratives from a range of sources—some written memoir and a few that are copies of interviews given to journalists.

The *Spirit of Enterprise* website not only offered a way to extend the life of the exhibition but provided a platform for further advocacy, as those involved in this memory work were increasingly convinced of its importance. The website's tagline is "A Project of National Significance," and statements in support of this claim were gathered from prominent Australians, which framed the project as part of a broader conversation about welcome and hospitality that connects with contemporary concerns about refugee and migration policy. The video embedded on the website home page features the late Malcolm Fraser who, as Australia's prime minister in the late 1970s, is associated with the end of the White Australia Policy. Fraser claims that the Enterprise Hostel story demonstrates that when new migrants are welcomed into a community, "They add to its diversity, diversity becomes a strength, and enriches all our lives."

In 2010, the campaign succeeded in attracting funding to undertake a consultation about a permanent memorial of some kind. The project was supported by the Springvale Neighbourhood House, a community meeting and support centre that had its genesis in the relationship between Enterprise Hostel residents and SCAAB in the 1980s. From the beginning, this consultation was framed by a desire to celebrate the good things about the Enterprise experience. The consultation report *"I'm Home!"* articulated two questions that guided the discussions: (1) Where is the most appropriate location to honour the Enterprise Hostel? and (2) What is the most appropriate medium to honour the Enterprise Hostel?

The experience of putting together the Immigration Museum exhibit and the website was the context out of which these questions emerged. The overwhelmingly positive response to this previous memory work, despite the committee's attempts to present a balance of good and bad stories, led to the positively framed consultation questions.

The consultation report was published with the emotive title of "*I'm Home!*."[11] It outlined a "vision" for a multi-stage commemorative project, the first two parts of which were the development of the memory space at Lexington Gardens and the cultivation of the "Enterprise Rose." Stage 3 would be the creation of a new place, possibly associated with a new community library, as "A living and ongoing memorial entrenched in daily life." Stage 4 suggested a walk that would "symbolically link" the old with the new.

The rose garden which became the focus of the memory space at Lexington Gardens is a reminder of the contextual nature of memory work. The main reason roses were included in this project was that there had been a rose garden at the entry point of the Enterprise Hostel. This was often the first thing people noticed about the hostel, and for some migrants it made a big impression. For those who lived or worked there for extended periods, the rose became a symbol of the good things about the hostel. The consultation report quotes former residents explaining how the roses became associated with hospitality and care:

> Roses so beautiful, the first thing we see when we come to hostel. Hostel open the door for us, beautiful country, thank you Australia. ... Roses are symbolic—pruned and cared for just like the people, and they all bloomed. ... At my place there's always a red rose.[12]

This quote shows the links made between the individual experience of the Enterprise Hostel and a broader narrative of Australian hospitality and migrant welcome. The cultivation of the "Enterprise Rose" has also had practical benefits, in the creation of a commercial, saleable object and a kind of logo that began to be used on promotional materials, including note cards and bookmarks.

The Enterprise Tribute Garden takes the form of a rose garden at the site of the former hostel, now the privately run Lexington Gardens retirement complex. At the entry point, near the car park, a red information panel gives some background to the history of the Enterprise Hostel and the broader Spirit of Enterprise history project. The garden beds are in the shape of petals and are planted with the "Enterprise Rose," and a spiral path leads to the central area, where two "petals" of red glass are printed with the image of two open hands below a map of the world. Water droplets run between the hands and the many countries on the map. A semicircular bench seat faces the panels. It is inscribed with numbers—one board for every 1000 migrants who arrived and stayed at the Enterprise Hostel.

As I will discuss further, the Enterprise memory work is both local and national in scope, and needs to be understood as networked heritage[13] in a number of different ways. Importantly, the Enterprise Hostel is part of a wide network of migration sites across Australia, in some ways providing a bridge between the older, post-war reception centres and contemporary immigration detention centres.

However, this memory work also has a very local existence, with the final stage of the project focusing on a heritage trail that creates a localized network of memory markers, following an "orientation" walk given weekly to new arrivals at the hostel by the late Sherron Dunbar, a staff member at SCAAB. The walk starts at the Enterprise Tribute Garden and includes six other markers: Springvale Rise (previously Springvale Primary School) where the Multicultural Teacher's Aide programme was founded; Centrelink; the Springvale health precinct; SCAAB; Springvale Neighbourhood House; and Springvale Shopping Centre. The final marker will be part of a new civic precinct at the site of the old Springvale Council. The old council buildings have been demolished, following Springvale's amalgamation into the City of Greater Dandenong, and the memory group has advocated for some form of commemoration of the Enterprise Hostel to be incorporated into the plans for the new building. An initial marker at SCAAB was a small plaque acknowledging Dunbar's important role installed in an "Enterprise Rose" garden, but between 2015 and early 2017, six more high profile markers were installed, each designed by Sinatra Murphy. Each marker is a tall, white, metal concertina with the top half a silhouette of inspiring words (Fig. 18.1). For example, the words on the Neighbourhood House sign are "friendly–empowering–encouraging–safe–culture–diverse–trusting–welcoming." The central fold at the bottom half includes an explanation of the importance of the marker and short history of the site in relation to the Enterprise Hostel.

Mobilizing Memory

The Spirit of Enterprise memory project developed at a time when Australia's migration policy, particularly towards refugees, was punitive and divisive. By the time the exhibition project began in the mid-2000s, refugees arriving in Australia were not offered transitional housing support of the kind available in the hostel era. Asylum seekers arriving by boat

Fig. 18.1 Enterprise Heritage Trail marker at Springvale Shopping Centre (design by Sinatra Murphy Pty Ltd). Photograph by Alison Atkinson-Phillips

were subject to mandatory detention in isolated locations or in offshore facilities. Although the Rudd Government initially softened the asylum seeker policy when it came to power in late 2007, over the decade that the memory project has been underway, asylum seeker and refugee policy in Australia has again become bitterly divisive. The desire to make use of the Enterprise Hostel story to offer an alternative vision of hospitality and welcome was not initially a conscious aim of the committee, but has grown over time. This strategic use of memory is evident in the promotional video *Spirit of Enterprise: A Project of National Significance*. For example, when Australian actor Simon Palomares describes his experience of arriving at the Enterprise Hostel as a young boy in the mid-1970s he states, "Every time I read about refugees and new migrants I always think about that day and the huge part Enterprise played in our lives."

In her history of the hostel, titled "Springvale—Rich Because of its Diversity," Merle Mitchell argues that, "Some people have described the Enterprise Migrant Hostel as the refugee and migrant gateway to the Australian community. Many of us describe it as Springvale's gateway to the world."[14] The *Spirit of Enterprise* website home page claims that it "demonstrates how strong, cohesive, vibrant communities can be built when migrants and refugees are warmly welcomed through unique, innovative settlement programs based on welcome, support and respect." This claim is repeated in various forms on each of the heritage markers that form the Enterprise Trail in Springfield. The celebration of diversity is a familiar trope in the celebratory multiculturalism that became dominant in Australia during the time the Enterprise Hostel was operational. Its continued emphasis by the memory team suggests not only a strategic adoption of this narrative, but a personal identification with it. Those involved in commemorating the Enterprise Hostel experience genuinely wanted to emphasize that it had given them the opportunity to meet people from different cultural backgrounds, and to have their lives and social environment enriched. Indeed, this was a positive experience for many of the migrants as well as the Anglo-Australians. One ex-resident of the Enterprise Hostel, Geraldina Alvarez-Poblete, reflected:

> When I left Chile in 1975, I had had very limited contact with people from other countries. I was so impressed by the diversity of people living in Victoria. ... I feel "privilege" by this experience.[15]

Having seen their community and their own lives transformed by the hostel and the people who passed through it, The Enterprise Migrant Hostel History Project committee was driven by a desire to have this history celebrated and acknowledged as a small but important part of the wider transformation of Australian society.

Despite the committee's goodwill and its commitment to diversity, it is important to recognize that the Spirit of Enterprise project fails to negotiate the violence of the "settlement" project it celebrates. The Enterprise Hostel was named for a colonial ship, the *Enterprize*, which sailed from Van Diemen's Land (Lutruwita/Tasmania) in 1835 with Victoria's first permanent settler-colonizers on board. The opening event of the *Worthwhile Enterprise* exhibition mobilized the concept of "settlement" strategically to emphasize continuity between the *Enterprize* and the Enterprise Hostel, and the integration of non-British migrants into the broader history of "settlement." A group of 40 ex-residents re-enacted their arrival by taking a boat ride on a replica of the *Enterprize* sailing ship.

The term "settlement" is a word that has been used widely within the field of Australian migration. Being settled or unsettled is about a feeling of comfort or discomfort; feeling "at home" or out of place. These are feelings inherently connected to migration. But in a settler-colonial context like Australia, settlement, like migration, can never be apolitical. As far back as 2002, Joseph Pugliese called for a "decolonising migrant historiography" that would not be complicit in the continuing dispossession of Aboriginal people.[16] He argued that the myth of *terra nullius* was an ongoing issue for the way Australians imagined their history, not in terms of a legal concept but as "something that filters down into the practices of everyday life" and renders Aboriginal people and their heritage invisible. The celebratory narrative of "diversity" draws heavily on the idea of a pre-multicultural Australia that was bland and lacked culture, in contrast with a contemporary multicultural society. What is hidden underneath that story is that the past was never monocultural, but is layered with cultural interactions predicated on uneven power relations.

Sara Wills has suggested that "between the [migrant] hostel and the [refugee detention] camp, there is possibly space for an ethical national conversation."[17] Despite its limitations, the Spirit of Enterprise project offers opportunities for such a space, or spaces. By focusing on the roses as a symbol of a moment of happy arrival, and by drawing on the continuity of the "settlement" narrative, the Enterprise project risks creating a celebratory narrative that smooths out the rough edges of its history. Yet, this activist memory work also potentially opens a door to a past that seemed finished. The archive overall demonstrates the project team's desire to present a range of perspectives on hostel experience—although I would acknowledge there are "epistemological implications"[18] for the presentation of oral history as a paraphrased narrative, without inclusion of the questions asked or any distinction between different kinds of first-person testimony, and alongside first-person written memoir and reproduced news articles.[19] While this memory work has been driven by a core team of memory activists, the archive hints at the sense of agency of individual participants, in their choices to speak and not speak. For example, the testimony narrative of "hostel mother" Isabel Stix states, "Isabel refuses to talk about the problems she had with some of them saying that their problems came from their experiences in the camps."

While the creation of the "Enterprise Rose" points to a focus on the moment of arrival as an "origin" story, Merle Mitchel suggests the Enterprise Tribute Garden has become a place for migrants to be able to remember and acknowledge the past they could not bring with them to Australia. Where the online testimonies offer an opportunity for the stories of Enterprise residents, staff and supporters to be made public, the Tribute Garden offered a physical, intimate space for stories to be shared between family members or friends. At the opening event in December 2012, one of those invited to speak was Peter Jong, whose mother arrived at Enterprise in the 1970s as one of a group of pregnant women evacuated from Timor-Leste. Jong said that it was only through his involvement with the memory project that he came to understand this history: "I can honestly say this whole project has turned my life around." Similarly, each heritage marker's planning and launch event has brought together a slightly different group of people, motivated to tell and share their own particular part of the Enterprise story. In very practical terms, the public artworks of the heritage trail have worked to "constitute a community."[20] In the process, the Spirit of Enterprise has opened up space for conversations about what makes such a community of value.

NOTES

1. "Enterprise Migrant Hostel History Project," *The Spirit of Enterprise: A Project of National Significance*, https://www.enterprisehostel.org.
2. Immigration Museum, *A Worthwhile Enterprise* (Melbourne, 2008).
3. Sinatra Murphy Pty Ltd, "*'I'm Home!' Honouring the Enterprise Hostel.*" Consultation Report, City of Greater Dandenong, 2011.
4. A newspaper article in *The Sun*, 11 August 1970, compares images of "THE OLD ... Dreary Nissen Huts" accommodation with the new style of accommodation at the hostel.
5. Sara Wills, "Between the Hostel and the Detention Centre: Possible Trajectories of Migrant Pain and Shame in Australia," in William Logan and Keir Reeves eds, *Places of Pain and Shame* (London and New York: Routledge, 2009), 268.
6. Jayne Persian, *Beautiful Balts* (Sydney: NewSouth Publishing, 2017).
7. Klaus Neumann, *Across the Seas* (Melbourne: Black Inc., 2015), 81.
8. "The Spirit of Enterprise" website contains a first person account of this experience from one of the asylum seekers, as well as the story of an Heng Phang, a Cambodian man who arrived with his family in the 1980s and was brought back to Enterprise to support the asylum seekers in the 1990s. The story was also briefly told in the *Worthwhile Enterprise* exhibition and catalogue, as part of the final chapter of Enterprise's existence.
9. "Living Treasures," City of Greater Dandenong, http://www.greaterdandenong.com/document/25684/living-treasures.

282   A. ATKINSON-PHILLIPS

10. Unfortunately, these interviews have survived primarily as summarized narratives, with a few verbatim quotes, rather than as original recordings or transcripts.
11. Sinatra Murphy, "*I'm Home!*," 2011.
12. Quoted in Murphy, "*I'm Home!*," 2011.
13. This term is taken from the work of Dennis Byrne; for example, "Affect and Empathy," in Paul Ashton and Jacqueline Z. Wilson eds, *Silent System: Forgotten Australians and the Institutionalisation of Women and Children* (Melbourne: Australian Scholarly Publishing, 2014), 71–80.
14. Merle Mitchell, "Springvale—Rich because of Diversity," in "*I'm Home!*," 3–6.
15. Geraldina Alvarez-Poblete, hosted on "Enterprise Migrant Hostel History Project" website, http://www.enterprisehostel.org/images/pdfs/Geraldina%20AlvarezPoblete.pdf.
16. Joseph Pugliese, "Migrant Heritage in an Indigenous Context: For a Decolonising Migrant Historiography," *Journal of Intercultural Studies* 23, no. 1 (2002), 5–18.
17. Sara Wills, "Between the Hostel and the Detention Centre," 277.
18. Peter Jackson, Graham Smith and Sarah Olive, "Families Remembering Food: Reusing Secondary Data" (2007), https://www.sheffield.ac.uk/polopoly_fs/1.145076!/file/FRF-reuse-paper-WP-.pdf.
19. See, for example, Alistair Thompson's work on migration life histories for a discussion of how the time and context of telling shapes life narratives: "Life Stories and Historical Analysis," in Simon Gunn and Lucy Faire eds, *Research Methods for History*, 101–17 (Edinburgh: Edinburgh University Press, 2012).
20. See Rosalyn Deutsche's conception of the work of public art in *Evictions: Art and Spatial Politics* (Cambridge, MA: MIT Press, 1996), 288.

BIBLIOGRAPHY

Byrne, Dennis. "Affect and Empathy: Thinking About the Power of Material Things to Move Visitors." In *Silent System: Forgotten Australians and the Institutionalisation of Women and Children*, edited by Paul Ashton and Jacqueline Z. Wilson 71–80. Melbourne: Australian Scholarly Publishing, 2014.

City of Greater Dandenong. "Living Treasures." Greater Dandenong: City of Opportunity. www.greaterdandenong.com/document/25684/living-treasures.

Deutsche, Rosalyn. *Evictions: Art and Spatial Politics*. Cambridge, MA: MIT Press, 1996.

Enterprise Migrant Hostel History Project. *The Spirit of Enterprise: A Project of National Significance*. http://www.enterprisehostel.org.

Immigration Museum. *A Worthwhile Enterprise: The Migrant Hostel in Springvale.* Exhibition Catalogue, Melbourne, VIC: Immigration Museum, 2008.

Jackson, Peter, Graham Smith, and Sarah Olive. "Families Remembering Food: Reusing Secondary Data." (2007) https://www.sheffield.ac.uk/polopoly_fs/1.145076!/file/FRF-reuse-paper-WP-.pdf.

Neumann, Klaus. *Across the Seas: Australian's Response to Refugees, A History.* Melbourne: Black Inc., 2015.

Persian, Jayne. *Beautiful Balts: From Displaced Persons to New Australians.* Sydney: NewSouth Publishing, 2017.

Pugliese, Joseph. "Migrant Heritage in an Indigenous Context: For a Decolonising Migrant Historiography," *Journal of Intercultural Studies* 23, no. 1 (2002): 5–18.

Sinatra Murphy Pty Ltd. *"'I'm Home!' Honouring the Enterprise Hostel."* Consultation Report, City of Greater Dandenong, 2011.

Thomson, Alistair. "Life Stories and Historical Analysis." In *Research Methods for History*, edited by Simon Gunn and Lucy Faire, 101–17. Edinburgh: Edinburgh University Press, 2012.

Wills, Sara. "Between the Hostel and the Detention Centre: Possible Trajectories of Migrant Pain and Shame in Australia." In *Places of Pain and Shame*, edited by William Logan and Keir Reeves 263–80. London and New York: Routledge, 2009.

CHAPTER 19

In Search of "Australia and the Australian People": The National Library of Australia and the Representation of Cultural and Linguistic Diversity

Klaus Neumann

"We are defined [...] by shared values of freedom, democracy, the rule of law and equality of opportunity—a 'fair go,'" then Australian Prime Minister Malcolm Turnbull wrote in his foreword to the National–Liberal coalition government's 2017 Multicultural Policy Statement.[1] The Australia

---

Research for this essay has been supported by Australian Research Council grant LP170100222. I thank my colleagues Jodie Boyd, Morgan Harrington, Ian McShane and Michael Piggott for their comments on a previous version of this paper. I am also indebted to the staff of the National Library of Australia for conversations about some of the ideas discussed in this chapter, while taking full responsibility for my interpretation of National Library policies.

K. Neumann (✉)
Hamburg Foundation for the Advancement of Research and Culture,
Hamburg, Germany

Deakin University, Melbourne, VIC, Australia

Hannah Arendt Institute, Dresden, Germany
e-mail: klaus.neumann@wiku-hamburg.de

© The Author(s) 2019
K. Darian-Smith, P. Hamilton (eds.), *Remembering Migration*,
Palgrave Macmillan Memory Studies,
https://doi.org/10.1007/978-3-030-17751-5_19

depicted in the Statement is one that has had a successful history, becoming, for example, "the most successful multicultural society in the world." It is one of the markers of successful multiculturalism that migrants "have the opportunity to contribute to our nation."

In English, there is no morphologically overt difference between inclusive and exclusive personal pronouns, yet the rhetoric of the Multicultural Statement implies that what "we" do and think can be taken as a given; "we" and "our nation" have already been demarcated and are firmly in place when the migrant arrives. The migrant is to identify with "our" history, while "we" are not expected to incorporate their histories into our understanding of who we are. The Multicultural Statement implies that today's migrants—their lives, but also their histories and memories—are to be absorbed into a fully formed Australian nation.

There is room in "our" history for memories of migration. After all, even British and Irish settlement, which is held responsible for "the establishment of our parliamentary democracy, institutions and law,"[2] was the result of migration. But some memories are more suitable than others: those that are incorporated into "our" history describe how "millions of people from all continents [...] have made Australia home,"[3] "ours" is a history that makes sense of how "we" became "the most successful multicultural society in the world." Thus, migrants' memories perform an important role in that they confirm that absorption and assimilation are possible.

Official discourses are rarely uniform; often they are characterized by internal contradictions between and within government policies, practices and rhetoric. In this chapter, I discuss a policy that is, potentially at least, not reconcilable with the approach that informs the 2017 Multicultural Statement, in that it offers an expansive view of Australia which challenges the conception of Australia as a territorially bounded nation-state and comprised only of its citizens. In the following I explore aspects of the mandate, policies and practices of the National Library of Australia (NLA) with regard to the collection of material about Australians from culturally and linguistically diverse backgrounds. The National Library's practices and the aspirations that inform them are significant because the NLA has long justifiably claimed to occupy "a leadership position that is unique among Australian cultural institutions, and in the international context."[4]

Since the turn of this century, archives, museums and libraries around the world have increasingly identified—and been identified—as "memory institutions."[5] The NLA's 2017–2018 Corporate Plan, for example, identified the building of "the nation's memory" as one of three strategic priorities for the Library.[6] How inclusive and comprehensive is that memory?

How inclusive could it be? What are the parameters of "the nation" to which that memory belongs?

The *National Library Act 1960* obliges the NLA to "maintain and develop a national collection of library material, including a comprehensive collection of library material relating to Australia and the Australian people."[7] In the second reading debate of November and December 1960, several speakers endorsed an idea put forward by the National Librarian Harold White, namely that an Australian national library ought to record the "life and development of the people."[8] The legislation does not define what is meant by "comprehensive." Even more importantly, it does not specify what constitutes "Australia," nor does it define the "Australian people."

To appreciate the relevant wording of the 1960 NLA Act, and the fact that it leaves much room for interpretation, it is useful to contrast it with that of the *National Museum of Australia Act 1980*. According to the latter, the National Museum of Australia (NMA) is, *inter alia*:

1. to develop and maintain a national collection of historical material; [...]
2. to exhibit material, whether in written form or in any other form, that relates to Australia's past, present and future; [...]
3. to conduct, arrange for or assist in research into matters pertaining to Australian history[9]

The 1980 NMA Act specifies that "historical material" is "material (whether in written form or in any other form) relating to Australian history," that "Australian history" encompasses both "the natural history of Australia" and "the history of the interaction of man [sic] with the Australian natural environment," and that "Australia" also includes all former and current external territories.[10]

Neither Act equates "Australia" with a territorially bounded nation-state; the "Australian natural environment" of the NMA Act refers to a physical entity that existed before it was thought of in terms of geopolitical boundaries, yet at the same time that Act's wording makes clear that geographical entities that are not usually thought of as part of Australia, such as Papua, have nevertheless been part of the "Australia" of concern to the NMA because of their geopolitical association. By referring specifically to Australia's former and current territories, the NMA Act also implies that other places, even if they have a strong association with Australia, or if they are under Australian control but not part of Australia in a geopolitical sense, are not covered by the NMA's mandate.

The NLA Act, on the other hand, makes no reference to Australia as a physical entity with geographical boundaries. Instead it refers to "Australia" as one of a pair: "Australia and the Australian people." Given that the NLA Act defines neither of them outside of this formula, they seem mutually dependent: Australia is the entity that belongs to and is defined by the Australian people, and the Australian people are defined by their relationship with Australia. Importantly, this mutual dependency is not that of a nation-state that rests on the sovereignty of a particular people and of a people constituted by that nation-state.[11]

I now turn to how the NLA's "function" (to use the term employed in the 1960 NLA Act) is interpreted in relevant Library policy. The National Library's first Collection Development Policy (CDP) dates from 1981.[12] The 2016 CDP is the most recent iteration of policies that have guided the National Library's approach to "maintain[ing] and develop[ing] a national collection." It does not mention "the Australian people," except when quoting the 1960 legislation. In the sections dealing with the NLA's Australian collections, there is no mention either of citizens. The policy does make several references to the Australian nation, however. When referring to the Australian published collections, the CDP stipulates that the Library is to collect material that reflects Australia's development as a nation or that relates to historical events that have informed "Australia as a modern nation."[13] Yet, in neither of these instances is the intention to collect material *exclusively* related to Australia *as a nation*. More common than the references to Australia as a nation are those to "Australian society," "Australian life" and "Australian culture"; in fact, here the language of the CDP harks back to Harold White's formula of the "life and development of the people."

All this suggests that the National Library's interpretation of its mandate is deliberately expansive and that the "national memory" is conceived as something significantly broader than the memory of the Australian nation-state and its citizens. The 2016 CDP makes it clear that for the National Library, the "Australian people" of the 1960 Act includes citizens and non-citizens, those living in Australia as well as former residents, and Indigenous peoples—including those inhabiting Australia before 1788. The 2016 Collection Development Policy does not exclude the possibility that "Australia" also includes physical places that were shaped by "Australians," yet were never part of Australia in a geopolitical sense, and that conversely the people whose lives are of concern to the National Library are all those who are part of "Australia" in a wider sense (including, e.g., those detained in Australia's regional processing centres, or the Afghan neighbours of Australians stationed in Tarin Kowt).

The 2005 CDP uses the term "multicultural" six times, and the term "multiculturalism" four times, saying, for example, that the National Library aims "to ensure [...] that Australia's ethnic diversity is documented and its multicultural heritage is preserved." Unlike its predecessors, the 2016 CDP does not use the terms "multicultural" or "multiculturalism,"[14] but it stresses the need "to reflect the full diversity and range of Australian life" and to represent "cultural and linguistic diversity."[15] In the heydays of Australian multiculturalism, in the 1980s and first half of the 1990s, the commitment of collecting institutions to adequately represent cultural diversity tended to be linked to the idea that people from culturally and linguistically diverse backgrounds needed to be allowed to see their own experience reflected in collections. The Hawke government adopted eight goals proposed in 1988 by the Advisory Council on Multicultural Affairs, including goal number 7, "All Australians should be able to develop and share their cultural heritage."[16] The government's 1989 National Agenda for a Multicultural Australia identified "cultural identity" as one of "three dimensions of multicultural policy." For the Agenda's authors, "cultural identity" meant "the right of all Australians, within carefully defined limits, to express and share their individual cultural heritage, including their language and religion."[17] The Agenda did not recognize that the documentation of cultural heritage by libraries and cultural institutions was essential to ensure that *all* Australians would be able to share such heritage.[18] Instead it argued that the failure of museums and other cultural institutions to represent Australia's diversity would devalue the self-esteem of Australians from migrant backgrounds.[19]

The National Library's 2016 CDP takes a different approach. Its opening sentence quotes the first priority of the 2016–2020 Corporate Plan:

> The Library aspires to enable Australians to understand their diverse social, cultural and intellectual histories by collecting and preserving Australian publications and unpublished collections—in print and digital forms—so that they can be enjoyed by current and future generations.[20]

That is, the Library is concerned not so much with the collection of material related to Australia's migrant heritage *for* people identifying with that heritage, but it wants *all* Australians, now *and in the future*, to be able to gain a comprehensive—and culturally and linguistically diverse—picture of Australian society, life and culture.

The ambition to interpret the 1960 NLA Act expansively has long been tempered by the National Library's budget. Particularly in recent years, when the efficiency dividend introduced by the Hawke Labor government in 1987 has put the national cultural institutions under significant pressure,[21] the Library's mandate to "maintain and develop [...] a *comprehensive* collection of library material relating to Australia and the Australian people" has appeared to be increasingly unrealistic. Without wishing to downplay the role of such resource constraints, here I would like to discuss a select number of structural issues that have meant that the Library's collection is not as representative of Australia's cultural and linguistic diversity as the 2016 CDP would like it to be.

According to the 2016 CDP, "The Library aims to comprehensively collect Australian publications in order to reflect the full diversity and range of Australian life depicted in the nation's published record, both contemporary and retrospective."[22] Under legal deposit legislation, publishers are required to lodge one copy of each published work with the Library[23]; since 2016, the Library has also been able to require publishers to provide digital copies. The Library reminds publishers of their obligations, and, if such reminders are unsuccessful, also resorts to purchasing items that should have been deposited, particularly in the case of self-published material. However, several provisos are in order.

First, the Library's book collection reflects the diversity of Australian life only as far as it is depicted in the published record. Self-publishing notwithstanding, that record is also a reflection of market forces. When it comes to published memoirs, for example, Australian commercial publishers privilege the memories of some Australians over those of others, favouring narratives that are perceived to appeal to a broad audience, such as rags-to-riches biographical stories rather than those that describe migration as a failure.

Second, the National Library collection could realistically aim to reflect the diversity of Australian life only as it is depicted in the *Australian* published record. Australian authors writing about their experience as migrants, for example, sometimes do so in books published outside Australia, in their home countries or elsewhere in the diaspora, and often in their native language.[24] They sometimes do so after having returned to their native country (which does not disqualify them from being Australian). While the National Library commissions agents to collect books published with Australian content outside Australia, including in languages other than English, the success of these agents' attempts to collect Australian material comprehensively is dependent on their access to accurate and comprehensive metadata provided by publishers and library cataloguers overseas.[25]

The following example illustrates the difficulties involved. In the mid-1960s, the Polish-born Holocaust survivor Janina David published two volumes of a memoir dealing with her life as a Jewish girl in Poland during and immediately after World War II.[26] David had left Poland in 1946, lived for a while in France, and in 1948, under the name Janina Dawidowicz, migrated to Australia.[27] She lived and worked in Melbourne, was awarded a scholarship to study social work at the University of Melbourne, and in 1955 became an Australian citizen. The books, published in London, became a global success, and the National Library included them in its collection. Three decades later, David published *Light Over the Water*,[28] the third instalment of her memoir, which the National Library did not collect, despite the fact that it dealt with her life in Australia. In 1958, David left Australia to return to France, and from there moved to the UK. The NLA's agent in the UK may not have been able to know that *Light Over the Water* has Australian content; the subject terms listed in the British Library catalogue seem to be informed by the aspects of David's biography that made her famous rather than by the content of the book, and include only the following: "David, Janina, 1930–; Jews—Poland—Biography; Refugees, Jewish—Biography; World War, 1939–1945—Refugees; World War 2 Refugees; Poland."[29] The ambition to trace the output of, and collect material about the lives of, former Australian residents presents even greater challenges in non-English-speaking contexts. Thus, three of David's books of fiction written in English, but published only in a German translation, have also not been identified by Australian libraries as Australian.[30]

Finally, the Library's "collecting and preserving" of material will in itself not enable users to understand Australians' diverse histories. The collected and preserved material needs to be discoverable and accessible. Discoverability depends on the quality of the metadata attached to Library material. That quality varies depending on the cataloguer's ability to interpret the Library item in question—which means that the metadata of catalogue entries for non-English language books by migrant authors are sometimes incorrect or inadequate. The terms used by many librarians in English-speaking countries to describe minority cultures have been notoriously problematic, as cataloguers have long relied on a universalizing and culturally biased set of subject headings provided by the Library of Congress.[31] The Library of Congress is also responsible for maintaining an authoritative list of MARC (MAchine Readable Cataloguing) codes which are used by libraries, including the NLA, to record information about the language of a particular library item. The most recent list has 484 codes, of which 55 are for groups of languages. The list privileges European languages; thus it lists almost 200 languages spoken in Melanesia and Southeast Asia under one code, "map" (Austronesian Other), while it has a separate code for Cornish, "cor."

At the National Library, books of fiction which comprise a large proportion of the English-language Australian published record dealing with the migrant experience are usually not assigned subject terms. The NLA catalogue would be of little help for a user wanting to find, for example, contemporary depictions of the experience of Yiddish-speaking migrants, who would not be directed towards classics such as *Alien Son* or *Light and Shadow*,[32] and would not be aware that David's novel, *A Part of the Main*, published in the UK, and held by the National Library of Australia (but curiously not by the British Library), is set in Melbourne, and that her main protagonist is a young migrant.[33]

The published record depicts the diversity of Australian life, but its depiction is neither comprehensive nor representative. However, the Library also collects unpublished material, and it creates material. Regarding the latter, the 2016 CDP lists as one of five priorities in Australian collecting: "Representation of the rich diversity of Australian society, in rural and regional as well as urban areas, and the experience and encounters of everyday life, including aspects of Australia that are inadequately documented."[34] Thus, the Library contracts photographers to take pictures of Australian life, society and culture, and it commissions oral histories. By commissioning pictures and oral histories—and, to a lesser extent, by collecting ephemera and manuscript and online material—the Library could compensate for gaps in its collection of published material.

The following example illustrates the unevenness of the National Library's collection, and the potential to compensate for gaps. The 2016 Australian census counted 4303 Australian residents born in Eritrea and 4583 speaking Tigrinya at home. However, according to its catalogue, in 2018 the National Library held no newspaper published in Eritrea or by Eritreans in Australia and only three books in Tigrinya (two of them Bibles, and one a chrestomathy). It held comparatively few books that contain information about the country left behind by recent Eritrean migrants to Australia, but comparatively many memoirs by or biographies of Australians of Eritrean background.[35] It held only one image depicting Eritreans in Australia, and no oral histories of Eritrean Australians.

The commissioning of whole-of-life oral history interviews with Eritrean Australians might compensate for gaps in other parts of the NLA collection. However, such an undertaking would raise further questions. What determines the representation of Eritrean Australians in the NLA's oral history collection as adequate? Should the Library use the representation of other recent migrant groups—for example, Karen, Bhutanese, Congolese or Colombians—as a benchmark? Should the number of oral histories collected by the Library per every 10,000 Australians be a guide? According to the latest figures on the NLA's website, the Library's collections included 22,989 oral history records, or approximately 10 for every 10,000 Australian residents.[36] However, this figure does not take into account that the oral history collection has grown over the course of several decades, including at a time when very few Eritreans lived in Australia. It also does not take into account that the oral history collection privileges professions in which Eritreans are underrepresented, including, for example, politicians, senior public servants and writers (in English). And any attempt to commission oral history interviews as a means of compensating for gaps elsewhere in the NLA collection may need to put relative values on different parts of the collection; for example, how many additional oral history interviews would make up for the fact that the NLA does not hold a single newspaper in Tigrinya or targeting an Australian Eritrean audience? Should the overrepresentation of memoirs written by Eritrean Australians in the past 20 years be an argument against the commissioning of oral histories?

The identification of gaps is also difficult because it would be necessary to measure Australia's diversity. The only statistics that could be used for such purposes are those provided by the Australian Bureau of Statistics (ABS). The ABS uses a five-yearly census to establish Australian residents' ancestry according to the Australian Standard Classification of Cultural and Ethnic Groups (ASCCEG). The most recent ASCCEG, which was used for the 2016 census, lists 275 categories, including one each for (mainland) Chinese (numbering more than 1.3 billion people), Papua New Guineans (numbering more than eight million people from more than 850 language groups), people from the Isle of Man, and Channel Islanders. Much like the MARC language codes of the Library of Congress, the ASCCEG categories privilege European identities.

Furthermore, any attempt to establish how representative the Library's collection is of the Australian population runs the risk of reproducing problematic ethnic or national labels. The difficulty of such an undertaking becomes obvious when considering the case of Janina David. As a former long-term Australian resident, she is an Australian in the expansive sense of the term that informs the 2016 CDP. The NLA would therefore want to comprehensively collect her output as a writer, irrespective of whether her writing is concerned with Australia. Should the catalogue identify her as a Polish Australian, because she was born in Poland? As a British Australian because she has spent most of her life in the UK? As a Jewish Australian because of her Jewish ancestry? As a refugee? As an Australian expatriate? As a Holocaust survivor? As a social worker, translator and writer of fiction?

I have drawn attention to some of the structural difficulties encountered by the Library when trying to implement its collection development policy not because these difficulties render the CDP an unrealistic document. Rather, I argue that the attempt to think through these difficulties could allow us to conceptualize expansive notions of "Australia" and "Australians" (or "the Australian people"). The formula of the 1960 NLA Act and its interpretation in the National Library's 2016 CDP could prompt us to think of "Australia" not primarily as a territorially bounded nation-state, nor only as an entity constituted by its citizens, but rather as the lands peopled by Australians in the broadest sense.

A contemplation of the difficulties encountered in attempts to rectify the perceived underrepresentation of Australians from culturally and linguistically diverse backgrounds in the National Library collections could also be instructive. How could Australia's diversity be measured without resorting to mutually exclusive categories (such as migrant/non-migrant; of British descent/of non-British descent; English-speaker/non-English speaker), and without relying on a list of ideologically and politically charged terms referring to nations and peoples?

Such interrogations of the contradictions of "multicultural" societies, as much as the necessarily imperfect solutions offered by "memory institutions" such as the National Library of Australia, are fashioning a more inclusive "we." They help us to conceptualize a nation whose boundaries are porous and whose identity is in flux, and to recognize that migrants' lives and memories keep transforming Australia.

NOTES

1. Australia, Federal Government, *Multicultural Australia: United, Strong, Successful: Australia's Multicultural Statement* (Canberra: Australian Government, 2017), 3, 7 and 13.
2. *Multicultural Australia*, 7.
3. *Multicultural Australia*, 7.
4. National Library of Australia, "2018–19 Corporate Plan: Covering Reporting Periods 2018–19 to 2021–22" (2018): 5.
5. Joan M. Schwartz, "'We Make Our Tools, and Our Tools Make Us': Lessons from Photographs for the Practice, Politics, and Poetics of Diplomatics," *Archivaria* 40 (1995): 40–74; Edwin Klijn and Yola de Lusenet, *In the Picture: Preservation and Digitisation of European Photographic Collections.* (Amsterdam: European Commission on Preservation and Access, 2000); Gabrielle Ritchie, "The Culture of Collecting: The National Library as a Memory Institution," *Historia* 47, no. 2 (2002): 511–30; Helena Robinson, "Remembering Things Differently: Museums, Libraries and Archives as Memory Institutions and the Implications for Convergence," *Museum Management and Curatorship* 27, no. 4 (2012): 413–29.
6. National Library of Australia, "2017–18 Corporate Plan: Covering reporting periods 2017–18 to 2020–21," 2017, 3.
7. *National Library Act 1960*: s. 6.
8. Kim Edward Beazley, *Commonwealth Parliamentary Debates (CPD)*, Representatives, 24 November 1960, 3239, Leonard James Reynolds, *CPD*, Representatives, 24 November 1960, 3258; William Henry Spooner, *CPD*, Senate, 29 November 1960, 1801. Robert Menzies referred to the library's function to collect material "illustrating the life and achievements of the people" (*CPD*, Representatives, 10 November 1960, 2724); H. L. White, "Source Material for Australian Studies," *Historical Studies: Australia and New Zealand* 7, no. 28 (1957): 453, 455.
9. *National Museum of Australia Act 1980*: s 6.
10. *National Museum of Australia Act 1980*: s 3, 1 and s 3, 2.
11. Robert French, "The Constitution and the People," in Robert French, Geoffrey Lindell, and Cheryl Saunders eds, *Reflections on the Australian Constitution*, 60–85. (Annandale: Federation Press, 2003).
12. National Library of Australia, *National Library of Australia Selection Policy*, (Canberra: National Library of Australia, 1981).
13. National Library of Australia, "2016 Collection Development Policy," 2016.

14. National Library of Australia, *Collection Development Policy*, (Canberra: National Library of Australia, 2005).
15. National Library of Australia, "2016 Collection Development Policy," Principles.
16. Office of Multicultural Affairs, Department of the Prime Minister and Cabinet, *National Agenda for a Multicultural Australia: Sharing Our Future* (Canberra: AGPS, 1989), vii.
17. *National Agenda for a Multicultural Australia*, vii.
18. Derek Whitehead, "Documenting Diversity: Acquisitions and Access to Material Reflecting a Multicultural Australia," in *Towards Federation 2001: Linking Australians and Their Heritage*, 263–69. (Canberra: National Library of Australia, 1993), 264.
19. Office of Multicultural Affairs, *National Agenda for a Multicultural Australia*, 47.
20. National Library of Australia, "2016 Collection Development Policy," Introduction.
21. Joint Committee of Public Accounts and Audit *The Efficiency Dividend and Small Agencies: Size Does Matter* (Canberra: Parliament of the Commonwealth of Australia, 2008), 56.
22. National Library of Australia, "2016 Collection Development Policy," Principles.
23. *Copyright Act 1968*: s. 195CD.
24. Katarzyna Kwapisz Williams, "Transnational Literary Cultures in Australia: Writers of Polish Descent," in Bruno Mascitelli, Sonia Mycak and Gerardo Papalia eds, *The European Diaspora in Australia: An Interdisciplinary Perspective*, 114–35 (Newcastle upon Tyne: Cambridge Scholars Publishing, 2016).
25. The NLA sources overseas publications with the help of contractors. In 2018, the only country in which the NLA maintains a physical presence to collect material is Indonesia.
26. Janina David, *A Square of Sky: The Recollections of a Childhood* (London: New Authors Limited, 1964); Janina David, *A Touch of Earth: A Wartime Childhood* (London: Hutchinson, 1966).
27. National Archives of Australia (Canberra): A12508, 50/435, National Archives of Australia (Melbourne): B78, DAWIDOWICZ J.
28. Janina David, *Light Over the Water: Post-war Wanderings* (London: Barnet Libraries in conjunction with JMLS, 1995).
29. The NLA purchased a copy of *Light Over the Water* in 2016. The catalogue metadata identify the book's author as Australian, but include the same incorrect subject terms as the British Library catalogue summarizing David's experiences as related to World War II.

19 IN SEARCH OF "AUSTRALIA AND THE AUSTRALIAN PEOPLE... 297

30. Janina David, *Leben aus zweiter Hand* (Frankfurt: Fischer Taschenbuch-Verlag, 1990), Janina David, *Die Perle der Weisheit* (München: Droemer Knaur, 1994); Janina David, *Eurydikes Augen* (Berlin: Berliner Taschenbuch-Verlag, 2004).
31. Sanford Berman, *Prejudices and Antipathies: A Tract on the LC Subject Heads Concerning People* (Metuchen: Scarecrow Press, 1971); Hope A. Olson, "The Power to Name: Representation in Library Catalogues," *Signs* 26, no. 3 (2001): 639–68.
32. Judah Waten, *Alien Son* (Sydney: Angus & Robertson, 1952); Herz Bergner, *Light and Shadow*, translated by Alec Braizblatt (Melbourne: Georgian House, 1963).
33. Janina David, *A Part of the Main* (London: Hutchinson, 1969).
34. National Library of Australia, "2016 Collection Development Policy," Principles.
35. Joseph Ribarow ed., *From Eritrea to Australia: The Recollections of Abraham Hadgu: A Refugee from Africa* (Melbourne: Inner Western Region Migrant Resource Centre, 2001); Brett Hilder, *The Sea of Chance* (Millers Point: Pier 9, 2007); Tewodros Fekadu, *No One's Son* (Fredonia: Leapfrog Press, 2012); Keiron Galloway, *Kemey de Han w'alu: Kibra's Story* (Sandy Bay: Tasmanian Council for Adult Literacy, 2014).
36. National Library of Australia, "Collection Statistics: Holdings by Type (as at the End of 2016–17)," n.d. [2017].

BIBLIOGRAPHY

Australia Federal Government. *Multicultural Australia: United, Strong, Successful: Australia's Multicultural Statement*. Canberra: Australian Government, 2017.

Bergner, Herz. *Light and Shadow*. Translated by Alec Braizblatt. Melbourne: Georgian House, 1963.

Berman, Sanford. *Prejudices and Antipathies: A Tract on the LC Subject Heads Concerning People*. Metuchen: Scarecrow Press, 1971.

Copyright Act 1968.

David, Janina. *A Square of Sky: The Recollections of a Childhood*. London: New Authors Limited, 1964.

David, Janina. *A Touch of Earth: A Wartime Childhood*. London: Hutchinson, 1966.

David, Janina. *A Part of the Main*. London: Hutchinson, 1969.

David, Janina. *Leben aus zweiter Hand*. Translated by Michaela Hubner. Frankfurt: Fischer Taschenbuch-Verlag, 1990.

David, Janina. *Die Perle der Weisheit*. Translated by Jakob Leutner. München: Droemer Knaur, 1994.

David, Janina. *Light Over the Water: Post-war Wanderings*. London: Barnet Libraries in conjunction with JMLS, 1995.

298　K. NEUMANN

David, Janina. *Eurydikes Augen*. Translated by Gesine Stempel. Berlin: Berliner Taschenbuch-Verlag, 2004.

Fekadu, Tewodros. *No One's Son*. Fredonia: Leapfrog Press, 2012.

French, Robert. "The Constitution and the People." In *Reflections on the Australian Constitution*, edited by Robert French, Geoffrey Lindell, and Cheryl Saunders, 60–85. Annandale: Federation Press, 2003.

Galloway, Keiron. *Kemey de Han w'alu: Kibra's Story*. Sandy Bay: Tasmanian Council for Adult Literacy, 2014.

Hilder, Brett. *The Sea of Chance*. Millers Point: Pier 9, 2007.

Joint Committee of Public Accounts and Audit. *The Efficiency Dividend and Small Agencies: Size Does Matter*. Canberra: Parliament of the Commonwealth of Australia, 2008.

Klijn, Edwin, and Yola de Lusenet. *In the Picture: Preservation and Digitisation of European Photographic Collections*. Amsterdam: European Commission on Preservation and Access, 2000.

National Library Act 1960.

National Library of Australia. *National Library of Australia Selection Policy*. Canberra: National Library of Australia, 1981.

National Library of Australia. *Collection Development Policy*. Canberra: National Library of Australia, 2005.

National Library of Australia. "2016 Collection Development Policy," 2016. https://www.nla.gov.au/collection-development-policy.

National Library of Australia. "Collection Statistics: Holdings by Type (as at the End of 2016–17)", n.d. [2017]. https://www.nla.gov.au/collections/statistics.

National Library of Australia. "2017–18 Corporate Plan: Covering Reporting Periods 2017–18 to 2020–21," 2017. https://www.nla.gov.au/sites/default/files/nla_corporate_plan_2017-18_final.pdf.

National Library of Australia. "2018–19 Corporate Plan: Covering Reporting Periods 2018–19 to 2021–22," 2018. https://www.nla.gov.au/sites/default/files/nla_corporate_plan_2018-19.pdf.

National Museum of Australia Act 1980.

Office of Multicultural Affairs, Department of the Prime Minister and Cabinet. *National Agenda for a Multicultural Australia: Sharing Our Future*. Canberra: AGPS, 1989.

Olson, Hope A. "The Power to Name: Representation in Library Catalogues." *Signs* 26, no. 3 (2001): 639–68.

Ribarow, Joseph ed. *From Eritrea to Australia: The Recollections of Abraham Hadgu: A Refugee from Africa*. Melbourne: Inner Western Region Migrant Resource Centre, 2001.

Ritchie, Gabrielle. "The Culture of Collecting: The National Library as a Memory Institution." *Historia* 47, no. 2 (2002): 511–30.

Robinson, Helena. "Remembering Things Differently: Museums, Libraries and Archives as Memory Institutions and the Implications for Convergence." *Museum Management and Curatorship* 27, no. 4 (2012): 413–29.

Schwartz, Joan M. "'We Make Our Tools, and Our Tools Make Us': Lessons from Photographs for the Practice, Politics, and Poetics of Diplomatics." *Archivaria* 40 (1995): 40–74.

Waten, Judah. *Alien Son*. Sydney: Angus & Robertson, 1952.

White, H. L. "Source Material for Australian Studies." *Historical Studies: Australia and New Zealand* 7, no. 28 (1957): 452–60.

Whitehead, Derek. "Documenting Diversity: Acquisitions and Access to Material Reflecting a Multicultural Australia." In *Towards Federation 2001: Linking Australians and Their Heritage*, 263–69. Canberra: National Library of Australia, 1993.

Williams, Katarzyna Kwapisz. "Transnational Literary Cultures in Australia: Writers of Polish Descent." In *The European Diaspora in Australia: An Interdisciplinary Perspective*, edited by Bruno Mascitelli, Sonia Mycak, and Gerardo Papalia, 114–35. Newcastle upon Tyne: Cambridge Scholars Publishing, 2016.

CHAPTER 20

Remembering the Child Migrant on Screen

Felicity Collins

The migrant story in Australian cinema is bittersweet. Oscillating between comic and tragic modes, feature films, mini-series and documentaries have highlighted non-British migration from Europe, after World War II, and from Asia, after the Vietnam War. In the 1960s, *They're a Weird Mob* (Michael Powell, 1966) established an enduring comic template for the European adult migrant's initiation into "the Australian way of life." Four decades later, comedies of social integration were displaced by accounts of family disintegration narrated in a tragic mode. In *Romulus, My Father* (Richard Roxburgh, 2007) a boy bears witness to his family's disintegration after migrating from Romania, and in *The Home Song Stories* (Tony Ayres, 2007) a son remembers his mother's disintegration after migrating from Hong Kong. In contrast, *Floating Life* (Clara Law, 1996) offers a tragi-comic perspective (through the eyes of younger sons) on the dispersal of the Chan family between Hong Kong, Australia and Germany. While the child's memory of migration has been significant in diasporic filmmaking, this chapter draws attention to a "pariah" figure—the child migrant who arrived in Australia alone, with "no birth certificate or documentation; no letters or photographs ... [and] nothing to tie them to the past except distant memories."[1]

F. Collins (✉)
La Trobe University, Melbourne, VIC, Australia
e-mail: f.collins@latrobe.edu.au

© The Author(s) 2019
K. Darian-Smith, P. Hamilton (eds.), *Remembering Migration*,
Palgrave Macmillan Memory Studies,
https://doi.org/10.1007/978-3-030-17751-5_20

Whether "deported" from a British orphanage to grow up in an Australian institution, or "rescued" from poverty in India to grow up in an Australian family, the child migrant is remarkably absent when it comes to "remembering migration." In the 2011 documentary series, *Immigration Nation: The Secret Story of Us*, the child migrant has no place, even in the "Populate or Perish" episode on immigration policy after World War II. This policy included a plan to bring 50,000 British "war babies" and "orphans" to fill Australia's "empty spaces" with "good British stock."[2] The outcome was an estimated 10,000 British children sent to farm schools and orphanages run by charities and churches, where they disappeared from the nation's migration story. For the British child migrant, finding a place in the "immigration nation" has depended not just on the oral historian but on the combined efforts of a British social worker, journalist and documentary producer—supplemented by Australian and British filmmakers. A more recent kind of child migrant, the inter-country adoptee, is also absent from Australia's migration story, becoming the focus of research into adoption rather than migration, and surfacing in popular culture in exceptional circumstances, primarily aided by the social worker, journalist, ghost writer and filmmaker.

The question posed by the child migrant—as pariah or outsider in the story of immigrant Australia—is best articulated by Judith Butler when she asks, "whose lives are grievable [and representable] and whose are not?"[3] Keeping in mind Butler's point that the social and political norms that define a grievable life "are enacted through visual and narrative frames,"[4] this chapter explores how two popular genres—the adventure-quest narrative and the memoir—have made child migrant lives representable and grievable. It argues that these popular genres are especially important for remembering the child migrant precisely because such lives leave "no public trace to grieve, or only a partial, mangled, and enigmatic trace."[5]

The following discussion begins with the discovery and intermedial remembering of the child migrant as a "pariah" figure who troubles public memory. It shows how the adventure-quest narrative frames the child migrant in similar ways in the mini-series, *The Leaving of Liverpool* (Michael Jenkins, 1992), and the feature film, *Lion* (Garth Davis, 2016). It then looks at how child migrant memories appear as "partial, mangled and enigmatic" in Margaret Humphrey's activist memoir, *Empty Cradles* (1994), republished as *Oranges and Sunshine* in 2011, and Saroo Brierley's ghost-written memoir *A Long Way Home* (2013), republished as *Lion* in 2016.

Discovering the British Child Migrant

The British child migrant came to public attention in Britain in July 1987 through two feature articles by Annabel Ferriman, published in *The Observer* and republished in Australian newspapers. The empire-building rationale of the British child migration scheme was further exposed when Granada Television broadcast *Lost Children of the Empire* (Joanna Mack, 1989). This documentary was supplemented by a book of the same title published by the Child Migrants Trust—set up in 1987 to bring public attention to the plight of adult child migrants.

Although the deportation of children to work in British colonies began in 1618 with 100 children sent to Virginia, the media revelation that this practice continued until the 1970s had particular resonance in Australia. Of the estimated 10,000 British children deported to Australia, a handful returned to Britain to find their families. Arriving in Britain with few or no documents and "mangled" childhood memories, their cause was taken up by social worker, Margaret Humphreys, who had been working with an adoption group in Nottingham. An initial contact with one adult child migrant and the sister of another took Humphreys to Australia in 1987, the first of many trips to conduct interviews with hundreds of child migrants. The gradual revelation of the extent and duration of British deportation of children during the twentieth century—to Canada (from 1900 until the 1930s), to Australia (from 1912, but mainly after World War II), and to a lesser extent New Zealand and Rhodesia (after World War II)—led Humphreys and her supporters to establish the Child Migrants Trust in order to fund the painstaking work of tracing the families of children deported through the British child welfare system, often without parental knowledge or consent. The Trust also attempted to investigate the institutions and charities responsible for implementing the child migrant scheme in Britain and Australia. In 1993, Humphreys was awarded the Order of Australia Medal in Canberra, surrounded by adult child migrants. At the time, as she noted in her memoir, both British and Australian governments were steadfastly refusing to acknowledge and take responsibility for what happened to child migrants in Australia.[6]

The prolonged struggle for political recognition and public memory of child migrants, especially those subjected to indentured labour and domestic servitude in rural Australia, took different forms over three decades. In 1987 the most urgent need was for adult child migrants to find living relatives in Britain, and to discover why they had been abandoned by those responsible for their emigration. In 1997, 2001 and 2004, survivor testimony offered a different narrative frame for recognizing and remembering the child migrant: enquires into the institutional care and abuse of children eventually led to public apologies from Australian Prime Minister Kevin Rudd in 2009, and British Prime Minister Gordon Brown in 2010.[7] A further forum for survivor testimony was provided by the Royal Commission into Institutional Responses to Child Sexual Abuse, announced by Prime Minister Julia Gillard in Australia in 2012, followed in 2014 with the announcement by British Home Secretary Theresa May of the Independent Inquiry into Child Sexual Abuse in England and Wales. Decades of work by journalists, survivor groups and steadfast advocates such as the Child Migrants Trust have played a vital role in obtaining further recognition and redress for child migrants, as recently as 2018.[8]

Intermedial Remembering of the Child Migrant

While the abuse of children in institutional care has been well documented over the last two decades,[9] the visual and narrative frames that made their lives representable and grievable have had less attention. Popular memory of the child migrant has relied on the "chat" media where an ephemeral news item is "worked through" in talk shows, becoming a social issue whose tropes are processed "into more narrativized, explained forms" including memoir and genre films.[10] An exemplary instance of intermedial remembering occurred in Australia with *Bringing Them Home*, the 1997 report on the Stolen Generations of Aboriginal and Torres Strait Islander children removed from their families.[11] The vigorous public debate over whether the children were "stolen" or "saved" gave rise to the influential feature film, *Rabbit-Proof Fence* (Phillip Noyce, 2002), which owed its story to Doris Pilkington-Garimara's 1996 memoir *Follow the Rabbit-Proof Fence*. This intermedial pattern of creating a public memory— whereby a buried history becomes a contentious social and political issue—is also evident in the child migrant story.

The 1987 articles on British child migrants published in *The Observer* not only paved the way for *Lost Children of the Empire*, they led to the Australian–British co-production of the historical mini-series, *The Leaving of Liverpool* (shown on ABC TV in Australia in 1992, but held back in Britain by the BBC until July 1993).[12] Researched and written by Australians, John Alsop and Sue Smith, and produced by Penny Chapman for the ABC, *The Leaving of Liverpool* dramatized the hope, shock, deprivation, violation, bewilderment and anger suffered by many of the child migrants at religious institutions such as the notorious Bindoon Boys Town run by Christian Brothers in Western Australia, and charitable institutions such as the Fairbridge Farm Schools, which "received" British children from 1935 to 1973. The child migrant stories told to Margaret Humphreys in interviews from 1986 to 1993 (and integrated into her 1994 memoir) provided material for *The Leaving of Liverpool*. In 2011, Humphreys' memoir was republished to coincide with the release of the British feature film, *Oranges and Sunshine*, directed by Jim Loach and starring Emily Watson as Humphreys. At the time of the film's release in Australia, adult child migrants appeared in the media speaking for themselves, alongside Humphreys, Loach and Watson.[13]

In the 1970s–1980s, another category of "child migrant" entered the mediasphere as inter-country adoption, as the "rescue" of children from poverty in countries such as India, came to public attention through a similar intermedial pattern. In the same year that Humphreys began working to reunite British child migrants with their families, a Bengali lawyer and social worker based in Calcutta, Mrs Saroj Sood, was arranging for a five-year-old boy, known then as Saru, to be adopted by Sue and John Brierley in Tasmania as part of an inter-country adoption programme run by the Indian Society for Sponsorship and Adoption (ISSA). Like the British child migrant scheme, ISSA was set up to "rescue" lost, abandoned and orphaned children from poverty, abuse and exploitation in Calcutta. Twenty-five years later, in 2012, Saroo Brierley's astonishing story of finding his way home to his Indian village (after a six-year search using Google Earth and Facebook) was taken up by news and current affairs programmes, then quickly transformed into the international bestselling memoir, *The Long Way Home* (written with Larry Buttrose, 2013). In 2016 the screenplay of Brierley's memoir resulted in the box office hit and Oscar-nominated film, *Lion* (Garth Davis).[14]

THE ADVENTURE-QUEST NARRATIVE IN *THE LEAVING OF LIVERPOOL* AND *LION*

While there are significant differences between the experiences of child migrants deported from Britain to Australia and child migrants who arrived in Australia as inter-country adoptees, their stories dramatized on screen share similar tropes, narrative turning points and frames of memory. Although twenty-five years passed between the 1992 broadcast of *The Leaving of Liverpool* and the 2017 Australian release of *Lion*, they share a narrative template commonly referred to as the adventure-quest. Both the mini-series and the film open with the cinematic immersion of the viewer-spectator in the pre-migration world of the child—a joyful and kinetic space of young bodies stretching the boundaries of "home." In *The Leaving of Liverpool*, "home" is the Star of the Sea Orphanage in Liverpool, where not everyone is an orphan and not all staff are benign, but where there is space to run free in games that involve conquest and the planting of the Union Jack by Bert (Kevin Jones), a radiant storyteller who loves Empire and "reads" from memory. In *Lion*, five-year-old Saroo (Sunny Pawar) has the freedom to go adventuring along railway tracks while scavenging for food with his older brother. Meanwhile, their mother works on a building site, carrying heavy rocks to take the edge off the family's extreme poverty. Responding to his first viewing of *Lion*, Salman Rushdie describes Sunny Pawar's performance as "a thing of intense beauty" that, like the filming of India itself, "rings true" with "not an instant of exoticism."[15] The same could be said of the performances by Kevin Jones (as Bert) and Christine Tremarco (as Lily) in the cool and misty landscapes of a northern English childhood that establish a "paradise lost" in *The Leaving of Liverpool*. The framing of pre-migration childhoods as vital worlds is the first step in making the lives of child migrants both grievable and representable in public memory.

Both *Liverpool* and *Lion* figure the moment of the child's separation from home (from England, from India) as the beginning of an adventure that goes badly wrong, scarring young lives. In *Liverpool*, the Star of the Sea children are lined up in an assembly hall and exhorted by a powerful patron to imagine a new life in the service of keeping the Commonwealth "British." Holding back, the excitable but wary children are half-tricked, half-coerced into "choosing" Canada, Australia, Rhodesia or New Zealand as their new home. While some already carry the scars of corporal punishment, the first migration-wound is delivered before the children leave the orphanage. Serving as a portent of things to come, each child's tonsils are removed in a clinically efficient operation that leaves them shocked and bleeding. In *Lion*, Saroo's separation from his brother is accidental but no less terrifying: after falling asleep on a station platform, while waiting for his brother to return, Saroo wakes up in an empty train carriage that transports him from his small town in the west of India to the city of Calcutta in the east. Unable to make himself understood in Bengali, Saroo catches train after train out of Howrah Station, but none of them takes him home. He learns to survive on the streets and riverbanks of Calcutta, evading predators until a timely rescue lands him in an orphanage. There, Saroo witnesses corporal punishment and sexual abuse but like Bert at Star of the Sea, he manages to evade the worst of it. And like Lily in *Liverpool*, Saroo knows he has a mother who will be desperate to find him. His consent, as a five-year-old, to be adopted by an unknown couple in a place called Tasmania is easily won in a context where the adventure of inter-country adoption is presented as a better option than Calcutta's streets or orphanage.

Both *Liverpool* and *Lion* reveal the child's pre-migration world as perilous, but also lively. Both foreground the child's "consent" to migrate as one based on the promise of opportunities closed to them in their country of birth. The two-part narrative structure of *Liverpool* and *Lion* opens two pathways through the migration experience. One leads into the depths of the labyrinth where the perils of the pre-migration world loom even larger in the new world, taking the child into unimaginable darkness and further descent. The other pathway entails a dangerous journey through the labyrinth that, after many hardships, delivers the adult child migrant "home," into the arms of the lost mother.

In *Liverpool* it is Bert who descends into the labyrinth—leaving his beloved England full of hope and Empire spirit only to labour in an arid, treeless, scorching landscape, breaking rocks and building a church for the Christian Brothers who, despite moments of generosity, betray Bert's trust and, in their depravations, forfeit all claim to godliness. It is Bert's best friend, Lily—his "sister" and "lover"—whose rebellious spirit propels her out of the labyrinth. Surviving the hazards of a punitive girls' home, an isolated sheep station and a well-meaning shearer, Lily achieves independence and a job in Sydney. While she keeps her childhood promise and rescues a now-broken Bert from the Christian Brothers, Lily cannot save him from the depths of the labyrinth. The mini-series ends with two poignant scenes. On the day of Queen Elizabeth's 1954 coronation visit to Sydney, Lily re-unites with her mother who has travelled to Australia to find her. In another part of the crowd, Bert runs amuck, renouncing Britain and using his knife to slice into his badly scarred arm, adding his own blood to Henry Lawson's "blood on the wattle." As the prison doors close on Bert, his descent into the labyrinth is complete and there is nothing Lily, or her mother, can do to save him.

308   F. COLLINS

In *Lion*, young Saroo appears to flourish with his kindly adoptive parents (Nicole Kidman and David Wenham) in Tasmania's green and misty landscapes and its glistening coves and beaches. His adopted brother, Mantosh, however, is less fortunate. Languishing in the Calcutta orphanage for two long years while his adoption goes through, Mantosh (like Bert in *Liverpool*) eventually falls prey to its horrors. He brings this ruinous childhood with him into the Brierley household, disturbing Saroo's small corner of paradise. As a young and moody adult, Saroo, after a series of misadventures, wrong turns and miscalculations, finds his way home through the labyrinth of Google Earth and Facebook to the village of Ganesh Talai, whose name he mispronounced, but struggled to keep hold of while growing up in Tasmania. In the adventure-quest, however, the return home comes at price: if Bert's blood is the price of Lily's happiness, Saroo's safe harbour in Tasmania is paid for, in narrative terms, by Mantosh. His miraculous return to Ganesh Talai has been paid for in advance by his beloved brother—hit by a train the same night that five-year-old Saroo was transported all the way to Calcutta.

A question arises from the narrative template that shapes both the fictionalized story of the British child migrant in *The Leaving of Liverpool*, and the autobiographical story of inter-country adoption in *Lion*. How is it that the adventure-quest works equally well for fictional and factual stories—for *Liverpool*'s exposé of a migration scheme that destroyed the lives it was supposed to save, and for *Lion*'s uplifting story of Saroo's miraculous return home, twenty-five years after his successful inter-country adoption?

Reviewing the literature on inter-country adoption, Susan Gair sheds light on the way that popular narrative templates have influenced attitudes towards inter-country adoption. She argues that the focus of the 1997 report on the Stolen Generations, on intergenerational trauma as an outcome of Indigenous children being "rescued" from their families and communities, had flow-on effects. One of these effects was the shift in perception of inter-country adoption—from "rescuing" impoverished children to serving the needs of childless couples in affluent nations.[16] One overlap with the adventure-quest's two pathways is evident in Gair's finding that "pre-arrival adversity and low parental socio-economic status" as well as "institutional experience prior to adoption" were more likely to impact on the success of inter-country adoption than factors such as "racism *by itself* and stigma of adoption."[17] On the return journey home and recognition by family and community (the desired outcome of the adventure-quest narrative), Gair cautions "against assumptions in the public adoption narrative that all intercountry adoptees need to return to their roots, to 'find out who they really' are."[18] A further conclusion of Gair's review is that the plasticity of the brain is significant for adoptee recovery from "pre-arrival adversity," especially in light of initial difficulties with learning, remembering and concentrating.[19] Here, the memoir, as a collaborative process involving narrator-informant, interviewer-advocate and ghost writer, exemplifies the "plasticity" and reparative potential of memory-work undertaken by the child migrant.

Memoir and Memory-Work

The reparative memory-work conducted by Humphreys in her role as social worker, advocate and director of the Child Migrants Trust was first given narrative form in the memoir, *Empty Cradles*. The memoir provided material for *The Leaving of Liverpool* and, later, for the biopic about Humphreys, *Oranges and Sunshine*. *Empty Cradles*, narrated by Humphreys (with writing assistance credited to Michael Robotham), advanced the work of the Child Migrants Trust, participating in what Katie Wright calls "therapeutic culture" in a politicized mode.[20] As the narrator, Humphreys' voice is descriptive and matter-of-fact rather than literary or self-reflexive. She directs our eye to the story on the page rather than to her own memories and feelings. She does, however, begin with an account of a childhood separation from her Wesleyan parents and the early loss of her father, grandparents, family doctor and mother. And towards the end, she acknowledges the price she and her family paid for her years of advocacy. The biopic, *Oranges and Sunshine*, exercises a similar restraint. Preparing for her lead role, Emily Watson declined to meet with Humphreys until the film was finished. Instead, she did her research by observing documentary footage of Humphreys in her professional role as a social worker, reuniting a former child migrant with a mother who had been lied to about the fate of her child. Publicizing the film together, Humphreys and Watson agreed that, in their respective roles as social worker and screen actor, they had a "covenant" with the child migrants whose life stories required a truthful telling and a truthful performance.[21] The screenplay's focus on the memory-work undertaken by a social worker with adult child migrants makes for a subtle and understated performance by Watson in a film which one reviewer has described as "too decent."[22] Watson's is a different kind of performance from that of the Australian actors (including David Wenham and Hugo Weaving) who, as adult child migrants, deliver memory-monologues. This performative approach asks the viewer-spectator to hear these monologues as *retelling*, refining and distilling survivor testimony as it morphs from the original interviews with Humphreys, to written memoir, to screen performance. Eschewing the intensely affective, melodramatic adventure-quest mode, the memoir and the biopic shatter any illusions about the benefits of Britain's child migrant scheme.

A different kind of memory-work underpins Saroo Brierley's memoir of his inter-country adoption and his reunion with his family in India.[23] The memoir opens with a prologue recounting Saroo's triumphal return to his childhood home in Ganesh Talai in 2012, only to find "They've gone." Fortunately, his mother is quickly found: after twenty-five years, she lives two minutes away. For the most part, the memoir is based on Brierley's adult memory-work in collaboration with ghost writer, Larry Buttrose. This work included a visit to India, together, looking for memory prompts and undertaking the fateful train journey, again, from Ganesh Talai to what is now Kolkata. In the opening chapter, "Remembering," Brierley reflects on the "night-thoughts" (calling up images of people and places in order not to forget) and other memory-work he did as a child with his adoptive mother and a teacher, making notes and drawing maps of the routes he took as a child through his village, along the river and to the railway station. Though not always accurate, these maps, notes and night-thoughts proved essential to the eventual success of Saroo's Google Earth and Facebook searches as an adult.

In the memoir, Saroo reflects on memory gaps, the lack of certainty about "the order in which incidents occurred," and "what I thought and felt then, as a child, and what I've come to think and feel" over twenty-six years of "repeated revisiting, searching the past for clues" and, perhaps, disturbing "some of the evidence." At the same time, he insists that much of "my childhood experience remains vivid in my memory."[24]

There is one interruption to the memoir's linear and cohesive account of Saroo's initial separation from home, his inter-country adoption and the long search that took him back to his birth family in Ganesh Talai. A chapter in the middle of the book reflects on the migration stories of his adoptive parents. His adoptive father's unproblematic migration with his family from Britain provides a sharp contrast to his adoptive mother's experience of growing up with a volatile Polish father and a Hungarian mother, whose turbulent life in Australia started in the migrant camp at

Bonegilla.[25] As a child of post-war migration in a family that broke apart, Sue Brierley's vision, at the age of twelve during "something like a breakdown"—of a "brown-skinned child standing by her side"—became an origin story for her later decision to pursue inter-country adoption.[26] Towards the end of the memoir, a liminal space appears in which memory's partial and enigmatic traces, clung to since childhood, solidify into media stories. When the news of Saroo's miraculous return home is picked up by the media in India, he discovers that "as I told my story over and over again, it began to feel as though it had happened to someone else."[27] This estrangement threatens the sense-memories and "mind-twisting" echoes of the "childhood ordeal" that fed Saroo's struggle not to forget.[28]

MEMORY TRACES AND GRIEVABLE LIVES

In *Recording Oral History* Valerie Raleigh Yow reminds us that although biographers seek to "*impose* a coherence on the wildly disparate events of a life," it has to be granted that "neither narrating subject nor biographer can reconstruct fully the life as it was lived." Yet, Yow concludes (quoting Jerome Brunner), we "guard the sense of coherence and continuity we have about ourselves" over time and space.[29] In the case of the child migrant, "partial, mangled and enigmatic trace[s]" work against the "coherence and continuity" imposed by popular genres. Such traces persist where memories fade, as Humphreys notes throughout her memoir. In the case of Harold Haig, the trace is enigmatic—a longing for mother/ for love, embodied "in his voice and body language."[30] For an unnamed child migrant, the trace is partial: as Humphreys writes, "She wanted me to describe how things [violets, daffodils, chimney pots] looked and smelt and felt" in the old country.[31] For Bert and Lily in *The Leaving of Liverpool*, the trace is partial—the swish of a green silk dress; and enigmatic—the outline of a woman's face appearing and fading in a fresco and drawing. For Saroo, while his experiences on the streets of Calcutta "seemed to be imprinted on my mind with great detail, the first big trauma—being trapped alone on a train … appeared instead to have overwhelmed me. I recalled it more in snapshots of distress."[32]

What kind of story would enshrine the child migrant in the story of the immigration nation? Or must this figure always be a fortunate survivor (Lily/Saroo) or an unfortunate victim (Bert/Mantosh) of institutionalized systems of child abuse, taken up by the media, narrativized in print and on screen, and then replaced by other stories? The British child migrant and the inter-country adoptee have contemporary resonances in Australia, with the Stolen Generations of Indigenous children and also with refugee and asylum-seeking children held in various forms of offshore detention by successive Australian governments since 2001. While adult survivors of child migration schemes have received formal apologies and promises of reparation, a new category of child migrant is being "quietly" removed from long-term detention on the island of Nauru to face an uncertain future in Australia. As Williams wrote in his 2011 review of *Oranges and Sunshine*,[33] "Perhaps one day there will be a film about our treatment of asylum-seekers and the incarceration of children in desert camps. How long should we wait?" In the political and media spheres, the function of this child migrant has been to "turn back the boats." With "snapshots of distress" circulating across media platforms, a new chapter in the story of the child migrant as an expendable life is unfolding. The visual and narrative frames that would make such lives representable are emerging elsewhere, in the transnational spectacle of forced migrations which no longer fit the templates developed by the twentieth-century immigration nation.

NOTES

1. Margaret Humphreys, *Oranges and Sunshine* (London: Corgi Books, 2011), 69.
2. *Immigration Nation: The Secret History of Us* (Renegade Films, 2011), https://www.sbs.com.au/immigrationnation.
3. Judith Butler, *Frames of War: When Is Life Grievable?* (London and New York: Verso, 2009), 74.
4. Butler, *Frames of War*, 75.
5. Butler, *Frames of War*, 75.
6. Humphreys, *Oranges and Sunshine*, 370–72.
7. See especially, Australian Senate Community Affairs References Committee, *Lost Innocents: Righting the Record Report on Child Migration* (Canberra: Senate Printing Unit, 2001) and *Forgotten Australians: A Report on Australians Who Experienced Institutional or Out-of-Home Care as Children* (Canberra: Senate Printing Unit, 2004).
8. On 22 October 2018, Australian Prime Minister Scott Morrison delivered a formal apology to adult survivors of institutional sexual abuse, including British child migrants. See Katie Wright, Shurlee Swain, and Kathleen McPhillips, guest editors, *Special Issue: The Royal Commission into Institutional Responses to Child Sexual Abuse, Journal of Australian Studies* 42, no. 2 (2018).

9. Shurlee Swain, *Histories of Australian Inquiries Reviewing Institutions Providing Care for Children* (Sydney: Royal Commission into Institutional Responses to Child Sexual Abuse, 2014).
10. John Ellis, "Television as Working Through," in Jostein Gripsrud ed., *Television as Common Knowledge* (London: Routledge, 1999), 55–57.
11. Human Rights and Equal Opportunity Commission. *Bringing Them Home: Report of the National Inquiry into the Separation of Aboriginal and Torres Strait Islander Children from Their Families* (Sydney: HREOC, 1997).
12. See Humphreys, *Oranges and Sunshine*, 336–39, for an account of the campaign to publicize *The Leaving of Liverpool* (Michael Jenkins, 1992) in Britain after the BBC tried to bury the mini-series in its summer schedule without publicity or helplines.
13. See for instance, ABC TV, *7.30 Report*, 23 May 2011. It includes an interview with child migrants, Sandra Anker and Harold Haig, as well as comments from Margaret Humphreys and Jim Loach, https://edutv-informit-com-au.ez.library.latrobe.edu.au/watch-screen.php?videoID=148379.
14. Garth Davis (Director), *Lion*, 2016.
15. Salman Rushdie, "Salman Rushdie Extols the Immigrant's Struggle of 'Lion,'" Guest Column, *Deadline Hollywood*, 21 February 2017, https://deadline.com/2017/02/salman-rushdie-lion-immigrant-struggle-guest-column-best-picture-1201917653.
16. Susan Gair, *Literature Review Providing an In-depth Overview of Existing Research on the Effects of Intercountry Adoption on Adoptees* (The Cairns Institute: James Cook University, 2015), 6–7.
17. Gair, *Literature Review*, 12–13.
18. Gair, *Literature Review*, 14.
19. Gair, *Literature Review*, 15–16.
20. Katie Wright, "Challenging Institutional Denial: Psychological Discourse, Therapeutic Culture and Public Inquiries," *Journal of Australian Studies* 42, no. 2 (2018): 177–90.
21. "DP/30: Oranges & Sunshine, Jim Loach, Emily Watson, Margaret Humphreys," DP/30: *The Oral History of Hollywood*, 21 October 2011. https://www.youtube.com/watch?v=TJBR-_kOmKI.
22. Evan Williams, "Forgotten Children of Jim Loach's *Oranges and Sunshine*," *The Weekend Australian*, 11 June 2011. https://www.theaustralian.com.au/arts/film/forgotten-children-of-jim-loachs-oranges-and-sunshine/news-story/e7311f7bb6692835ecac5b45f40b0743.
23. Saroo Brierley, *Lion* (Australia: Penguin Random House, 2016); first published as *A Long Way Home* (Australia: Penguin Group, 2013).
24. Brierley, *Lion*, 13.

25. Brierley, *Lion*, 99–111.
26. Brierley, *Lion*, 106–07.
27. Brierley, *Lion*, 189.
28. Brierley, *Lion*, 144.
29. Valerie Raleigh Yow, *Recording Oral History: A Guide for the Humanities and Social Sciences*, 2nd edition (Walnut Creek, CA: Altamira Press, 2015), 221–22.
30. Humphreys, *Oranges and Sunshine*, 70.
31. Humphreys, *Oranges and Sunshine*, 14–15.
32. Brierley, *Lion*, 119.
33. Williams, "Forgotten Children of Jim Loach's *Oranges and Sunshine*."

BIBLIOGRAPHY

ABC TV. *7.30 Report*, 23 May 2011. "Oranges and Sunshine." https://edutv-informit-com-au.ez.library.latrobe.edu.au/watch-screen.php?videoID=148379.

Australian Senate Community Affairs References Committee. *Lost Innocents: Righting the Record Report on Child Migration*. Canberra: Senate Printing Unit, 2001.

Australian Senate Community Affairs References Committee. *Forgotten Australians: A Report on Australians Who Experienced Institutional Out-of-Home Care as Children*. Canberra: Senate Printing Unit, 2004.

Bean, Philip, and Joy Melville. *Lost Children of the Empire*. London and Sydney: Unwin Hyman, 1989.

Brierley, Saroo, with Larry Buttrose. *Lion*. Australia: Penguin Random House, 2016.

Butler, Judith. *Frames of War: When Is Life Grievable?* London and New York: Verso, 2009.

Davis, Garth (Director). *Lion*, 2016.

"DP/30 Oranges & Sunshine, Jim Loach, Emily Watson, Margaret Humphreys." *DP/30: The Oral History of Hollywood*. 21 October 2011. https://www.youtube.com/watch?v=TJBR-_kOmKI.

Ellis, John. "Television as Working Through." In *Television as Common Knowledge*, edited by Jostein Gripsrud, 55–57. London: Routledge, 1999.

Gair, Susan. *Literature Review Providing an In-depth Overview of Existing Research on the Effects of Intercountry Adoption on Adoptees*. The Cairns Institute: James Cook University, 2015. https://researchonline.jcu.edu.au/50165.

Hill, David. "Oranges and Sunshine Sparks Class Action." Interview. *7.30 Report*. ABC News (Australia). 14 June 2011. https://www.youtube.com/watch?v=_EyQyB4oUJU.

Human Rights and Equal Opportunity Commission. *Bringing Them Home: Report of the National Inquiry into the Separation of Aboriginal and Torres Strait Islander Children from their Families.* Sydney: HREOC, 1997.

Humphreys, Margaret. *Oranges and Sunshine.* London: Corgi Books, 2011 (first published as Empty Cradles: One Woman's Fight to Uncover Britain's Most Shameful Secret. London: Doubleday, 1994).

Immigration Nation: The Secret History of Us. Renegade Films, 2011. https://www.sbs.com.au/immigrationnation.

Jenkins, Michael (Director). *The Leaving of Liverpool.* Australian Broadcasting Corporation and British Broadcasting Corporation, 1992.

Royal Commission into Institutional Responses to Child Sexual Abuse. Final Report. Sydney, 2017.

Rushdie, Salman. "Salman Rushdie Extols the Immigrant's Struggle of 'Lion.'" Guest Column. *Deadline Hollywood.* 21 February 2017. https://deadline.com/2017/02/salman-rushdie-lion-immigrant-struggle-guest-column-best-picture-1201917653.

Swain, Shurlee. *Histories of Australian Inquiries Reviewing Institutions Providing Care for Children.* Sydney: Royal Commission into Institutional Responses to Child Sexual Abuse, 2014.

Williams, Evan. "Forgotten Children of Jim Loach's *Oranges and Sunshine.*" Review. *The Weekend Australian,* 11 June 2011. https://www.theaustralian.com.au/arts/film/forgotten-children-of-jim-loachs-oranges-and-sunshine/news-story/e7311f7bb6692835ecac5b45f40b0743.

Wright, Katie. "Challenging Institutional Denial: Psychological Discourse, Therapeutic Culture and Public Inquiries." *Journal of Australian Studies* 42, no. 2 (2018): 177–90.

Wright, Katie, Shurlee Swain, and Kathleen McPhillips, guest editors. *Special Issue: The Royal Commission into Institutional Responses to Child Sexual Abuse. Journal of Australian Studies* 42, no. 2 (2018).

Yow, Valerie Raleigh. *Recording Oral History: A Guide for the Humanities and Social Sciences,* 2nd edition. Walnut Creek, CA: Altamira Press, 2015.

CHAPTER 21

Politicizing the Past: Memory in Australian Refugee Documentaries

Sukhmani Khorana

In Australia, public debate on the issue of asylum seekers has been vexed and polarizing of late, and especially since the introduction of mandatory detention for maritime arrivals in 1992. Moreover, what distinguishes this policy from other nations of the global north is that despite being a signatory to the 1951 United Nations Refugee Convention, Australia is the only country where there is "mandatory immigration detention for all unlawful non-citizens."[1] Such a policy has come about as there has been consensus on both sides of politics that "asylum seekers pose a threat to the integrity of Australia's borders or to its social fabric, that fear of asylum seekers is legitimate, and that a policy of deterrence is an appropriate response."[2] Klaus Neumann notes that the policy of deterrence is occasionally questioned when the courts insist that it must not violate Australian law or when the public sporadically shows compassion for individual asylum seekers, especially children. In the most recent of such cases, the Victorian Supreme Court approved a $70m compensation payout to current and former Manus Island asylum seekers over their illegal detention in dangerous conditions.[3] Although this has been reported to be the largest human rights class action settlement in Australia, it has not impacted

S. Khorana (✉)
University of Wollongong, Wollongong, NSW, Australia
e-mail: skhorana@uow.edu.au

© The Author(s) 2019
K. Darian-Smith, P. Hamilton (eds.), *Remembering Migration*,
Palgrave Macmillan Memory Studies,
https://doi.org/10.1007/978-3-030-17751-5_21

317

318   S. KHORANA

federal government policy or the opposition party's official stance in any way.

It is likely that the failure of institutions like law and party politics to sufficiently address the issue has led to a surge of interest among asylum seeker advocates, as well as ex-refugees, to invoke the power of narrative instead. While the empathy evoked by screen-based storytelling can often be transient, de-politicized and individually mobilized,[4] it is sometimes worth returning to the texts in question. This is because some of these creative narratives are historical documents of place and memory, and such memorialization—however mediated—has the capacity to render a different patina to the refugee issue for the wider public in times to come.

REPRESENTATION OF REFUGEES AND THE AUSTRALIAN MEDIA

The representation of refugees in the Australian media—especially their mediation through news discourses—has been the subject of a good deal of critical attention since the early 2000s.[5] In the context of refugee-themed screen narratives, Anna Szorenyi examines the practice of collecting photographs of refugees in "coffee-table books" and concludes that the format and accompanying text tend to produce readings that lean towards spectacle.[6] In a similar vein, Terence Wright's investigation of media images and fiction films based on refugee stories uncovered that the former have origins in Christian iconography, while the latter conform to the visual conventions of the road movie genre.[7] The last finding is also echoed in Australia-based refugee film *Lucky Miles*,[8] focusing on male asylum seekers, which, Jon Stratton argues, results in it "making the Australian government appear less hostile, less morally culpable, and therefore enabling white Australian audiences to feel better about themselves and the government that represents them."[9]

The emphasis on spectacle notwithstanding, there has been a marked shift in the production and distribution practices of refugee-themed films in Australia, led by Heather Kirkpatrick's documentary *Mary Meets Mohammad* in 2013. In this documentary, there is an ethical focus on refugee participation, and the filmmaker organized a series of community screenings to reach audiences beyond the film festival and boutique cinema circuit.[10] In the wake of this, there has been a spate of refugee-oriented documentaries, often recollecting stories of fleeing persecution, memorializing the moment of arrival in Australia (or elsewhere), and recounting the ongoing issue of attempting to belong in the new community. They include *Freedom Stories*,[11] *Chasing Asylum*,[12] *Constance on the Edge*,[13] and *Cast from the Storm*.[14] These films are classified as documentaries, and have links to community screenings (in varied forms) on their official websites. For the purpose of this chapter, I will examine relevant excerpts from *Constance on the Edge*, as well as an earlier short film titled *Villawood Mums*. This is because both texts are concerned with the particular history of their refugee protagonists, and how this was met with the policy and politics of the time of their arrival in Australia. Such memorializing does not uncritically celebrate the past, but, rather, highlights how policy and representation continue to politicize refugee lives.

Constance on the Edge: Facing Trauma and Embracing Community

This feature-length documentary is directed by Belinda Mason, who sees people from refugee backgrounds as "survivors."[15] In my online interview with Mason, I was told that the film was "one of seven documentary films selected for the 2014 philanthropic Good Pitch Australia initiative."[16] She explained that Good Pitch brings together "filmmakers with foundations, not-for-profits, campaigners, philanthropists, policy-makers, brands, educators, broadcasters and media to forge powerful alliances around ground breaking films that will have a significant impact in relation to issues of social importance—and benefit the partners, the development of the films and society as a whole." This means that the documentary was funded and produced with the explicit intention of influencing public discourse and policy on the asylum seeker issue. Mason also informed me that the film has a clearly defined "impact strategy" to ensure that it is seen by a broad national audience. The aim of wide distribution is to "foster more welcoming communities for people with refugee backgrounds; help create educational resources for schools, police, health services, local government and community services; and promote the provision of better support services and job opportunities for people with refugee backgrounds."

In terms of the stated impact, Mason's account is that they held over 80 successful screenings around the country during Refugee Week in 2017. She added that in Wagga, where the film was shot, there were numerous sold out screenings. The filmmaking team also carried out detailed surveys

320 S. KHORANA

on viewers' experience of the film at the end of most screenings. According to Mason, there were very positive responses to this, and "the majority of people surveyed [said] they have a better understanding of the refugee experience and many of them feel compelled to act, by volunteering, or donating to refugee organisations." Independent reviewers, such as *The Guardian's* Luke Buckmaster have also commended the film. He pays tribute to the rapport between the filmmaker and the subject, and concludes that the text is "another reminder that deep-seated trauma cannot be turned off like a switch; another portrayal of the road to recovery being long, rocky and circuitous."[17] It is this acknowledgement of the past, and its re-surfacing in the present and the future that deems this text worthy of attention.

The film begins with the audience being informed that Constance, a middle-aged woman of Sudanese descent, was resettled in Wagga Wagga (a regional town in the Australian state of New South Wales) eight years ago, and has been living there with her family since then. This is followed by a close shot of Constance saying to camera that while she was in a refugee camp, she was fighting for human rights, but now her struggle seems to be for belonging. In effect, the film shows that refugee trauma can emerge many years after resettlement, and also impact subsequent generations in positive and negative ways.[18]

Towards the beginning of the documentary, the narrator's voiceover mentions that while in a refugee camp in Kenya, Constance interpreted for FilmAid as she speaks four languages. While she has faced the trauma of war, she is framed as someone who has resilience as well as cultural capital. Later in the film, one of Constance's daughters, Vicky, finds out that she has been accepted into a nursing programme at Charles Sturt University. Constance is very happy and says that Vicky is digging the road to university for others in her family to follow. She also charts the possible futures of her other children, remarks that they are growing up, and adds that they will "fit like Australians." She then jokes that this means they might develop racist attitudes towards new immigrants in the future. In this way, what appears at first to be a straightforward account of refugee integration, with Vicky's university admission turns into a multidimensional tale of the politicized present from Constance's perspective.

Constance's engagement with the town of Wagga Wagga and its community is conveyed through two main sequences. In the first, she attempts to be a bridge between the refugees and the police, and is invited to the police station by a female officer called Sandy. Constance mentions that the local Sudanese community is having trouble with the police (largely due to the latter's perceptions). She adds that this is in contrast to what the African-origin refugees were told about Australian police officers being very friendly. After introducing Constance to her colleagues, Sandy remarks that she feels a lot of empathy for Constance, and adds that most refugees have a "fight or flight" reaction to the police due to their prior experiences. Later in the film, we see Constance's affective relationship with the regional city itself on display as she walks down the main street, looks through clothing stores, and dons bangles. When asked by a counsellor present at an African community event to complete the sentence "I feel at home when I am … " Constance replies that the answer for her is seeing colour at second-hand shops. This encounter with the spaces of the town is as important as the ones with its residents to manifest belonging and embed it in the local, albeit through a connection to Constance's history.

Villawood Mums: Memories of Arrival

Directed by Guido Gonzalez and Saif Jari, *Villawood Mums* is a short documentary which was produced in 2010 as part of *The Stories Project* of CuriousWorks. The latter is a media and arts organization based in western Sydney which works collaboratively with local communities, including those from marginalized backgrounds. According to its website, it is especially interested in stories "from communities that are largely invisible in mainstream media and seeking to be heard." In her thesis on multicultural digital stories in Australia, Trimboli notes that CuriousWorks "does not begin from an assumed position of neutrality."[19] In addition, the organization is particularly mindful of the power it produces when it intervenes in communities, as well as its own impact on constructions of 'community' and 'cultural diversity'.[20]

The Stories Project in turn came about to facilitate "an online exchange of short films and stories between refugee youth living in urban Sydney and young Aboriginal filmmakers in Jigalong, Western Australia."[21] *Villawood Mums* is one of the films from the project that was screened widely, as well as published online. Given the length and community-orientation of the film, there are no official reviews available. However, it can still be viewed online via the CuriousWorks website and is listed as a resource by a number of advocacy organizations. These include the "Resource Kit" for Refugee Week 2018, and the educational website Roads to Refuge (a partnership between the New South Wales Department

322   S. KHORANA

of Education, and University of New South Wales Centre for Refugee Research).

Villawood Mums is effective as a work of refugee memory, as it demonstrates the changes in policy and treatment of refugees over a period of ten years. According to Haviland, "Without any additional commentary this short film powerfully revealed the impact of government immigration policies on the experiences of people who are granted refugee status in Australia, at a time when current refugee policies were a source of great tension across the country." In the context of looking at a range of digital stories made by or about migrants in her study, Trimboli concludes that *Villawood Mums* "provides a tension that we do not often see in the digital story archive of multicultural Australia."[22] This implies that the narrative reverses the trajectory of the once displaced, now happily resettled refugee in a manner similar to *Constance on the Edge*. In the present case, it is the shifting policies of the host country that are the identified reason for ongoing trauma, as opposed to the persecution faced in the homeland.

The story of *Villawood Mums* begins with a woman pushing a trolley in a suburban supermarket. A male voiceover says that his mum Maria fled Chile in the 1980s as she was fleeing persecution. This is followed by footage of another woman entering a grocery store, and the voiceover stating that his mother Zahoor fled Iraq in 1995, as she was escaping the Saddam Hussein regime. Next, we are told that Maria arrived at Villawood Hostel with three sons and heavily pregnant with the filmmaker Guido's sister. Saif adds that his mother arrived at what was by then Villawood Detention Centre in 1998, and with nothing but a suitcase and her family. This is the beginning of the study in contrasts, as the women are subsequently shown in similar shots (picking up milk from a fridge at the supermarket), with the voiceover declaring that the first was welcomed as a refugee, while the second was not.

The middle sequence consists of interviews with the two women in their homes, interspersed with old family photographs. Maria mentions that the officers from immigration treated them well, and that they were polite. The rooms they were given were akin to small apartments. She stayed in the hostel for seven months, and her daughter was born on the premises. The staff took good care of her, and fussed over her kids.

Seated on a couch in her living room, Zahoor says that even though there is no freedom in Iraq, the reality of leaving everything you know is very hard. When they arrived in Australia, they were very tired and scared. She was interviewed right away by the female immigration official at the airport, who forced her to answer questions even though she had a migraine and was unable to talk at the time. She then recalls being in the Villawood Detention Centre, and that it was like a jail as it was surrounded by big fences. She ironically mentions that she left the prison that was Iraq, only to find herself in another one. Zahoor recollects another story where her little daughter took a sick pigeon to the security guards who decided to give honey dips to the bird. This made her daughter remark with surprise that the birds were treated better than she was.

In the final sequence, Maria says that when she visited Villawood many years later, she found the conditions there to be terrible in comparison with when she resided there on her family's arrival in Australia. She adds that this was not the freedom that Australia once promised, and she found it painful to see the hostel transformed. We then switch back to Zahoor, who remarks that when they were in the detention centre, there was a great deal of uncertainty, as they did not know when they could leave. When she was given a permanent visa one morning, she felt as though she was flying. Before the credits roll, Maria's son Guido enters the frame (in their home kitchen) as the text on the screen tells us that she has been working as a cleaner, and then as a caretaker since settling in Australia. In the case of Zahoor, a similar shot is repeated. The text mentions that while she worked as an accountant in Iraq, she has struggled to find work in Australia. She supports the family through housework and is also studying English and computer literacy at a technical and further education (TAFE) institution. What the film shows, rather than didactically tells, is a story of a refugee resettling in conditions where the past that haunts her is the moment of her arrival in the land of promised freedom and human rights. It begs the question of why trauma is only interpreted as the injustice experienced in a distant location, and whether different accounts of memory will be considered in the public discourse on asylum seekers.

REFUGEE KNOWLEDGE AND NATIONAL MEMORY

While *Villawood Mums* is still available online via the CuriousWorks website, it does raise the question of what we do with these new media archives beyond making them? How do we show them widely, and meaningfully insert these kinds of narratives into the national canon? To begin with, we must critique the production of knowledge about refugees, regardless of which side of the political divide they emerge from. Prem Rajaram concludes that this knowledge is heavily bureaucratized:

> ... the extrapolation of refugee experience from individual social and histori-
> cal contexts and the creation of a veneer of objectivity and dislocation,
> occurs in a text designed to impart exhortatory information without prob-
> lematizing—indeed, making invisible—the author's position.[23]

This kind of emphasis on objective information also produces visual com-
modification of the refugee experience. It renders the refugee speechless,
thereby reinforcing a state-centric political imagination in which "refugees
become a site where certain forms of knowledge are reproduced and justi-
fied."[24] Another related impact of the disassociation of first-hand refugee
narratives from their historical contexts is the de-politicization of these
stories in the present, including in some advocacy campaigns. According
to Nando Sigona, such de-politicization happens in two ways: "at the
micro-level, by neglecting and/or denying the importance of the political
in their experience of exile; and at the macro level, by concealing behind
the discourse of the West's humanitarianism present and past involvement
in producing the causes of conflict and forced migration."[25] In terms of
the films being examined in this chapter, the political is present at the
micro-level, as all of the featured refugee women (and their respective
families) are depicted as being subjects of the politics of their home and
host countries. However, these and other refugee-themed texts in Australia
have more work to do in terms of highlighting macro-level politicization
through the nation's collusion with the United States, and the latter's role
in various conflicts in the Middle East in particular.

In addition to politicizing the nation within a global framework,
refugee-oriented narratives in Australia could also have a bearing on framing the national past, especially as it pertains to the policies affecting asylum seekers and economic migrants. In other words, more nuance could
be added to the somewhat simplistic rendition of a refugee-friendly nation
in the aftermath of the Vietnam War, followed by a sudden shift of direc-
tion after the events of September 11, 2001. While *Villawood Mums*
appears to indicate that these policies were changing several years before
the World Trade Centre collapse and the consequent worldwide rise in
Islamophobia, it does not have the space to probe the reasons for this
shift. According to Andreas Huyssen in a piece that examines media amnesia and cultural nostalgia at the turn of the twentieth century, "One of
modernity's permanent laments concerns the loss of a better past, the
memory of living in a securely circumscribed place, with a sense of stable
boundaries and a place-bound culture with its regular flow of time and a

core of permanent relations."[26] He adds that such days have always been "a dream rather than a reality, a phantasmagoria of loss generated by modernity itself rather than by its prehistory."[27] Therefore, the illusion of the loss of a more humane past ought to be alluded to in order to adequately account for the present.

GLOBAL LESSONS FOR AUSTRALIAN HUMANITARIAN NARRATIVES

In terms of what constitutes the politics of the present itself, recent ethnographic work on asylum seekers stranded in Hungary (en route to Germany) differentiates between vertical and horizontal political endeavours. According to Annastiina Kallius et al.:

> Once in Hungary, migrants encountered an escalating tension between depoliticizing narratives of crisis and concrete political action that sought to facilitate mobility. State agencies and humanitarian volunteer groups framed mobility in terms that emphasized a vertical form of politics, which rests on a series of binaries—notably citizen–foreigner and politics–humanitarianism—distinguishing groups to be acted on and the institutions that do the acting.[28]

In addition, they contrast the oftentimes paternalistic action of several humanitarian groups with the "horizontal solidarities" involving "private citizens working with migrants, standing with them in their protests, sheltering people, and transporting them to the western border."[29] Later in the piece and towards the end of this "crisis," the difference between humanitarian impulses and collaborative efforts becomes more blurred. What this points to, for the sake of refugee narratives in contexts like Australia, is not entirely shutting down the vertical humanitarian story, but facilitating its movement to a horizontal plane. This could be done through a recalibration of what national memory stands for in the twenty-first century, and how it is inadvertently (globally) mediated.

Using similar ethnographic and discursive tools, Seth Holmes and Heidi Castañeda look at the recent "refugee crisis" in Germany to try to unpack the particularities of the refugee story, and the varied responses of the citizens of the nation-state. They observe that although the definition of "refugee" is codified in the 1951 United Nations Convention of the Status of Refugee, "how states respond to asylum seekers always reflects geopolitical interests that reinscribe ideas about which groups deserve support and at which historical moments."[30] This illustrates that historical memory (or attempts to overwrite it) merit more attention in Australia and elsewhere, especially when considering our mediated and political responses to those seeking asylum.

At the height of this migrant crisis in Europe, an Italian documentary called *Fire at Sea* was receiving international accolades as it was nominated for an Academy Award in 2017, and won the Golden Bear at the Berlin International Film Festival in the same year. The primary reason for this acclaim was not just the fact that the film dealt with migrant boats arriving on the Sicilian island of Lampedusa, but that it did so indirectly through assembling seemingly mundane footage from the lives of a local boy and a doctor, who treats him as well as the traumatized refugees. This leads reviewer Andrew Pulver to conclude that, "Rosi's film is a collection of tiny details that morph, almost by osmosis, into a shocking excavation of the mechanics of crisis."[31] Similarly, in a review for *The New York Times*, A. O. Scott suggests that socially-minded documentaries can be as formulaic as genre films, and that this sort of "dutiful and conventional" cinema often offers "raising awareness" itself as a solution.[32] He argues that *Fire at Sea* clearly departs from such trite tropes by being impressionistic and cultivating alertness such that, "At the end, you understand something about the texture and organization of life in Lampedusa, and about the effect that migration has had on the island."[33]

While a rendition of the crisis such as Rosi's may be considered apolitical by some, it is in fact an innovative cinematic technique for an island with a long history of boat arrivals. In other words, memory work can sometimes be performed through more tangential techniques, and not just the first-person narration of the migrant or the refugee. This is not to discount the value of first-hand experience, representation and production. As noted in the Australian case studies examined in this chapter, these can often bring previously unrepresented stories to light, humanize asylum seekers and politicize the present policy situation. Other research on digital storytelling and participants' agency suggests that it allows the exploration and ownership of previously unarticulated experiences and enables the emergence of new meanings about the refugees' lives.[34] However, if the aim of the narrative is to interrupt the national canon and shift public discourse on the issue of asylum seekers, stories documenting first-person accounts may not be enough. It is for this reason that Australian filmmakers interested in advocating on behalf of asylum seekers should consider tales that manifest horizontal solidarities and mundane lives to historicize the past and imagine a different future.

NOTES

1. Sarah Brown, "What Is Mandatory Detention?," *The Asylum and Refugee Law Project*, https://uqrefugeeresearch.wordpress.com/2013/07/08/what-is-mandatory-detention.
2. Klaus Neumann, "The Politics of Compassion," *Inside Story*, 1 March 2012, http://insidestory.org.au/the-politics-of-compassion.
3. Ben Doherty, "Manus Island: Judge Approves $70m Compensation for Detainees," *Guardian Australia*, 6 September 2017, https://www.theguardian.com/australia-news/2017/sep/06/judge-approves-70m-compensation-for-manus-island-detainees.
4. Sukhmani Khorana, "The Problem with Empathy," *Overland Literary Magazine*, 1 October 2015, https://overland.org.au/2015/10/the-problem-with-empathy.
5. Sharon Pickering, "Common Sense and Original Deviancy: News Discourses and Asylum Seekers in Australia," *Journal of Refugee Studies* 14, no. 2 (2001): 169–86; Peter Gale, "The Refugee Crisis and Fear: Populist Politics and Media Discourse," *Journal of Sociology* 40, no. 4 (2004): 321–40; Natascha Klocker and Kevin Dunn, "Who's Driving the Asylum Debate: Newspaper and Government Representations of Asylum Seekers," *Media International Australia* 109, no. 1 (2003): 71–92.
6. Anna Szörényi, "The Images Speak for Themselves? Reading Refugee Coffee-Table Books," *Visual Studies* 21, no. 1 (2006): 24–41.
7. Terence Wright, "Moving Images: The Media Representation of Refugees," *Visual Studies* 17, no. 1 (2002): 53–66.
8. *Lucky Miles*, directed by Michael James Rowland, Blink Films, 2007.
9. Jon Stratton, "'Welcome to Paradise': Asylum Seekers, Neoliberalism, Nostalgia and *Lucky Miles*," *Journal of Media and Cultural Studies* 23, no. 5 (2009): 629–45.
10. Sukhmani Khorana, "Self-distribution and *Mary Meets Mohammad*: Towards Ethical Witnessing," *Studies in Australasian Cinema* 9, no. 1 (2015): 66–76.
11. *Freedom Stories*, directed by Steve Thomas, Flying Carpet Productions, 2015.
12. *Chasing Asylum*, directed by Eva Orner, Nerdy Girl Films, 2016.
13. *Constance on the Edge*, directed by Belinda Mason, Constance on the Edge Pty Ltd, 2016.
14. *Cast from the Storm*, Directed by David Mason, Missing Archive Production, 2016.

15. *Constance on the Edge* Official Website, "Interview with Director Belinda Mason," http://constanceontheedge.com/the-film, accessed 27 June 2018.
16. Belinda Mason, "Re: Constance on the Edge Answers," received by Sukhmani Khorana, 8 September 2017.
17. Luke Buckmaster, "Constance on the Edge Review—A Vivid, Big-hearted Portrait of Refugee Life in Australia," *The Guardian*, 3 May 2017, https://www.theguardian.com/film/2017/may/03/constance-on-the-edge-review-a-vivid-big-hearted-portrait-of-refugee-life-in-australia.
18. *Constance on the Edge*, official website.
19. Daniella Trimboli, "Mediating Everyday Multiculturalism: Performativity and Precarious Inclusion in Australian Digital Storytelling" (PhD diss., University of British Columbia, 2016).
20. Trimboli, "Mediating Everyday Multiculturalism," 194.
21. Maya Haviland, *Side by Side?: Community Art and the Challenge of Co-creativity* (New York and Oxon: Taylor & Francis: 2016).
22. Trimboli, "Mediating Everyday Multiculturalism," 197.
23. Prem Kumar Rajaram, "Humanitarianism and Representations of the Refugee," *Journal of Refugee Studies* 15, no. 3 (2002): 248.
24. Rajaram, "Humanitarianism," 251.
25. Nando Sigona, "The Politics of Refugee Voices: Representations, Narratives, and Memories," in Elena Fiddian-Qasmiyeh, Gil Loescher, Katy Long and Nando Sigona eds, *The Oxford Handbook of Refugee and Forced Migration Studies* (Oxford: Oxford University Press, 2014), 372.
26. Andreas Huyssen, "Present Pasts: Media, Politics, Amnesia," *Public Culture* 12, no. 1 (2000): 34.
27. Huyssen, "Present Pasts," 34.
28. Annastiina Kallius, Daniel Monterescu, and Prem Kumar Rajaram, "Immobilizing Mobility: Border Ethnography, Illiberal Democracy, and the Politics of the 'Refugee Crisis' in Hungary," *American Ethnologist* 43, no. 1 (2016): 26.
29. Kallius et al., "Immobilizing Mobility," 27.
30. Seth M. Holmes, and Heide Castañeda, "Representing the 'European Refugee Crisis' in Germany and Beyond: Deservingness and Difference, Life and Death," *American Ethnologist* 43, no. 1 (2016): 17.
31. Andrew Pulver, "Why Fire at Sea Sailed Away with the Berlin Film Festival's Golden Bear," *The Guardian*, 22 February 2016, https://www.theguardian.com/film/2016/feb/22/fire-at-sea-berlin-film-festival-golden-bear-gianfranco-rosi-migrant-crisis.
32. A. O. Scott, "'Fire at Sea' is not the Documentary You'd Expect About the Migrant Crisis. It's Better," *The New York Times*, 20 October 2016, https://www.nytimes.com/2016/10/21/movies/fire-at-sea-review.html.

33. Scott, "Fire a Sea."
34. Caroline Lenette, Leonie Cox, and Mark Brough, "Digital Storytelling as a Social Work Tool: Learning from Ethnographic Research with Women from Refugee Backgrounds," *The British Journal of Social Work* 45, no. 3 (2013): 988–1005.

BIBLIOGRAPHY

Brown, Sarah. "What is Mandatory Detention?" *The Asylum and Refugee Law Project.* https://uqrefugeeresearch.wordpress.com/2013/07/08/what-is-mandatory-detention.

Buckmaster, Luke. "Constance on the Edge Review—A Vivid, Big-hearted Portrait of Refugee Life in Australia." *The Guardian*, 3 May 2017. https://www.theguardian.com/film/2017/may/03/constance-on-the-edge-review-a-vivid-big-hearted-portrait-of-refugee-life-in-australia.

Constance on the Edge. Official Website, "Interview with Director Belinda Mason." Accessed 27 June 2018. http://constanceontheedge.com/the-film.

Doherty, Ben. "Manus Island: Judge Approves $70m Compensation for Detainees." *Guardian Australia*, 6 September 2017. https://www.theguardian.com/australia-news/2017/sep/06/judge-approves-70m-compensation-for-manus-island-detainees.

Gale, Peter. "The Refugee Crisis and Fear: Populist Politics and Media Discourse." *Journal of Sociology* 40, no. 4 (2004): 321–40.

Gonzalez, Guido, and Saif Jari (Directors). *Villawood Mums.* CuriousWorks Stories Project, 2010.

Haviland, Maya. *Side by Side?: Community Art and the Challenge of Co-creativity.* New York and Oxon: Taylor & Francis, 2016.

Holmes, Seth M., and Heide Castañeda. "Representing the 'European Refugee Crisis' in Germany and Beyond: Deservingness and Difference, Life and Death." *American Ethnologist* 43, no. 1 (2016): 12–24.

Huyssen, Andreas. "Present Pasts: Media, Politics, Amnesia." *Public Culture* 12, no. 1 (2000): 21–38.

Kallius, Annastiina, Daniel Monterescu, and Prem Kumar Rajaram. "Immobilizing Mobility: Border Ethnography, Illiberal Democracy, and the Politics of the 'Refugee Crisis' in Hungary." *American Ethnologist*, 43, no. 1 (2016): 25–37.

Khorana, Sukhmani. "Self-distribution and *Mary Meets Mohammad*: Towards Ethical Witnessing." *Studies in Australasian Cinema* 9, no. 1 (2015a): 66–76.

Khorana, Sukhmani. "The Problem with Empathy." *Overland Literary Magazine*, 1 October 2015b. https://overland.org.au/2015/10/the-problem-with-empathy.

Kirkpatrick, Heather (Director). *Mary Meets Mohammad.* Waratah Films, 2013.

Klocker, Natascha, and Kevin Dunn. "Who's Driving the Asylum Debate: Newspaper and Government Representations of Asylum Seekers." *Media International Australia* 109, no. 1 (2003): 71–92.

Lenette, Caroline, Leonie Cox, and Mark Brough, "Digital Storytelling as a Social Work Tool: Learning from Ethnographic Research with Women from Refugee Backgrounds." *The British Journal of Social Work*, 45, no. 3 (2013): 988–1005.

Mason, Belinda (Director). *Constance on the Edge*. Constance on the Edge Pty Ltd, 2016.

Mason, Belinda. "Re: Constance on the Edge Answers." Received by Sukhmani Khorana, 8 September 2017.

Mason, David (Director). *Cast from the Storm*. Missing Archive Production, 2016.

Neumann, Klaus. "The Politics of Compassion." *Inside Story*, 1 March 2012. http://insidestory.org.au/the-politics-of-compassion.

Orner, Eva (Director). *Chasing Asylum*. Nerdy Girl Films, 2016.

Pickering, Sharon. "Common Sense and Original Deviancy: News Discourses and Asylum Seekers in Australia." *Journal of Refugee Studies* 14, no. 2 (2001): 169–86.

Pulver, Andrew. "Why Fire at Sea Sailed Away with the Berlin Film Festival's Golden Bear." *The Guardian*, 22 February 2016. https://www.theguardian.com/film/2016/feb/22/fire-at-sea-berlin-film-festival-golden-bear-gianfranco-rosi-migrant-crisis.

Rajaram, Prem Kumar. "Humanitarianism and Representations of the Refugee." *Journal of Refugee Studies* 15, no. 3 (2002): 247–64.

Rosi, Gianfranco (Director). *Fire at Sea*. 01 Distribution, 2016.

Rowland, Michael James (Director). *Lucky Miles*. Blink Films, 2007.

Scott, A. O. "'Fire at Sea' Is Not the Documentary You'd Expect About the Migrant Crisis. It's Better." *The New York Times*, 20 October 2016. https://www.nytimes.com/2016/10/21/movies/fire-at-sea-review.html.

Sigona, Nando. "The Politics of Refugee Voices: Representations, Narratives, and Memories." In *The Oxford Handbook of Refugee and Forced Migration Studies*, edited by Elena Fiddian-Qasmiyeh, Gil Loescher, Katy Long and Nando Sigona, 369–82. Oxford: Oxford University Press, 2014.

Stratton, Jon. "'Welcome to Paradise': Asylum Seekers, Neoliberalism, Nostalgia and *Lucky Miles*." *Journal of Media and Cultural Studies* 23, no. 5 (2009): 629–45.

Szörényi, Anna. "The Images Speak for Themselves? Reading Refugee Coffee-Table Books." *Visual Studies* 21, no. 1 (2006): 24–41.

Thomas, Steve (Director). *Freedom Stories*. Flying Carpet Productions, 2015.

Trimboli, Daniella. "Mediating Everyday Multiculturalism: Performativity and Precarious Inclusion in Australian Digital Storytelling." PhD diss., University of British Columbia, 2016.

Wright, Terence. "Moving Images: The Media Representation of Refugees." *Visual Studies* 17, no. 1 (2002): 53–66.

CHAPTER 22

Memory and Meaning in the Search for Chinese Australian Families

Sophie Couchman and Kate Bagnall

In 1960, Gwen Num wrote one of the earliest published Chinese Australian family histories, a short article about her father, Daniel Poon Num (1872–1928), which appeared in the journal *Nation*.[1] Poon Num arrived in Adelaide around the turn of the twentieth century, and joining his elder brother in the fruit and vegetable trade, he soon became a notable figure in the Adelaide Chinese community. He was baptized in the Church of Christ in 1904, took an active part in Chinese community politics and, in 1908, married a white South Australian, Gertrude Smith.[2] Nearly sixty years after Gwen Num's article and more than a century after Daniel Poon Num's arrival in Australia, Daniel and Gertrude's grandson Richard visited Qiaotou, a cluster of villages in rural Kaiping County in Guangdong Province. Within the family, memory of Poon Num's exact birthplace was lost, but Qiaotou is the likely candidate. Over the course of the nineteenth century, many men of the Poon clan from Qiaotou made their way to southern Australia, settling in Melbourne and across western Victoria to Adelaide.

S. Couchman (✉)
La Trobe University, Melbourne, VIC, Australia
e-mail: sophie.couchman@gmail.com

K. Bagnall
University of Wollongong, Wollongong, NSW, Australia
e-mail: kate.bagnall@gmail.com

© The Author(s) 2019
K. Darian-Smith, P. Hamilton (eds.), *Remembering Migration*,
Palgrave Macmillan Memory Studies,
https://doi.org/10.1007/978-3-030-17751-5_22

331

Fig. 22.1 Richard Num paying his respects at a shrine in Qiaotou village, Kaiping, with Megan Neilson looking on. Photograph by Sophie Couchman

In Qiaotou, Richard came face to face with his Cantonese heritage, wandering through laneways and past paddy fields, speaking with local villagers and paying his respects at a small village shrine (Fig. 22.1). His visit was made as part of a heritage tour, run by the authors, which gives Australian family historians an opportunity to retrace their Cantonese ancestors' steps through the *qiaoxiang* counties of the Pearl River Delta region of Guangdong Province.[3] Richard's cousin David had joined us on the tour the previous year, and the cousins' journeys marked a significant moment in their individual searches for their family's Chinese past. After years of tracking ancestors through the Australian archives, sometimes over generations, descendants can be left with an uncomfortable gap in their family narrative following a loss of language, culture and intergenerational memory. Visiting the *qiaoxiang* can help descendants satisfy an intellectual curiosity and spark their historical imagination, as well as filling an emotional need to understand more about the lives of their ancestors.

In this chapter, we discuss the endeavours of Chinese Australian family historians in uncovering their Cantonese roots, including by travelling to their ancestral homelands in China, and we reflect on the practice of personal memory-making in the wake of national and familial forgetting.[4] The family historians are descended from immigrants from southern China, primarily from Guangdong Province, who came to Australia between the 1850s and 1950s; many are of mixed heritage and/or several generations removed from their original migrant ancestors. Growing up in a nation that predominantly celebrates its white British history, these descendants have faced powerful forces of forgetting which have shaped both Australia's national remembering and their own lives.[5] The twin forces of memory and forgetting are multifaceted, shifting as they pass between the individual and the family, and bending as they are shaped by collective and national memory.[6]

Descendants' sense of connection to the Chinese language, culture and identity of their ancestors, or their lack thereof, comes from what has been forgotten and what has been remembered—the intergenerational memory passed down through their families. We present a case study that explores, through the lens of memory and forgetting, the ways that Chinese Australian family historians build new meanings and understandings through genealogical research and "roots tourism" in China.[7] Although their motivations might initially be personal ones—an individual quest to know more about their own ancestry—their endeavours also provide a means of overcoming national forgetting through the restoration of historical memory, research in the archives and the creation of new personal and familial memories through travel.

Revealing Chinese Australian Family Histories

Although the first known Chinese Australian family was formed in the 1820s,[8] stories of such families remained largely untold in the public sphere until the late twentieth century, both overlooked and hidden through the years of White Australia.[9] Before the 1980s there were only a handful of published accounts of Chinese Australian families, prompting Monica Tankey to publish several articles in the early 1980s about the family of her great-grandfather, John Tan Kee (c.1830–1902), who arrived in New South Wales as an indentured labourer from Amoy (Xiamen) in 1851. Tankey issued a rallying cry for further research by Chinese Australian family historians as a means of "rewriting ... our history books".[10] Other descendants around Australia were also starting to uncover their families' Chinese pasts, and the shift away from White Australia towards ideas of multiculturalism from the mid-1970s, together with new interests in social and oral history, created an imaginative space for their family stories to be voiced. These early family historians, like those researching Indigenous and convict pasts,[11] came to understand that their personal accounts made an important contribution to new ways of viewing Australia's history.

Interest in multicultural and migration histories in the 1980s and 1990s led to projects dedicated to Australia's Chinese history and heritage, including community museums such as the Museum of Chinese Australian History in Melbourne (established 1985), the Golden Dragon Museum in Bendigo (established 1991) and the Northern Territory Chinese Museum (established 1992). Descendants and family historians were among the strongest advocates for these projects, which gave them the opportunity to work with history and heritage professionals in sharing their family stories with a broader public. Capturing personal and intergenerational memories were an important part of this. Oral historians Morag Loh, Diana Giese and Janis Wilton recorded interviews with members of the Chinese Australian community,[12] prompting descendants to speak at conferences, record life stories and publish family histories.[13] The Museum of Chinese Australian History's 1993 conference on "Histories of the Chinese in Australasia and the South Pacific" also became a model for subsequent Chinese Australian history conferences—now more than twenty-five in total—which have been multidisciplinary and welcoming of family historians as speakers and audience.[14] Over time, the work of family historians, public historians and academic historians in the field of Chinese Australian history has become entwined, with each enhancing the other.[15]

Chinese Australian family historians find great value in connecting with each other. Many are members of their local family history societies, but mainstream groups still largely focus on British and Irish ancestry and so lack the knowledge and resources to help those researching families from other backgrounds. Those researching Chinese ancestors also face particular practical and emotional challenges, including in coming to terms with Australia's complex and confronting history of anti-Chinese laws, policies and ideologies, and consequent losses of family culture and knowledge. To fill the gap, in the early 2000s a number of dedicated Chinese Australian family and community history groups were formed, including Chinese Australian Family Historians of Victoria (CAFHOV) in Melbourne, the

Chinese Australian Historical Association in Brisbane (now defunct), the Chinese Australian Historical Society and the Chinese Heritage Association of Australia, both based in Sydney. These groups provide forums for sharing the challenges and successes of members' research through talks, meetings and publications, as well as connecting online through genealogical websites and social media.

The Search for Belonging

The experience of living in a country that excluded Chinese migrants and their descendants from its national memory has resonated through generations of Chinese Australian families. Sometimes the forgetting has come with the natural progression of time, a discarding of things no longer relevant, while in other cases it was a deliberate act of erasure of intergenerational identity and memory. The large majority of early Chinese in Australia were men, and many of those who formed Australian families partnered with women of European or Indigenous heritage, who were then largely responsible for the raising of children. In the face of racist sentiments and policies during the White Australia period, and as circumstances permitted, many mixed-race children and grandchildren distanced themselves from their Chinese heritage in a desire to blend in. They changed their names, moved to places where their heritage was unknown, discarded family papers and invented stories to explain "foreign" colouring or to hide gaps in the family story.[16] Family photographs were a particular target of this purposeful forgetting, with portraits being destroyed or defaced.[17] For families with two Chinese parents the apparent abandonment or forgetting of language, culture and familial past came about as the result of acculturation and assimilation as they made a life for themselves and their children in a new land.[18] Even when younger generations wanted to know about the family's past, their questions could be deflected.[19] These processes of forgetting began with individuals and flowed across and between generations, the outcome being that many Australian descendants have little or no cultural connection with their Chinese ancestors.

Through their research, Chinese Australian family historians, many of whom grew up in the 1950s and 1960s, look to make sense of fractured family pasts that do not easily fit with the Australian history they were taught as school children or read in history books. Theirs is a search for belonging in a society which, for a century or more, actively discriminated against their ancestors through laws and policies relating to immigration, citizenship, social welfare and employment, among other things. Despite its geographic proximity, for many Australians raised in the White Australia/Cold War era of the mid-twentieth century, China was at best an exotic mystery and at worst a threatening source of communism, compounding a sense that Chinese immigrants and their descendants were outsiders. For Kevin Wong Hoy, a fourth-generation Queenslander, the place of Chinese as outsiders or unwanted immigrants meant that "locating one's place in the history of Australia [could] be an intellectual challenge as well as emotionally confronting".[20] The very records they use to reconstruct their family histories have also been shaped or produced by exclusion and discrimination; for example, ships' passenger lists that give numbers of Chinese passengers but no names, and identity documents issued under the discriminatory Immigration Restriction Act. Chris Lee, who searched through church records for her grandfather, Anglican missionary James Lee Wah (1832–1909), found the archives steeped in "the attitudes of colonial and racial superiority" and wrote that their absence of emotion was another silencing of Australia's Chinese past.[21]

Confronting historical discrimination in the archives and addressing the absence of Chinese Australians in many published histories gives the work of Chinese Australian family historians a political, as well as an emotional, edge. For many, their quest is more than simply constructing a family tree; it is an effort to understand the historical context of White Australia and earlier anti-Chinese policies, to make sense of mysteries and fractured identities within their families, and to commemorate or recognize the contributions of early Chinese migrants to Australia.[22] They also seek acknowledgement that they are as Australian as anyone else. Recent mainstream media programmes that include Chinese Australian family stories—whether they be from Australia's national broadcaster, the ABC,[23] or commercial television programmes like *Who Do You Think You Are?*—help to validate this position.

Reclaiming Lost Connections of Language and Place

Most Chinese in nineteenth and early twentieth-century Australia came as economic "sojourners"; their ultimate goal was to return to their families who remained in south China. These men maintained links with their families at home through financial remittances, letters, newspapers and return visits and, were they to die in Australia, they hoped for their bones to be sent back for reburial in their ancestral village. Many, of course, never returned to their homeland, while others oscillated between Australia and China, visiting family, doing business and educating children. Some men eventually brought their wives and children to Australia and built new lives and futures here; others still left families they had formed in Australia to return to China in ill-health or old age, effectively disappearing from their children's and grandchildren's lives. The "sojourning" tradition of overseas Chinese has been a central theme of Chinese Australian histories,[24] and so family historians learn about the significance and meaning of the ancestral home, and of the ongoing ties between the village and those who went overseas. They trace their ancestors' comings and goings using Australian travel and immigration records, yet they are often left to wonder whether a decision to stay or return was intended or was imposed by circumstance and history. Many also struggle to imagine their ancestors' lives in Guangdong and hope that undertaking research in China will provide answers to family mysteries that Australian archives cannot answer. The realities of genealogical research in China mean that a visit in person to the ancestral village is often the only way to do this.

With the Japanese invasion of Guangdong in the late 1930s, the ravages of World War II and the closure of mainland China by the Communist Party from 1949, return visits became increasingly difficult for Chinese Australians, and during these tumultuous times many families overseas lost contact with relatives in China. The People's Republic of China remained largely closed off to foreign visitors for more than thirty years, but from the mid-1970s small numbers of Australians began to visit once again to reconnect with family or to experience the land and culture of their ancestors. The *qiaoxiang* counties of Guangdong were not mainstream tourist destinations, however, and basic tourist needs of transportation, hotels, guide books and maps were limited, if not non-existent. The local Overseas Chinese Affairs Office (僑務辦公室 *Qiaowu Bangongshi*) could assist in facilitating a visit to a home village, if this was known, but many Australians were content with seeing major tourist sites in cities like Beijing and Guangzhou on trips usually organized by the government-run China Travel Service.

Today travel to Guangdong is much easier, yet challenges remain for those seeking to trace their ancestry back to a precise location. Language is perhaps the greatest roadblock. Many descendants, even children of migrant parents, have no or only limited Chinese-language skills, and they often do not know the name of their ancestor or their home village, both of which are needed to successfully undertake genealogical research in

China. This information has not been passed down in many families, and Australian records, such as naturalization applications and marriage registrations, seldom provide enough detail—Chinese characters for personal or place names are rare, meaning that it can be hard to reconcile an Australian version of a name with its "proper" Chinese one. Without an ancestor's name in Chinese characters a descendant is unlikely to locate them in historical Chinese-language newspapers, community records and memorial tablets in Australia, or in genealogies or other records in China. Without the name of the ancestral village they cannot visit their ancestor's Chinese birthplace and former home, their ancestral hall or grave site, nor find their clan and family genealogies (族譜 *zupu* and 家譜 *jiapu*), nor further information about their ancestors' origins and life in China.

Chinese Australian family historians work hard to overcome these difficulties. They scour birth, death and marriage certificates, immigration and citizenship records, and the backs of photographs and old envelopes looking for Chinese signatures, addresses and variations in spellings of names and places. They track down grave sites in Australia which might have Chinese inscriptions, explore business and family connections looking for leads and speak with family members and elders in the Chinese Australian community hoping for details.[25] With some information—a possible family and village name—there are online resources that can help identify and locate the ancestral village, including Chinese genealogy websites and forums, maps from Baidu and Google China, and the Roots Village Database, a searchable index of clan names and *qiaoxiang* villages.[26] Despite their best endeavours, however, many family historians still do not succeed, leaving them with a longing to make a tangible connection to China and the pre-migration lives of their ancestors.

Retracing Ancestral Journeys: From Australia to Guangdong

As public historians who have lived in China and worked closely with Chinese Australian family historians over many years, we saw the challenges that family historians faced, but also knew of the rich heritage and culture that survives in the Cantonese *qiaoxiang* towns and villages; we also knew the profound shift in perspective that viewing Australia's Chinese history from south China brings.[27] Kate first lived in Guangdong in the late 1990s, an experience that prompted her interest in Chinese Australian history, and she became keen to try something like the "In Search of Roots" programme, established by Him Mark Lai and Albert Cheng in San Francisco in 1991, but designed for Chinese Australian family historians, particularly those who were disconnected from their Chinese origins and so could not trace their ancestral village.[28]

We have run a Chinese Australian Hometown Heritage Tour annually since 2017, each time taking a group of around sixteen to Hong Kong and Guangdong for about ten days. Participants on the tour have included those who do not know their ancestral village at all, those who know only the county their ancestors came from, and those who know the specific ancestral village or villages. The tour starts in Hong Kong, the port where most early Chinese boarded ships to Australia, before travelling by river ferry to Jiangmen and then by bus through the *qiaoxiang* districts of Kaiping, Taishan, Xinhui, Zhongshan and Zhuhai. We visit local museums, including those that focus on overseas Chinese history, and spend two days at Cangdong, a UNESCO award-winning heritage project in Kaiping run by Dr Selia Tan of Wuyi University. In Cangdong we learn about village history and architecture, and participate in cultural activities such as cooking, handicrafts and music. We also visit other different kinds of overseas Chinese villages, including the impressive World Heritage-listed *diaolou* (碉樓 watchtowers) in Kaiping, drawing out Australian connections. Importantly, we work with tour members who know the name of their ancestral village to organize for them to visit independently or as part of the tour.

Visiting the *qiaoxiang* helps Chinese Australian family historians fill emotional and narrative gaps in their family histories and create new memories and cultural knowledge. It is not possible to bring back the family memory that has been lost, but in the *qiaoxiang*, descendants can trace their ancestors' migration journeys, imagine life for them in their home village and see the effects, both positive and negative, that 150 years of emigration has had on the local villages, towns and cities. With a better understanding of the complexities of Cantonese history and a greater feel for the culture and language, the Chinese side of Australian family histories is illuminated and personified, as are the experiences of Cantonese families who lost contact with loved ones who went to Australia long ago. One 2017 tour member, Jenny, reflected on her Chinese great-great-grandfather, saying "suddenly he was a real person," while Megan, who came on the 2018 tour, noted that "while a relative may never have returned as intended, in person or as bones, our journey and our presence signified that overseas family were interested and were returning now." Megan is the great granddaughter of interpreter and storekeeper Chin Kit (1830–1902), who established his long-term home in Launceston, and she is yet to find details of his ancestral village in Taishan. She looked on as Richard paid his respects at the village shrine in Qiaotou (Fig. 22.1). Megan might not know her precise ancestral home in China, but she came away from the tour with new memories and understandings of what their lives could have been like.

Conclusion

The national forgetting of Australia's Chinese past originated in the construction of an imagined white nation where migrant Chinese and Australians of Chinese heritage, including those of mixed race, were excluded and discriminated against. Since the 1980s, Australian family historians have been uncovering the presence and identity of Chinese ancestors and seeking to understand their place in Australian history. These family historians have felt a disconnect between national narratives and family experience, and so have worked alongside history and heritage professionals in forging a space for Chinese Australians within Australian public and popular history. By recovering family memory, enhancing it through research and sharing their family histories in public, they offer alternatives to national histories that previously excluded their ancestors. Some struggle, however, to overcome the loss of language, culture and intergenerational memory exacerbated by decades of discrimination and marginalization. Severed family connections between Australia and China, and the deliberate or inadvertent loss of knowledge of family information have left some with a profound sense of loss or disconnection. "Roots tourism" in the form of visiting the *qiaoxiang* counties of Guangdong can help overcome gaps in the family story, enabling Chinese Australian family historians to experience, connect and imagine, even if they cannot *know* for sure.

Notes

1. Gwen Num, "A Life with a Difference," *Nation* 57 (November 1960): 17–18.
2. Cora Num, "A Chinese Family in South Australia," Typescript in possession of the authors (2010).

3. The term *qiaoxiang* (僑鄉) refers to the ancestral or home villages of emigrant Chinese and the rural districts in which these villages are found.
4. We use the term "Chinese Australian family historians" to describe people who are researching or are descended from at least one Chinese ancestor who lived in Australia.
5. Paula Hamilton, "The Knife Edge: Debates about Memory and History," in Kate Darian-Smith and Paula Hamilton eds, *Memory and History in Twentieth Century Australia* (Melbourne: Oxford University Press, 1994), 23.
6. Kate Darian-Smith and Paula Hamilton, "Memory and History in Twenty-First Century Australia: A Survey of the Field," *Memory Studies* 6, no. 3 (2013): 370–83.
7. Tingting Elle Li and Bob McKercher, "Developing a Typology of Diaspora Tourists: Return Travel by Chinese Immigrants in North America," *Tourism Management* 56 (2016): 106–13; Naho Maruyama and Amanda Stronza, "Roots Tourism of Chinese Americans," *Ethnology: An International Journal of Cultural and Social Anthropology* 49, no. 1 (2010): 23–44; Andrea Louie, "Crafting Places Through Mobility: Chinese American 'Roots Searching' in China," *Identities: Global Studies in Culture and Power* 8, no. 3 (2001): 343–79.
8. Valerie Blomer, *An Alien in the Antipodes: The Story of John Shying* (Self-published, 1999), https://web.archive.org/web/20020713123504/http://www.multiline.com.au/~bvl/Stories/Shying.htm.
9. Kate Bagnall, "Rewriting the History of Chinese Families in Nineteenth-Century Australia," *Australian Historical Studies* 42, no. 1 (2011): 62–77.
10. Monica Tankey, "A Blueprint for Action," *The Australian Journal of Chinese Affairs* 6 (July 1981): 195; Monica Tankey, "English on the Outside and Chinese on the Inside," *Australia–China Review* 11 (February 1983): 9–10.
11. Tanya Evans, "Secrets and Lies: The Radical Potential of Family History," *History Workshop Journal* 71 (April 2011): 49–73; Graeme Davison, "Ancestors: The Broken Lineage of Family History," in *The Use and Abuse of Australian History* (St. Leonards: Allen & Unwin, 2000), 80–109.
12. Morag Loh, "Testimonies from White Australia: Oral History Interviews and Chinese Immigrants and their Descendants," *The La Trobe Journal* 90 (December 2012): 112–71; Janis Wilton, *Hong Yuen: A Country Store and its People* (Armidale: Multicultural Education Coordinating Committee and Armidale College of Advanced Education, 1988); Diana Giese, *Astronauts, Lost Souls and Dragons: Voices of Today's Chinese Australians in Conversation with Diana Giese* (St Lucia: University of Queensland Press, 1997).

13. Norma King Koi, "Discovering My Heritage: An Oral History of My Maternal Family—The Ah Moons of Townsville," in Paul Macgregor ed., *Histories of the Chinese in Australasia and the South Pacific* (Melbourne: Museum of Chinese Australian History, 1995), 287–95; Kevin Wong Hoy ed., *Collected Papers on the Yet Foy Family of Queensland* (Melbourne: Self-published, 1999); Rosalie Hiah and Warren Lee Long, "Taking Our Chinese Family History to the Wider Community: Producing the Kwong Sue Duk Family History Video Documentary," in Pookong Kee, Chooihon Ho, Paul Macgregor and Gary Presland eds, *Chinese in Oceania* (Melbourne: ASCADAPI, Museum of Chinese Australian History, and Centre for Asia-Pacific Studies, VUT, 2002), 77–86.

14. Macgregor ed., *Histories of the Chinese in Australasia and the South Pacific*.

15. Sophie Couchman, "Introduction," in Sophie Couchman and Kate Bagnall eds, *Chinese Australians: Politics, Engagement and Resistance* (Leiden: Brill, 2015), 6; Tanya Evans, "Secrets and Lies: The Radical Potential of Family History."

16. Barbara Moore, "The Case of the Missing Sisters," *Ancestral Searcher* 17, no. 2 (1994): 61–63.

17. Chris Lee, "Unfolding the Silence: James Lee Wah (1832–1909) Chinese Goldfields Miner and Anglican Missionary," in Sophie Couchman ed., *Secrets, Silences and Sources: Five Chinese-Australian Family Histories* (Melbourne: Asian Studies, La Trobe University, 2005), 29; Morag Loh, "Testimonies from White Australia: Oral History Interviews and Chinese Immigrants and their Descendants," *The La Trobe Journal* 90 (December 2012): 119.

18. Doreen Cheong, "East–West Fusion," in Nikki Loong ed., *From Great Grandmothers to Great Granddaughters: The Stories of Six Chinese Australian Women* (Katoomba: Echo Point Press, 2006), 34; Darryl Low Choy, "That's Not a Chinese Name," in Chek Ling ed., *Plantings in a New Land: Stories of Survival, Endurance and Emancipation* (Brisbane: Society of Chinese Australian Academics in Queensland, 2001), 62–78.

19. Norma King Koi, "Discovering My Heritage: An Oral History of My Maternal Family—The Ah Moons of Townsville," in *Histories of the Chinese in Australasia and the South Pacific*, 287–95.

20. Kevin Wong Hoy, "Chinese-Australian History vs Huaqiao History: Chinese in North Queensland," in *Secrets, Silences and Sources*, 5.

21. Chris Lee, "Unfolding the Silence: James Lee Wah (1832–1909) Chinese Goldfields Miner and Anglican Missionary," in *Secrets, Silences and Sources*, 22.

22. Claire Faulkner, *Conquest: An Inside Story—The Integration of a Colonial Chinese-Australian Family Cluster* (Australia: Self-published, 2013); Joanne Olsen and Keith Shang, *With His Gold in a Little Velvet Bag: The*

Story of a Chinaman and a Bonnie Lassie from Edinburgh (Lindfield, NSW: Self-published, 2013).

23. Jason Fang, "200 Years of Chinese-Australians: First Settler's Descendants Reconnect with Their Roots," *ABC Online*, 10 June 2018, https://web. archive.org/web/20181016015635/http://www.abc.net.au/news/ 2018-06-10/first-chinese-settlers-descendants-reconnect-with-their-roots/9845804; Jane Lee, "The Story of William Ah Ket, the First Chinese-Australian Barrister," *ABC Online*, 30 August 2018, https:// web.archive.org/web/20181016020045/http://www.abc.net.au/ news/2018-08-30/william-ah-ket-the-first-chinese-australian-barrister/10160198.

24. Eric Rolls, *Sojourners: Flowers and the Wide Sea* (St Lucia: University of Queensland Press, 1992).

25. Jon Kehrer, "Honourable Ancestors: My Search for the Chinese Connection," *The Ancestral Searcher* 27, no. 4 (2004): 328–33.

26. *Chinese Genealogy*, http://siyigenealogy.proboards.com; *Roots Village Database Search*, http://villagedb.friendsofroots.org/search.cgi.

27. Kate Bagnall, "Golden Shadows on a White Land: An Exploration of the Lives of White Women Who Partnered Chinese Men and Their Children in Southern Australia, 1855–1915," PhD diss. (Sydney: University of Sydney, 2006); Kate Bagnall, "Landscapes of Memory and Forgetting: Indigo and Shek Quey Lee," *Chinese Southern Diaspora Studies* 6 (2013): 7–24; Sophie Couchman ed., *Secrets, Silences and Sources*.

28. Albert Cheng and Him Mark Lai, "The 'In Search of Roots' Program: Constructing Identity through Family History Research and a Journey to the Ancestral Land," in Susie Lan Cassel ed., *The Chinese in America: A History from Gold Mountain to the New Millennium* (Walnut Creek: Altamira Press, 2002), 293–307.

Bibliography

Bagnall, Kate. "Golden Shadows on a White Land: An Exploration of the Lives of White Women Who Partnered Chinese Men and Their Children in Southern Australia, 1855–1915." PhD diss., University of Sydney, 2006.

Bagnall, Kate. "Rewriting the History of Chinese Families in Nineteenth-Century Australia." *Australian Historical Studies* 42, no. 1 (2011): 62–77.

Bagnall, Kate. "Landscapes of Memory and Forgetting: Indigo and Shek Quey Lee." *Chinese Southern Diaspora Studies* 6 (2013): 7–24.

Blomer, Valerie. *An Alien in the Antipodes: The Story of John Shying.* Self-published, 2006. https://web.archive.org/web/20020713123504/http://www.multi-line.com.au/~bvl/Stories/Shying.htm.

Cheng, Albert, and Him Mark Lai. "The 'In Search of Roots' Program: Constructing Identity through Family History Research and a Journey to the Ancestral Land." In *The Chinese in America: A History from Gold Mountain to the New Millennium*, edited by Susie Lan Cassel, 293–307. Walnut Creek: Altamira Press, 2002.

Cheong, Doreen. "East–West Fusion." In *From Great Grandmothers to Great Granddaughters: The Stories of Six Chinese Australian Women*, edited by Nikki Loong, 31–40. Katoomba: Echo Point Press, 2006.

Couchman, Sophie, ed. *Secrets, Silences and Sources: Five Chinese-Australian Family Histories*. Melbourne: Asian Studies, La Trobe University, 2005.

Couchman, Sophie. "Introduction." In *Chinese Australians: Politics, Engagement and Resistance*, edited by Sophie Couchman and Kate Bagnall, 1–21. Leiden: Brill, 2015.

Darian-Smith, Kate, and Paula Hamilton. "Memory and History in Twenty-First Century Australia: A Survey of the Field." *Memory Studies* 6, no. 3 (2013): 370–83.

Davison, Graeme. "Ancestors: The Broken Lineage of Family History." In *The Use and Abuse of Australian History*, 80–109. St. Leonards: Allen & Unwin, 2000.

Evans, Tanya. "Secrets and Lies: The Radical Potential of Family History." *History Workshop Journal* 71 (April 2011): 49–73.

Fang, Jason. "200 Years of Chinese-Australians: First Settler's Descendants Reconnect with Their Roots." *ABC Online*, 10 June 2018. https://web.archive.org/web/20181016015635/http://www.abc.net.au/news/2018-06-10/first-chinese-settlers-descendants-reconnect-with-their-roots/9845804.

Faulkner, Claire. *Conquest: An Inside Story—The Integration of a Colonial Chinese-Australian Family Cluster*. Australia: Self-published, 2013.

Giese, Diana. *Astronauts, Lost Souls and Dragons: Voices of Today's Chinese Australians in Conversation with Diana Giese*. St Lucia: University of Queensland Press, 1997.

Hamilton, Paula. "The Knife Edge: Debates about Memory and History." In *Memory and History in Twentieth Century Australia*, edited by Kate Darian-Smith and Paula Hamilton. Melbourne: Oxford University Press, 1994.

Hiah, Rosalie, and Warren Lee Long. "Taking Our Chinese Family History to the Wider Community: Producing the Kwong Sue Duk Family History Video Documentary." In *Chinese in Oceania*, edited by Pookong Kee, Chooi-hon Ho, Paul Macgregor, and Gary Presland, 77–86. Melbourne: ASCADAPI, Museum of Chinese Australian History, and Centre for Asia-Pacific Studies, VUT, 2002.

Kehrer, Jon. "Honourable Ancestors: My Search for the Chinese Connection." *The Ancestral Searcher* 27, no. 4 (2004): 328–33.

King Koi, Norma. "Discovering My Heritage: An Oral History of My Maternal Family—The Ah Moons of Townsville." In *Histories of the Chinese in Australasia and the South Pacific*, edited by Paul Macgregor, 287–95. Melbourne: Museum of Chinese Australian History, 1995.

Lee, Chris. "Unfolding the Silence: James Lee Wah (1832–1909) Chinese Goldfields Miner and Anglican Missionary." In *Secrets, Silences and Sources: Five Chinese-Australian Family Histories*, edited by Sophie Couchman, 17–30. Melbourne: Asian Studies, La Trobe University, 2005.

Lee, Jane. "The Story of William Ah Ket, the First Chinese-Australian Barrister." *ABC Online*, 30 August 2018. https://web.archive.org/web/2018 1016020045/http://www.abc.net.au/news/2018-08-30/william-ah-ket-the-first-chinese-australian-barrister/10160198.

Li, Tingting Elle, and Bob McKercher. "Developing a Typology of Diaspora Tourists: Return Travel by Chinese Immigrants in North America." *Tourism Management* 56 (2016): 106–13.

Loh, Morag. "Testimonies from White Australia: Oral History Interviews and Chinese Immigrants and their Descendants." *The La Trobe Journal* 90 (December 2012): 112–71.

Louie, Andrea. "Crafting Places Through Mobility: Chinese American 'Roots Searching' in China." *Identities: Global Studies in Culture and Power* 8, no. 3 (2001): 343–79.

Low Choy, Darryl. "That's Not a Chinese Name." In *Plantings in a New Land: Stories of Survival, Endurance and Emancipation*, edited by Chek Ling, 62–78. Brisbane: Society of Chinese Australian Academics in Queensland, 2001.

Macgregor, Paul, ed. *Histories of the Chinese in Australasia and the South Pacific*. Melbourne: Museum of Chinese Australian History, 1995.

Maruyama, Naho, and Amanda Stronza. "Roots Tourism of Chinese Americans." *Ethnology: An International Journal of Cultural and Social Anthropology* 49, no. 1 (2010): 23–44.

Moore, Barbara. "The Case of the Missing Sisters." *Ancestral Searcher* 17, no. 2 (1994): 61–63.

Num, Cora. "A Chinese Family in South Australia." Typescript in possession of the authors, 2010.

Num, Gwen. "A Life with a Difference." *Nation* 57 (November 1960): 17–18.

Olsen, Joanne, and Keith Shang. *With His Gold in a Little Velvet Bag: The Story of a Chinaman and a Bonnie Lassie from Edinburgh*. Lindfield, NSW: Self-published, 2013.

Rolls, Eric. *Sojourners: Flowers and the Wide Sea*. St Lucia: University of Queensland Press, 1992.

Tankey, Monica. "A Blueprint for Action." *The Australian Journal of Chinese Affairs* 6 (July 1981): 189–95.

Tankey, Monica. "English on the Outside and Chinese on the Inside." *Australia–China Review* 11 (February 1983): 9–10.

Wilton, Janis. *Hong Yuen: A Country Store and its People*. Armidale: Multicultural Education Coordinating Committee and Armidale College of Advanced Education, 1988.

Wong Hoy, Kevin. "Chinese-Australian History vs Huaqiao History: Chinese in North Queensland." In *Secrets, Silences and Sources: Five Chinese-Australian Family Histories*, edited by Sophie Couchman, 3–16. Melbourne: Asian Studies Program, La Trobe University, 2005.

Wong Hoy, Kevin, ed. *Collected Papers on the Yet Foy Family of Queensland*. Melbourne: Self-published, 1999.

Index[1]

A

Abul Fazal Abbas shrine, 175
Adelaide, 8, 93–100, 110, 206, 331
Advisory Council on Multicultural
  Affairs, 289
Affective storytelling, 260–262
Affective ties, 95
Afghanistan, 8, 167–170, 172, 173,
  175, 176
Afghan refugee, 79
Agutter, Karen, 7, 228
Albury Museum and Library, 210
Alcoholics Anonymous (AA), 67
Alexakis, Effy, 4
Alsop, John, 304
Alternative histories, 77
Alvarez-Poblete, Geraldina, 279
Anderson, David, 260
Andrews, Graeme, 207
Andrews, Kevin, 160
Anne's International Kitchen, 83
Anomie, 193

Anti-Semitism, 35
Antze, Paul, 131
Anzac tradition, 1
Armstrong, Helen, 223
Arnhem Bay, 173
Ashton, Paul, 282n13
Assmann, Aleida, 156, 157, 161
Assmann, Jan, 95
Australian, 2, 4–6, 10, 11, 19, 22–25,
  32, 33, 35–37, 48, 49, 52, 53, 60,
  66, 76–80, 82–85, 98–100, 108,
  109, 112, 117, 124, 126, 128,
  133, 144, 148, 156, 160–162,
  167, 173–177, 186, 187, 189,
  191–194, 203, 207, 210,
  220–223, 256, 257, 262, 264,
  274–276, 278–280, 286–294,
  301–304, 306, 309, 312, 331–340
Australian Broadcasting Control
  Board, 77–78
Australian Bureau of Statistics (ABS),
  2, 293

---

[1] Note: Page numbers followed by 'n' refer to notes.

© The Author(s) 2019
K. Darian-Smith, P. Hamilton (eds.), *Remembering Migration*,
Palgrave Macmillan Memory Studies,
https://doi.org/10.1007/978-3-030-17751-5

347

348 INDEX

Australian Census, 48, 292
Australian Generations Oral History
    Project, 61, 71n21
Australian Generations project, 48, 61
Australian Heritage Commission, 223
Australian Heritage Strategy, 224
Australian Institute of Multicultural
    Affairs, 93
Australian Labor Party (ALP), 188
Australian Lesbian and Gay Life
    Stories, 47–50, 55
Australian media, 77, 191, 318–319
Australian Migration History Network,
    11
Australian Migration Officers, 126,
    133
Australian National Maritime
    Museum, 8
Australian Standard Classification of
    Cultural and Ethnic Groups
    (ASCCEG), 293

B

Baldassar, Loretta, 102n23, 103n29
Beautiful Balts, 3
Behind the Wire, 266
Benalla Migrant Camp, 225–227
Benjamin, Walter, 241
Blainey, Geoffrey, 191
Bonegilla Migrant Centre, 226
Border protection policy, 3
Bornat, Joanna, 60
Bosworth, Richard, 38
Boyd, Nan Alamilla, 48
Breyley, Gay, 108
Brierley, Saroo, 302, 305, 308, 310
Brierley, Sue and John, 305, 311
Bringing Them Home Report, 304
Britain, 2, 31, 76, 77, 262, 303–305,
    307, 310, 313n12
British immigrants, 19

British Migrants: Instant Australians?,
    262, 263, 267
Broadcast media, 78
Brown, Gordon, 304
Brunner, Jerome, 311
Buckmaster, Luke, 320
Burns, Ken, 196
Burra Charter, 224, 225
Burrell, Kathy, 31, 32
Butler, Judith, 302
Butler, Kelly Jean, 4
Buttrose, Larry, 305, 310
Byrne, Denis, 223

C

Café di Stasio, 239
Calwell, Arthur, 111
Camera operators, 76
Canfield, Robert, 171
Cangdong, 339
Cantonese families, 339
Cartoons, 79
Castellorizo, 143
Cast from the Storm, 319
Cave, Colin, 21–25
Cave, Heather, 22, 25
Cave, Mark, 36
Cave, Phyllis, 17–19, 21, 26, 27n8
Chapman, Penny, 304
Chasing Asylum, 319
Cheng, Albert, 339
Child migrants, 3, 10, 115, 301–312
Child Migrants Trust, 303, 304,
    309
Child refugees, 60
Chinese Australian Family Historians
    of Victoria (CAFHOV), 334
Chinese Australian Historical Society,
    335
Chinese Australian Hometown
    Heritage Tour, 339

INDEX

Chinese Australians, 11, 80, 81, 188, 331–340
Chinese Heritage Association of Australia, 335
Chinese Museum, 9
Chin Kit, 340
Chops and Changes, 206
Cigler, Michael, 32
Cilia, Ninette, 81
Clarke, Annie, 231n7
Co.As.It Italian Historical Society and Museo Italiano, 9
Cohen, Daniel G., 30
Cohler, Betram J., 49
Collection Development Policy (CDP), 288–290, 292, 294
Collective memory, 11, 107–108, 110, 143, 146, 155, 159–163, 208, 210, 211, 213, 214
Colour broadcasting, 80
Commonwealth Special Intelligence Bureau, 34
Communications sector, 76
Constance on the Edge, 319–322
Convention on the Protection and UNESCO Promotion of the Diversity of Cultural Expressions, 220
Corbin, Juliet, 157
Coronation Street, 76
Corporate Plan, 286, 289
Crawford Productions, 82
Creative visualization, 262–264
Critical heritage studies, 219
Crossing Place permanent exhibition, 210, 216n23
Cultural diversity, 2, 76, 78, 81, 197, 256, 289, 321
Cultural memory, 157, 161, 237
Cultural representation, 77
Current affairs, 76, 305
Cyber "communities," 11

D
Dalley, Valery, 212
Damousi, Joy, 60
Danforth, Lorin M., 147
David, Janina, 291, 292, 294
Davies, Stuart, 205
De Stefanis, Marina, 81
Dellios, Alexandra, 10, 110, 115
Dell'Oso, Anna Maria, 79, 80
Department of Immigration, 112, 113, 115, 228
Depression, the, 97
Des Pres, Terrence, 168
Di Fabrizio, Don, 228
Diasporic memory, 1, 124
Digital streaming, 81
Displaced persons (DP), 3, 4, 7, 29–38, 62, 107–112, 115–117, 158, 273
Documentaries, 1, 5, 10, 29, 80, 82, 100, 167, 174, 185, 190, 192, 194–196, 301–303, 309
Doganieri, Maria, 81, 82
Douglas, Kate, 67
Duggan, Heather, 272, 274
Dunbar, Sherron, 277
D'Urbano, Michelina, 81
Dynamics of memory, 157–161

E
Earl Grey Irish Scheme, 111
Eltahir, Magdi, 207
Empty Cradles, 302, 309
Enterprise Hostel, 271–279
Enterprise Migrant Hostel, 271, 278
Enterprise Tribute Garden, 272, 276, 280
Epic Theatre, 81
Eritrean Australians, 292, 293
Espin, Oliva, 108
Estonia, 3

350 INDEX

Ethiopia, 80, 156
Ethnic entrepreneurs, 83
Ethnic stereotypes, 77
Ethno-regional approach, 142
European soccer, 84

F
Family Secrets, 237, 238
Ferriman, Annabel, 303
Field, Sean, 176
Films, 1, 10, 11, 32, 78, 79, 81, 82, 84,
   107, 109, 110, 116, 213, 256–
   258, 263, 301, 302, 304–306,
   309, 312, 318–324, 326
Fire at Sea, 326
First Peoples exhibition, 265
First-person narratives, 77, 203–214,
   264
Floating Life, 301
Florina, 8, 141, 142, 144–149,
   151n16
Foley, Dennis, 249
Foley, Michael, 196
Forced migration, 123–134, 156, 168,
   213, 312, 324
Forgotten Australians and Former
   Child Migrants, 3
Fortier, Anne-Marie, 96–98
Fraser, Malcolm, 190, 275
Freedom Stories, 319
Fremantle Museum, 208
Funseth, Robert, 127

G
Gair, Susan, 308, 309
Galbally Report, 190, 191
Gendered silence, 110–111
Giese, Diana, 334
Gippsland Immigration Park, 227,
   228, 230

Gippsland Migrant Resource Centre,
   67
Global diaspora, 11
Golden Dragon Museum, 334
Gonzalez, Guido, 321
Good, Gwen, 19
Good Pitch Australia, 319
Gordon, Milton, 156
Gorman-Murray, Andrew, 49, 50
Government Holding Centres, 112
Grecian Scene, 84
Greece, 8, 60, 76, 84, 141–146, 148,
   149, 151n16, 228
Greek Affair, 83
Greek Australians, 84, 143, 223
Greek Civil War, 142, 145, 146
Greek Cypriot, 83
Greek Macedonians, 141–149
Greek Variety Show, 78, 83, 84
Grenville, Kate, 241
Grinchenko, Gelinada, 31
Guangdong Province, 331–333

H
Haig, Harold, 311
Halbwachs, Maurice, 36, 155, 161
Hamilton, Paula, 213, 264
Hammerton, A. James, 18, 60
Hammerton, Jim, 34
Hartling, Poul, 129
Hartnell, Barry John, 212
Hawke government, 289
Hazara, 167–177
   community, 168
   refugees, 8, 167–177
Hellenic Museum, 9
Heritage tour, 332
Heritage Victoria, 226, 227
Heritage Week, 224, 225
Herzfeld, Michael, 146
Heyes, T. H. E., 113

Hirsch, Marianne, 6, 242
HMAS *Wollongong*, 174
Holocaust survivors, 6, 186, 291, 294
Holovka, Peter, 212
The Home Song Stories, 301
Hostel Stories Project, 111
Hosteltler, Andrew, 49
Howard, John, 173, 221, 222
Hughes, John, 31, 37
Humanitarian entrants, 130, 156, 159, 160
Humanitarian programme, 3, 156, 273
Humanitarian refugees, 2
Human Rights and Equal Opportunity Commission, 110–111
Humphreys, Margaret, 303, 305, 309–311
Husseini, Nurjan, 174
Husseini, Sayyed Shahi, 174
Huyssen, Andreas, 1, 324

I

Ibrahimi, Niamatullah, 178n14, 178n15, 178n17
Identity: Yours, Mine, Ours, 213, 258, 260
Il Corriere d'Australia, 83
"I'm Home!" consultation report, 275, 276
Immigration Museum, 8, 10, 213, 224, 255–257, 259–262, 265–267, 271, 273–275
Immigration Nation:The Secret Story of US, 302
Immigration Restriction Act, 186, 336
Independent Inquiry into Child Sexual Abuse in England and Wales, 304
Indian Society for Sponsorship and Adoption, 305

Indigenous Australians, 77, 264
Indo-Chinese refugees, 191
In Search of Lost Time, 249
In Search of Roots, 339
Intergenerational memory, 143, 332–334, 340
International conglomerates, 83
International education, 11
International Refugee Organization (IRO), 30, 35, 39n4, 113, 116
Islamic Museum of Australia, 9
Italian, 5, 29, 78, 79, 81–84, 94–99, 191, 196, 227, 228, 326
  market gardeners, 93–100
  migrants, 79, 81, 82, 94, 96
Italian Australians, 93

J

James, Daniel, 94
Janiszewski, Leonard, 4
Jari, Saif, 321
Jennings, Rebecca, 50
Jewish immigrants, 186
Jewish Museum of Australia, 9
Jobbins, Ted, 84
Johnston, Chris, 231n7, 231n8
Jonatis, Elena, 108
Jones, Kevin, 306
Jong, Peter, 281

K

Kaiping, 331, 332, 339
Kakmi, Dmetri, 79
Kennedy, Roger, 245, 251n12
Kirkpatrick, Heather, 318
Kleiss, Donna, 111
Kopijn, Yvette J., 168
Kouvaros, George, 11
Kuhn, Annette, 237, 238

352 INDEX

L

Lai, Him Mark, 339
Lam, Cuc, 80
Lambek, Michael, 131
Lang, Jack, 188
Laplanche, Jean, 237, 244, 245
Latvia, 3
The Leaving of Liverpool, 10, 302, 304–309, 311
Lee, Chris, 336
Lee Wah, James, 336
Let's Go Greek, 84
Lexington Gardens, 276
Library of Congress, 291, 293
Lienz cossacks, 35
Light Over the Water, 291
Linguistic and cultural diversity, 78
Lion (film), 10, 302, 305–309
Lithuania, 3
Little Italy, 96
Local content, 78
Loh, Morag, 334
Long Way Home, 302, 305
Longley, Kateryna Olijnyk, 30, 31, 36, 38
Lost Children of the Empire, 303, 304
Love (exhibition), 265
Luciano, Antonio (Tony), 83, 84
Lucky Miles, 318
Luibheid, Eithne, 47

M

Macedonia, 141, 145–147
Macquarie University, 5
Mainstream production organizations, 78
Makeas, Sam, 207
Making Multicultural Australia, 10, 190–192, 196
Manus Island, 317
Maritime museums, 9

Marr, David, 173
Marshall, Barrie, 239
Martin, Jean, 4
Mary Meets Mohammad, 318
Mason, Belinda, 319, 320
Maynes, Mary Jo, 62
McDowell, Linda, 31
McShane, Ian, 206, 221
Media moguls, 83
Media Press, 84
Melbourne Immigration Museum, 255–267
Melbourne Olympic Games, 75
Memoirs, 1, 4, 10, 11, 20, 21, 76, 77, 80, 81, 85, 107, 275, 280, 290–293, 302–305, 309–311
Memory studies, 1, 75, 237, 242
Memory text, 237, 238
Menji, Tatek, 80
Merenda, Francesca, 190
Merton, Robert, 193
Metcalfe, Susan, 179n31
Metropolitan Community Church, 54
Michaels, Harry, 83, 84
Microhistory, 94, 101n10
Migrant Heritage Centre, 5
Migrant market gardening families, 93
Migrant mothers, 107–117, 226, 227
Migrant technicians, 76
Migrant television producers, 77, 83
Migrant testimonies, 2
Migration and Cultural Diversity Collection, 256
Migration heritage, 1, 219, 222–227, 229, 230
Migration Heritage Centre, 224
Migration Museums, 8, 206
Milano, Mario, 81
Mirhady, Vera, 49
Mitchell, Merle, 272–274, 278
Mondale, Walter, 125
Monuments to migrant groups, 227

Moving Stories, 19
Mujahideen, 169, 170
Multicultural Australia: United, Strong, Successful, 222
Multiculturalism, 8, 10, 21, 32, 85, 108, 109, 117, 186, 190, 191, 206, 210, 221–223, 229, 256, 279, 286, 289, 334
Multicultural Museums Victoria, 9
Multicultural Policy Statement, 285
Murdoch, Rupert, 84
Murphy, Sinatra, 272, 277
Museum archives, 204, 206
Museum of Chinese Australian History, 334
Museums Victoria, 8, 256, 267

N

National Agenda for a Multicultural Australia, 289
National apology, 3, 115
National Apology to Victims and Survivors of Institutional Child Sexual Abuse, 3
National Archives, 37, 38
National Film and Sound Archive (NFSA), 77, 86n10
National identity, 60, 77, 147
National Inquiry into the Separation of Aboriginal and Torres Strait slander Children from their Families, 111
National Library Act 1960, 287
National Library of Australia (NLA), 4, 5, 10, 29, 47, 48, 86n10, 192
National Maritime Museum, 206
National memory, 1, 288, 323–325, 333, 335
National Museum of Australia (NMA), 8, 206, 287

National Museum of Australia Act 1980, 287
National network, 77
National stories, 8, 75–85, 226
NBN television studios, 84
Neighbours, 80
Netflix, 81
Network Ten, 83
Neumann, Klaus, 10, 167, 273, 317
A New Australia: Post-War Immigration to Western Australia, 208
New Economic Zones, 125, 128, 129
New Zealand, 48, 50, 51, 126, 303, 306
Newman, John, 194
Nguyen, Hong Duc, 258
Nguyen, Van Long, 128
Nicholson Street, 247, 248, 250
Noorzai, Salim, 79
Northern Territory Chinese Museum, 334
Novick, Lynn, 196
NSW Education Department, 192
NSW Parks and Wildlife Service, 231n6
Num, Gwen, 331
Number 96, 83

O

Once My Mother, 109–110, 114
Once Upon a Time in Cabramatta (OUATIC), 192, 196, 197
Once Upon a Time in Carlton, 196
Once Upon a Time in Punchbowl, 193, 196
Operation Relex, 173
Oral History, 1, 18, 29–38, 47–55, 60, 76, 93–100, 107, 124, 142, 168, 190, 203–214, 219, 256, 272, 292, 302, 334

354 INDEX

Oral history project, 29, 31, 47, 48, 93–95, 99, 100, 142, 210, 223
Oranges and Sunshine, 302, 305, 309, 312
Orderly Departure Program (ODP), 124–128, 133, 134, 135n2
Origlass, Nick, 188

P

Pacific Solution, 173
Palomares, Simon, 81, 278
Panorama Productions, 83
Park, Robert, 193
Parsons, Deborah, 84
Partington, Jennie, 51
A Part of the Main, 292
Partridge, Sophie, 51
Payne, Anne Maree, 110, 111
Pedagogy of listening, 203, 210, 213
Pedagogy of looking, 203, 207–209
Pedagogy of reading, 203, 207
Pennay, Bruce, 115
People's Republic of China, 135n2, 337
Perks, Rob, 216, 217
Perks, Robert, 133, 204, 205
Photography, 3, 24, 190, 242
Phuong Ngo, 192, 193
Pickett, Joan, 19
Pilkington-Garimara, Doris, 304
Play School, 80
Policy of multiculturalism, 2, 77, 190, 221
Polish Australian culture, 65
Polish immigrants, 62
Poon Num, Daniel, 331
Porritt, Barbara, 3
Portelli, Alessandro, 30, 55, 99
Post-memory, 6
Powerhouse Museum, 224

Presenters, 76, 78
Price, Rita, 79, 81
Prinsen, Deirdre, 226
Proust, Marcel, 247–249
Public history, 18, 100, 185, 225
Public Records Office of Victoria, 227
Pugliese, Joseph, 82, 280
Pulver, Andrew, 326

Q

Qiaotou, 331, 332, 340
Qiaoxiang, 332, 337–340

R

Rabbit-Proof Fence, 304
Rebeiro, Joyce, 274
Recording Oral History, 311
Redfern, 188, 189
Report into Post-Arrival Programs for Migrants, 190
Repositories of knowledge, 93
Republic of Vietnam Armed Forces (RVNAF), 131
Review of Post-Arrival Programs and Services for Migrants, 78
Ricoeur, Paul, 4
Robotham, Michael, 309
Romero Centre, 175
Romulus, My Father, 301
Roots tourism, 11, 333, 340
Roots Village Database, 338
Rothberg, Michael, 156, 163
Royal Commission into Institutional Responses to Child Sexual Abuse, 3, 304
Royal Terrace, 247–250
Rudd, Kevin, 278, 304
Rushdie, Salman, 306
Ruxton, Bruce, 129

S

Santamaria, B. A., 81
Santowiak, Donat, 61–69, 71n21
Satellite television, 79
Scarba House orphanage, 187
Scarfone, Dominique, 245, 246
Schymitzek, Andreas, 212
Screen Australia, 85
The Secret River, 241
Senate Select Committee on the
    Encouragement of Australian
    Productions for Television, 77
Sham-Ho, Helen, 192, 194, 195
Shapcott, Tom, 37
Shared social identity, 93–100
SIEV X, 179n30
Sikh Heritage Trail, 8
Silver City, 29, 38n1
Simic, Zora, 108
The Simpsons, 80
Sitcoms, 78, 79
Skalkos, Theo, 84
Skilled migrants, 3, 76
Skippy the Bush Kangaroo, 79
Skrzynecki, Peter, 37
Sloan, Stephen, 265
Sluga, Glenda, 30
Small business models, 83
Small screen, 75–85, 264
Smith, Sue, 304
Smyth, Sabine, 115
Snowy Mountains Hydro Electric
    Scheme, 222
Social cohesion, 99, 196, 222, 260
Social history museums, 204, 205
Sood, Mrs Saroj, 305
South Sudan, 158, 162, 163
South Sudanese, 8, 155–163
South Sudanese identity, 158, 159,
    161, 162
Soviet spies, 34
Special Broadcasting Service (SBS), 2,
    78, 80, 82–84, 192, 193

The Spirit of Enterprise, 271–281
Springvale Historical Society, 274
Srimgeour, Janet, 258
St Kilda, 239–244, 250
State Electricity Commission, 62, 66,
    229
State Library of New South Wales, 5
Stefanovic, Sofija, 80
Stinson, Father, 114
Stix, Isabel, 280
Stolen Generations, 111, 119n39,
    265, 304, 308, 312
The Stories Project, 321
Stratton, Jon, 318
Strauss, Anselm, 157
Streaming services, 79
Sumber Lestari, 173
Sun, Erica, 80
Switzerland, 82
Sydney, 5, 8, 17, 18, 21, 22, 24, 25,
    50, 52–55, 78, 83, 84, 157,
    163n4, 186, 189, 192, 193, 224,
    273, 307, 321, 335

T

Tampa, 3, 173
Tan Kee, John, 333
Tan, Selia, 339
Tankey, Monica, 333
Technologies of memory, 11
Television (TV), 1, 7, 10, 52, 76–80,
    82, 85, 174, 192–194, 196, 304,
    336
  history, 76–79, 85
  industry, 76–78, 86n10
  news, 76
Temporary Protection Visa (TPV),
    169, 174, 175
Ten Pound Poms, 18
Thang Ngo, 192, 194, 195
*They Cannot Take the Sky:Stories from
    Detention*, 266

356 INDEX

They're a Weird Mob, 301
Thompson, Paul, 60
Thomson, Alistair, 7, 48, 60, 61, 71n21, 95, 133
Tigrinya, 292, 293
Timor Leste, 281
Tonight, Italian Style, 82
Tonkin, Susan, 224
Transcultural theories of memory, 6
Transnational communication, 100
Tremarco, Christine, 306
Trezise, Jan, 274
Turkiewicz, Sophia, 109, 110, 112, 115, 116
Turnbull Liberal government, 222
Turnbull, Malcolm, 222, 285
Turner, Catherine (Cate), 50
TV:Make it Australian, 77

U
UNESCO Convention for the Safeguarding of the Intangible Cultural Heritage, 220–221
UNHCR, *see* United Nations High Commissioner for Refugees
United Nations, 125, 145
United Nations High Commissioner for Refugees (UNHCR), 124–126
United Nations Refugee Convention, 317
United States, 76, 77, 81, 83, 94, 125–126, 128, 129, 193, 324
University libraries, 4
Uranquinty Accommodation Centre Hospital, 113

V
Veneto (region), 7, 93, 94, 97–99
Veneto market gardeners, 94–100

Victorian Heritage Register (VHR), 225
Victorian Multicultural Commission, 275
Videocassette technology, 80
Vietnamese, 3, 7, 123–134, 136n31, 191–195
    refugees, 3, 7, 123–134, 136n31
    settlement, 192, 193
(The) Vietnam War, 7, 123–125, 190, 196, 301, 324
Villawood Detention Centre, 273, 322, 323
Villawood Mums, 319, 321, 323, 324
Vu Van Bao, 123, 127

W
Wacol Holding Centre, 111
Wagga Wagga, 320
Wall of Recognition, Morwell, South-Eastern Victoria, 227
Walsh, Kate, 206
Watson, Emily, 305, 309
Watson, Sheila, 259
Weaving, Hugo, 310
Wenham, David, 308, 310
West Sale Migrant Camp, 67
West Sale Migrant Memorial Project, 67
White Australia, 186, 187, 191, 257, 273, 333–336
White Australia Policy, 2, 134, 186, 275
White, Harold, 287, 288
Whitlock, Gillian, 9
Wilderman, Betty, 272, 274
Wilkinson, Marian, 173
Williams, Katarzyna, 108
Williams, Paul, 261
Wills, Sara, 6, 38, 280
Wilton, Janis, 38, 334
Witcomb, Andrea, 10, 261

INDEX 357

Wong Hoy, Kevin, 336
Wong, Jessie, 187, 188
World Championship Wrestling, 81
World Heritage-listed, 339
World News, 78
World War II, 1, 2, 29, 34, 93, 94, 97,
    107, 109, 142, 146, 187, 191, 226,
    264, 291, 296n29, 301–303, 337
Worthwhile Enterprise (exhibition),
    272, 273, 279, 281n8
Wright, Dorothy, 19
Wright, Katie, 309
Wyner, Izzy, 188

Y

Yiannopoulos, Anastasios (Stan
    Young), 84
York, Barry, 38n2, 81
YouTube, 81
Yow, Valerie Raleigh, 59, 311
Yue, Audrey, 52
Yugoslavia, 80, 82, 189
Yung, Joey, 53

Z

0/10 Network, 83, 84